Oliver Cowdery

SCRIBE, ELDER, WITNESS

ESSAYS FROM BYU STUDIES AND FARMS

Oliver Cowdery

SCRIBE, ELDER, WITNESS

EDITED BY

JOHN W. WELCH AND LARRY E. MORRIS

THE NEAL A. MAXWELL INSTITUTE FOR RELIGIOUS SCHOLARSHIP

BRIGHAM YOUNG UNIVERSITY
PROVO, UTAH

John W. Welch (J.D., Duke University) is Professor of Law at the J. Reuben Clark Law School, Brigham Young University and editor in chief of *BYU Studies*.

Larry E. Morris is a writer and editor with the Neal A. Maxwell Institute for Religious Scholarship at Brigham Young University.

Cover design by Jacob D. Rawlins

On the Cover
Background: The Testimony of the Three Witnesses from the printer's manuscript of the Book of Mormon. Courtesy of the Community of Christ Archives.

Foreground: A newly discovered daguerreotype of Oliver Cowdery. Courtesy Prints and Photographs Division, Library of Congress.

The Neal A. Maxwell Institute for Religious Scholarship
Brigham Young University
200 WAIH
Provo, Utah 84602

10 09 08 07 06   10 9 8 7 6 5 4 3 2 1

Library of Congress Cataloging-in-Publication Data

Available upon request

ISBN: 0-8425-2661-7
ISBN-13: 978-0-8425-2661-6

CONTENTS

Acknowledgments

Since Oliver Cowdery played a crucial role in the publication of the Book of Mormon (as well as many other early Church publications), it is fitting that the articles published over the years by *BYU Studies* and FARMS about Oliver Cowdery should be gathered and published in celebration of his 200th birthday. Thanks to Andrew Skinner and Alison Coutts of the Maxwell Institute for their support of this project. We also appreciate the authors who contributed to this volume; they have established a rich tradition of Cowdery scholarship.

Some of these pieces include revisions by the author; most of them, however, have been reproduced as they were originally published. (Information on the original publication is given at the end of each article, before the notes.) Rather than impose a single editorial style on articles printed over a period of almost forty years, we have generally retained previous styles. Although certain details, especially in articles produced decades ago, are now in need of updating, we are convinced that the research behind these essays holds up remarkably well.

Thanks to Julie Adams, Brette Jones, Kelsey Lambert, Josh Probert, Heather Seferovich, and Sandra Thorne for their hard work on this volume. We are particularly indebted to Paula Hicken and Shirley Ricks for their help with copyediting, proofreading, and permissions and to Jacob Rawlins and Alison Coutts, who handled typesetting, design, and a multitude of other tasks.

John W. Welch and Larry E. Morris
Provo, Utah
October 2006

Chronology

1830-31	serves as Church Recorder
Oct. 1830–Feb. 1831	serves mission to Ohio with Parley P. Pratt, Peter Whitmer Jr., and Ziba Peterson (first major mission of the Church)
Aug. 28, 1831	ordained high priest by Sidney Rigdon
Nov. 1831–July 1833	assists W. W. Phelps with publishing Church periodicals in Missouri
July 1833–fall 1837	preaches, publishes, and assists in Church administration in Kirtland, Ohio
Dec. 5, 1834	ordained assistant president of the High Priesthood
1835–37	serves as Church Recorder a second time
Apr. 3, 1836	sees a vision of the Savior with Joseph Smith, followed by visits from Moses, Elias, and Elijah (recorded in D&C 110)
Sept. 3, 1837	sustained as assistant counselor to the First Presidency
late 1837	grows estranged from Joseph, particularly over the Prophet's economic and political program
Apr. 12, 1838	excommunicated in absentia by the high council at Far West, Missouri
fall 1838	moves from Missouri back to Kirtland
early 1840	begins practicing as an attorney in Ohio
fall 1840	moves from Kirtland to Tiffin, Ohio, and practices law there
Dec. 1842	visited by brother-in-law Phineas H. Young, who informs his brother Brigham and the Twelve that Oliver's "heart is still with us" and makes consistent efforts over the next six years to effect Oliver's reconciliation
Oct. 1845	writes Brigham Young and offers legal and personal services to the Church

late 1846   travels to Washington, DC, to visit political
             contacts

Apr. 1847   moves from Tiffin to Elkhorn, Wisconsin,
             and practices law there with brother Lyman

late 1847   receives a letter from Brigham Young and
             the Twelve (by way of Phineas) inviting
             him to be rebaptized

Feb. 1848   responds favorably to Brigham Young's
             letter

Oct. 1848   leaves Elkhorn

Oct. 21, 1848   bears his testimony to the Saints camped
                 near Council Bluffs, Iowa

Nov. 12, 1848   rebaptized by Apostle Orson Hyde, presi-
                 dent of the Quorum of the Twelve

Jan. 1849   departs Iowa to visit Whitmer family in
             Richmond, Missouri

June 1849   informs Phineas that he will not be able to
             travel to Utah this year, as planned

summer 1849   health steadily deteriorates, probably from
               effects of tuberculosis

Mar. 3, 1850   dies at age 43 in Richmond, Missouri,
                reaffirming his testimony of the Book of
                Mormon on his deathbed

A Brief Biography of Oliver Cowdery

Richard Lloyd Anderson

Oliver Cowdery (1806–1850) was next in authority to Joseph Smith in 1830 (D&C 21:10–12), and was a second witness of many critical events in the restoration of the gospel. As one of three Book of Mormon witnesses, Oliver Cowdery testified that an angel displayed the gold plates and that the voice of God proclaimed them correctly translated. He was with Joseph Smith when John the Baptist restored to them the Aaronic Priesthood and when Peter, James, and John ordained them to the Melchizedek Priesthood and the apostleship, and again during the momentous Kirtland Temple visions (D&C 110).

Oliver came from a New England family with strong traditions of patriotism, individuality, learning, and religion. He was born at Wells, Vermont, on October 3, 1806. His younger sister gave the only reliable information about his youth: "Oliver was brought up in Poultney, Rutland County, Vermont, and when he arrived at the age of twenty, he went to the state of New York, where his older brothers were married and settled. . . . Oliver's occupation was clerking in a store until 1829, when he taught the district school in the town of Manchester" (Lucy Cowdery Young to Andrew Jenson, March 7, 1887, Church Archives).

While boarding with Joseph Smith's parents, he learned of their convictions about the ancient record that their son was again translating after Martin Harris had lost the manuscript in 1828. The young teacher prayed and received answers that Joseph Smith mentioned

Oliver Cowdery (1806–1850), scribe to Joseph Smith and witness of the Book of
Mormon (1829), Second Elder of the Church (1830), and Assistant President of the
Church (1834), editor, and lawyer. Cowdery was with Joseph Smith when the Aaronic
and Melchizedek priesthoods and keys were restored. After ten years of separation from
the Church, he was rebaptized. He died at age forty-three, faithful to his testimony.
Photograph, c. 1848, C. W. Carter Collection.

in a revelation (D&C 6:14–24). The Prophet's first history states the "Lord appeared unto . . . Oliver Cowdery and shewed unto him the plates in a vision and . . . what the Lord was about to do through me, his unworthy servant. Therefore he was desirous to come and write for me to translate" (*Papers of Joseph Smith* 1:10).

From April 7 through the end of June 1829, when they finished the translation, Joseph dictated while Oliver wrote, with "utmost gratitude" for the privilege (*Messenger and Advocate* 1:14). Oliver penned a letter then, expressing deep love for Christ, a lifetime theme. He later told how he and Joseph interrupted their work as they were translating the record of the Savior's post-resurrection American ministry, and how, as they prayed about baptism, they heard the "voice of the Redeemer" and were ministered to by John the Baptist, who gave them authority to baptize (JS—H 1:71, note).

In 1835 Oliver helped Joseph Smith correct and publish the revelations for the Doctrine and Covenants. Section 27 lists the major priesthood messengers of the restoration: John the Baptist, whom "I have sent unto you, my servants, Joseph Smith, Jr., and Oliver Cowdery, to ordain you unto this first priesthood" (D&C 27:8); and "Peter, James, and John, whom I have sent unto you, by whom I have ordained you and confirmed you to be apostles and especial witnesses of my name, and bear the keys of your ministry" (D&C 27:12).

The lesser priesthood was restored on May 15, 1829, two weeks before the Prophet and Cowdery moved to the Whitmers' in New York to complete the translation of the Book of Mormon (*History of the Church* 1:39–41, 48–49). The higher priesthood also came before this move; David Whitmer remembered he was ordained as an elder only weeks after their first arrival at his upstate farm (Whitmer, p. 32). The ancient apostles appeared with priesthood keys as Joseph and Oliver traveled between their Pennsylvania home and Colesville, New York (D&C 128:20), where Joseph Knight, Sr., lived. Knight remembered their seeking help to sustain them while translating in April or May (Jessee, p. 36).

After the move to the Whitmer farm, the angel showed the plates to Joseph Smith and the Three Witnesses in June 1829. Oliver supervised

the printing of the Book of Mormon that fall and winter. After the publication of the book on March 26, the Church was organized on April 6,
1830. Oliver spoke in the meeting the next Sunday, which was "the first
public discourse that was delivered by any of our number" (*History of
the Church* 1:81).

Few exceeded Cowdery in logical argument and elevated style.
Moreover, his speeches and writings carry the tone of personal
knowledge. Generally serving as editor or associate editor in the first
publications of the Church, Oliver wrote with unusual consistency
through two decades of published writings and personal letters.
He insisted that a relationship with God required constant contact:
"Whenever [God] has had a people on earth, he always has revealed
himself to them by the Holy Ghost, the ministering of angels, or
his own voice" (*Messenger and Advocate* 1:2). Oliver Cowdery led
the Lamanite Mission, the first major mission of the Church (D&C
28:8, 30:5), which doubled Church membership and took the Book
of Mormon to Native Americans. After the temple site was designated in Jackson County in 1831, he traveled there with copies of
the revelations for their first printing. Because publishing was vital
for spreading the gospel and instructing members, Oliver was called
to work with William W. Phelps, an experienced editor (D&C 55:4;
57:11–13). After Missouri ruffians destroyed the press, Cowdery
returned to Ohio to counsel with Church leaders, who assigned him
to relocate Church publications there. Because of the importance
of accurate information, he and Sidney Rigdon remained in Ohio
in 1834 when many faithful men marched to Missouri with Zion's
Camp to assist the Saints in returning to their homes and land in
Jackson County.

In 1830–1831, Oliver Cowdery served as the first Church
Recorder, a calling he again resumed between 1835 and 1837. Even
in other years, he often kept the official minutes of meetings and
was often editor and contributor for the first Church newspapers.
He wrote articles for the *Messenger and Advocate* that helped document early LDS history. From June to October 1830, Oliver served

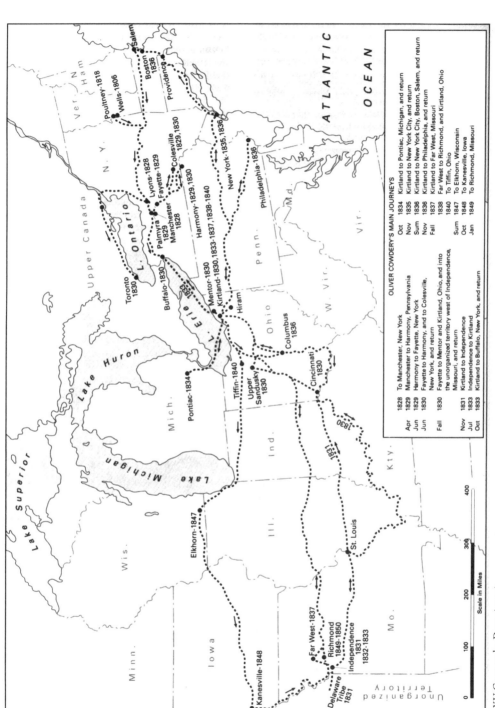

ATLANTIC OCEAN

OLIVER COWDERY'S MAIN JOURNEYS

1828	To Manchester, New York	Oct 1834	Kirtland to Pontiac, Michigan, and return
Apr 1829	Manchester to Harmony, Pennsylvania	Nov 1835	Kirtland to New York City, and return
Jun 1829	Harmony to Fayette, New York	Sum 1836	Kirtland to New York City, Boston, Salem, and return
Jun 1830	Fayette to Harmony, and to Colesville, New York, and return	Nov 1836	Kirtland to Philadelphia, and return
		Fall 1837	Kirtland to Far West, Missouri
Fall 1830	To Mentor and Kirtland, Ohio, and into the unorganized territory west of Independence, Missouri, and return	1838	Far West to Richmond, and Kirtland, Ohio
		1840	To Tiffin, Ohio
Nov 1831	Kirtland to Independence	Sum 1847	To Elkhorn, Wisconsin
Jul 1833	Independence to Kirtland	Oct 1848	To Kanesville, Iowa
Oct 1833	Kirtland to Buffalo, New York, and return	Jan 1849	To Richmond, Missouri

Salem
Boston 1836
Poultney-1818
Wells-1806
Providence 1836

Lyons-1828
Colesville 1829, 1830
Fayette-1829
New York-1835, 1836
Palmyra 1829
Manchester 1828
Harmony-1829, 1830
Harmony-1830, 1833-1837, 1838-1840
Philadelphia-1836

Toronto 1830
Buffalo-1830
Mentor-1830
Kirtland-1830, 1833-1837, 1838-1840
Hiram

Pontiac-1834
Tiffin-1840
Upper Sandusky 1830
Columbus 1836
Cincinnati 1830

Elkhorn-1847
St. Louis

Kanesville-1848
Far West-1837
Richmond 1849-1850
Independence 1832-1833
Delaware Tribe 1831

Lake Superior
Lake Huron
Lake Michigan
L. Ontario
L. Erie

Upper Canada
N. H.
Ver N
N. Y.
Penn.
Md.
Vir.
W. Vir.
Ohio
Ind.
Ky.
Mich.
Wis.
Minn.
Iowa
Ill.
Mo.
Unorganized Territory

Scale in Miles
0   100   200   300   400

as scribe while the Prophet completed important portions of the Joseph Smith Translation of the Bible.

An 1830 revelation named Oliver Cowdery next only to Joseph Smith in priesthood leadership (D&C 20:2–3), a status formalized in December 1834, when he was ranked above Sidney Rigdon, who had long served as Joseph's first counselor. Each would "officiate in the absence of the President, according to his rank and appointment, viz.: President Cowdery first; President Rigdon second, and President Williams third" (*Papers of Joseph Smith* 1:21). Cowdery wrote that this calling was foretold in the first heavenly ordination, though Missouri printing duties had intervened: "This promise was made by the angel while in company with President Smith, at the time they received the office of the lesser priesthood" (*Papers of Joseph Smith* 1:21; cf. *History of the Church* 1:40–41). His office next to the Prophet—sometimes called "associate president"—was given to Hyrum Smith in 1841 (D&C 124: 194–6) after Cowdery's excommunication.

Oliver's Church career peaked from 1834 to 1836. Minutes and letters picture him as a highly effective preacher, writer, and administrator. His 1836 journal survives, showing his devotion to religion and family, his political activities, his study of Hebrew, and the spiritual power he shared at the completion of the Kirtland Temple. Cowdery's last entry in this journal, penned the day of the temple dedication, says of the evening meeting: "I saw the glory of God, like a great cloud, come down and rest upon the house. . . . I also saw cloven tongues like as of fire rest upon many . . . while they spake with other tongues and prophesied" (Arrington, p. 426).

Oliver also alluded to more. A year later he penned an editorial "Valedictory." After mentioning "my mission from the holy messenger" prior to the organization of the Church, he wrote that such manifestations were to be expected, since the Old Testament promised that God would "reveal his glorious arm" in the latter days "and talk with his people *face to face*" (*Messenger and Advocate* 3:548). The words he italicized match his recent temple vision of Christ on April 3, 1836, which he experienced in company with the Prophet (D&C

110:1–10). This was also the time that these first priesthood leaders received special priesthood keys from Moses, Elias, and Elijah, completing restoration of the "keys of the kingdom" (D&C 27:6–13) and completing Cowdery's mission as "second witness" to such restoration. Oliver had deep confidence in divine appearances. In 1835 he charged the newly appointed Twelve: "Never cease striving until you have seen God face to face" (*History of the Church* 2:195).

Despite these profound spiritual experiences, Oliver's letters reveal a crisis of personal and family estrangement from Joseph Smith by early 1838. The Three Witnesses had seen an angel with Joseph Smith, but later they tended to compete rather than cooperate with his leadership. Cowdery disagreed with the Prophet's economic and political program and sought a personal financial independence that ran counter to the cooperative economics essential to the Zion society that Joseph Smith envisioned. Nonetheless, when Oliver was tried for his membership, he sent a resignation letter in which he insisted that the truth of modern revelation was not at issue: "Take no view of the foregoing remarks, other than my belief on the outward government of this Church" (*Far West Record*, pp. 165–66).

This trial was related to the excommunications of Oliver's brothers-in-law John Whitmer and David Whitmer, also at this time; this paralleled Oliver's earlier support of the Whitmer family in the matter of Hiram Page's competing revelations (D&C 28:11–13). The Church court considered five charges against Cowdery: inactivity, accusing the Prophet of adultery, and three charges of beginning law practice and seeking to collect debts after the Kirtland bank failure.

Oliver's charge of adultery against the Prophet was simplistic, for Oliver already knew about the principle of plural marriage. Rather than deny the charge, the Prophet testified that because Oliver had been his "bosom friend," he had "intrusted him with many things" (*Far West Record*, 168). Brigham Young later said that the doctrine was revealed to Joseph and Oliver during the Book of Mormon translation (cf. Jacob 2:30); clearly a fuller understanding of the principle of plural marriage came by 1832, in connection with

Joseph Smith's translation of Genesis (cf. D&C 130:1–2). Brigham Young added that Oliver impetuously proceeded without Joseph's permission, not knowing "the order and pattern and the results" (Charles Walker Journal, July 26, 1872, Church Archives). Oliver married Elizabeth Ann Whitmer in 1832, and problems with polygamy apparently influenced him and the Whitmer family to oppose the principle later.

In 1838, following his excommunication, Oliver returned to Ohio, though he did not, as a fictitious deed states, then pay Bishop Edward Partrige $1,000 for the temple lot in Independence on behalf of his children, John, Jane, and Joseph Cowdery. Such children never existed; Oliver had no such money and showed no interest in Jackson County then or later. In fact, he continued law study and practiced in Kirtland, but in 1840 he moved to Tiffin, Ohio, where he became a prominent civic leader as an ardent Democrat. His law notices and public service regularly appeared in local newspapers, and he was personally sketched in the warm recollections of the prominent Ohio lawyer William Lang, who apprenticed under Cowdery and described him as being of slight build, about five and a half feet tall, clean, and courteous. Professionally, Cowdery was characterized as "an able lawyer," well informed, with "brilliant" speaking ability; yet "he was modest and reserved, never spoke ill of anyone, never complained" (Anderson, 1981, p. 41).

In 1847 Oliver moved to Wisconsin, where he continued his law practice and was almost elected to the first state legislature, in spite of newspaper accounts ridiculing his published declaration of seeing the angel and the plates. In his ten years outside the Church, Cowdery never succumbed to the considerable pressure to deny his Book of Mormon testimony. Indeed, letters to his LDS relatives show that he was hurt at the Church's rejection but remained a deep believer. Feeling that his character had been slandered, he asked for public exoneration, explaining that anyone would be sensitive about reputation "had you stood in the presence of John with our departed Brother Joseph, to receive the Lesser Priesthood, and in the presence of Peter, to receive the Greater" (Gunn, pp. 250–51).

These statements contradict a pamphlet that Oliver was alleged to have published in 1839 as a "Defense" for leaving the Church. Surfacing in 1906, it portrays Oliver as confused about seeing John the Baptist. But no original exists, nor does any reference to it in Cowdery's century. Its style borrows published Cowdery phrases but rearranges his conclusions. A clumsier forgery is the "Confession of Oliver Overstreet," which claims that the author was bribed to impersonate Cowdery and return to the Church. Abundant documents show that Oliver returned to Council Bluffs, Iowa, in 1848 with his wife and young daughter.

Diaries and official minutes record Oliver Cowdery's words in rejoining the Church. He sought only rebaptism and fellowship, not office. He publicly declared that he had seen and handled the Book of Mormon plates and that he was present with Joseph Smith on the occasions when "holy angels" restored the two priesthoods (Anderson, *BYU Studies*, 1968, p. 278). The High Council questioned him closely about his published letter (to David Whitmer) in which Oliver claimed that he retained the keys of priesthood leadership after Joseph Smith's death. That was his opinion, Oliver said, before seeing the Nauvoo revelation giving all powers to Hyrum Smith "that once were put upon him that was my servant Oliver Cowdery" (D&C 124:95). "It was that revelation which changed my views on this subject" (Anderson, *IE*, Nov. 1968, p. 19).

Because they had started for Council Bluffs late in the season, the Cowdery family were forced to winter in Richmond, Missouri, where most of the Whitmer family lived. Letters throughout 1849 repeat Oliver's hope to move west and also disclose his lack of means. They speak of his coughing up blood, a long-term respiratory condition that finally took his life March 3, 1850. The circuit court recorded a resolution of fellow lawyers that in the death of "Oliver Cowdery, his profession has lost an accomplished member, and the community a valuable and worthy citizen" (Anderson, 1981, p. 46).

David Whitmer and other relatives living near Oliver Cowdery in his final year later claimed that he disagreed with many Kirtland and Nauvoo doctrines, but Oliver's documented criticisms at this time concern only intolerance and a continuing concern about polygamy. Although David Whitmer considered Joseph a fallen prophet, in 1848 Cowdery said publicly and privately "that Joseph Smith had fulfilled his mission faithfully before God until death" (Geo. A. Smith to Orson Pratt, *MS* 11 [Oct. 20, 1848]: 14), and "that the priesthood was with this people, and the 'Twelve' were the only men that could lead the Church after the death of Joseph" (Anderson, *IE*, Nov. 1968, p. 18). In his last known letter, Oliver accepted an assignment from the Twelve to lobby in Washington and acknowledge the leadership of the "good brethren of the [Salt Lake] valley" (Gunn, p. 261).

Oliver's wife, Elizabeth Ann Whitmer Cowdery (1815–1892), had known him when he was taking dictation during the translation of the Book of Mormon, before their marriage. Said she of his lifelong commitment: "He always without one doubt . . . affirmed the divinity and truth of the Book of Mormon" (Anderson, 1981, p. 63). This confidence stood the test of persecution, poverty, loss of status, failing health, and the tragic deaths of five of his six children. Dying at forty-three, Oliver was surrounded by family members who told how he reaffirmed the divinity of the Book of Mormon and the restored priesthood—and voiced total trust in Christ. Just before rejoining the Church, he penned his inner hopes to fellow witness David Whitmer: "Let the Lord vindicate our characters, and cause our testimony to shine, and then will men be saved in his kingdom" (Oliver Cowdery to David Whitmer, July 28, 1847, *Ensign of Liberty*, 1:92).

Editors' note: This article was originally published in the *Encyclopedia of Mormonism*, 1:335–40. Full bibliographical information for the internal citations can be found in the bibliography at the end of this volume or in the original article, p. 340.

Oliver Cowdery's Vermont Years and the Origins of Mormonism

Larry E. Morris

$\mathcal{M}$ost of what is known about Oliver Cowdery's youth comes from a well-known summary offered by his sister Lucy Cowdery Young:

> Now in regard to Oliver he was born in the Town of Wells in the state of Vermont[.] when he was three years of age Father married my Mother she resided in the Town of Poultney so Oliver was brought up in Poultney Rutland County Vermont and when he arrived at the age of twenty he went to the State of New York where his older brothers were married and Settled and in about two years my father moved there.[1]

Cowdery biographers have generally repeated these brief facts before darting to Oliver's initial meeting with Joseph Smith in April 1829. A close look at the record, however, reveals a rich family history behind Lucy's simple summary—a history that includes the death of Oliver's mother, the blending of three families, four moves between two states, and a plague that took a dear aunt and uncle.

All of these details in turn shed light on two controversial theories bearing on the origins of Mormonism. The first alleges that Joseph Smith Sr. and William Cowdery participated in a divining-rod incident known as the "Wood Scrape," forming associations that impacted their sons' founding of the Church a quarter of a century later.[2] The second purports that young Oliver knew minister Ethan Smith, read his work *View of the Hebrews,* and passed on knowledge of the book—or a copy of the book itself—to Joseph, who borrowed freely from it in producing the Book of Mormon.[3] Both theories have spawned considerable discussion and research. The well-documented history of the William Cowdery family in Vermont, however, shows that both theories are long on speculation and short on fact.

William Cowdery's Forty Years in Vermont

Oliver's youth is best understood in the context of the four decades his father spent in Vermont (interrupted by a three-year stay in New York). William Cowdery Jr. was born in East Haddam, Connecticut, on September 5, 1765. Around 1787 he and his wife, Rebecca Fuller (born on January 2, 1768, also in East Haddam), moved to Wells, Vermont, where Rebecca's brother-in-law and sister, Rufus and Huldah Fuller Glass, had recently settled.[4] Around 1827, William moved his family to western New York. Although this period has received little attention in biographies of Oliver Cowdery,[5] it is fairly well documented, with at least thirty references to William Cowdery in original Vermont records and additional information in Cowdery family histories.

Wells, Vermont[6]

- October 17, 1788—birth of Warren Cowdery[7]
- September 1789—William Cowdery included in the list of free men in Wells[8]
- February 16, 1791—birth of Stephen Cowdery[9]
- April 1791–February 1793—various land sales to William Cowdery[10]
- February 20, 1792—William Cowdery sworn to position of surveyor of highways[11]
- July 1793—William Cowdery's livestock earmarks identified in the town minutes[12]
- October 4, 1793—birth of Dyer Cowdery[13]
- August 13, 1796—birth of Erastus Cowdery[14]
- December 19, 1797—William Cowdery files an affidavit with the town clerk discussing four stray sheep: "The owner is desired to prove property pay charges and take them away."[15]

- June 30, 1799—birth of Sally Cowdry[16]
- 1800—William Cowdre family listed in Wells census[17]
- March 12, 1802—birth of Lyman Cowdry[18]
- March 1803—William Cowdery sworn to position of surveyor of highways[19]
- June 16, 1804—birth of Olive Cowdery[20]
- October 3, 1806—birth of Oliver Cowdery[21]
- January 1807–November 1808—various land sales from William Cowdery. The last known reference to William in the Wells town record is a sale to Socrates Hotchkiss on November 9, 1808, that included "all the land and buildings standing on the farm on which I the grantor now live."[22]

Middletown, Vermont
- Early 1809—Cowdery family moves to Middletown[23]
- September 3, 1809—death of Rebecca Fuller Cowdery[24]
- March 18, 1810—marriage of William Cowdery and Keziah Pearce Austin[25]

Williamson, New York
- Summer 1810—family moves to Williamson, Ontario County, New York[26]
- 1810—William Cowdry family listed in Ontario, New York census[27]
- December 18, 1810—birth of Rebecca Marie Cowdery[28]

Middletown, Vermont
- 1813–1814—family returns to Middletown[29]
- June 3, 1814—birth of Lucy Pearce Cowdery[30]
- February 23, 1815—land sale from William Cowdery to Moses Copeland[31]
- January 17, 1817—birth of Phoebe Cowdery[32]

Poultney, Vermont
- August 2, 1818—baptism of Rebecca Marie, Lucy, and Phoebe[33]
- 1820—William Cowdery family listed in Poultney census[34]

Oliver Cowdery was born in Wells on October 3, 1806, after a summer of drought in southwestern Vermont. According to a Wells historian, "No rain fell from seeding time to harvest. Crops were almost a complete failure."[35]

The Cowdery and Rufus Glass homes were just a mile apart, giving the eight children in each family a good chance to get well acquainted with their cousins. There must have been frequent trips back and forth between the two homes, with the cousins enjoying boiled bag pudding or hot maple syrup served on platters of snow.[36]

William Cowdery and Rufus Glass were landowners who probably raised beef cattle, sheep, and hogs. William and his six sons no doubt cleared land with crude axes, planted hay and grain in the thin topsoil, and hoped the short Vermont growing season would yield a good harvest. In late winter and early spring they tapped maple trees, collecting enough sugar to last the entire year. Like their neighbors, the family probably cooked meals of potatoes, turnips, pumpkins, beans, and ground corn over an open hearth.[37]

William came from a religious family. His father, William Sr., and his mother, Hannah Emmons, both belonged to the Congregational Church.[38] William Sr. served as a deacon in the Reading, Vermont, Congregational Church, preaching sermons after the death of

Marker at the birthplace of Oliver Cowdery, Wells, Vermont. Courtesy Richard Neitzel Holzapfel.

the minister.[39] Oliver probably met his grandfather Cowdery (his only surviving grandparent) and listened firsthand to his Calvinist exhortations.

Oliver was two years old when the family left Wells early in 1809, but the move to Poultney—often thought to have taken place immediately—did not occur for another decade. The family moved first to a farm in Middletown, a township a few miles directly northeast of Wells. Oliver's mother, Rebecca, may have been sick with a chronic cough when they left Wells. Her health did not improve. Nine months later, in a portent of Oliver's own future, Rebecca died of consumption, most likely tuberculosis, at the age of forty-three. Oliver died, probably from the same disease, also at forty-three.[40]

One historian of Wells has suggested that after Rebecca's death, two-year-old Oliver went to live with his aunt Huldah Glass, his mother's older sister.[41] Various records indicate that Oliver may have lived with the Glass family for at least two extended periods, first from 1809 to 1813 and again between 1820 and 1822. The 1810 census record for William Cowdery, for example, lists only one male child under ten, although Lyman and Oliver were both in that age bracket. Furthermore, the Glass census record for 1810 lists two boys under ten, even though the Glass boys were all over ten. Oliver's living with the Glass family would be consistent with both census reports.[42]

Even if Oliver temporarily lived with the Glass family (proved possible but hardly certain by known records), William Cowdery still had seven other children to care for. Sometime in the six months after Rebecca's death, he courted Keziah Pearce Austin, a Middletown widow, who came from a respected Poultney family. They were married in Middletown on March 18, 1810. The union eventually combined three families—a child from Keziah's first marriage and eight Cowdery children were eventually joined by William and Keziah's three daughters.[43]

As Vermont historian Charles T. Morrissey details, "The years immediately preceding and following the War of 1812 provided all sorts of troubles for Vermont," including a depressed economy that likely factored in the family's migration by ox team to western New York in the summer of 1810.[44] William and Keziah's first child, Rebecca Marie, was born in Williamson, New York, that December.

Young Oliver, whose early years had already been traumatized by the loss of his mother, faced a double blow just four years later when a plague descended on Wells and the surrounding communities. Both Glass parents fell ill, first with chills and a high fever, followed by violent coughing, vomiting, and diarrhea. Huldah died on March 21, 1813, at the age of fifty-one, and fifty-seven-year-old Rufus succumbed two weeks later.[45] (This epidemic was probably part of an outbreak of typhoid fever that struck the entire Connecticut River Valley between 1812 and 1815, claiming six thousand lives and affecting both seven-year-old Joseph Smith, who endured an excruciating leg operation, and his sister Sophronia, who almost died.)[46] Oliver's cousin, seventeen-year-old Arunah Glass, was left to care for himself, his three younger sisters, and possibly for six-year-old Oliver.

William Cowdery brought his family back to Vermont in 1813 or 1814, possibly because of the deaths of Rufus and Huldah (the Vermont economy certainly had not improved and was not the reason they returned). The Cowderys returned to Middletown, and the records of three events provide evidence of their continual Middletown residence for the next few years: the birth of Lucy Pearce in June 1814, William's property sale in February 1815, and Phoebe's birth in January 1817. They were therefore in Middletown—and Oliver was nine years old—during the summer of 1816, "the year without a summer" when a foot of snow fell on about June 8, and fifteen sheep froze to death in a Wells barn. (This was also the third successive year of crop failures for the Joseph Smith Sr. family, driving them from Vermont to western New York.)[47]

Oliver faced several adjustments during the Middletown years. His oldest brother, Warren, married Patience Simonds in 1814 and had moved to Freedom, New York, by 1816.[48] The next year, Oliver's siblings Dyer, Erastus, and Sally had joined Warren in New York.[49] Along with his new sisters, Oliver also had a new stepbrother to get used to, Silas Austin, who was seven years his senior. Silas Austin is mentioned in a journal entry Oliver made in 1836 on a trip through Ohio: "On my way I called on Silas Austin . . . he received me with a smile, and wished me to remember him."[50]

Lucy Cowdery Young's summary of Oliver's youth does not mention Middletown, but this is understandable since she was only three or four when the family left Middletown and moved a few miles west to the township of Poultney. This was familiar territory to Lucy's mother, Keziah, who had lived in Poultney both before and after her marriage to Harrington Austin. The Cowderys arrived in Poultney by 1818, and Rebecca Marie, Lucy, and Phoebe were baptized that August in the same Congregational Church that Keziah had joined in 1803.[51] According to Lucy, the family remained in Poultney for close to a decade, with Oliver leaving for western New York around 1825 and the remaining members of the family following two years later.

Few details of the Poultney years are known, but William Cowdery was a literate man who emphasized his children's education. At least four of his six sons became either doctors or lawyers. And although the upbringing and education of the Cowdery children is virtually undocumented, a local history of Wells written in 1869 contains a reference to Oliver's education: "We well remember this same Oliver Cowdery when in our boyhood. . . . He attended school in the District where we reside in 1821 and 1822."[52]

The possibility of Oliver's attending school in Wells is curious because the Cowderys resided in Poultney during these years. Available records once again indicate, however, that Oliver may have been temporarily residing with his cousin, Arunah Glass, who had married in 1817. One reason could have been Arunah's inheritance of the debts of his deceased parents. As Richard L. Bushman has pointed out, New Englanders of this period lived precarious economic lives, often owing money to or being owed by scores of individuals. "A person could be prospering while alive and suddenly be insolvent at death."[53] Arunah apparently lived on the edge of poverty, at one point receiving assistance from others in the community,[54] and Oliver may well have attended school while helping Arunah support a wife, son, and three sisters.

Locations in Vermont and New York significant to the early life of Oliver Cowdery.

During the year of Joseph Smith's first vision, 1820, Oliver turned fourteen. The Poultney census record for that year does not list any boys at all residing with the William Cowdery family, while the four daughters still at home are accurately represented. (Oliver's five brothers were all old enough to be living away from home by this time.) Interestingly, the Wells census record for Arunah Glass lists one boy between ten and sixteen, as well as one boy under ten—and Arunah's only son was three.[55] Though not unimpeachable, those census records indicate that Oliver might have resided in Wells, where he took advantage of educational opportunities. The Wells school district records also support the theory that Oliver attended school there. In 1822, for example, two students between the ages of four and eighteen are listed in the Arunah Glass household, but Arunah had only one child at the time (Rufus, born in 1817), and his younger sisters were all over eighteen. In 1823 one student is listed for the Glass family.[56] Therefore, available records corroborate the claim that Oliver attended school in Wells in the early 1820s.

Oliver would have attended school during the long winter term, possibly studying composition and figures under Almon Hopson, an instructor who taught in Wells for twenty years. The school day began with reading of the Bible, and reading was stressed more than any other subject. Quill pens were difficult to make, and paper was "very course [*sic*] and scarce."[57] In this spare setting, young Oliver began to acquire the skills of logic and language that served him so well in future years.

Oliver left Vermont around 1825, but the exact year is not known. Lucy claims he left when he was twenty, and he turned twenty in October 1826. However, Lucy mistakenly states that Oliver was born in 1805, so she could have thought that he turned twenty in 1825.[58] Whatever the exact date, Oliver had grown to young manhood in the Green Mountain State, and his family's time there becomes a source of controversy in discussions of both the Wood Scrape and *View of the Hebrews*.

The Wood Scrape

The Wood Scrape actually took place in Middletown, Vermont, seven years before William Cowdery moved there (and four years before Oliver's birth). According to nineteenth-century Middletown historian Barnes Frisbie, Nathaniel Wood, a preacher who had tried unsuccessfully to become pastor of Middletown's Congregational Church, and several of his relatives broke from the Congregational Church and claimed they were "modern Israelites or Jews, under the special care of Providence; that the Almighty would . . . visit their enemies . . . with his wrath and vengeance." In 1799, with the Wood movement gathering momentum, a man named Winchell, who contemporaries claimed was a fugitive and a counterfeiter, arrived on the scene and initiated the group to the use of the hazel rod, a small shrub cut with two prongs. "From the use of this stick Winchell and the Woods pretended to divine all sorts of things to suit their purpose."[59]

With increasing zeal, Winchell and the Woods were soon using the rod to dig for buried treasure and search for missing persons. The frenzy reached its apex on the night of January 14, 1802, with the rodsmen preparing for a cataclysmic earthquake—even writing Passover messages on their doorposts—and with local "Gentiles" calling out the militia and standing guard for "destroying angels." "There was no sleep that night among the inhabitants;

fear, consternation, great excitement and martial law prevaile[d] throughout the night," historian Frisbie wrote in 1867.[60] But there was no earthquake, and the disgraced Wood group dispersed. Justus Winchell was "warned out" of town, and the Woods, who had previously been prominent citizens—with a former town selectman, constable, and justice of the peace among their numbers—bolted to New York.

Frisbie saw the roots of Mormonism in the Wood movement, claiming that Joseph Smith Sr. and William Cowdery were both involved with Winchell in Vermont around 1800 and that they resumed that association two decades later in New York.

> There we find these men [Joseph Smith Sr. and William Cowdery] with the counterfeiter, Winchell, searching for money over the hills and mountains with the hazel rod, and their sons Joe and Oliver, as soon as they were old enough, were in the same business, and continued in it until they brought out the "vilest scheme that ever cursed the country."[61]

Frisbie himself, however, admitted that the evidence for these claims was thin. Describing Joseph Smith Sr.'s involvement in the Scrape, Frisbie wrote, "I have been told that [he] resided in Poultney . . . and that he was in it [the Wood movement]. . . . Of this I cannot speak positively, for the want of satisfactory evidence."[62] Similarly, Frisbie cannot place William Cowdery directly in the Wood movement:

> Winchell, I have been told, was a friend and acquaintance of Cowdry's, but of this I cannot be positive, they were intimate afterwards; but Winchell staid at Cowdry's some little time, keeping himself concealed. . . . Winchell next turns up in Middletown . . . and here he began to use the hazel rod (whether he had before used it at Cowdry's, in Wells, I cannot say).[63]

Furthermore, as Richard Lloyd Anderson has pointed out, Frisbie's Smith-Cowdery discussion appears separately from his main summary of the Wood Scrape. In that narrative, Frisbie offered a detailed description of the incident—with specific names, dates, and locations—but said nothing at all about Smith or Cowdery, nor did his star witness, Laban Clark, a preacher who was temporarily in Middletown at the time of the Wood movement. In 1867, Clark wrote a letter to Frisbie discussing the "rod-men" that further complicated the picture by claiming the counterfeiter was named Wingate, not Winchell. Frisbie also explained that before 1860 he interviewed more than thirty men and women who were living in Middletown in 1800. According to Frisbie's summary, these survivors said nothing of a counterfeiter or of Cowdery.[64]

Despite Frisbie's seeming lack of evidence, his concept of a Winchell-Smith-Cowdery association has been revived by D. Michael Quinn, who considers it likely that Winchell mentored the Smiths in the occult and that Oliver Cowdery's "gift of working with the rod" came by way of Winchell's influence on William Cowdery.[65] In reaching these conclusions, Quinn assumes: (1) William Cowdery was involved in the Wood Scrape; (2) William Cowdery gained knowledge of working with the rod from Winchell and transmitted that knowledge to Oliver; (3) Joseph Sr. moved temporarily from eastern to western Vermont around 1800 and also got involved in the Wood Scrape; and (4) Joseph Sr. was reunited with Winchell in New York in the early 1820s. A close examination of the existing documents, however, fails to support any of these assumptions.

1. William Cowdery was never actually identified as a rodsman or as a participant in the Wood Scrape. Quinn's assertion that William was "described as a divining rodsman by his Vermont neighbors"[66] is not accurate. Frisbie claimed only that Winchell briefly stayed with Cowdery three years before the Wood Scrape, and the historian of Middletown was uncertain whether Winchell used the rod at that time. Frisbie, therefore, had jumped to a conclusion when he argued that "Oliver Cowdery's father was in the Wood Scrape,"[67] and Quinn compounds this mistake by frequently asserting that Cowdery was identified as a Vermont rodsman.

As for the three Wells residents mentioned in an 1869 history of Wells, none made specific claims about William Cowdery. Nancy Glass (who was ten years old in 1800) wrote to the authors, "If any

one [of the Cowdery family] was engaged in it, it must have been
the old gentleman; I rather think it was, but won't be positive."
The other two, Joseph Parks (fourteen years old in 1800) and Mrs.
Charles Garner (age unknown), merely verified that Cowdery was
"connected with the rodsmen."[68] All of this, recalled nearly seventy
years after the fact, could simply be a confirmation that Winchell
stayed with Cowdery. As Anderson has convincingly summarized,
"William Cowdery's knowing a man who knew the Woods does not
make him a participant. Indeed, Oliver's father is absent from all
sources preceding Frisbie. . . . The main group of Middletown survivors of the 1800 period—'more than thirty men and women'—were
interviewed up to 1860, and they said nothing of a counterfeiter or
of Cowdery."[69]

Existing records of William Cowdery's stay in Wells offer no
indication that he was involved in the Wood Scrape. Winchell was
"warned out" of Middletown, and the Woods were pressured to
leave—"seeing the 'slow moving finger of scorn' pointed towards
them from all their neighbors; and fearing, moreover, that the heavy
hand of the law would fall on them for their misdeeds."[70] Meanwhile,
Cowdery remained in Wells and appears to have been a respected
citizen both before and after the Wood Scrape. In 1803, a year after
the Wood Scrape, he was named as a surveyor of highways, a position he had held in the previous decade.

After leaving Wells, William moved to Middletown, the last
place one would expect a disgraced rodsman to go—especially with
huge mounds of dirt throughout the area serving as conspicuous
reminders of Winchell's money-digging fiasco. And, in contrast
to Nathaniel Wood's excommunication from the Middletown
Congregational Church, William was married to Middletown resident Keziah Austin in the same church, by Congregational minister
Henry Bigelow, whom Frisbie called "truly orthodox, and firm in
his religious sentiments."[71] Nor can William and Keziah's move to
New York be taken as an attempt to flee Middletown, because they
returned three years later and remained in Middletown for another
four years.

2. As Quinn himself has noted, "the historical record is silent about how or when Oliver Cowdery obtained the divining rod he was already using for revelation before April 1829."[72] In fact, a revelation given to Joseph Smith within weeks of Oliver's arrival in Pennsylvania in April 1829 offers all that is known on this subject: "Now this is not all, for you have another gift, which is the gift of working with the rod: behold it has told you things: behold there is no other power save God, that can cause this rod of nature, to work in your hands."[73] According to Anderson, "No known source tells whether Oliver did money digging before becoming the Book of Mormon scribe."[74] In fact, Anderson argues that the rod had many uses in addition to locating hidden treasure. Even during the Wood Scrape, diviners used the rod to seek spiritual answers of all kinds, including healings and answers to prayers.[75] Whether Winchell's money-digging activities almost thirty years earlier had anything to do with Oliver's use of the rod is unknown. Perhaps, as Bushman has suggested, Oliver employed the rod to locate water and minerals, like many of his New England contemporaries.[76]

3. The connection of the Smith family to the Wood Scrape appears even more tenuous since Joseph Sr.'s well-documented history does not include a move to Poultney, Vermont. Since Frisbie asserted (based on an unidentified source who offered no specific details) that Joseph Sr. lived in Poultney and participated in the Wood Scrape, and since *a* Joseph Smith is listed in the 1800 census for Poultney, Quinn speculates that Joseph Sr. "may have visited Poultney or Middletown while the Wood movement was developing from the spring of 1800 to January 1802."[77] Vermont civic and religious records, however, place Joseph Sr. across the state in Tunbridge in 1798 (birth of Alvin); in February 1800 (birth of Hyrum); and in May 1803 (birth of Sophronia).[78] The name of *a* Joseph Smith is also listed in the 1800 Tunbridge census,[79] but since the listing does not accurately describe the family of the Prophet's father, Quinn counters that the Poultney Joseph Smith listing seems just as likely a record of Joseph Smith Sr. But as Dan Vogel has perceptively observed, Lucy Mack Smith offers a solution to this conundrum

when she stated that the family relocated temporarily to Randolf, Vermont (about ten miles northwest of Tunbridge), after Hyrum's birth.[80] The family could have been in transit when the census was taken, which would account for their not being listed. Furthermore, in her entire history, which is full of names and dates, Lucy never mentions Rutland County or Poultney. Finally, Poultney records clearly indicate that the Joseph Smith listed in the 1800 census had been a long-time resident. A Joseph Smith is included in the tax rolls for 1792, 1793, 1794, 1795, 1797, and 1798 (the last year such records are available).[81] Thus, Quinn's allegation that Joseph Sr. participated in the Wood Scrape runs counter to several historical documents and rests entirely on a speculation that suffered from a "want of satisfactory evidence," in the words of Barnes Frisbie.[82]

4. Additionally, Joseph Sr. cannot be linked with Winchell in New York. Three years after the Smith family moved to Palmyra, New York, the *Palmyra Register* noted that the post office was holding an unclaimed letter for "Justus Winchel." A similar notice appeared in the *Wayne Sentinel* almost five years later (July 7, 1824). Relying on these notices—and on Frisbie's claim of a Smith-Winchell connection in New York (a claim for which Frisbie offers neither documents nor witnesses)—Quinn concludes that "Winchell followed Joseph Sr. from Vermont to New York" and that Winchell was likely one of two "occult mentors to the Smiths."[83] But Quinn's assertion fails three fundamental tests. First, there is no evidence that Winchell lived in the Palmyra area. Two unclaimed letters over a five-year period do not prove residence and may point to the very opposite; and, as Quinn notes, Winchell's whereabouts at the time of the 1820 census are unknown.[84] Second, a case has not been made that the Justus Winchel named in the newspaper notices is the same Justus Winchell who was warned out of Vermont in 1802. Winchell's son, Justus Jr., lived within twenty miles of Palmyra from 1817 to 1820, and a German-born Justus Winchell (no known relation) moved to within twenty-five miles of Palmyra sometime after 1820. Quinn can place *the* Justus Winchell no closer than Wayne, New York—twenty-one miles from Palmyra—where he died in 1823.[85]

Third, nothing links Winchell with New York money-digging activities. It is particularly telling that the manifold affidavits collected by the likes of Philastus Hurlbut, Chester C. Thorne, and Arthur B. Deming—all of whom attempted to link the Smiths with shady occult practices, money digging, and fraud (the very accusations made against Winchell in Vermont)—say nothing about anyone named Winchell.[86]

Nor can William Cowdery be linked with Winchell in New York. This is a crucial point because Quinn relies heavily on Frisbie, who insists that Winchell, Smith, and Cowdery were in the Wood Scrape in Vermont and were reunited in Palmyra.[87] But, according to Quinn, Winchell's alleged Palmyra visit or residence does not begin until 1819 and ends with his death in 1823, and William and Oliver Cowdery were clearly in Vermont during this period, as shown above. Thus, the Winchell-Cowdery-New York claim falls flat in the face of the documentary evidence.

The primary historical documents fail to support Frisbie's—and Quinn's—Winchell-Smith-Cowdery allegations. Historian David M. Ludlum states the case succinctly: "The strands of connection between the Wood Scrape and the Palmyra outcroppings are too tenuous to withstand historical criticism."[88]

View of the Hebrews

Ethan Smith (1762–1849), no relation to Joseph, was a prominent New England minister who published a number of sermons and books. From 1821 to 1826, he served as minister of the Poultney, Vermont, Congregational Church, and during that period published his best-known work, *View of the Hebrews*. This book "combines scriptural citations and reports from various observers among American Indians and Jews to support the claim that the Indians were the descendants of the Lost Ten Tribes of Israel."[89] By the early twentieth century, and down to the 1980s, suggestions of a relationship between *View of the Hebrews* and the Book of Mormon were made by several authors.[90]

Proponents of this theory have pointed out that the William Cowdery family lived in Poultney when *View of the Hebrews* was published, and some have claimed an Ethan Smith-Cowdery association. Book of Mormon enthusiast Thomas Stuart Ferguson concluded, for instance, that the Cowdery family "had a close tie with Ethan Smith."[91] The most intensive examination of the possible Ethan Smith-Cowdery association appears in David Persuitte's *Joseph Smith and the Origins of the Book of Mormon*, published in 1985. Persuitte calls attention to a brief note in the Records of Baptisms for the Congregational Church in Poultney:

> 1818
>
> August 2   Mr. Cowdry's children viz Rebecka Maria Lucy and Phebe[92]

Noting the connection of the Cowdery family to the Poultney Congregational Church that Ethan Smith would preside over three years later, Persuitte claims, "It is reasonable to expect, then, that Oliver Cowdery eventually became acquainted firsthand with Ethan Smith."[93] However, Persuitte makes two mistaken assumptions in reaching this conclusion. First, he assumes the Cowderys moved to Poultney soon after William and Keziah's marriage[94]—an understandable assumption given Lucy Cowdery Young's letter—and second, that the Cowderys had a long-standing association with the Poultney Congregational Church.

To support this second assumption, Persuitte refers to two church records—an 1810 vote "to give Mrs. Keziah Cowdry a letter of recommendation"[95] and the 1818 baptismal record mentioned above. Persuitte reasons that since the Cowderys associated with the Poultney Congregational Church from 1810 to 1818, they probably continued in the church until 1825. As shown, however, the family resided in Middletown, Vermont, or Williamson, New York, from 1809 to 1817 or 1818 and was therefore not at all likely to form a close association with the Poultney church during this period.

Convinced that he has established an Oliver Cowdery-Ethan Smith connection, Persuitte quickly attempts to link Ethan Smith's ideas to the origin of the Book of Mormon:

> Since Pastor Smith wrote his book to convince his fellow Americans of the religious importance of his ideas about the American Indians, we can speculate that he also used his pulpit to expound on them. In the congregation, Oliver Cowdery might thus have heard and been deeply impressed . . . [and] there was a reasonable period of time in which Oliver Cowdery could have supplied Joseph with a copy [of *View of the Hebrews*]. . . . Though Joseph later claimed that he did not meet Oliver until the spring of 1829, he might have said that to preclude any appearance of collusion. It is also possible that some other individuals were involved in the collaboration and that Oliver worked with them first and not directly with Joseph until later.[96]

In the face of such speculative musing (which is void of documentation), a close look at the historical records proves highly instructive:

- William and Keziah's three daughters—Rebecca Marie, Lucy Pearce, and Phoebe—were all baptized on the same day, at the ages of seven, four, and one, raising questions of how often the family attended church services. (William's orthodox parents, by contrast, had him baptized when he was one month old.[97])
- Keziah's known contact with the Poultney Congregational Church in 1803[98] (when she joined), 1810, and 1818 all occurred with the same pastor in office, the Reverend Mr. Leonard, a popular minister who served from 1803 to 1821.[99] There is no record of her having contact with any other Poultney minister.
- Keziah lived in Poultney during the 1790s but was a resident of Middletown in 1800 and also in 1810, when she married William Cowdery.[100] She did not return to Poultney until 1817 or 1818. It is therefore likely that the May 26, 1810, letter of recommendation was obtained (possibly from Poultney church members who had known her years earlier) in relation to the move to New York, which took place in the summer of 1810.[101]

- Although Keziah was a member of the Poultney Congregational Church, and her three daughters were baptized, no other Pearce, Austin, or Cowdery family members are mentioned in church records.[102]
- The baptismal entry in 1818 is the last record of Cowdery association with the Poultney Congregational Church, and no document has been found linking Ethan Smith to any member of the Cowdery family. Even Persuitte acknowledges that Oliver's three half-sisters were baptized three years before Smith became pastor.[103]
- No document has been found linking Oliver Cowdery to the Congregational Church or the writings of Ethan Smith.[104]

All of this does not prove that the Cowderys did not know Ethan Smith or that Oliver Cowdery was not aware of *View of the Hebrews*. What it does suggest, however, is that the theory of an Ethan Smith-Cowdery association is not supported by the documents and that it is unknown whether Oliver knew of or read *View of the Hebrews*. (Oliver's possible acquaintance with Ethan Smith is further diminished by his likely residence in Wells from 1820 to 1822, as discussed earlier.)

Nevertheless, some historians have continued to speculate that Oliver may have somehow obtained a copy of *View of the Hebrews* in Poultney and given it to Joseph Smith sometime before 1827, when Joseph reported obtaining the gold plates. Persuitte, for example, launches into a lengthy scenario according to which Oliver meets with Ethan Smith and is allowed free access to his library. When Oliver leaves Vermont in 1825, he takes with him the enlarged edition of *View of the Hebrews,* as well as a romance written by Ethan Smith (although no record exists of this volume). Soon Oliver meets with Joseph, and "the two get the idea of using Ethan Smith's romance as the basis of a history of ancient America that they can sell for profit."[105] They incorporate material from *View of the Hebrews* as well. Persuitte omits specific dates and locations from his Joseph/Oliver conspiracy, which he admits is "purely speculative."[106] Still, in a book that gives the appearance of treating historical matters seriously, taking such creative license seems out of place.

In a more recent—and more surprising—attempt to link Joseph Smith with *View of the Hebrews* through Oliver Cowdery, Richard S. Van Wagoner offers another amazing series of speculations. His springboard is an 1830 editorial in the *Ashtabula (Ohio) Journal* which states, "For we had known Cowdry some seven or 8 years ago, when he was a dabbler in the art of Printing, and principally occupied in writing and printing pamphlets, with which, as a pedestrian pedlar, he visited the towns and villages of western N. York, and Canada."[107]

Van Wagoner first suggests that young Oliver Cowdery may have been "employed by Smith & Shute, the Poultney firm that printed *View of the Hebrews*." Next he conjectures that Oliver was a "traveling agent" for Smith & Shute and that Oliver "had copies of the 1823 edition of *View of the Hebrews* in his knapsack when he visited his relatives the Smiths." This, in Van Wagoner's estimation, explains how Joseph, in the autumn of 1823, began telling his family interesting details about the ancient inhabitants of America.[108]

While Persuitte's scenario of Joseph receiving *View of the Hebrews* offers no dates, locations, or documents, Van Wagoner includes four specific details that do not withstand scrutiny.

1. The *Ashtabula Journal*'s identification of Oliver as a "pedestrian pedlar" could be a case of mistaken identity. As Scott Faulring has noted, "Benjamin Franklin Cowdery was an older relative of Oliver who went through repeated hard luck in printing ventures in western New York. Before 1830, he had published eight newspapers, and about this time others in the trade evidently felt him 'poorly qualified to speak for the printers.'"[109]

2. Oliver Cowdery himself indicated he did not learn the printing trade until 1829. In December of that year he was assisting with the printing of the Book of Mormon and wrote to Joseph Smith, "It may look rather strange to you to find that I have so soon become a printer."[110] In addition, a nineteenth-century history of Poultney mentions several people associated with printing in Poultney

(including Horace Greeley, who began work as a *Northern Spectator* apprentice in 1826), but does not mention Oliver.[111]

3. Oliver Cowdery was only sixteen when the supposed 1823 Smith & Shute employment and trip to western New York would have been necessary. However, there is no record of Oliver being in New York between 1815 and 1824. Had he gone to western New York in 1823, he most likely would have visited his older brother Warren, who had been practicing medicine in the area for at least six years. In his apothecary ledger, Warren noted the names of Dyer, Erastus, and Sally Cowdery, but there is no mention of Oliver. Nor is a boy Oliver's age listed in the 1820 census record for Warren Cowdery.[112]

4. There is no evidence that Oliver met the Smiths before 1828 or that he then knew they were related (Oliver Cowdery was a third cousin to Lucy Mack Smith). Similarly, Lucy says the Joseph Sr. family met Oliver for the first time in 1828 and does not mention any awareness of their distant family connection.[113]

Like other attempts to establish an Ethan Smith-Oliver Cowdery-Joseph Smith connection, Van Wagoner's version lacks support from primary documents.

Conclusion

In the cold spring of 1829, when Samuel Smith and Oliver Cowdery set out on a 130-mile journey from Palmyra, New York, to visit the Prophet in Harmony, Pennsylvania, traveling through miserable weather—"raining, freezing, and thawing alternately, which had rendered the roads almost impassable"[114]—Oliver was only twenty-two years old. Contrary to well-known theories regarding the Wood Scrape and *View of the Hebrews,* his family history offered no evidence of preparation for the establishment of a new religion. And while his family's history is well documented, his personal life seemed ordinary, with his birth record as the only primary Vermont document mentioning him by name. All of that was about to change. He faced an extraordinary future, full of "days never to be forgotten."[115]

Notes

The author wishes to thank Richard L. Anderson, of Brigham Young University, and Ruth Czar and Kathy Hutson, of the Poultney Historical Society, for their help with this article. This article was originally printed in *BYU Studies* 39/1 (2000): 106–29.

1. Lucy Cowdery Young to Brigham H. Young, March 7, 1887, Family and Church History Department Archives, The Church of Jesus Christ of Latter-day Saints (hereafter Church Archives).

2. The earliest account of the Wood movement is in a newspaper article entitled "The Rodsmen," published in *Vermont American*, May 7, 1828. This article summarizes the Wood Scrape but does not name any of the participants, nor does it mention a counterfeiter. This was followed by Barnes Frisbie, *The History of Middletown, Vermont* (Rutland, VT: Tuttle, 1867), 43–64. Recollections by Wells residents are recounted in *Hiland Paul and Robert Parks, History of Wells, Vermont, for the First Century after Its Settlement* (Rutland, VT: Tuttle, 1869; repr., Wells, VT: Wells Historical Society, 1979), 79–82. For in-depth analyses of the Wood Scrape, see Richard Lloyd Anderson, "The Mature Joseph Smith and Treasure Searching," *BYU Studies* 24 (fall 1984): 489–560; David Persuitte, *Joseph Smith and the Origins of the Book of Mormon* (Jefferson, NC: McFarland, 1985), 56–59, 234–38; D. Michael Quinn, *Early Mormonism and the Magic World View*, rev. and enl. (Salt Lake City: Signature Books, 1998), 35–36, 121–30; Dan Vogel, ed., *Early Mormon Documents* (Salt Lake City: Signature Books, 1996), 1:599–621.

3. Ethan Smith's *View of the Hebrews* was originally published in Poultney, Vermont, by Smith and Shute, the first edition in 1823 and the second in 1825. It was recently reprinted. See *View of the Hebrews: 1825*, 2nd ed. complete text by Ethan Smith, edited with an introduction by Charles D. Tate Jr. (Provo, UT: BYU Religious Studies Center, 1996). Linkage with the Book of Mormon was first suggested by psychologist I. Woodbridge Riley, *The Founder of Mormonism* (New York: Dodd, Mead, 1903), 124–25. B. H. Roberts discussed the question of whether *View of the Hebrews* could have influenced the writing of the Book of Mormon in his papers entitled "A Book of Mormon Study" and "A Parallel," in *B. H. Roberts: Studies of the Book of Mormon*, ed. Brigham D. Madsen (Urbana: University of Illinois Press, 1985), reviewed by John W. Welch in *Pacific Historical Review* 55 (November 1986): 619–23. For various discussions on Ethan Smith's possible influence on the Book of Mormon or lack thereof, see Fawn Brodie, *No Man Knows My History*, 2nd ed. (New York: Knopf, 1971), 46–49; Richard L. Bushman, *Joseph Smith and the Beginnings of Mormonism* (Urbana: University of Illinois Press, 1984), 134–38; Robert N. Hullinger, *Joseph Smith's Response to Skepticism* (Salt Lake City: Signature Books, 1992), 55–59, 183–89; Robert N. Hullinger, "Lost Tribes of Israel and the Book of Mormon," *Lutheran Quarterly* 22 (August 1970): 319–29; Francis W. Kirkham, *A New Witness for Christ in America: The Book of Mormon* (Independence, MO: Zion's Printing and Publishing, 1951), 2:391–96; Stan Larson, *Quest for the Gold Plates: Thomas Stuart Ferguson's Archaeological Search for the Book of Mormon* (Salt Lake City: Free Thinker Press, 1996), 144–49; Spencer J. Palmer and William L. Knecht, "*View of the Hebrews*: Substitute for Inspiration?" *BYU Studies* 5 (1964): 105–13; Persuitte, *Origins of the Book of Mormon*, reviewed by L. Ara Norwood in *Review of Books on the Book of Mormon* 2 (1990): 187–204; Richard S. Van Wagoner, *Sidney Rigdon: A Portrait of Religious Excess* (Salt Lake City: Signature Books, 1994), 463–67, reviewed by

David J. Whittaker in *Journal of Mormon History* 23 (spring 1997): 189–95; Dan Vogel, *Indian Origins and the Book of Mormon: Religious Solutions from Columbus to Joseph Smith* (Salt Lake City: Signature Books, 1986), 18–69, reviewed by Kevin Christensen in *Review of Books on the Book of Mormon* 2 (1990): 214–57; John W. Welch, "*View of the Hebrews*: 'An Unparallel,'" in *Reexploring the Book of Mormon*, ed. John W. Welch (Salt Lake City: Deseret Book and FARMS, 1992), 83–87. For specific discussions of B. H. Roberts's writings, see Brigham D. Madsen, "Reflections on LDS Disbelief in the Book of Mormon as History," *Dialogue* 30 (fall 1997): 87–97; Truman G. Madsen, "B. H. Roberts and the Book of Mormon," *BYU Studies* 19 (summer 1979): 427–45; Truman G. Madsen and John W. Welch, "Did B. H. Roberts Lose Faith in the Book of Mormon?" (Provo, UT: FARMS, 1985).

4.   Mary Bryant Alverson Mehling, *Cowdrey-Cowdery-Cowdray Genealogy* (Frank Allaben Genealogical, 1911), 79. Mehling compiled parts of her book in the 1880s and obtained information from Oliver Cowdery's daughter, Marie Louise Cowdery Johnson. See also William Hyslop Fuller, *Genealogy of Some Descendants of Edward Fuller of the Mayflower* (Palmer, MA: Fiske, 1908), 199; Grace E. Pember Wood, *A History of the Town of Wells, Vermont* (Wells, VT: By the author, 1955), 87.

5.   Three biographies of Oliver Cowdery have been published: Stanley R. Gunn, *Oliver Cowdery: Second Elder and Scribe* (Salt Lake City: Bookcraft, 1962); Phillip R. Legg, *Oliver Cowdery: The Elusive Second Elder of the Restoration* (Independence, MO: Herald Publishing House, 1989); and Joseph Hyrum Greenhalgh, *Oliver Cowdery: The Man Outstanding* (n.p., [1964]). In addition, Andrew Jenson published a key biographical essay of Oliver Cowdery in *Latter-day Saint Biographical Encyclopedia: A Compilation of Biographical Sketches of Prominent Men and Women in The Church of Jesus Christ of Latter-day Saints* (Salt Lake City: Andrew Jenson History, 1901–36), 1:246–51. None of these publications refers to original Vermont documents and none mentions the Cowdery family's stay in Middletown.

6.   All Wells documents except the census report are from the Wells Town Record, an unpublished document located in the Wells, Vermont, town clerk's office. Much of the Wells record is available at the LDS Family History Library in Salt Lake City. Russell R. Rich conducted on-site research in Wells in 1974 and discovered several references to William Cowdery in the Vermont records for this period. William Cowdery's name is variously spelled *Cowdry, Cowdrey,* and *Cowdre.*

7.   Mormon historians have generally accepted Mehling's claim that Warren was born in Poultney, Vermont. Mehling, *Cowdrey-Cowdery-Cowdray Genealogy*, 170. However, the Wells Town Record states that Warren was born in Wells. Wells Town Record, Record of Births, 146. While another section of the Wells record clouds the picture by stating that Warren was born in Reding (probably referring to Reading, Vermont), the secondary sources state he was born in Wells. See Wells Town Record, Record of Births, 229–30.

8.   Wells Town Record, List of the Free Men in Wells, September 1789, 105.

9.   Wells Town Record, Record of Births, 229–30.

10.   Wells Town Record, Land Records, April 12, 1791 (238), April 20, 1791 (236), April 22, 1791 (224), November 22, 1792 (414), February 28, 1793 (423).

11.   Wells Town Record, Minutes of Town Meeting, February 20, 1792, 292.

12.   Wells Town Record, Record of Ear Marks for Livestock, July 1793, 102.

13.   Wells Town Record, Record of Births, 150–51.

14. Wells Town Record, Record of Births, 152–53.

15. Wells Town Record, Affidavit from William Cowdery, December 19, 1797, 159.

16. Wells Town Record, Record of Births, 154–55.

17. Bureau of the Census, "Population Schedules of the Second Census of the United States, 1800," Wells, Vermont, prepared by the National Archives and Records Service (Washington, DC, 1960), 264.

18. Wells Town Record, Record of Births, 156–57.

19. Wells Town Record, Minutes of Town Meeting, March [?] 1803, 185. Apparently, William Cowdery was also elected tithingman in Wells on one or two occasions. Thanks to Richard Lloyd Anderson for this information.

20. Wells Town Record, Record of Births, 158–59.

21. Wells Town Record, Record of Births, 158–59.

22. Wells Town Record, Land Records, January 8, 1807 (99), January 9, 1807 (376–77), December 24, 1807 (72), December 24, 1807 (441), November 9, 1808 (16).

23. Paul and Parks, *History of Wells*, 81; Fuller, *Some Descendants of Edward Fuller*, 199.

24. Mehling, *Cowdrey-Cowdery-Cowdray Genealogy*, 95.

25. The original marriage record for William Cowdery and Keziah Pearce Austin was found in the Middletown Springs town clerk's office by Deborah Morris in August 1998. It is also available on microfilm at the LDS Family History Library. See Middletown Springs (VT) Town Record, Births, Marriages, and Deaths, vol. 2, 34 (March 18, 1810).

26. Carl A. Curtis, "Cowdery Genealogical Material," 1970, 1, Special Collections and Manuscripts, Harold B. Lee Library, Brigham Young University, Provo, Utah (hereafter cited as BYU Special Collections). Curtis was the son of Caroline Eleanor Cowdery Curtis, the daughter of Warren A. Cowdery (and niece of Oliver Cowdery).

27. Bureau of the Census, "Population Schedules of the Third Census of the United States, 1810," Ontario, New York, prepared by the National Archives and Records Service (Washington, DC, 1958), 786. Richard Lloyd Anderson informed me that William Cowdery was included in this census.

28. Mehling, *Cowdrey-Cowdery-Cowdray Genealogy*, 186.

29. Curtis, "Cowdery Genealogical Material," 1.

30. Mehling, *Cowdrey-Cowdery-Cowdray Genealogy*, 187.

31. Middletown Springs Land Records, 1814–21, 391. This record indicates that William Cowdery lived in Middletown in 1815 and sold thirty acres of land situated in the northern part of Middletown to Moses Copeland.

32. Mehling, *Cowdrey-Cowdery-Cowdray Genealogy*, 188.

33. "Historical and Genealogical Material, Poultney, Vermont, Part I, Historical," 1052, typescript, Poultney town clerk's office, Poultney, Vermont.

34. Bureau of the Census, "Population Schedules of the Fourth Census of the United States, 1820," Poultney, Vermont, prepared by the National Archives and Records Service (Washington, DC, 1959), 250.

35. Wood, *History of the Town of Wells*, 29.

36. Wood, *History of the Town of Wells*, 7–8.

37. Wood, *History of the Town of Wells*, 8.

38. Karl P. Stofko, *Vital Statistics Records from the Records of the First Church of Christ, Congregational in East Haddam, Connecticut, 1704–1850*, 37; *Second Congregational*

Church and Ecclesiastical Society (East Haddam Connecticut), Church Records, 1733–1931, 22.

39. Mehling, *Cowdrey-Cowdery-Cowdray Genealogy*, 79.

40. For the death of Rebecca, see Paul and Parks, *History of Wells*, 81. Scott H. Faulring has concluded that Oliver Cowdery was suffering from chronic pulmonary tuberculosis when he died. See Scott H. Faulring, "The Return of Oliver Cowdery," in *The Disciple as Witness: Essays on Latter-day Saint History and Doctrine in Honor of Richard Lloyd Anderson*, ed. Stephen D. Ricks, Donald W. Parry, and Andrew H. Hedges (Provo, UT: FARMS, 2000), 172 n. 106.

41. Elmer J. Culp, "Early Vermont Roots of Mormonism," 1980, 5, photocopy in BYU Special Collections. In a talk given to the Pawlett Historical Society on February 6, 1980, Culp argued that "there is evidence that Oliver went to live with them [the Glass family]" (5), but he does not say what that evidence is.

42. Bureau of the Census, "Population Schedules of the Third Census of the United States, 1810," Wells, Vermont, prepared by the National Archives and Records Service (Washington, DC, 1960), 26; Bureau of the Census, "Population Schedules of the Third Census of the United States, 1810," Ontario, New York, 786.

43. Keziah Pearce was born in Canaan, Litchfield, Connecticut, on July 1, 1773. Mehling, *Cowdrey-Cowdery-Cowdray Genealogy*, 95–96. Her father, Phineas Pearce, moved to Poultney, Vermont, "soon after the surrender of Burgoyne." Joseph Joslin, Barnes Frisbie, and Frederick Ruggles, *A History of the Town of Poultney, Vermont* (Poultney, VT: Journal Printing Office, 1875), 319. The Phineas Pearce family (spelled Pierce) is listed in the 1790 U.S. Census for Poultney (Bureau of the Census, "Population Schedules of the First Census of the United States, 1790," Poultney, Vermont, prepared by the National Archives and Records Service [Washington, DC, 1965], 245.) Keziah married Harrington Austin sometime in the 1790s; they lived in Poultney for a time, but by the time of the 1800 census, they were residents of Middletown (with Harrington listed in the 1800 Middletown census as "Horrington"). For the birth of Silas Austin, son of Harrington and Keziah, see Helen McGauphy and Pauline Austin, professional researcher files, correspondence in possession of the author; Edith Austin Moore, *Unplaced Austin Records* (n.p.: By the author), 3:149. Harrington died between 1800 and 1810. The marriage record lists Keziah as a resident of Middletown, so it is possible that she resided in Middletown from 1800 to 1810.

44. Charles T. Morrissey, *Vermont: A Bicentennial History* (New York: Norton, 1981), 109. According to Cowdery tradition, the family left Middletown in the summer of 1810, returned in 1813 or 1814, traveling by ox team. See Curtis, "Cowdery Genealogical Material."

45. Fuller, *Some Descendants of Edward Fuller*, 199; Margaret R. Jenks, *Wells Cemetery Inscriptions, Rutland County Vermont* (Kirkland, WA: By the author, 1980), 19.

46. See Lucy Mack Smith, *Biographical Sketches of Joseph Smith, the Prophet, and His Progenitors for Many Generations* (London: published for Orson Pratt by S. W. Richards, 1853), 59–66; Bushman, *Beginnings of Mormonism*, 32; LeRoy S. Wirthlin, "Nathan Smith (1762–1828) Surgical Consultant to Joseph Smith," *BYU Studies* 17 (spring 1977): 319–37. Charles T. Morrissey discusses an 1813 epidemic of spotted fever, or cerebrospinal meningitis; see Morrissey, *Vermont*, 109.

47. According to Richard L. Bushman, the cold weather during the summer of 1816

"is generally attributed to the volcanic explosion of Tambora on Sumbawa in 1815, which blew fifteen cubic kilometers of volcanic ash." See Bushman, *Beginnings of Mormonism*, 200. For more about the "poverty year" of 1816, see Smith, *Biographical Sketches*, 66; Paul and Parks, *History of Wells*, 20; Morrissey, *Vermont*, 109 n. 99.

48. On Warren's marriage, see Mehling, *Cowdrey-Cowdery-Cowdray Genealogy*, 170.

49. Stephen Cowdery's whereabouts during this period are unknown. He is not mentioned in Warren's records nor is he included in the 1820 census for either William or Warren. See Curtis, "Cowdery Genealogical Material," Warren Cowdery Ledger, 1.

50. Leonard J. Arrington, "Oliver Cowdery's Kirtland, Ohio, 'Sketch Book,'" *BYU Studies* 12, no. 4 (1972): 414. Silas Austin was born in Poultney in 1799 to Harrington Austin and Keziah Pearce. He married Emily Buckland in Licking County, Ohio, in 1819 and spent most of his life there. He worked as a blacksmith and served in the Mexican-American War. He and Emily had four children. Emily died in 1875 and Silas in 1886. They are buried in Harrison, Licking County, Ohio. See Helen McGauphy and Pauline Austin, professional researcher files; Licking County History and Court Records, Newark, Ohio; Moore, *Unplaced Austin Records*, 3:149.

51. "Members, The Congregational Church, Poultney, Vermont, 1782 to 1898, copied from Mr. Edward C. Ripley's Papers," typescript, 1067, Poultney town clerk's office, Poultney, Vermont.

52. Paul and Parks, *History of Wells*, 79.

53. Bushman, *Beginnings of Mormonism*, 21.

54. In 1826, Lyman Stevens of Wells was authorized by "the overseers of the poor" to assist Arunah Glass, but Arunah was to pay his own doctor's bill (indicating the family suffered health problems that compounded their financial difficulties).

55. Bureau of the Census, "Population Schedules of the Fourth Census of the United States, 1820," Wells, Vermont, prepared by the National Archives and Records Service (Washington, DC, 1959), 259.

56. Wells Town Record, Land Records, 380. For 1823, see Land Records, 383. There is no district record for 1824, and Arunah is not listed in the record for 1825, but for 1826 and 1827 two students are listed with the Glass household. This could not have been Oliver because he was over eighteen—and also because he was apparently in New York at the time. See Wells Town Record, Land Records, 604, 651. Arunah Glass reportedly lived in Wells until 1855, when he moved to Illinois, dying there in 1860 at the age of 64. See Wood, *History of the Town of Wells*, 55.

57. Wood, *History of the Town of Wells*, 20–21.

58. Young to Young, March 7, 1887.

59. Frisbie, *History of Middletown*, 47.

60. Frisbie, *History of Middletown*, 54. Frisbie gives the year as 1801, but as Dan Vogel argues, "The year 1801 is probably an error since the earliest account of the Wood movement cites the date as January 14, 1802 (*Vermont American*, May 7, 1828)." See Vogel, *Early Mormon Documents*, 1:609 n. 15.

61. Frisbie, *History of Middletown*, 62. Frisbie adds, though, that the fact that Joseph Sr. "was a rods-man under the tuition of this counterfeiter after he went to Palmyra has been proven to my satisfaction, at least" (62).

62. Frisbie, *History of Middletown*, 62.

63. Frisbie, *History of Middletown*, 46–47.

64. Frisbie, *History of Middletown*, 42–63.
65. Quinn, *Magic World View*, 37.
66. Quinn, *Magic World View*, 318.
67. Frisbie, *History of Middletown*, 62.
68. Paul and Parks, *History of Wells*, 81, 82.
69. Anderson, "Mature Joseph Smith," 522.
70. "The Rodsmen," *Vermont American*.
71. Frisbie, *History of Middletown*, 93.
72. Quinn, *Magic World View*, 38.

73. Book of Commandments 7:3. The Book of Commandments was a collection of the Prophet Joseph Smith's early revelations, published in 1833. These revelations were incorporated in the Doctrine and Covenants in 1835. The verse concerning Oliver and the rod now reads: "Now this is not all thy gift; for you have another gift, which is the gift of Aaron; behold, it has told you many things; Behold, there is no other power, save the power of God, that can cause this gift of Aaron to be with you" (D&C 8:6–7).

74. Anderson, "Mature Joseph Smith," 528.
75. Anderson, "Mature Joseph Smith," 524–25.
76. Bushman, *Joseph Smith and the Beginnings of Mormonism*, 98.
77. Quinn, *Magic World View*, 125.
78. Vogel, *Early Mormon Documents*, 1:635, 638.
79. Vogel, *Early Mormon Documents*, 1:639.

80. Lucy Smith, "Preliminary Manuscript," 1845, 25, Church Archives. In her published work, Lucy dates the move to Randolf in 1802. However, the published account offers no support for a temporary residence in Poultney, because Lucy's account has the family renting the Tunbridge farm and moving directly from there to Randolf. See Smith, *Biographical Sketches*, 45.

81. "Historical and Genealogical Material," 165–84.

82. Quinn fails to account for the obvious anti-Mormon bias of Frisbie, who at one point refers to "this monster—Mormonism" (Frisbie, *History of Middletown*, 64), which makes his theories about Mormon origins suspect. Quinn also fails to explore the implications of his own claim that in 1800 Joseph Smith was "the most common name in America" (*Magic World View*, 125). The 1800 census lists eleven Joseph Smiths in Vermont and well over a hundred combined total in Vermont, New Hampshire, Massachusetts, and New York. According to Vogel, none of these census records is an exact match for the makeup of the Joseph Sr. family. See Vogel, *Early Mormon Documents*, 1:640. This makes locating the family solely on the basis of census records impossible.

83. Quinn, *Magic World View*, 125, 132.
84. Quinn, *Magic World View*, 124–26.
85. Quinn, *Magic World View*, 126–27.

86. Quinn attempts unsuccessfully to link Winchell with Luman Walters, named by Pomeroy Tucker as a money-digging associate of Joseph Smith. Stating that the family of Philastus Hurlbut "*may have been related*" to the family of Walters and that Hurlbut "*may have been related*" to Winchell, Quinn suddenly invents the phrase "Walter(s)-Winchell" as if the two are interchangeable. See Quinn, *Magic World View*, 122–23; emphasis added. However, he offers no documents associating the two men; nor does he acknowledge that even if Hurlbut was related to both of them (which itself is purely

speculative), it would not necessarily mean they were related to each other. Quinn does not consider the possibility that Frisbie confused Winchell with Walters. Persuitte suggests that "it seems to be a reasonable conclusion that Walters was Wingate/Winchell" (*Origins of the Book of Mormon*, 238). For information on the affidavits collected by Hurlbut, Thorne, and Deming, see Vogel, *Early Mormon Documents*, 2:13–77, 167–81, 185–214.

87. Frisbie, *History of Middletown*, 61–62.

88. David M. Ludlum, *Social Ferment in Vermont, 1791–1850* (New York: Columbia University Press, 1939; New York: AMS Press, 1966), 242, cited in Quinn, *Magic World View*, 386.

89. Richard C. Roberts, "View of the Hebrews," in *Encyclopedia of Mormonism*, ed. Daniel H. Ludlow (New York: Macmillan, 1992), 4:1509.

90. See note 3 above.

91. Thomas Stuart Ferguson to Ron Barney, January 10, 1983, cited in Stan Larson, "The Odyssey of Thomas Stuart Ferguson," *Dialogue* 23 (spring 1990): 83.

92. "Historical and Genealogical Material, Poultney," 1052.

93. Persuitte, *Origins of the Book of Mormon*, 8.

94. Persuitte, *Origins of the Book of Mormon*, 235. Persuitte correctly notes that the Cowderys lived in Middletown before moving to Poultney but mistakenly believes the family arrived in Poultney in 1810. Brigham Madsen makes a much more serious error when he writes that Oliver Cowdery "had lived in Poultney for twenty-two years until 1825" (Roberts, *Studies of the Book of Mormon*, 27). This calculation misses Oliver's birth date by three years (he was born in 1806, not 1803) and has Oliver in Poultney fifteen years longer than he actually was.

95. Persuitte, *Origins of the Book of Mormon*, 270. Persuitte reports that in 1977 he took photos of Poultney Congregational Church records and that they included information about the letter of recommendation and also state that William and Keziah's three daughters were baptized in 1818 "on the faith of the mother" (*Origins of the Book of Mormon*, 270, 7). Persuitte obtained these records from the Poultney Historical Society but reports that they were stolen in the winter of that year. I could not find them when I searched the Historical Society's holdings and the town clerk's office in 1999.

96. Persuitte, *Origins of the Book of Mormon*, 8, 57.

97. Stofko, *Records of the First Church of Christ, Congregational in East Haddam*, 37.

98. "Members, The Congregational Church," 1067.

99. Joslin, Frisbie, and Ruggles, *History of the Town of Poultney*, 104.

100. Bureau of the Census, "Population Schedules of the Second Census of the United States, 1800," Middletown, Vermont, prepared by the National Archives and Records Service (Washington, DC, 1960), 110; marriage record for William Cowdery and Keziah Austin, March 18, 1810, Middletown Town Record, Births, Marriages, and Deaths, 2:34.

101. Curtis, "Cowdery Genealogical Material," 1.

102. "Members, The Congregational Church," 1065–71.

103. Persuitte, *Origins of the Book of Mormon*, 8.

104. Emily A. Ross to William Powell, April 22, 1976, Church Archives. Asked to research whether Oliver Cowdery was a member of Ethan Smith's congregation, Poultney resident Emily Ross was unable to locate any connection in the documentary record.

106. Persuitte, *Origins of the Book of Mormon*, 254. The original manuscript of the Book of Mormon offers strong evidence that Oliver acted simply as scribe, not coauthor. See Royal Skousen, "Translating the Book of Mormon: Evidence from the Original Manuscript," in *Book of Mormon Authorship Revisited: The Evidence for Ancient Origins*, ed. Noel B. Reynolds (Provo, UT: FARMS, 1997), 61–93.

107. *Cleveland Herald*, November 25, 1830, clipping in Milton V. Backman Jr. and others, comps., "Contemporary Accounts of the Latter-day Saints and Their Leaders Appearing in Early Ohio Newspapers," 2 vols., vol. 2, BYU Special Collections.

108. Van Wagoner, *Sidney Rigdon*, 465–66. Apparently following Brigham Madsen's lead, Van Wagoner erroneously claims Oliver Cowdery resided in Poultney from 1803 to 1825. Of course, Oliver was not actually born until 1806. Since Van Wagoner is discussing the possibility that Oliver was a traveling agent for Smith & Shute, this three-year mistake is crucial. It seems unlikely for Oliver to have had such a job at age sixteen, his actual age in 1823.

109. Scott H. Faulring to Larry E. Morris, October 29, 1998. The information on Benjamin Franklin Cowdery comes from Milton W. Hamilton, *The Country Printer, New York State, 1785–1830*, 2nd ed. (Port Washington, NY: Friedman, 1964), 265–66, 92.

110. Oliver Cowdery to Joseph Smith, December 28, 1829, Joseph Smith Letterbook, 1:5, microfilm, Joseph Smith Papers, Church Archives.

111. Joslin, Frisbie, and Ruggles, *History of the Town of Poultney*, 89–94.

112. Curtis, "Cowdery Genealogical Material," Warren Cowdery Ledger, 2; Bureau of the Census, "Population Schedules of the Fourth Census of the United States, 1820," LeRoy, New York, prepared by the National Archives and Records Service (Washington, DC, 1959), 150.

113. Smith, *Biographical Sketches*, 128.

114. Smith, *Biographical Sketches*, 130.

115. "Oliver Cowdery to W. W. Phelps," September 7, 1834, [Letter I], *Messenger and Advocate* 1 (October 1834): 14.

THE COMING FORTH
OF THE BOOK OF MORMON

John W. Welch

*T*he translation of the Book of Mormon, completed by Joseph Smith in June 1829, was an amazing feat. By any standard, this 588-page holy book is extraordinary. Isaiah's words, "a marvelous work and a wonder" (Isa. 29:14), which can be translated from the Hebrew more literally as "a miraculous work and a miracle," readily describe the coming forth of this key restoration text.

Divine manifestations of several kinds directed the rapid course of the translation. Through angelic ministrations, the gift of powers to translate, the guidance of visions, and in many other ways, the hand of God was evident in the truly astounding work of bringing forth the ancient Nephite record. Through the Book of Mormon came many crucial revelations opening the heavens for all to receive: vital testimonies of the divinity of Jesus Christ, abundant declarations of God's plan of salvation, heavenly dispensations of ethical teachings, and prophetic patterns for religious rites and ordinances. It is impossible to imagine Mormonism without the Book of Mormon. Its translation was a key event that unlocked a treasury of God's dealings with mankind in the past and, in so doing, opened the way for his work to go forward in the present and on into the future.

While the embedding had occurred centuries earlier, the unfolding process commenced in September 1823, when Joseph Smith Jr. was visited several times by the angel Moroni, who informed him that God "had a work for [him] to do" (Joseph Smith—History 1:33).

THE TESTIMONY OF THREE WITNESSES.

Be it known unto all nations, kindreds, tongues, and people, unto whom this work shall come, that we, through the grace of God the Father, and our Lord Jesus Christ, have seen the plates which contain this record, which is a record of the people of Nephi, and also of the Lamanites, his brethren, and also of the people of Jared, which came from the tower of which hath been spoken; and we also know that they have been translated by the gift and power of God, for his voice hath declared it unto us; wherefore we know of a surety, that the work is true. And we also testify that we have seen the engravings which are upon the plates; and they have been shewn unto us by the power of God, and not of man. And we declare with words of soberness, that an Angel of God came down from heaven, and he brought and laid before our eyes, that we beheld and saw the plates, and the engravings thereon; and we know that it is by the grace of God the Father, and our Lord Jesus Christ, that we beheld and bear record that these things are true; and it is marvellous in our eyes: Nevertheless, the voice of the Lord commanded us that we should bear record of it; wherefore, to be obedient unto the commandments of God, we bear testimony of these things.—And we know that if we are faithful in Christ, we shall rid our garments of the blood of all men, and be found spotless before the judgement seat of Christ, and shall dwell with him eternally in the heavens. And the honor be to the Father, and to the Son, and to the Holy Ghost, which is one God. Amen.

OLIVER COWDERY,
DAVID WHITMER,
MARTIN HARRIS.

The angel went on to state that a book written upon gold plates containing the fullness of the gospel was deposited in a stone box in a nearby hill, and that in due time he, Joseph Smith, would be given stewardship over that book. This extensive record had been compiled mainly by the final Nephite leader, Mormon, who lived in the fourth century AD. Painstakingly, he had engraved onto the final set of plates carefully quoted, purposefully abridged, and paraphrased materials that he drew from a much larger collection of historical and religious records that had been written by his predecessors over the previous centuries. Most prominently, Mormon's account featured numerous instances of angelic and divine manifestations, including appearances of Jesus Christ during the year after his resurrection. In about AD 385, Mormon, after adding his own concluding narrative, gave the plates to his son Moroni (who died about AD 421). After appending his abridgement of the Jaredite records, a few ecclesiastical documents, and his own farewell, Moroni finally deposited the plates in the Hill Cumorah in modern-day western New York. On September 22, 1827, Moroni released those plates to Joseph, thus inaugurating one of the most important stages in the Restoration of the gospel.

Numerous approaches can and should be taken in approaching the Book of Mormon. This complex book has been read and scrutinized in many ways: textually, doctrinally, historically, comparatively, literarily, legally, statistically, geographically, philosophically, practically, biographically, intellectually, prayerfully, and spiritually—to name some of the most obvious. The richness of this book inevitably invites several questions: How was this book written? Where did it come from? Joseph Smith testified that he translated the Book of Mormon miraculously, by the gift and power of God. Is that testimony credible?

The set of over two hundred documents in the full version of *Opening the Heavens* assembles data pertinent to that ultimate question. A number of these documents pertaining to Oliver Cowdery's role in the translation also appear here. In particular, from these contemporaneous historical records, this study seeks to determine, as precisely as possible, when the Book of Mormon was translated and how long it took to complete this impressive task. The overwhelming accumulation of the consistent historical details provided by eyewitness participants and local observers leads to the solid conclusion that the Book of Mormon was translated in a very short period of time. Oliver played a crucial role in this process. Inside of three astonishingly compressed months, Joseph Smith produced the Book of Mormon. Its text simply emerged as it fell from his lips, line after line, recorded by his attentive scribe. The rapidity of the translation left no time for steps normally taken in producing translations.

The historical records corroborating the translation of the Book of Mormon are indeed copious and quite detailed. In addition to several contemporaneous references in the Doctrine and Covenants to the translation as it was underway, accounts were left by many of the participants, eyewitnesses, or observant people who were closely associated with the unfolding translation. These people include Joseph Smith and Emma Smith, and especially the Three Witnesses of the Book of Mormon—Martin Harris, Oliver Cowdery, and David Whitmer. The thirty-seven accounts given by Joseph Smith and Oliver Cowdery are notably specific and powerfully consistent.[1]

Consisting of 202 documents, the entire collection is presented in the document section of *Opening the Heavens*, and a portion of these documents has been reproduced here. Underlining is reproduced from the original document. Editorial marks include angle brackets < > to indicate insertions made by the author of the document. Strikeouts are shown by ~~strikeouts~~. Brackets [ ] indicate editorial comments.

By way of introducing these documents, an annotated chronology is first given, detailing the main events and heavenly manifestations that transpired during the translation and publication of the Book of Mormon from 1829 through 1830. Despite a few minor uncertainties in this historical data, most of the information falls clearly into a single logical sequence of events. The historical record abundantly sustains the basic narrative concerning the coming forth of the Book of Mormon. The sheer number of witnesses, friendly or otherwise, who were aware of this work as it progressed and who sensed its importance enough to speak or write to others about it, renders alternative accounts of fabrication or deception unlikely. At least, perpetrating such a ruse would have necessarily involved the willing collusion of many others who do not appear prone to have been willing coconspirators.

In sum, it is shown that nearly all the 590 pages printed in the 1830 edition of the Book of Mormon were translated, dictated, and written all within an extremely short and intensely busy period of time, from April 7 to the last week of June 1829. Virtually no excess time existed during those three months for Joseph Smith to plan, to ponder about, to research around, to hunt for sources, to organize data, to draft, to revise, or to polish the pages of the original manuscript of this book. Although Joseph became aware of and began contemplating this assignment in September 1823, and while he translated the 116 pages containing the book of Lehi from April 12, 1828, to June 14, 1828, which were sadly lost that summer, once Joseph and Oliver set to work on April 7, 1829, the pages of the Book of Mormon flowed forth in rapid succession. The text of the Book of Mormon was dictated one time through, essentially in final form. This was done despite significant interruptions and distractions. Such a feat, in and of itself, constitutes a considerable achievement, given the length, quality, and complexity of the Book of Mormon alone.

Further details concerning Oliver's involvement in this monumental work, as well as the description of the plates, the complex structure of the Book of Mormon, and what can be gathered concerning Joseph Smith's means and methods of translating the Book of Mormon, can be found conveniently at the beginning of published editions of the book, in standard histories of the Church,[2] in the *Encyclopedia of Mormonism*, or in other surveys of scholarship about the Book of Mormon.[3]

Dates listed in the chronology are, for the most part, historically verifiable, but some have been approximated. Taken together these details coalesce into a clear picture of the miraculous time of translation of the Book of Mormon.

Chronology of Events from April 1829 to April 1830 relating to the Translation and Publication of the Book of Mormon

April 5, 1829. Oliver Cowdery arrived in Harmony to assist Joseph with the translation of the Book of Mormon.[4] Joseph told Oliver "his entire history as far as it was necessary for his information in those things which concerned him." Oliver was given assurances that "the words or the work which thou hast been writing are true" (D&C 6:17, 1833 ed.), and he was offered "a gift, if you desire of me, to translate, even as my servant Joseph." Joseph and Oliver probably started writing at or shortly after Mosiah 1.[5] Oliver and Joseph met for the first time in person on April 5, 1829. Joseph Knight reports this event: "Next Spring Oliver Cowdry a young man from palmyra Came to see old Mr Smith, Josephs father, about this work and he sent him Down to pensylveny to see Joseph and satisfy him self. So he Came Down and was soon Convinced of the truth of the work."[6] A few paragraphs later, Knight expressly places this event in "the spring of 1829."[7] Lucy Smith's published reminiscences indicate that Oliver had only secondhand information about Joseph before April 1829, stating that after Oliver "had been in the school but a short time, when he began to hear from all quarters concerning the plates, and as soon began to importune Mr. Smith upon the subject, but for a considerable length of time did not succeed in eliciting any information."[8] David Whitmer, who was first to hear of Joseph Jr. among the Whitmers, recalled speaking with Oliver about the matter in 1828. Oliver was then a teacher in Palmyra and boarded with the Joseph Smith Sr. family for a time until the school term ended in March 1829.[9] During this time, Joseph Jr. was in Harmony.

Oliver explicitly dates his first meeting with Joseph Smith Jr. as April 5, 1829: "Near the time of the setting of the Sun, Sabbath evening, April 5th, 1829, my natural eyes, for the first time beheld this brother."[10] On the same page printed in 1834, Oliver said he had endured many "fateagues and privations . . . for the gospel's sake, since 1828, with this brother." Apparently Oliver had begun suffering criticism as early as 1828 for his interest in Joseph and the plates.

In 1835 he said he had known Joseph intimately for "almost seven years."[11] From 1829 to 1835 is seven years inclusive. Clear evidence supports April 5, 1829, as the date for the first meeting of Oliver Cowdery and Joseph Smith.

April 6, 1829. Oliver recorded: "On Monday the 6th, I assisted [Joseph] in arranging some business of a temporal nature."[12]

April 7, 1829. Oliver began writing as scribe to Joseph Smith, as he remained for the greater part of the translation. He said he transcribed it all "with the exception of a few pages." Joseph remembered that Oliver wrote "with little cessation." Oliver later recalled, "These were days never to be forgotten—to sit under the sound of a voice dictated by the *inspiration* of heaven, awakened the utmost gratitude of this bosom! Day after day I continued, uninterrupted, to write from his mouth, as he translated . . . 'The book of Mormon.'"[13] Sometime during April 1829, Doctrine and Covenants 6, 7, 8, and 9 were received, and Joseph made a trip to Colesville. Oliver unsuccessfully attempted to translate.

Mid to Late April. Oliver wrote two letters to David Whitmer, telling him that "he was convinced that Smith had the records" and giving "a few lines of what they had translated" and assuring David "that he knew of a certainty that [Joseph] had a record of a people that inhabited this continent, and that the plates they were translating gave a complete history of these people."

About May 10, 1829. Around this time, Joseph and Oliver ran out of provisions. They went to Colesville (Coleville) to see if Joseph Knight would help them with some provisions, but he was in "Cattskill."[14] An account attributed to Joseph Smith might relate to this same trip to Colesville, although an occasion in 1830 is possible:

> When I first commenced this work, and had got two or three individuals to believe, I went about thirty miles with Oliver Cowdery, to see them. We had only one horse between us. When we arrived, a mob of about one hundred men came upon us before we had time to eat, and chased us all night; and we arrived back again [in

Harmony] a little after daylight, having traveled about sixty miles in all, and without food.[15]

Joseph and Oliver returned to Harmony and looked to see "if they Could find a place to work for provisions, But found none. They returned home and found me [Joseph Knight] there with provisions, and they ware glad for they ware out."[16] Joseph Knight brought writing paper (foolscap) and other provisions for the translation and visited "several times" during May, traveling the distance of at least thirty miles each way (from his farm in Broome County).[17] Joseph was admonished by the Lord to "be patient until you shall accomplish it."

May 10–15, 1829. The work progressed steadily until Joseph and Oliver reached the account of the ministry of the resurrected Christ to the inhabitants of ancient America in 3 Nephi. "After writing the account given of the Savior's ministry to the remnant of the seed of Jacob, upon this continent,"[18] the question arose in the minds of the Prophet and his scribe concerning the mode and authority of baptism.

May 15, 1829. The Aaronic Priesthood was restored to Joseph Smith and Oliver Cowdery by John the Baptist. Oliver and Joseph baptized each other as commanded by God (see D&C 13).[19]

May 15–25, 1829. Apparently after the completion of 3 Nephi, the final form of Doctrine and Covenants 10 (particularly 10:38–70) was essentially dictated.[20] Doctrine and Covenants 10:41 appears to instruct Joseph to translate the Small Plates of Nephi at a time when he had already translated the account of the reign of King Benjamin: "You shall translate the engravings which are on the plates of Nephi, down even till you come to the reign of king Benjamin, or until you come to that which you have translated." Katharine Smith Salisbury confirmed in 1895 that Joseph had "fasted and prayed several days" and the angel told him "to begin where he had left off." This would eventually bring him to the portion he still "retained" from his translation apparently of the first pages of the book of Mosiah, which he had not given to Martin Harris (D&C 10:41).[21]

May 25, 1829. Oliver Cowdery baptized Samuel Smith,[22] both having possibly arrived in Harmony in April.[23] The translation continued after Samuel's baptism.[24] Hyrum visited a few days later.[25] Doctrine and Covenants 11 was then received; Doctrine and Covenants 11:19 told Hyrum to be patient: "You may assist in bringing to light those things of which has been spoken—yea, the translation of my work."

May 15–31, 1829. During this time, Joseph and Oliver may have gone to Colesville again.[26] This may have been the time when the Melchizedek Priesthood was restored as Joseph and Oliver were returning from Colesville, but the dating of that event is uncertain.[27] It would take about a day to travel from Harmony to Colesville. At this time Oliver wrote a third letter to David Whitmer telling him "to come down into Pennsylvania and bring him and Joseph to my father's house, giving as a reason therefor that they had received a commandment from God to that effect" through the Urim and Thummim. David came, met Joseph Smith for the first time, and remained in Harmony "long enough to satisfy himself of the divine inspiration of Smith."

June 1–3, 1829. Joseph and Oliver moved with David Whitmer from Harmony to Fayette, Seneca County, New York, to the home of Peter Whitmer. The journey from Harmony to Fayette (ninety-eight miles direct) would have taken about three days.[28] Emma came a short time afterward.

June 4–end of June 1829. The translation of the Book of Mormon commenced the day after their arrival and was finished in the upstairs room of Peter Whitmer's home by July 1, "about one month" later. Some of the Whitmers helped as scribes: "They continued so, boarded and lodged us according to arrangements; and John Whitmer, in particular, assisted us very much in writing during the remainder of the work."[29] Christian Whitmer is also mentioned as a scribe. Oliver B. Huntington records in his journal a conversation in 1897 with Sarah (Sally) Heller Conrad, who may have been a cousin of the Whitmers and who was at the Whitmer home during these days. She recalled seeing the men "come down from translating room several times when they looked so exceedingly white and strange that she inquired of Mrs. Whitmer the cause of their unusual appearance." She soon embraced the gospel.[30] An affidavit of Elizabeth Ann Whitmer Cowdery also pertains to this period: "I often sat by and saw and heard them translate and write for hours together. Joseph never had a curtain drawn between him and his scribe while he was translating."[31] Concerning the translation in Fayette, David Whitmer reported a time when Joseph was "put out about . . . something that Emma, his wife, had done." As a result, "he could not translate a single syllable. He went downstairs, out into the orchard and made supplication to the Lord; was gone about an hour—came back to the house, and asked Emma's forgiveness and then came upstairs where we were and the translation went on all right."[32]

June 11, 1829. Before this date, Joseph and Oliver had translated all the Plates of Mormon and the title page inscribed by Moroni. On this day, the copyright for the Book of Mormon was secured at the office of the Federal District Court Clerk, Richard R. Lansing. The application contains the title page of the forthcoming book.[33]

June 5–14, 1829. Doctrine and Covenants 14, 15, 16 (revelations for David Whitmer, John Whitmer, and Peter Whitmer Jr.) were received around this time; Doctrine and Covenants 18 was then also received by Joseph Smith, Oliver Cowdery, and David Whitmer.[34]

June 14, 1829. Oliver wrote a letter to Hyrum from Fayette, stating, among other things: "Remember the worth of souls is great in the sight of God" (compare D&C 18:10); "behold the Lord your god . . . suffered the pains of all men that all men might repent and come unto him. . . . behold he commandeth all men . . . every where to repent" (compare 2 Ne. 9:21–23); "that there they may be willing to take upon them the name of Christ for that is the name by which they shall be called at the Last day and if we know not the name by which we are called I fear" (compare Mosiah 5:9–10); and instructing Hyrum to baptize all men, women, and children over the age of accountability (compare Moro. 8).[35]

Mid-June 1829. The translation continued. John Whitmer "assisted us very much in writing during the remainder of the work," and previous to that David Whitmer had offered "his own assistance when convenient."[36] Finishing was "slow work, and they could write only a few pages a day." Hyrum Smith, David Whitmer, and Peter Whitmer Jr. were baptized sometime in the middle of June 1829 in Seneca Lake, Fayette Township, Seneca County, New York.[37] Discussions were also held in mid-June "with many from time to time who were willing to hear us, and who desired to find out the truth as it is in Christ Jesus, and apparently willing to obey the Gospel, when once fairly convinced and satisfied in their own minds. . . . From this time forth many became believers, and some were baptized whilst we continued to instruct and persuade as many as applied for information."[38] A document entitled "Articles of the Church of Christ" was prepared by Oliver Cowdery around this time or later in 1829.[39]

Around June 20, 1829. In Fayette, the Three Witnesses were shown the plates (D&C 17:1–4). It appears that this manifestation was prompted by the translation of 2 Nephi 27:12,[40] which reads, "the eyes of none shall behold it save it be that three witnesses shall behold it, by the power of God, besides him to whom the book shall be delivered; and they shall testify to the truth of the book and the things therein." A few days later in Manchester, New York, near the Smith log home, the Eight Witnesses were allowed to see and handle the plates. Lucy Mack Smith said that she also, at one point, saw and handled the plates.

June 26, 1829. The *Wayne Sentinel* published the Book of Mormon title page, perhaps obtaining the text from the federal copyright application. Probably around this time, Martin Harris approached E. B. Grandin to see if he would publish the book, but Grandin declined, considering it financially a "losing speculation."[41]

July 1, 1829. The translation was completed, and the plates were returned to the angel. David Whitmer later stated that "the translation at my father's occupied about one month, that is from June 1st to July 1st, 1829."[42]

July 1829. Thurlow Weed, owner-editor of the *Rochester Telegraph*, was approached twice, but he likewise declined to print the book.[43] Sometime during July 1829, the printer's manuscript of the Book of Mormon was begun by Oliver Cowdery.

August 25, 1829. Harris mortgaged his farm.[44] Around this same time the contract with Grandin for the printing of the Book of Mormon was possibly signed.[45] It was agreed that five thousand copies would be printed, which was an unusually large press run for that day.[46] Harris promised to deliver the sum of $3,000 to Grandin within eighteen months. If Harris defaulted, his land was to be "sold at public auction to satisfy the demand."[47] Hyrum delivered the first manuscript installment, and typesetting commenced "in August."[48]

Fall 1829. The original typesetter was John H. Gilbert, and proofs were printed by J. H. Bortles until December. Grandin then hired Thomas McAuley, a "journeyman pressman." McAuley and Bortles did the "balance of the press-work" until March 1830.[49] Martin Harris, Hyrum Smith, and Oliver Cowdery visited Grandin's office frequently during this period; Joseph, returning to Harmony on October 4, came only once for a short visit to Grandin's office.[50] Manuscript pages were hand delivered and retrieved frequently. Oliver "held and looked over the manuscript when most of the proofs were read."[51]

November 6, 1829. Oliver wrote a letter to Joseph in Harmony: "The printing goes rather Slow yet as the type founder has been sick but we expect that the type will be in and Mr. Granden still think[s] ~~we~~ <he> will finish printing by the first of feb[r]uary." In a postscript Cowdery noted his progress in preparing the Printer Manuscript: "P S I have Just got to alma['s] commandment to his son in coppying the manuscrip," that is, to Alma 36.[52]

January 1830. Abner Cole (alias Obediah Dogberry), in his *Palmyra Reflector*, January 2, 13, and 22, printed several extracts of the Book of Mormon from sheets he pilfered at Grandin's printing office (where his own newspaper was printed).[53] This made it necessary for Joseph to return to Palmyra from Harmony and to assert his copyright privileges in order to stop this unauthorized publication of sections of the Book of Mormon.[54] During that winter,[55] Joseph apparently sent Oliver Cowdery and Hiram Page to Kingston, Ontario, Canada, to try to sell the Book of Mormon copyright.[56]

January 16, 1830. Joseph Smith Jr. entered into an agreement with Martin Harris which reads:

> I hereby agree that Martin Harris shall have an equal privilege with me & my friends of selling the Book of Mormon of the Edition now printing by Egbert B Grandin until enough of them shall be sold to pay for the printing of the same or until such times as the said Grandin shall be paid for the printing the aforesaid Books or copies[.]
>
> Manchester January the 16th 1830—/s/ Joseph Smith Jr
> Witness /s/ Oliver H P Cowdery.[57]

February 12, 1830. Lucius Fenn of Covert, Seneca County, New York, wrote to Birdseye Bronson in Winchester, Connecticut, that the publication of the Book of Mormon was widely awaited; it was expected to tell when "the Millenniam day . . . is a goeing to take place." About this time, according to David Whitmer, Joseph gave the seer stone to Oliver Cowdery.

March 26, 1830. The printing and binding were finished and the book was offered for sale to the public on March 26, 1830. After printing the complete title page of the Book of Mormon, the newspaper notice continued: "The above work, containing about 600 pages, large Duodecimos, is now for sale, wholesale and retail, at the Palmyra Book Store, by Howard & Grandin."[58] Prices at Grandin's Bookstore seem to have ranged from $1.25 to $1.75 per book.[59]

April 6, 1830. The Church of Christ was organized. Affirmations were given that the Book of Mormon was translated by the power of God, and that by repenting, humbling himself, and having faith, Joseph received the power to translate. In the ensuing years, Joseph described and bore testimony of the translation process on several occasions.

Documenting the Translation Chronology

Joseph Smith, as recorded by Oliver Cowdery (1831)

> Br. Hyrum Smith said that he thought best that the information of the coming forth of the book of Mormon be related by Joseph himself to the Elders present that all might know for themselves.

Br. Joseph Smith jr. said that it was not intended to tell
the world all the particulars of the coming forth of the book of
Mormon, & also said that it was not expedient for him to relate
these things &c.[60]

Joseph Smith (1832)

[The] Lord appeared unto a young man by the name of Oliver
Cowdry and shewed unto him the plates in a vision and also the
truth of the work and what the Lord was about to do through
me his unworthy servant therefore he was desirous to come and
write for me to translate now my wife had written some for me
to translate and also my Brother Samuel H Smith but we had be
come reduced in property and my wives father was about to turn
me out of doors & I had not where to go and I cried unto the Lord
that he would provide for me to accomplish the work whereunto
he had commanded me.[61]

Joseph Smith, as recorded by Oliver Cowdery (1835)

[The messenger] said this history was written and deposited not
far from that place, and that it was our brother's privilege, if obedient to the commandments of the Lord, to obtain, and translate
the same by the means of the Urim and Thummim, which were
deposited for that purpose with the record.[62]

Joseph Smith, as recorded by Oliver Cowdery (1835)

[Joseph Smith] was ministered unto by the angel, and by his direction he obtained the Records of the Nephites, and translated
by the gift and power of God.[63]

Joseph Smith, as recorded by Oliver Cowdery (1835)

The angel said, ". . . they cannot be interpreted by the learning
of this generation; consequently, they would be considered of no
worth, only as precious metal. Therefore, remember, that they are
to be translated by the gift and power of God. By them will the
Lord work a great and a marvelous work."[64]

Joseph Smith (1839)

He [the angel] said there was a book deposited written upon gold
plates, giving an account of the former inhabitants of this conti-

nent and the source from whence they sprang. He also said that the fullness of the everlasing Gospel was contained in it as delivered by the Saviour to the ancient inhabitants.

Also that there were two stones in silver bows and these (put <stones fastened> in to a breast plate) which constituted what is called the Urim & Thummin deposited with the plates, and <the possession and use of these stones> that was what constituted seers in ancient or former times and that God <had> prepared them for the purpose of translating the book....

... Immediately after my arrival there [Pennsylvania] I commenced copying the characters of all the plates. I copied a considerable number of them and by means of the Urim and Thummin I translated some of them which I did between the time I arrived at the house of my wife's father in the month of December [1827], and the February following.

Mr [Martin] Harris ... returned again to my house about the twelfth of April, Eighteen hundred and twenty eight, and commenced writing for me while I translated from the plates, which we continued untill the fourteenth of June following, by which time he had written one hundred and sixteen <pages> of manuscript on foolscap paper....

I did not however go immediately to translating [in the winter of 1828], but went to laboring with my hands ... in order to provide for my family.

Two days after the arrival of Mr Cowdery (being the seventh of April [1829]) I commenced to translate the book of Mormon and he commenced to write for me....

... During the month of April I continued to translate, and he to write with little cessation, during which time we received several revelations....

Whilst continuing the work of translation during this month of April; Oliver Cowdery became exceedingly anxious to have the power to translate bestowed upon him and in relation to this desire the following revelations were obtained [D&C 8, 9; see excerpts above]....

We still continued the <work of> translation, when in the ensuing month (May, Eighteen hundred and twenty nine) we on a certain day went into the woods to pray and inquire of the Lord respecting baptism for the remission of sins as we found mentioned in the translation of the plates. . . .

. . . my wife's father's family . . . were willing that I should be allowed to continue the work of translation without interruption: And therefore offered and promised us protection from all unlawful proceedings as far as in them lay.

. . . we also showed him [Samuel Smith] that part of the work which we had translated, and labored to persuade him concerning the Gospel of Jesus Christ. . . .

. . . Mr Joseph Knight Senr. . . . very kindly and considerately brought us, a quantity of provisions, in order that we might not be interrupted in the work of translation . . . which enabled us to continue the work. . . .

. . . we accepted the invitation and accompanied Mr [David] Whitmer to his father's house, and there resided untill the translation was finished, . . . and John Whitmer, in particular, assisted us very much in writing during the remainder of the work. . . .

In the course of the work of translation, we ascertained that three special witnesses were to be provided by the Lord, to whom he would grant, that they should see the plates from which this work (the Book of Mormon) should be translated, and that these witnesses should bear record of the same. . . .

. . . when immediately afterwards we heard a voice from out of the bright light above us, saying "These plates have been revealed by the power of God, and they have been translated by the power of God; the translation of them which you have seen is correct, and I command you to bear record of what you now see and hear." . . .

Mean time we continued to translate, at intervals, when not necessitated to attend to the numerous enquirers, that now began to visit us. . . .

I wish also to mention here, that the Title Page of the Book of Mormon is a literal translation, taken from the very last leaf, on the left hand side of the collection or book of plates, which contained the record which has been translated.[65]

Emma Smith Bidamon, as interviewed by Joseph Smith III (1879)

Q. Who were scribes for father when translating the Book of Mormon?

A. Myself, Oliver Cowdery, Martin Harris, and my brother, Reuben Hale.

Q. Was Alva Hale one?

A. I think not. He may have written some; but if he did, I do not remember it. . . .

Q. What of the truth of Mormonism?

A. I know Mormonism to be the truth; and believe the Church to have been established by divine direction. I have complete faith in it. In writing for your father I frequently wrote day after day, often sitting at the table close by him, he sitting with his face buried in his hat, with the stone in it, and dictating hour after hour with nothing between us.

Q. Had he not a book or manuscript from which he read, or dictated to you?

A. He had neither manuscript nor book to read from.

Q. Could he not have had, and you not know it?

A. If he had had anything of the kind he could not have concealed it from me.

Q. Are you sure that he had the plates at the time you were writing for him?

A. The plates often lay on the table without any attempt at concealment, wrapped in a small linen table cloth, which I had given him to fold them in. I once felt of the plates, as they thus lay on the table, tracing their outline and shape. They seemed to be pliable like thick paper, and would rustle with a metalic sound when the edges were moved by the thumb, as one does sometimes thumb the edges of a book.

Q. Where did father and Oliver Cowdery write?

A. Oliver Cowdery and your father wrote in the room where I was at work.

Q. Could not father have dictated the Book of Mormon to you, Oliver Cowdery and the others who wrote for him, after having first written it, or having first read it out of some book?

A. Joseph Smith [and for the first time she used his name direct, having usually used the words, "your father," or "my husband"] could neither write nor dictate a coherent and well-worded letter; let alone dictating a book like the Book of Mormon. And, though I was an active participant in the scenes that transpired, and was present during the translation of the plates, and had cognizance of things as they transpired, it is marvelous to me, "a marvel and a wonder," as much so as to any one else.

Q. I should suppose that you would have uncovered the plates and examined them?

A. I did not attempt to handle the plates, other than I have told you, nor uncover them to look at them. I was satisfied that it was the work of God, and therefore did not feel it to be necessary to do so.

Major Bidamon here suggested: Did Mr. Smith forbid your examining the plates?

A. I do not think he did. I knew that he had them, and was not specially curious about them. I moved them from place to place on the table, as it was necessary in doing my work.

Q. Mother, what is your belief about the authenticity, or origin of the Book of Mormon?

A. My belief is that the Book of Mormon is of divine authenticity— I have not the slightest doubt of it. I am satisfied that no man could have dictated the writing of the manuscripts unless he was inspired; for, when acting as his scribe, your father would dictate to me hour after hour; and when returning after meals, or after interruptions, he would at once begin where he had left off, without either seeing the manuscript or having any portion of it read to him. This was a usual thing for him to do. It would have been improbable that a learned man could do this; and, for one so ignorant and unlearned as he was, it was simply impossible.[66]

Emma Smith Bidamon, as recorded by Joseph Smith III (1879)

She wrote for Joseph Smith during the work of translation, as did also Reuben Hale, her brother, and O[liver]. Cowdery; that the larger part of this labor was done in her presence, and where she could see and know what was being done; that during no part of it was did Joseph Smith have any Mss. [manuscripts] or Book of any kind from which to read, or dictate, except the metalic plates, which she knew he had.[67]

Emma Smith Bidamon, as recorded by Joseph Smith III (1900)

My mother [Emma Smith] told me that she saw the plates in the sack; for they lay on a small table in their living room in their cabin on her father's farm, and she would lift and move them when she swept and dusted the room and furniture. She even thumbed the leaves as one does the leaves of a book, and they rustled with a metalic sound. Yes, mother did some of the writing for father while he was translating[.] She testified that father found and had the plates, and translated them as the history states; that she had no doubt as to the truth of it.[68]

Oliver Cowdery, as recorded by Ashbel Kitchell (1830)

Oliver Lowdree . . . stated that he had been one who had been an assistant in the translation of the golden Bible, and had also seen the Angel, and had been commissioned by him to go out and bear testimony, that God would destroy this generation.[69]

Oliver Cowdery to W. W. Phelps (1834)

Near the time of the setting of the Sun, Sabbath evening, April 5th, 1829, my natural eyes, for the first time beheld this brother. He then resided in Harmony, Susquehanna county Penn. On Monday the 6th, I assisted him in arranging some business of a temporal nature, and on Tuesday the 7th, commenced to write the book of Mormon. These were days never to be forgotten—to sit under the sound of a voice dictated by the *inspiration* of heaven, awakened the utmost gratitude of this bosom! Day after day I continued, uninterrupted, to write from his mouth, as he translated, with the *Urim* and *Thummim*, or, as the Nephites whould have said, "Interpreters," the history, or record, called the "The book of Mormon."[70]

Oliver Cowdery, as interviewed by Josiah Jones (1841)

In the last part of October, 1830, four men appeared here by the names of [Oliver] Cowdery, [Parley P.] Pratt, [Peter] Whitmar and [Ziba] Peterson; they stated they were from Palmyra, Ontario county, N.Y. with a book, which they said contained what was

engraven on gold plates found in a stone box, in the ground . . .
and was found about three years ago by a man named Joseph
Smith Jr. who had translated it by looking into a stone or two
stones, when put into a dark place, which stones he said were
found in the box with the plates. They affirmed while he looked
through the stone spectacles another sat by and wrote what he
told them, and thus the book was all written. . . .

He [Cowdery] stated that Smith looked into or through the
transparent stones to translate what was on the plates. I then
asked him if he had ever looked through the stones to see what
he could see in them; his reply was that he was not permitted to
look into them. I asked him who debarred him from looking into
them; he remained sometime in silence; then said that he had
so much confidence in his friend Smith, who told him that he
must not look into them, that he did not presume to do so lest he
should tempt God and be struck dead.[71]

Oliver Cowdery, as recorded by Reuben Miller (1848)

Friends and brethren my name is Cowdrey, Oliver Cowdrey, In
the early history of this church I stood Identified with her. And
[was] one in her councils. . . .

I wrote with my own pen the intire book of mormon (Save a
few pages) as it fell from the Lips of the prophet [Joseph Smith].
As he translated <it> by the gift and power of god, By [the] means
of the urum and thummim, or as it is called by that book holy
Interperters. I beheld with my eyes. And handled with my hands
the gold plates from which it was translated. I also beheld the
Interperters. That book is true. Sidney Rigdon did not write it.
Mr [Solomon] Spaulding did not write it. I wrote it myself as it fell
from the Lips of the prophet.[72]

Oliver Cowdery, as recounted by George Q. Cannon (1881)

When I was a boy I heard it stated concerning Oliver Cowdery, that
after he left the Church he practised law, and . . . in a court in Ohio,
the opposing counsel thought he would say something that would
overwhelm Oliver Cowdery, and . . . alluded to him as the man that
had testified and had written that he had beheld an angel of God,
and that the angel had shown unto him the plates from which the

Book of Mormon was translated. He supposed, of course, that it would cover him with confusion ... but ... he [Oliver Cowdery] arose in the court, and in his reply stated that, whatever his faults and weaknesses might be, the testimony which he had written, and which he had given to the world, was literally true.[73]

Oliver Cowdery, as recorded by Edward Stevenson (1886)

He testified that he beheld the plates, the leaves being turned over by the angel, whose voice he heard, and that they were commanded as witnesses to bear a faithful testimony to the world of the vision that they were favored to behold, and that the translation from the plates in the Book of Mormon was accepted of the Lord, and that it should go forth to the world and no power on earth should stop its progress.[74]

Oliver Cowdery, as recorded by William M. Frampton (1901)

Brother Cowdery looked up[on] the people for a short time without speaking, his manner caused deep attention then in a distinct and very impressive voice, said "My name is Cowdery, Oliver Cowdery, in an early day I was identified with this Church in her councils, I wrote the Book Of Mormon, Spaulding did not write it, Sidney Rigdon did not write it, I wrote it (with the exception of a few pages) with this right hand, (extending his hand) as the inspired words fell from the lips of Joseph Smith.[75]

Oliver Cowdery, as interviewed by Samuel Whitney Richards (1907)

He [Oliver Cowdery] represents Joseph as sitting by a table with the plates before him. and he reading the record with the Urim & Thummim. Oliver, his scribe, sits close beside to hear and write every word as translated. This is done by holding the translators over the words of the written record, and the translation appears distinctly in the instrument, which had been touched by the finger of God and dedicated and consecated for the express purpose of translating languages. This instrument now used fully performed its Mission. Every word was made distinctly visible even to every letter, and if Oliver did not in writing spell the word correctly it remained in the translator until it was written correctly. This was the Mystery to Oliver, how Joseph being compar[a]tively ignorant could correct him in spelling, without seeing the word written, and he would not be satisfied until he should be permitted or have the gift to translate as well as Joseph.[76]

Oliver Cowdery, as interviewed by Jacob F. Gates (1912)

I am a dying man, and what would it profit me to tell you a lie? I know . . . that this Book of Mormon was translated by the gift and power of God. My eyes saw, my ears heard, and my understanding was touched, and I know that whereof I testified is true. It was no dream, no vain imagination of the mind,—it was real.[77]

David Whitmer, as interviewed by the *Kansas City Journal* (1881)

After several months Cowdery told me he was going to Harmony, Pa.—whither Joseph Smith had gone with the plates on account of persecutions of his neighbors—and see him about the matter. He did go and on his way stopped at my father's house and told me that as soon as he found out anything either truth or untruth he would let me know. After he got there he became acquainted with Joseph Smith, and shortly after, wrote to me telling me that he was convinced that Smith had the records and that he (Smith) had told him that it was the will of heaven that he (Cowdery) should be his scribe to assist in the translation of the plates. He went on and Joseph translated from the plates and he wrote it down. Shortly after this Cowdery wrote me another letter in which he gave me a few lines of what they had translated, and he assured me that he knew of a certainty that he had a record of a people that inhabited this continent, and that the plates they were translating gave a complete history of these people. When Cowdery wrote me these things and told me that he had revealed knowledge concerning the truth of them, I showed these letters to my parents, and brothers and sisters. Soon after I received another letter from Cowdery, telling me to come down into Pennsylvania and bring him and Joseph to my father's house, giving as a reason therefor that they had received a commandment from God to that effect. I went down to Harmony, and found everything just as they had written me. The next day after I got there they packed up the plates and we proceeded on our journey to my father's house where we arrived in due time, and the day after we commenced upon the translation of the remainder of the plates. I, as well as all of my father's family, Smith's wife, Oliver Cowdery, and Martin Harris were present during the translation. The translation was by Smith and the manner as follows:

"He had two small stones of a chocolate color, nearly egg shaped and perfectly smooth, but not transparent, called interpreters, which were given him with the plates. He did not use the plates in the translation, but would hold the interpreters to his eyes and cover his face with a hat, excluding all light, and before his eyes would appear what seemed to be parchment, on which would appear the characters of the plates in a line at the top, and immediately below would appear the translation in English, which Smith would read to his scribe, who wrote it down exactly as it fell from his lips. The scribe would then read the sentence written, and if any mistake had been made the characters would remain visible to Smith until corrected, when they faded from sight to be replaced by another line. The translation at my father's occupied about one month, that is from June 1 to July 1, 1829."

"Were the plates under the immediate control of Smith all the time?"

"No, they were not. I will explain how that was. When Joseph first received the plates he translated 116 pages of the book of 'Lehi,' with Martin Harris as scribe. When this had been completed they rested for a time, and Harris wanted to take the manuscript home with him to show to his family and friends. To this Joseph demurred, but finally asked the Lord if Harris might be allowed to take it. The answer was 'no.' Harris teased Joseph for a long time and finally persuaded him to ask the Lord a second time, pledging himself to be responsible for its safe keeping. . . . [T]hrough some carelessness [Martin Harris] allowed it to be stolen from him. This incurred the Lord's displeasure, and he sent an angel to Joseph demanding the plates, and until Joseph had thoroughly repented of his transgressions would not allow him to have the use of them again. When Joseph was again allowed to resume the translation the plates were taken care of by a messenger of God, and when Joseph wanted to see the plates this messenger was always at hand. The 116 pages of the book of 'Lehi' which were stolen were never recovered, nor would the Lord permit Joseph to make a second translation of it.

"A few months after the translation was completed, that is in the spring of 1830, Joseph had the book published and this (showing a well worn volume) is a copy of the first edition which I have had in my possession ever since it was printed."[78]

David Whitmer (1881)

To the Editor of the [Kansas City] Journal.

RICHMOND, Mo., June 13 [1881].—I notice several errors in the interview had with me by one of your reporters as published in the *Daily Journal* of June 5th, '81, and wish to correct them.

. . . In regard to my going to Harmony, my statement was that "I found everything as Cowdery had written me, and that they packed up next day and went to my father's, (did not say 'packed up the plates') and that he, Smith, (not 'we') then commenced the translation of the remainder of the plates." I did not wish to be understood as saying that those referred to as being present were all of the time in the immediate presence of the translator, but were at the place and saw how the translation was conducted. I did not say that Smith used "two small stones," as stated nor did I call the stone "interpreters." I stated that "he used one stone (not two) and called it a sun stone." The "interpreters" were as I understood taken from Smith and were not used by him after losing the first 116 pages as stated. It is my understanding that the stone referred to was furnished him when he commenced translating again after losing the 116 pages.

My statement was and now is that in translating he put the stone in his hat and putting his face in his hat so as to exclude the light and that then the light and characters appeared in the hat together with the interpretation which he uttered and was written by the scribe and which was tested at the time as stated.[79]

David Whitmer, as interviewed by the *Chicago Times* (1881)

It was not until June, 1829, that he met the future prophet who visited his fathers house, and while there completed the translation of the "Book of Mormon;" and thus he became conversant with its history, having witnessed Smith dictate to Oliver Cowdery the translation of the characters that were inscribed on the plates, said by Mr. Anthon, our Egyptian scholar, to resemble the characters of that ancient people. Christian Whitmer, his brother, occasionally assisted Cowdery in writing, as did Mrs. Joseph Smith, who was a Miss Hale before she was married. . . .

After the plates had been translated, which process required about six months, the same heavenly visitant appeared and reclaimed the gold tablets of the ancient people, informing Smith that he would replace them with other records of the lost tribes that had been brought with them during their wanderings from the Asia, which would be forthcoming when the world was ready to receive them. . . .

The tablets or plates were translated by Smith, who used a small oval kidney-shaped stone, called Urim and Thummim, that seemed endowed with the marvelous power of converting the characters on the plates, when used by Smith, into English, who would then dictate to Cowdery what to write. Frequently, one character would make two lines of manuscript, while others made but a word or two words. Mr. Whitmer emphatically asserts as did Harris and Cowdery, that while Smith was dictating the translation he had no manuscript notes or other means of knowledge save the seer stone and the characters as shown on the plates, he being present and cognizant how it was done.[80]

David Whitmer, as interviewed by William H. Kelley and G. A. Blakeslee (1882)

I know Joseph Smith was a prophet of God, and he translated the Book of Mormon by the inspiration of God from the plates of the Nephites. . . .

. . . He [Joseph Smith] *had* to trust in God. He could not translate unless he was humble and possessed the right feelings towards every one. To illustrate, so you can see. One morning when he was getting ready to continue the translation, something went wrong about the house and he was put out about it. Something that Emma, his wife, had done. Oliver and I went up stairs, and Joseph came up soon after to continue the translation, but he could not do anything. He could not translate a single

syllable. He went down stairs, out into the orchard and made supplication to the Lord; was gone about an hour—came back to the
house, asked Emma's forgiveness and then came up stairs where
we were and the translation went on all right. He could do nothing save he was humble and faithful.[81]

David Whitmer, as interviewed by E. C. Briggs (1884)

"The boys, Joseph and Oliver, worked hard, early and late,
while translating the plates. It was slow work, and they could
write only a few pages a day."

Of Joseph he continued:

"He could not do a thing except he was humble, and just
right before the Lord."

I said, "Why not?"

He replied:

"The Urim and Thummim would look dark; he could not see
a thing in them."

"How did it appear in them?" we asked.

His answer was:

"The letters appeared on them in light, and would not go off
until they were written correctly by Oliver. When Joseph could
not pronounce the words he spelled them out letter by letter."[82]

David Whitmer, as interviewed by James H. Hart (1884)

"In regard to the translation," said Mr. Whitmer, "it was a
laborious work for the weather was very warm, and the days were
long and they worked from morning till night. But they were both
young and strong and were soon able to complete the work.

"The way it was done was thus: Joseph would place the seer-
stone in a deep hat, and placing his face close to it, would see, not
the stone, but what appeared like an oblong piece of parchment,
on which the hieroglyphics would appear, and also the translation
in the English language, all appearing in bright luminous letters.
Joseph would then read it to Oliver, who would write it down as
spoken. Sometimes Joseph could not pronounce the words correctly, having had but little education; and if by any means a mistake was made in the copy, the luminous writing would remain
until it was corrected. It sometimes took Oliver several trials to

get the right letters to spell correctly some of the more difficult words, but when he had written them correctly, the characters and the interpretation would disappear, and be replaced by other characters and their interpretation.

"When the seer-stone was not placed in the hat, no characters or writing could be seen therein, but when so placed then the hieroglyphics would appear as before described. Some represented but one word, or name, some represented several, and some from one to two lines.

"Emma, Joseph's wife, came to my father's house a short time after Joseph and Oliver came, and she wrote a little of the translation, my brother Christian wrote some, but Oliver wrote the greater portion of it."[83]

David Whitmer, as interviewed by George Q. Cannon (1884)

In speaking of the translating he [David Whitmer] said that Joseph had the stone in a hat from which all light was excluded. In the stone the characters appeared and under that the translation in English and they remained until the scribe had copied it correctly. If he had made a mistake the words still remained and were not replaced by any other.[84]

David Whitmer, as interviewed by the *St. Louis Republican* (1884)

"Yes," said Mr. Whitmer, "I have no objections to giving the particulars of my early life. . . . The translation was done in my father's house; at least two months of the time, was thus taken up with it there. Oliver Cowdery was the principal amanuensis. . . .

"Joseph Smith dictated every word in the book. The understanding we have about it was that when the book was discovered an angel was present and pointed the place out. In translating from the plates, Joseph Smith looked through the Urim and Thummim, consisting of two transparent pebbles set in the rim of a bow, fastened to a breastplate. He dictated by looking through them to his scribes."[85]

Notes

Editors' note: This article includes multiple excerpts from *Opening the Heavens*, edited by John W. Welch and Erick B. Carlson, 77–213.

1.   See generally, Richard Lloyd Anderson, *Investigating the Book of Mormon Witnesses* (Salt Lake City: Deseret Book, 1981); Milton V. Backman Jr., *Eyewitness Accounts of the Restoration* (Orem, UT: Grandin Book, 1983; reprint Salt Lake City: Deseret Book, 1986).

2.   See Joseph Smith—History in the Pearl of Great Price; Joseph Smith Jr., *History of The Church of Jesus Christ of Latter-day Saints*, ed. B. H. Roberts, 2nd ed., rev., 7 vols. (Salt Lake City: Deseret Book, 1971) (hereafter cited as *History of the Church*); Richard L. Bushman, *Joseph Smith and the Beginnings of Mormonism* (Urbana: University of Illinois Press, 1984); B. H. Roberts, *A Comprehensive History of The Church of Jesus Christ of Latter-day Saints, Century One*, 6 vols. (Provo, UT: Corporation of the President, The Church of Jesus Christ of Latter-day Saints, 1965).

3.   For example, Monte S. Nyman and Lisa Bolin Hawkins, "Book of Mormon: Overview," 1:139–43; Royal Skousen, "Book of Mormon Manuscripts," 1:185–86; Grant R. Hardy and Robert E. Parsons, "Book of Mormon Plates and Records," 1:195–201; John W. Welch and Tim Rathbone, "Book of Mormon Translation by Joseph Smith," 1:210–13, in *Encyclopedia of Mormonism*. For a thorough discussion of the coming forth of the Book of Mormon, its structure, and the various religious and scholarly receptions or reactions it evoked, see Terryl L. Givens, *By the Hand of Mormon: The American Scripture that Launched a New World Religion* (Oxford: Oxford University Press, 2002).

4.   *History of the Church*, 1:32; Oliver Cowdery, "Letter I," *Messenger and Advocate*, October 1834, 14; Lucy Mack Smith, *Biographical Sketches of Joseph Smith, the Prophet, and His Progenitors for Many Generations* (London: Published for Orson Pratt by S. W. Richards, 1853), 128–31. Lucy Mack Smith, Prelim. MS 1, cited in Lavina Fielding Anderson, ed., *Lucy's Book* (Salt Lake City: Signature Books, 2001), 438, states that Joseph had been praying for assistance and had been assured by the angel of the Lord that a scribe "should be forthcoming in a few days."

5.   Two theories exist about the order in which the Book of Mormon was translated in 1829. The book of Lehi was translated and lost in 1828. In March 1829, the translation resumed with both Samuel Smith and Emma acting as scribe for a few pages. In April 1829, Oliver Cowdery arrived and the pace of the work accelerated. Where in the text did Joseph begin at this time? Did he pick up where the 116 pages had left off (around the time of King Benjamin near Mosiah 1), or did he start at the beginning of the Small Plates (with 1 Nephi 1)? A few considerations make the "Mosiah-first" theory more plausible than the "Nephi-first" theory.

First, which scripture triggered the experience of the Three Witnesses in June 1829, toward the end of the translation? Was it Ether 5:2–4 or 2 Nephi 27:12, 22? If they were translating 2 Nephi in June, this would strongly indicate that they had begun with Mosiah in April and had returned after finishing Moroni in May to translate the Small Plates of Nephi in June. On the other hand, if they were translating the book of Ether in June, this would support the Nephi-first theory, since in the few days remaining in June after the experience of the Three Witnesses there would have been only enough time left to finish Ether and Moroni.

The *History of the Church* first appeared in print as a serial in the *Times and Seasons* in 1842. "History of Joseph Smith," *Times and Seasons* 3 (March 15, 1842): beginning on p. 726. A blank was left in the sentence that was to tell which passage in the Book of Mormon inspired the manifestation to the Three Witnesses. "History of Joseph Smith,"

Times and Seasons 3 (September 1, 1842): 897a. Joseph Smith, "History of the Church," A-1, Family and Church History Department Archives, The Church of Jesus Christ of Latter-day Saints (hereafter cited as Church Archives), likewise has a blank at this point. Page 25 of one of the manuscripts of the *History of the Church*, however, contains a note that the relevant scripture was found "in the 1st ed. . . . page 110 [2 Nephi 27]." This information was added to the manuscript some time after 1852, as is evident since that scribe also refers to a European edition of the Doctrine and Covenants of that date. Smith, "History of the Church," A-2, 25. Therefore, the earliest recorded understanding saw 2 Nephi 27 as the scripture involved. B. H. Roberts chose to refer principally to Ether 5 in the published edition of *History of the Church*, 1:52, but he also mentioned 2 Nephi 11:3 in this context. Significantly, the scripture in 2 Nephi 27 authorizes more precisely what in fact transpired with the witnesses (as discussed above under the date "Around June 20, 1829"), all making it more likely that 2 Nephi 27 was the more relevant scripture authorizing the manifestation to the Witnesses than Ether 5.

Second, the Mosiah-first theory allows five weeks (from April 7 to May 15) for the translation of Mosiah 1 through the account of the ministry of Christ among the Nephites in 3 Nephi. The book was then finished at about the same rate in June. Under the Nephi-first theory, however, all the material from 1 Nephi 1 through the account in 3 Nephi would have to have been translated within that time, requiring a faster rate. Correlatively, the Mosiah-first theory leaves a significant amount of material to be translated after May 15, which accommodates the fact that the translation continued at Harmony for two more weeks and that "many pages" were translated at the Whitmer house in Fayette. One report indicates that John Whitmer acted as scribe for as many as "sixty pages." Zenas H. Gurley, "Synopsis of a Discourse Delivered at Lamoni, Iowa," reported by S. F. Walker, *Saints' Herald* 26 (December 15, 1879): 370b.

Third, the title page of the Book of Mormon was translated before June 11, 1829, the date on which this text appears on the copyright application. Since the title was written by Moroni and was found at the end of the Plates of Mormon ("I wish to mention here that the title-page of the Book of Mormon is a literal translation taken from the very last leaf, on the left hand side of the collection or book of plates, which contained the record which has been translated," *History of the Church*, 1:71), it would appear that books up to and including the title page, namely 4 Nephi, Mormon, Ether, Moroni, and the title page itself, were translated after May 15 but before June 11. This supports the Mosiah-first theory.

Fourth, the handwriting on the original manuscript for 1 Nephi is neither Oliver Cowdery's nor Emma Smith's. It may be Reuben Hale's, which would support the Nephi-first theory, but it is also possible that it is one of the Whitmers', which would favor the Mosiah-first theory.

In light of the foregoing, the Mosiah-first theory seems more likely than the Nephi-first theory. Accepting this view, see George Reynolds, "History of the Book of Mormon," *Contributor* 5 (November 1883): 41–47; (February 1884): 161–68; (June 1884): 321–27; (July 1884): 361–67; Stanley R. Larson, "A Most Sacred Possession: The Original Manuscript of the Book of Mormon," *Ensign* 7 (September 1977): 87–88; Max H. Parkin, "A Preliminary Analysis of the Dating of Section 10," in *Sidney B. Sperry Symposium, January 27, 1979* (Provo, UT: Brigham Young University, 1979), 76; Bushman, *Beginnings of Mormonism*, 105; John W. Welch, ed. *Reexploring the Book of Mormon* (Salt

Lake City: Deseret Book; Provo, UT: FARMS, 1992), 1–8. Royal Skousen, *The Original Manuscript of the Book of Mormon* (Provo, UT: FARMS, 2001), 33, notes that "there is some evidence that Joseph Smith translated the small plates of Nephi at the very end of the process," but defers further discussion for a future publication. Ruminating about the implications and ideologies of some discussions of the Mosiah-first theory, see Alan Goff, "Positivism and the Priority of Ideology in Mosiah-First Theories of Book of Mormon Production," *FARMS Review* 16, no. 1 (2004): 11–36, arguing that the Mosiah-first theory need not pose any compositional difficulty.

6.   Dean Jessee, "Joseph Knight's Recollection of Early Mormon History," *BYU Studies* 17, no. 1 (1976): 35.

7.   Jessee, "Joseph Knight's Recollection," 36.

8.   Lucy Mack Smith, *Biographical Sketches*, 128; Lucy Mack Smith, Prelim. MS 1, cited in Anderson, *Lucy's Book*, 432, says "He had not been in the place long till he began to hear about the plates from all quarters and immediately he commenced importuning Mr. Smith upon the subject but he did not succeed in eliciting any information from him for a long time."

9.   Oliver apparently began boarding with Joseph Sr., in 1828. Larry C. Porter, "The Prophet's New York Years: Restoration, Publication, and Organization, 1829–1830," lecture, October 18, 1984, Brigham Young University, Provo, Utah.

10.   Cowdery, "Letter I," 14. Oliver apparently mentions his "natural eyes" because he had seen the plates and perhaps Joseph before in a vision; see above at February 1829.

11.   Oliver Cowdery to W. W. Phelps, "Letter VIII," *Messenger and Advocate*, October 1835, 196.

12.   Cowdery, "Letter I," 14.

13.   Cowdery, "Letter I," 14.

14.   Jessee, "Joseph Knight's Recollection," 36.

15.   *History of the Church*, 5:219, taken from Willard Richards's Journal. It is possible, however, that this trip to Colesville occurred after May 25, but this would allow little time for Joseph Knight to have made "several" visits (*History of the Church*, 1:47) before Joseph and Oliver left for Fayette on June 1. The account in *History of the Church*, 1:97, contains most of the same elements, making an 1830 date equally likely, although then the reference to only "two or three" believers seems odd; see below at May 15–31, 1829.

16.   Jessee, "Joseph Knight's Recollection," 36.

17.   *History of the Church*, 1:47.

18.   Cowdery, "Letter I," 15.

19.   "One morning however they sat down to their usual work when the first thing that presented itself to Joseph was a commandment from God that he and Oliver should repair to the water each of them be baptized they immediately went down to the susquehana river and obeyed the mandate given them through the urim and Thumim." Lucy Mack Smith, Prelim. MS 1, cited in Anderson, *Lucy's Book*, 439.

20.   The dating of D&C 10 has been discussed on several occasions. Stanley R. Larson, "A Study of Some Textual Variations in the Book of Mormon comparing the Original and the Printer's Manuscripts and the 1830, the 1837, and the 1840 Editions" (master's thesis, Brigham Young University, 1974), 17–18n15, stated:

> The date of section 10 has become a problem. When the original manuscript
> of the "History of Joseph Smith" was written, the discussion about this section

was accidentally omitted. This omission was soon noticed and two additional sheets with the text of the revelation and the correct date of May 1829 were inserted into the history; but unfortunately it was placed in the wrong context. This incongruity caused later editors to attempt to rectify the situation by altering the date of the revelation to "the summer of 1828." During the lifetime of Joseph Smith the date was consistently reported as May 1829. The Book of Commandments in 1833 first printed this revelation in its proper chronological order and with the correct date.

See also Stephen Snow, "Queries," *Mormon History Association Newsletter* 44 (June 1980): 15; Max H. Parkin, "Queries," *Mormon History Association Newsletter* 45 (November 1980): 2–4; Parkin, "Dating of Section 10," 68–84; Lyndon W. Cook, *The Revelations of the Prophet Joseph Smith* (Provo, UT: Seventy's Mission Bookstore, 1981), 17, 122; Robert J. Woodford, "The Historical Development of the Doctrine and Covenants," 3 vols. (Ph.D. diss., Brigham Young University, 1974), 1:200–205. Lyndon Cook and Max Parkin argue for an 1828 date for the first part of D&C 10, with additional material being added in 1829. For example, Parkin points out several clear similarities between D&C 10:49–70 and 3 Nephi that support their concurrent dating. If references to receiving the "gospel" in D&C 10:62 and 11:16, 19 refer to the impending translation of "which was ministered unto" the Nephites in 3 Nephi, and if, similarly, the statement in 18:17 was made at a time after Joseph, Oliver, and David had received 3 Nephi, then those sections bracket the translation of 3 Nephi, as Monte Nyman points out. On the other hand, it is possible that 10:62, which speaks of "that which you have received," is already speaking of the account of the ministry of Christ among the Nephites in 3 Nephi.

21. See Dean C. Jessee, "The Original Book of Mormon Manuscript," *BYU Studies* 10, no. 3 (1970): 260, 277–78, citing also D&C 5:30. See further, note 5 above.

22. *History of the Church*, 1:44. Lucy Mack Smith, Prelim. MS 1, cited in Anderson, *Lucy's Book*, 439, however, gives the impression that Samuel was baptized on the same day as were Joseph and Oliver.

23. Lucy Mack Smith, *Biographical Sketches*, 130. *History of the Church*, 1:44, however, reports that Samuel did not come to visit until a few days after May 15.

24. Lucy Mack Smith, *Biographical Sketches*, 131.

25. *History of the Church*, 1:44–45.

26. It is possible, but not likely, that Joseph had to appear in court in Colesville at this time, as remembered by Addison Everett in his letter of February 17, 1881, St. George, Utah, to Oliver B. Huntington, recorded in Oliver Boardman Huntington, Journal no. 14, January 31, 1881, L. Tom Perry Special Collections, Harold B. Lee Library, Brigham Young University, Provo, Utah (hereafter cited as Perry Special Collections), and discussed in Larry C. Porter, "The Restoration of the Aaronic and Melchizedek Priesthoods," *Ensign* 26 (December 1996): 43–44. See also Lucy Mack Smith, *Biographical Sketches*, 135, but the reference is vague ("After Samuel left them, they still continued the work as before, until about the time of the trial that took place in New York"). No records for such a trial are presently known. The sources seem to be confusing various events with an inconclusive hearing in Lyons, Wayne County, New York (Lucy Mack Smith, Prelim. MS 1, cited in Anderson, *Lucy's Book*, 441–45), or with a Bainbridge, New York, trial in 1830.

27. See sources discussed in Porter, "Aaronic and Melchizedek Priesthoods," 33–44. See also Roberts, *Comprehensive History*, 1:183. Richard L. Bushman discusses the date of this event in *Beginnings of Mormonism*, 163, esp. n. 55.

28. As reported by Joseph F. Smith, David Whitmer told him and Orson Pratt that Joseph prophesied to Oliver "a perfect description of what David did on the way" before David arrived. Joseph F. Smith, Statement, written April 25, 1918, 2, Church Archives. They traveled on "an ordinary wagon with two long poles in it at each end across the end gates of the wagon box, and then two boards laid across that for seats on those hickory poles. Joseph and Emma were on the hind seat and Oliver and David on the front seat." Joseph F. Smith, Statement, 2. The plates were carried to Fayette by Moroni in a bundle on his back. Joseph F. Smith, Statement, 3, Lucy Mack Smith, Prelim. MS 1, cited in Anderson, *Lucy's Book*, 450, does not include Emma on this trip to Fayette (Waterloo). See also Lyndon W. Cook, ed., *David Whitmer Interviews: A Restoration Witness* (Orem, UT: Grandin Book, 1991), 114–15, 197.

29. *History of the Church*, 1:49. John Whitmer later said that he wrote "sixty pages." John Whitmer, interview by Zenas Gurley, in "Synopsis of a Discourse," 370b. At this time, Joseph translated with some aid from a seer stone or the Urim and Thummim, though these instruments were not essential. He used "no manuscript notes or other means."

30. She married David Edwin Bunnell in the Peter Whitmer home on April 15, 1830, and was the mother of Stephen Bunnell of Provo, Utah. See Oliver B. Huntington, "History of the Life of Oliver B. Huntington," typescript, 49–50, Perry Special Collections; Pearl Bunnell Newell, interview by Carma DeJong Anderson, January 1970, 3–4, Perry Special Collections, provides a similar reminiscence of Sally Conrad; marriage date of Sally Conrad courtesy of Helen Bunnell Weeks of Orem, Utah. See article by Richard L. Anderson, "The House Where the Church Was Organized," *Improvement Era* 73 (April 1970): 16–25, for full discussion of the one-and-a-half story log house with attic and of the Whitmers and their relatives.

31. Copy contained on obverse of William E. McLellin to "My Dear Friends," February 1870, Community of Christ Library-Archives; cited in Cook, ed., *David Whitmer Interviews*, 233–34.

32. David Whitmer, Statement of September 15, 1882, to William Kelley and G. A. Blakeslee, in Braden and Kelley Debate February 12 to March 8, 1884 (St. Louis: Christian Publ., 1884), 186; also cited in Roberts, *Comprehensive History*, 1:131.

33. Copies of the two originals prepared by Lansing are found in the Church Archives and in the Library of Congress in Washington, D.C., respectively.

34. *History of the Church*, 1:48–51.

35. Original no longer extant. Copy found in Joseph Smith Letterbook 1, part 1, 5–6.

36. *History of the Church*, 1:49. Zenas Gurley's interview with John Whitmer, reported by Gurley in "Synopsis of a Discourse," 370b; John stated "that he had written [as scribe] sixty pages" of the Book of Mormon [about thirty pages of manuscript?].

37. *History of the Church*, 1:51; D&C 27:12. On January 14, 1885, David Whitmer stated: "Sometime in June 1829 Joseph ordained Oliver Cowdery to be an Elder, and Oliver ordained Joseph to be an Elder in the church of Christ. And during that year Joseph both baptized and ordained me an elder in the church of Christ." Z. H. Gurley, "Questions asked of David Whitmer at His Home in Richmond, Ray County, Missouri,

1885," 4, Church Archives. Brigham Young later stated that the first Apostles of this dispensation were Joseph Smith Jr., Oliver Cowdery, and David Whitmer. See discussion of Porter, "Prophet's New York Years," citing a Smith family prayer and Brigham Young. David Whitmer later maintained that he continued to hold that apostleship. "The Book of Mormon," *Chicago Tribune*, December 17, 1885, 3, col. 5; cited in Cook, ed., *David Whitmer Interviews*, 179.

38. *History of the Church*, 1:51.

39. An early "copy" of the Articles of the Church of Christ initialed by O. C., bearing the date 1829 and discussed by Woodford, "The Historical Development" 1:287–91, is held in Church Archives. It is unclear of what, if anything, it is a copy, or when the copy or its original was written. It quotes the sacrament prayers in Moroni 4–5 and the sacramental instructions in 3 Nephi 18:28–32 that were translated late in May 1829, and in some other ways the document resembles D&C 20, but the two documents are not directly connected. Doctrine and Covenants 20 took its basic present form in June 1830. For a full discussion, see Scott H. Faulring, "An Examination of the 1829 'Articles of the Church of Christ' in Relation to Section 20 of the Doctrine and Covenants," *BYU Studies* 43, no. 4 (2004): 57–91.

40. The other possibility is Ether 5:2–4. Ether 5, however, only expressly states that "unto three," that is, a total of three, "shall they be shown." 2 Nephi 27, on the other hand, provides that "three witnesses shall behold it, by the power of God, *besides* him to whom the book shall be delivered" (italics added), and 27:13–14 refers to the eight witnesses. Since 2 Nephi 27 authorizes more precisely what in fact eventually happened regarding the witnesses, it appears that it was not until that passage was translated that the manifestations to the witnesses ensued. This comports further with the earliest notes on the manuscript history of the Church, discussed further in note 5.

41. Pomeroy Tucker, *Origin, Rise, and Progress of Mormonism* (New York: D. Appleton, 1867), 4, quoted in Francis W. Kirkham, *A New Witness for Christ in America*, 2 vols. (Independence, MO: Zion's Printing and Publishing, 1942), 1:109. John H. Gilbert, "Memorandum made by John H. Gilbert Esq., Sep 8, 1892 Palmyra, N.Y.," Palmyra King's Daughters Free Library, Palymyra, New York, later remembered that Martin Harris approached Grandin twice "in the forepart of June, 1829," although this seems a little too early. See generally *History of the Church*, 1:71.

42. "Mormonism," *Kansas City Daily Journal*, June 5, 1881, 1, reprinted in "Mormonism," *Millennial Star* 43 (July 4, 1881): 421–23 and (July 11, 1881): 437–39; cited in Cook, ed., *David Whitmer Interviews*, 58–71.

43. Larry C. Porter, "A Study of the Origins of the Church of Jesus Christ of Latter-day Saints in the States of New York and Pennsylvania, 1816–1831" (Ph.D. diss., Brigham Young University, 1971; Provo, UT: BYU Studies, 2000), 86–87, citing Thurlow Weed, *Life of Thurlow Weed, Including His Autobiography and a Memoir*, 2 vols., ed. Harriet A. Weed (Boston: Houghton Mifflin, 1884), 1:358–59. One Rochester publisher did agree to print it. See Bushman, *Beginnings of Mormonism*, 107, citing Tucker, *Origin*, 51–53.

44. The mortgage is dated August 25, 1829, signed August 26, 1829, and was recorded on September 11, 1829. See Miner T. Patton, "The Gold That Paid for the Printing of the First Book of Mormon," unpublished manuscript with copies of documents, August 1983, Sun City, Arizona; with appreciation to Ken Godfrey for this item.

45. Peter Crawley, "A Bibliography of The Church of Jesus Christ of Latter-day Saints in New York, Ohio, and Missouri," *BYU Studies* 12, no. 4 (1972): 471. The nature of the contract, however, is uncertain.

46. Gayle G. Ord, "From Golden Plates to Printing Press," 1972, 11, Church Archives: "A cross sampling of 'first editions for 138 books published between 1880 and 1882 [still show that] only 28 per cent of these exceeded 1,500 copies. About 15 per cent were 2,500 or more, and the maximum printing' . . . 6,000 copies—was reserved for one particularly successful book," quoting Donald Sheehan, *This Was Publishing* (Bloomington, IN: Indiana University Press, 1952), 30.

47. Mortgages, book 3, p. 325, Wayne County Courthouse, Lyons, New York, cited in Porter, "Origins of the Church," 88.

48. Gilbert, "Memorandum," 3. John H. Gilbert to F. M. Lyman, October 23, 1887, cited in Kirkham, *New Witness for Christ*, 225; Porter, "Origins of the Church," 88–89.

49. Gilbert, "Memorandum," 3; see Ord, "Golden Plates to Printing Press," 24–43; Richard Lloyd Anderson, "Gold Plates and Printer's Ink," *Ensign* 6 (September 1976): 71–76; Wilford C. Wood, comp., *Joseph Smith Begins His Work*, 2 vols. (Salt Lake City: Deseret News Press, 1958–62), 1:introductory pages.

50. Joseph Smith Jr. to Oliver Cowdery, October 22, 1829, in Dean C. Jessee, ed. and comp., *The Personal Writings of Joseph Smith*, rev. ed. (Salt Lake City: Deseret Book; Provo, UT: Brigham Young University Press, 2002), 251. Gilbert, "Memorandum," 2–3, 4.

51. Gilbert, "Memorandum," 3.

52. Oliver to Joseph, November 6, 1829, Joseph Smith Letterbook, part 1, p. 8. Original letter not extant—copy is in Joseph's handwriting and follows his own spelling and punctuation.

53. 1 Nephi 1:1–2:3, 2:4–15, and Alma 43:22–40, respectively.

54. Russell Rich, "The Dogberry Papers and the Book of Mormon," *BYU Studies* 10/3 (1970): 319–20; Kirkham, *New Witness for Christ*, 271, confuses the dates and contents.

55. They went "over on the ice." Mr. J. L. Traughber, letter, in Wilhelm (von Wymetal) Wyl, *Mormon Portraits*, vol. 1, *Joseph Smith the Prophet* (Salt Lake City: Tribune, 1886), 311.

56. Wyl, *Mormon Portraits*, 311. See generally, Roberts, *Comprehensive History*, 1:162–66.

57. "Note on the sale of the book of Mormon, now printed," January 16, 1830, Simon Gratz Collection, Historical Society of Pennsylvania, Philadelphia.

58. "The Book of Mormon," *Palmyra, N.Y., Wayne Sentinel*, March 26, 1830.

59. Porter, "Prophet's New York Years." Hyrum sold copies to missionaries for $1.25, who sold them for about $2.50. Hyrum Smith, Diaries [and Account Book] 1831–1844, 35, 37–38, Church Archives.

60. Minutes of conference at Orange, Ohio, October 25, 1831, in Donald Q. Cannon and Lyndon W. Cook, eds., *Far West Record* (Salt Lake City: Deseret Book, 1983), 23. For one explanation of Joseph's reticence to share his vision publicly, see Richard L. Bushman, "The Visionary World of Joseph Smith," *BYU Studies* 37, no. 1 (1997–98): 194–97.

61. Dean Jessee, *Papers of Joseph Smith*, 2 vols. (Salt Lake City: Deseret Book, 1992), 1:10.

62. Oliver Cowdery to W. W. Phelps, "Letter IV," *Messenger and Advocate*, February 1835, 80.

63. Oliver Cowdery, Introduction to blessings, September 1835, in Patriarchal Blessing Book, 1:8–9, Church Archives; cited in Dan Vogel, ed. *Early Mormon Documents*, 5 vols. (Salt Lake City: Signature Books, 1996–2003), 2:452.

64. Oliver Cowdery to W. W. Phelps, "Letter VIII," *Messenger and Advocate*, October 1835, 198–200.

65. Joseph Smith, "History of the Church," A-1, Church Archives; published in Jessee, *Papers of Joseph Smith*, 1:278–300; Joseph Smith—History 1:59, 62, 67, 75; and *History of the Church*, 1:12–71.

66. Joseph Smith III, "Last Testimony of Sister Emma," *Saints' Herald* 26 (October 1, 1879): 289–90; and Joseph Smith III, "Last Testimony of Sister Emma," *Saints' Advocate* 2 (October 1879): 50–52. Joseph Smith III wrote that Emma reviewed the answers he had recorded for her. The answers "were affirmed by her" on the day before he left Nauvoo. Emma's husband Lewis C. Bidamon asserted that Emma's answers were "substantially what she had always stated" at times when they discussed the translation of the Book of Mormon.

67. Joseph Smith III to James T. Cobb, February 14, 1879, Community of Christ Library-Archives; cited in Vogel, *Early Mormon Documents*, 1:544.

68. Joseph Smith III to Mrs. E. Horton, March 7, 1900, Community of Christ Library-Archives; cited in Vogel, *Early Mormon Documents*, 1:546–47.

69. "A Mormon Interview," transcribed from Ashbel Kitchell, Pocket Journal (May [March] 7, 1831?), photocopy, Perry Special Collections. Kitchell was describing a visit of Oliver Cowdery that occurred in fall 1830.

70. Oliver Cowdery to W. W. Phelps, *Messenger and Advocate*, October 1834, 14. The letter was dated September 7, 1834. Phelps replied on December 25, 1834, declaring his spiritual anticipation of the Book of Mormon in 1823. *Messenger and Advocate*, February 1835, 65–67.

71. Josiah Jones, "History of the Mormonites," *Evangelist* 9 (June 1, 1841): 132–34. Jones wrote his history of the Mormons while living at Kirtland in 1831. According to the biographical blurb accompanying the article, Jones was "one of the faithful few belonging to the church of Kirtland, who refused to follow Rigdon when he made a surrender of himself and his flock to the Mormons."

72. Reuben Miller Journal, October 21, 1848, holograph, microfilm, Church Archives. Miller recorded Cowdery's testimony at a conference held at Council Bluffs. For more information on Reuben Miller, see Richard Lloyd Anderson, "Reuben Miller, Recorder of Oliver Cowdery's Reaffirmations," *BYU Studies* 8, no. 3 (1968): 277–93.

73. George Q. Cannon, in *Journal of Discourses*, 26 vols. (Liverpool: F. D. Richards, 1855–86), 22:254, September 18, 1881. Several others, including Brigham Young, Charles M. Nielsen, and Seymour B. Young, also gave accounts of this incident, but none of the accounts are firsthand. Historian Richard Lloyd Anderson, *Investigating the Book of Mormon Witnesses* (Salt Lake City: Deseret Book, 1981), 59–60, considers the Cannon account the most correct.

74. Edward Stevenson, "The Three Witnesses to the Book of Mormon," *Millennial Star* 48 (July 5, 1886): 420.

75. William M. Frampton to John E. Booth, September 15, 1901, typescript, microfilm, Church Archives.

76. Samuel W. Richards Statement, May 21, 1907, holograph, 2–3, Church Archives.

77.   Jacob F. Gates Affidavit, January 30, 1912, 1, Church Archives. Jacob Gates's testimony of his meeting with Oliver Cowdery was recorded by his son, Jacob F. Gates.

78.   *Kansas City Daily Journal*, June 5, 1881.

79.   David Whitmer to the editor, *Kansas City Daily Journal*, June 19, 1881; cited in Cook, ed., *David Whitmer Interviews*, 71–72.

80.   *Chicago Times*, October 17, 1881; cited in Cook, ed., *David Whitmer Interviews*, 74–76.

81.   Interview conducted on January 15, 1882, in Richmond, Missouri; published in the *Saints' Herald* 29 (March 1, 1882): 68.

82.   E. C. Briggs, Letter to the Editor, *Saints' Herald* 31 (June 21, 1884): 396–97.

83.   James H. Hart, "About the Book of Mormon," *Deseret Evening News*, March 25, 1884.

84.   George Q. Cannon, interview, February 27, 1884, George Q. Cannon Journal, Church Archives; cited in Cook, ed., *David Whitmer Interviews*, 108.

85.   *St. Louis Republican*, July 16, 1884; cited in Cook, ed., *David Whitmer Interviews*, 143.

Translating and Printing the Book of Mormon

Royal Skousen

Part 1: The Translation

Evidence from the Original Manuscript

*I*n this section I discuss what the original manuscript of the Book of Mormon tells us about how Joseph Smith translated the Book of Mormon. Historical statements by witnesses of the translation process also provide valuable information about how Joseph Smith translated, but sometimes these statements are unreliable. In many respects, the physical evidence from the original manuscript provides, as we shall see, an important means of verifying historical statements.[1]

This physical evidence and the witness statements that it confirms also shed light on the question of the authorship of the Book of Mormon. They do not support theories that Joseph Smith composed the text himself or that he took the text from some other source. Instead the physical evidence and witness statements are most compatible with the account that Joseph himself gave, that he translated the Book of Mormon "by the gift and power of God."[2]

Witnesses of the translation process make two kinds of claims. First of all, they provide valuable evidence of what they actually saw taking place. Generally speaking, their actual observations are consistent with the physical evidence in the original manuscript. On the other hand, these witnesses frequently made claims about matters ey themselves could not observe. For instance, some described what they believed Joseph Smith actually saw in the interpreters; and many claimed that Joseph Smith could not go on until the scribe had written down letter-for-letter what Joseph saw. It turns out that these kinds of claims are not supported by the original manuscript. Of course, the witnesses themselves did not see what Joseph saw. Here they were either offering their own conjecture or perhaps recalling what Joseph might have told them. Nonetheless, all seemed to believe that Joseph Smith actually saw words in English, and there is evidence in the original manuscript to support this idea.

This paper will not encompass a complete rehearsal of the witnesses' statements. Instead, I will provide, when needed, brief quotes from the fuller statements, which can be found in a number of sources.[3]

Statements from Witnesses of the Translation

During the translation process, the witnesses were able to observe, in an open setting, the following:

- Joseph Smith placing the interpreters (either the Urim and Thummim or the seer stone) in a hat and placing his face into the hat
- Joseph Smith dictating for long periods of time without reference to any books, papers, manuscripts, or even the plates themselves
- Joseph Smith spelling out unfamiliar Book of Mormon names
- After each dictated sequence, the scribe reading back to Joseph Smith what was written so that Joseph could check the correctness of the manuscript
- Joseph Smith starting a dictation session without prompting from the scribe about where the previous session had ended

The translation process that these witnesses observed was an open one—that is, others in the room could observe the dictation from Joseph Smith to the scribe. But early on in the translation, from late 1827 to early 1828, it appears that Joseph Smith used a different process while translating. During this time Joseph first copied some of the characters directly from the plates onto sheets of paper, from which sheets he would then translate his transcribed characters into English by means of the Urim and Thummim:

> By this timely aid was I enabled to reach the place of my destination in Pennsylvania, and immediately after my arrival there I commenced copying the characters of <all> the plates. I copied a considerable number of them and by means of the Urim and Thummim I translated some of them . . .[4]

In the above quote, the angled brackets < > surrounding *all* represent a crossout.

During this early period, the plates were uncovered while Joseph Smith translated (or at least while he copied the characters from the plates to paper); and since no one was permitted to see the plates until later, Joseph took precautions to prevent anyone from seeing him working directly with the plates. Martin Harris, in a couple of early statements, said that a blanket or curtain separated Joseph Smith from him at the time he (Harris) obtained a sample transcript and translation to take to Professor Anthon in New York City.[5]

In place of this early method, Joseph Smith soon turned to a method of translation that depended directly on the interpreters alone, so that the plates did not have to be viewed, and thus the translation could be done openly. All witnesses that refer to the translation of the lost 116 pages and our current Book of Mormon text (Emma Smith, Martin Harris, and members of the Whitmer family) openly observed this translation process—one without a curtain or blanket separating Joseph from his scribe. In fact, according to Emma Smith, the plates were wrapped up and not directly used.[6]

On the basis of the witnesses' statements, we can identify the following stages in the translation process:

1. Joseph Smith sees (in some way) the English text,
2. Joseph Smith reads off the text to the scribe,
3. the scribe hears the text,
4. the scribe writes the text.

Evidence from the original and printer's manuscripts suggests that the only revealed stage in the translation process was what Joseph Smith himself saw by means of the interpreters. Witnesses seemed to have believed that Joseph Smith actually saw an English text in the interpreters, but it is possible that Joseph saw the text, so to speak, in his "mind's eye." But in any event, all other stages—from Joseph Smith reading off that text to the scribe's writing it down—potentially introduced human error and had to be carefully monitored.

There appear to be three possible kinds of control over the dictation of the Book of Mormon text:

1. *Loose control:* Ideas were revealed to Joseph Smith, and he put the ideas into his own language (a theory advocated by many Book of Mormon scholars over the years).

2. *Tight control:* Joseph Smith saw specific words written out in English and read them off to the scribe—the accuracy of the resulting text depending on the carefulness of Joseph Smith and his scribe.

3. *Iron-clad control:* Joseph Smith (or the interpreters themselves) would not allow any error made by the scribe to remain (including the spelling of common words).

One can also conceive of mixtures of these different kinds of control. For instance, one might argue for tight control over the spelling of specific names, but loose control over the English phraseology itself.

A number of statements from the witnesses definitely show that virtually all of them believed in the iron-clad theory:

Joseph Knight (autograph [between 1833 and 1847]):

> But if it was not Spelt rite it would not go away till it was rite, so we see it was marvelous.[7]

Emma Smith (Edmund C. Briggs interview, 1856):

> When my husband was translating the Book of Mormon, I wrote a part of it, as he dictated each sentence, word for word, and when he came to proper names he could not pronounce, or long words, he spelled them out, and while I was writing them, if I made a

mistake in spelling, he would stop me and correct my spelling, although it was impossible for him to see how I was writing them down at the time.[8]

Martin Harris (Edward Stevenson's 1881 account):

> By aid of the seer stone, sentences would appear and were read by the Prophet and written by Martin, and when finished he would say, "Written," and if correctly written, that sentence would disappear and another appear in its place, but if not written correctly it remained until corrected, so that the translation was just as it was engraven on the plates, precisely in the language then used.[9]

David Whitmer (Eri B. Mullin interview, 1874):

> . . . the words would appear, and if he failed to spell the word right, it would stay till it was spelled right, then pass away; another come, and so on.[10]

David Whitmer (James H. Hart interview, 1884):

> Sometimes Joseph could not pronounce the words correctly, having had but little education; and if by any means a mistake was made in the copy, the luminous writing would remain until it was corrected. It sometimes took Oliver several trials to get the right letters to spell correctly some of the more difficult words, but when he had written them correctly, the characters and the interpretation would disappear and the interpretation would disappear [*a dittography?*], and be replaced by other characters and their interpretation.[11]

A similar example advocating iron-clad control is the secondary witness of Samuel W. Richards (in a statement recorded over fifty-eight years later, on 25 May 1907).[12] According to Richards, Oliver Cowdery explained to him during the winter of 1848–49 how Joseph Smith had translated:

1. Every word was distinctly visible even down to every letter;
2. and if Oliver omitted a word or failed to spell a word correctly, the translation remained on the "interpreter" until it was copied correctly.

As we shall see, the first statement is apparently true, but the second one is definitely false.

Evidence in the Manuscripts

We now turn to the original manuscript and what it can specifically tell us about the translation process. In a number of instances, it provides valuable support (or at least consistent evidence) for some events that witnesses actually saw. This manuscript also provides valuable evidence for procedures that none of the witnesses described in any of their statements.

The Original Manuscript Was Written from Dictation

Errors in the original manuscript (O) are based on the scribe mishearing what Joseph Smith dictated rather than visually misreading while copying from another manuscript. Consider, for instance, the difficulty the scribe had in hearing the difference between *and* and *an*. In 1 Nephi 13:29 of O the scribe (designated as scribe 2) wrote down the following:

> & because of these things which are taken away out of the gosple
> of the Lamb & exceeding great many do stumble

Obviously, scribe 2 misheard "an exceeding great many" as "and exceeding great many". The use of the ampersand (&) shows that the error was not based on visual similarity. Hearing *an,* the scribe interpreted it as the casual speech form *an'* for *and.*

A mishearing could also occur when the actual word was rather infrequent and the scribe replaced it with a more frequent but phonetically similar word, as in the following example from 1 Nephi 17:48 of O, when Oliver Cowdery wrote *weed* rather than *reed:*

> & whoso shall lay their hands upon me shall wither even as a
> dried weed

In this example, as well as in the previous one, the scribe of the original manuscript did not catch the error.

In the following example Oliver Cowdery immediately corrected a misheard word in Alma 57:22 of O. The incorrect *meet* is crossed out (angled brackets are used to represent crossouts) and the correct *beat* is inserted above the crossout (as indicated by the caret):

> for it was they who did <m^eet> \beat/ the Lamanites

One particular difficulty for the scribe occurred whenever Joseph Smith pronounced unstressed *'em* (for either *them* or *him*). In the following two examples, Oliver Cowdery first interpreted *'em* as *him*, then immediately corrected it by writing *them*:

> & behold they saw him <a> comeing & they hailed him but he sayeth unto <him> them fear not (Alma 55:8)

> wherefore Akish administered it unto his kindreds & friends leading {<%him%>|them} away by fair promises (Ether 8:17)

In the first instance, Oliver Cowdery simply crossed out the *him* and wrote the correct *them* immediately afterwards on the same line. In the second case, Oliver erased the incorrect *him* (represented as <%him%>) and then overwrote the erasure with *them* (the percent sign with angled brackets stands for erasure; curly brackets are used to represent overwriting). Both examples show the problems Oliver was having in interpreting the unstressed *'em* of Joseph Smith's dictation.

Sometimes a following word, when read aloud, interfered with the scribe's ability to hear the correct reading. For instance, in Alma 41:14 Oliver Cowdery wrote *Sons* instead of *Son* in O (he later corrected the error in the printer's manuscript [P]). In this example, underlining is used to highlight the textual change:

> therefore my <u>Sons</u> see that ye are merciful unto your Brethren (O)
> > <u>Son</u> (P)

The source of this error is the following word *see,* whose initial *s* would have made it hard for Oliver Cowdery to hear any difference between *son see* and *sons see*. This passage comes from Alma's discourse to his son Corianton; he is speaking to only one son. In other places in this passage (listed below) *son* is correctly transcribed in both O and P because the context does not lead to ambiguity; in these cases *son* is immediately followed by either a vowel or a consonant other than *s:*

> now my Son I do not say that their resurrection cometh at the resurrection of Christ (Alma 40:20)

> & now my Son this is the restoration of which has been spoken (Alma 40:24)

> & now my Son I have somewhat to say concerning the restoration (Alma 41:1)

> I say unto thee my Son that the plan of restoration is requisite with the Justice of God (Alma 41:2)

> & now behold my Son do not risk one more offence against your God (Alma 41:9)

> & now my Son all men that are in a state of Nature . . . (Alma 41:11)

> & now my Son I perceive there is somewhat more which doth worry your mind (Alma 42:1)

> now behold my son I will explain this thing unto thee (Alma 42:2)

> & now remember my Son if it were not for the plan of redemption . . . (Alma 42:11)

In Alma 41:13 ("O my Son this is not the case"), the text is not fully extant to show whether *Son* or *Sons* was in O; P definitely has *Son*.

In contrast to these examples from O, the errors that are found in P show that it was visually copied. We have examples where Oliver Cowdery incorrectly read O when copying it to produce P. In each case, the error leads to a more difficult reading. As before, underlining is used to indicate the textual change.

> yea & I <u>always</u> knew that there was a God (O) > <u>also</u> (P) (Alma 30:52)

> & Parhoran retained the Judgment seat which caused much rejoiceing among the Brethren of Parhoran & also <u>among</u> the People of liberty (O) > <u>many</u> (P*) > <u>many of</u> (Pjg, 1830) (Alma 51:7)

> [The correct spelling of the name should be *Parhoron;* the first four occurrences of this name in O were spelled *Parhoron* (Alma 50:40, 52:2–3), not *Pahoran* (as it appears in the current text) or *Parhoran* (as shown above in Alma 51:7); the symbol *P** refers to the original hand in P, while *Pjg* refers to a correction (in the printer's manuscript) made by John Gilbert, the compositor for the 1830 edition.]

and he also saw other multitudes pr*ssing their way towards that great and specious bilding (O) > feeling (P) (1 Nephi 8:31)

All of these errors are due to visual similarity. In the first two examples Oliver Cowdery miscopied his own hand in O. In the second example, Oliver wrote "many the People of liberty" in P, which made no sense, so the 1830 compositor, John Gilbert (whose marks are designated here by *Pjg*), inserted the *of* to improve the reading. And in the last example, the hand in O is scribe 3's. This scribe's open *p* has a high ascender, which makes his *p* look like an *f.* The *e* vowel is missing. And the first *s* in *pressing* was an elongated *s* (represented as **s* in the above transcription), which Oliver interpreted as an *l.*

Immediate corrections in the printer's manuscript also show the influence of visual similarity in producing P. Here I list some of the clear examples found in P that show an incorrect word crossed out and the correct visually similar word from O inserted or written immediately afterwards:

<sanct^ified> \satisfied/ (Mosiah 15:9)

<deliver> declare (Mosiah 27:37)

<curse^d> \caused/ (Alma 8:13)

<sacra^ment> \sacrifice/ (Alma 34:10)

<prisoner^s> \provisions/ (Alma 56:27)
    [This same correction is also found in Alma 57:11 and 57:15.]

<suppose>^ \suffer/ (Alma 58:22)

<cau^se> \cease/ (Helaman 4:25)

<burne^d> \buried/ (3 Nephi 8:25)

<rewa^rd> \rearward/ (3 Nephi 20:42)

Joseph Smith Was Working with at Least Twenty
to Thirty Words at a Time

There is some evidence in the original manuscript for the minimal amount of text Joseph Smith had access to as he was dictating. Consider, first of all, the evidence from scribal anticipations. Frequently the scribe, in attempting to keep up with Joseph's dictation, jumped ahead of the actual text. As an example, we have the following case of Oliver Cowdery anticipating the text in Alma 56:41 of O:

> & it came to pass that again <we saw the Lamanites> when the
> light of the morning came we saw the Lamanites upon us

This example suggests that Joseph and Oliver started out together, but by the time Oliver finished writing "& it came to pass that again" Joseph had moved along far enough that he was then dictating "we saw the Lamanites upon us" and Oliver started to write that down when he realized he had skipped the intervening text "when the light of the morning came," so he immediately crossed out "we saw the Lamanites" and wrote the correct sequence, possibly with Joseph repeating the correct text for him. If this explanation is correct, then it indicates that Joseph Smith had at least twenty words in view as he was dictating.

It is also possible that this error was produced by Joseph Smith as he was dictating; that is, Joseph himself may have accidentally skipped the phrase "when the light of the morning came" and then corrected himself. In either case, the implication remains that Joseph had access to at least twenty words.

Another kind of evidence for the length of dictation can be seen in a change of scribe found in Alma 45:22 of O; Oliver Cowdery (OC) suddenly stops acting as scribe and Joseph Smith (JS) himself takes over the scribe's task for twenty-eight words:

OC: . . . therefore Helaman & his Brethren went forth to establish the church again in all the land

JS: yea in every citty throughout all the land which was possessed by the people of Nephi and it came to pass that they did appoint priests and teachers

OC: throughout all the land over all the churches . . .

These twenty-eight words in Joseph Smith's hand are written very carefully. And except for one spelling variant (*citty*), all the extant words are spelled according to standard orthography.

One possible explanation for this momentary switch in scribes is that it represents Oliver Cowdery's unsuccessful attempt to translate. It even suggests that Oliver, like Peter the apostle walking on the water, succeeded at first. For instance, verse 5 of section 9 in the Doctrine and Covenants implies an initial success on Oliver's part:

> And, behold, it is because that you did not continue as you commenced, when you began to translate, that I have taken away this privilege from you.

Nonetheless, there is, in my opinion, some difficulty with the suggestion that these twenty-eight words in Alma 45 represent Oliver Cowdery translating. One problem is that the switch to Joseph Smith's hand occurs in the middle of the narrative, in fact, in the middle of a sentence (although at a point of semiclosure). One would think that Oliver Cowdery's attempt to translate would have come at a more suitable break in the narrative.

My explanation for this scribal switch is that there was a sudden need for the scribe to break off and Joseph Smith had to get down what he was currently viewing in the interpreters, so he wrote it down himself. The reason Joseph would have had to do this is possibly explained by Emma Smith's claim in her 1879 interview with her son Joseph Smith III that his father, Joseph Smith Jr., started dictation sessions without prompting:

> I am satisfied that no man could have dictated the writing of the manuscripts unless he was inspired; for, when acting as his

scribe, your father would dictate to me hour after hour; and when
returning after meals, or after interruptions, he would at once begin where he had left off, without either seeing the manuscript
or having any portion of it read to him. This was a usual thing
for him to do. It would have been improbable that a learned man
could do this; and, for one so ignorant and unlearned as he was,
it was simply impossible.[13]

This ability to continue without prompting suggests that before ending a dictation session or going on to the next portion of text, Joseph
Smith would have to finish getting copied down all of what he was
viewing; otherwise the uncopied part would be lost. In other words,
Joseph had to deal with what was in front of him and could not quit
until what he was seeing was transcribed.

Joseph's careful handwriting for these twenty-eight words as
well as his accurate spelling for several difficult words (*throughout,
possessed, appoint*) suggests that he might have been visually copying and not listening to someone else dictating the text (unless that
person was also spelling out English words for Joseph). In other early
holographic writings of Joseph Smith, we find numerous examples
suggesting that Joseph was not a particularly good speller. Yet in
those writings he does consistently spell *through* correctly. In documents dating from 1832, 1833, and 1839, he writes only *through,* so
the correct spelling of *throughout* in Alma 45 may simply be due
to the fact that Joseph already knew how to spell this word.[14] Early
on, in 1833, Joseph Smith spelled *possess* as *posess,* with a single *s* in
the middle of the word. Yet later, in 1840, he had apparently learned
how to spell *possession* correctly, with two *s*'s instead of one.[15] And
an 1832 spelling of *appointed* is also correctly written by Joseph
Smith.[16] So ultimately this brief passage in Alma 45 has too few
words in Joseph Smith's hand to demonstrate that he was visually
copying from an orthographically correct text. In a cursory examination, I have found only one holographic writing of Joseph's that
contains an incorrect spelling (that is, *posess*) for one of the three
potentially difficult words in this short passage. And of course, we

must remember that Joseph did misspell *city* as *citty* in this passage from Alma 45. So the spelling evidence is not conclusive.

Still, if this explanation is right (that the generally correct spelling of the text in Joseph Smith's hand here in the original manuscript suggests visual copying), then Joseph Smith was viewing at least these twenty-eight words.

Joseph Smith Could See the Spelling of Names

Several witnesses to the translation process claimed that Joseph Smith sometimes spelled out names to the scribe. And we find evidence in the original manuscript in support of this process. Frequently the first occurrence of a Book of Mormon name is first spelled phonetically, then that spelling is corrected; in some instances, the incorrect spelling is crossed out and followed on the same line by the correct spelling, thus indicating that the correction is an immediate one. For example, in Alma 33:15 the text of O reads as follows:

> for it is not written that Zenos alone spake of these things but
> <Zenock> Zenoch also spake of these things

Oliver Cowdery first wrote *Zenock* using the expected *ck* English spelling for the *k* sound when preceded by a short vowel. But then Oliver crossed out the whole word and immediately afterwards, on the same line, wrote *Zenoch,* thus indicating that the spelling agrees with the biblical name *Enoch.* This example also suggests that Joseph Smith spelled out the *ch* sequence for Oliver Cowdery, although it is possible that Joseph could have repronounced the *ch* sequence with the incorrect *ch* sound rather than with the correct *k* sound in order to help Oliver get it down right.

But there are also examples for which it is impossible to find a repronunciation that will guarantee the correct spelling. For instance, in Helaman 1:15 Oliver Cowdery first wrote the name *Coriantumr* phonetically, as *Coriantummer,* then he crossed it all out and wrote out the correct spelling, *Coriantumr:*

> & they were lead by a man whose name was <Coriantummer>
> Coriantumr

In this case, no matter how slowly or carefully Joseph Smith might have repronounced *Coriantumr,* it would have been impossible for him to have indicated that there was no vowel between the *m* and *r* at the end of the name except by actually spelling out the separate letters *m* and *r.* Nor could Oliver Cowdery have guessed this spelling since no word (or name) in English ends in *mr.* In fact, Oliver ends the correct spelling *Coriantumr* with a large flourish on the final *r,* which Oliver produces nowhere else in either the original or the printer's manuscript. This addition probably reveals Oliver Cowdery's frustration at having to guess at such a weird spelling.[17]

Emma Smith and David Whitmer claimed that Joseph Smith sometimes spelled out, in addition to names, English words that were difficult to pronounce:

Emma Smith (Edmund C. Briggs interview, 1856):

> When my husband was translating the Book of Mormon, I wrote a part of it, as he dictated each sentence, word for word, and when he came to proper names he could not pronounce, or long words, he spelled them out . . .[18]

David Whitmer (*Chicago Tribune* interview, 1885):

> In translating the characters Smith, who was *illiterate* and but little versed in Biblical lore, was ofttimes compelled to spell the words out, not knowing the correct pronunciation . . .[19]

There appears to be no firm evidence in what remains of the original manuscript to support this claim of Emma Smith and David Whitmer. Long English words found in what remains of the original manuscript are frequently misspelled, as in the following sampling from 1 Nephi (where misspelled letters are underlined):

Oliver Cowdery:

2:3	obedi<u>a</u>nt
2:11	i<u>mm</u>ag<u>i</u>onations
4:20	treasur<u>ey</u> (3 times)
16:19	fat<u>ea</u>gued
17:30	expedi<u>a</u>nt

| 17:51 | miricles |
| 19:10 | espesially |

Scribe 2:

3:16	inheritence
13:5	tortereth
13:23	covanants (2 times)
15:20	passified

Scribe 3:

4:20	treashury
4:34	dilligent
4:36	desirus
5:2	inherritance
5:8	surity (2 times)
5:9	sacrafice
5:13	prophasies
5:14	jenealeja
5:14	desendant
6:2	sofiseth
7:1	fammaly
7:8	exampel
7:12	exersise
8:21	concorses
10:2	dilagence
10:4	masiah
11:6	hosana
11:26	condesension
11:34	apostels
12:4	tumultius

Of all these examples, only the spelling for *genealogy* lends support to the idea that Joseph Smith spelled out English words. Scribe 3's spelling *jenealeja* for *genealogy* definitely suggests some difficulty in dealing with this word. In 1 Nephi we have the following spellings for *genealogy* in the original manuscript:

Reference	Scribe	Spelling
3:3	Oliver Cowdery	genealogy
3:12	scribe 2	genealogy
5:14	scribe 3	jenealeja
5:16	scribe 3	genealogy
6:1	scribe 3	genealogy
19:2	Oliver Cowdery	genealogy

The fact that both Oliver Cowdery and scribe 2 were readily able to spell *genealogy* correctly suggests that they had no difficulty in dealing with this word, nor did Joseph Smith in pronouncing it. But the first time scribe 3 tries to spell *genealogy* (in 1 Nephi 5:14), he writes *jenealeja,* a very naive spelling. This scribe's use of *j* in place of *g* suggests that he had no idea how to spell this word—and perhaps he didn't recognize or even know the word. But a short time later, when the word is used in verse 16, it suddenly appears in its standard spelling (as also in 6:1). This sudden change implies that someone—possibly Joseph Smith—could have told scribe 3 how to spell this word.

In any event, if Joseph Smith did spell out long English words, it appears to have been fairly infrequent. The lack of consistent evidence for spelling out words of English does not, however, necessarily contradict Emma Smith's statement. Emma's description refers to when she was acting as scribe, which presumably would have been at the beginning of the original book of Lehi (which formed part of the 116 manuscript pages that were later lost). Joseph Smith's pronunciation of long English words might have improved sufficiently as the 116 pages were being dictated that eventually he hardly ever needed to spell out difficult English words. Even in the beginning there probably wouldn't have been that many words causing him difficulty. Having learned how to pronounce the difficult words, he would have simply relied on the scribe to correctly spell the words he dictated, except for unfamiliar names.

The original manuscript suggests that the spelling of names could have been checked whenever the scribe felt unsure of the spelling. This situation would naturally occur with the first occurrence of an unfamiliar name in the text. (It could also occur after a substantial hiatus, during which the scribe might have forgotten the spelling.) As an extended example of this phenomenon, consider the spelling of *Amalickiah* in the book of Alma. The first couple of occurrences are spelled correctly, but then Oliver Cowdery (the scribe here) starts spelling the second and third vowels of *Amalickiah* as *e*'s. At first Oliver catches these errors and corrects them. But eventually he apparently remembers that once the scribe has made sure that the first occurrence of a name is spelled correctly, there is really no need to worry about spelling variance in subsequent occurrences of the name. In this case, the first spelling *Amalickiah* establishes the correct spelling. As long as this is kept in mind, there is no problem if subsequent occurrences of *Amalickiah* are spelled differently. So after the first handful of occurrences, Oliver rather consistently spells *Amalickiah* as *Ameleckiah,* although sometimes he immediately corrects the second *e* to an *i;* or sometimes he later corrects the first *e* to an *a* (always with a heavier ink flow).

In the following list, we have all the occurrences of *Amalickiah* and in order of appearance. Correct spellings are marked with an asterisk (*); some examples are not fully extant in O and are represented by a question mark (?); an *e* corrected to an *a* is written as {e|a}; a plus sign (+) means that the change of *e* to *a* was done in heavier ink; {e|i} stands for an *e* corrected to an *i;* and finally, parentheses containing blank spaces means that the text here is not extant:

correct spelling, without overwriting:

*		46:3	Amalickiah
*		46:4	Amalickiah

overwriting of *e*'s begins:

*+		46:5	Am{e|a}l{e|i}ckiah
*+		46:6	Am{e|a}l{e|i}ckiah
	?	46:7	—

overwriting suddenly ends; *e*'s not corrected at all:

	46:10	Ameleckiah
	46:11	Amelickiah

?	46:28	—
	46:28	Ameleckiahites
?	46:29	—
?	46:29	—
	46:30	Amaleckiah
	46:30	Ameleckiah
	46:30	Ameleckiah
	46:31	Ameleckiah
?	46:32	—
	46:33	Ameleckiah
	46:35	Ameleckiahites
	47:1	Amaleckiah

overwriting briefly returns with some consistency:

+	?	47:3	Am{e	a}( )ckiah
*+		47:4	Am{e	a}lickiah
*+		47:8	Am{e	a}lickiahs
*+		heading	Am{e	a}lickiah
*+		47:11	Am{e	a}lickiah
	?	47:12	—
+		47:13	Am{e	a}leckiah
*+		47:13	Am{e|a}l{e|i}ckiah

overwriting becomes fairly inconsistent:

+	47:13	Am{e	a}leckiah
	47:14	Amel{e	i}ckiah
	47:15	Amel{e	i}ckiah
*	47:15	Amal{e	i}ckiah
	47:16	Ameleckiah
	47:18	Ameleckiah
*+	47:19	Am{e|a}l{e|i}ckiah
	47:20	Amel{e	i}ckiah

overwriting becomes quite sporadic and infrequent:

	47:21	Amelickiah
	47:21	Ameleckiah
	47:22	Amel{e|i}ckiah

	47:25	Ameleckiah
	47:27	Ameleckiah
?	47:27	—
	47:30	Ameleckiah
	47:32	Amel{e|i}ckiah
	47:33	Ameleckiah
	47:34	Ameleckiah
	47:35	Amaleckiah
	heading	Amel{e|i}ckiah
	48:1	Ameleckiah
+	48:7	Am{e|a}leckiah
	49:9	Amel{e|i}ckiahites
*+	49:10	Am{e|a}l{e|i}ckiah
?	49:11	—
	49:25	Amel{e|i}ckiah
?	51:9	—
?	51:11	—
?	51:12	—
	heading	Ameleckiah
+	51:23	Am{e|a}leckiah
	51:23	Amelickiah
*+	51:25	Am{e|a}l{e|i}ckiah
	51:27	Amelickiah
	51:30	Amelickiah
	51:32	Ameleckiah
	51:33	Ameleckiah
?	51:37	( )el( )
	52:1	Ameleckiah
*+	52:3	Am{e|a}lickiah
	52:3	Ameleckiah
	heading	Ameleckiah
	54:16	Amelickiah
	55:5	Ameleckiah
?	62:35	—

Quite obviously, the scribe can make errors. There is definitely no iron-clad control over the text.

The spelling *Ameleckiah* also provides evidence that Joseph Smith was pronouncing this name with stress on the first syllable, with the result that the second and third vowels were reduced to the indistinct schwa vowel ("uh"). If Joseph Smith had been pronouncing *Amalickiah* as we do currently, with stress on the second syllable, then Oliver Cowdery would have consistently and correctly spelled at least the second vowel.

Most of the witnesses believed that Joseph Smith or the interpreters had some ability to know what the scribe was writing. They may well have occasionally observed Joseph Smith correcting the scribe without directly looking at the manuscript. Yet this interference was not automatic, nor did it prevent the scribe from making mistakes.

The Scribe Repeated Back the Text to Joseph Smith

According to David Whitmer (as found in his own 1887 publication *An Address to All Believers in Christ*), a dictation of words was followed by a checking sequence in which the scribe would read back the text to Joseph Smith. If an error was discovered, Joseph Smith would presumably then read off the correct text once more until he was satisfied that the scribe had written it down correctly:

> Brother Joseph would read off the English to Oliver Cowdery, who was his principal scribe, and when it was written down and repeated to Brother Joseph to see if it was correct, then it would disappear, and another character with the interpretation would appear.[20]

David Whitmer also referred to this repetition in an 1881 interview published in the *Kansas City Journal*:

> He did not use the plates in the translation, but would hold the interpreters to his eyes and cover his face with a hat, excluding all light, and before his eyes would appear what seemed to be parchment, on which would appear the characters of the plates in a line at the top, and immediately below would appear the translation

in English, which Smith would read to his scribe, who wrote it down exactly as it fell from his lips. The scribe would then read the sentence written, and if any mistake had been made, the characters would remain visible to Smith until corrected, when they faded from sight, to be replaced by another line.[21]

The specific evidence from the original manuscript is consistent with the claim that the scribe read back what had been written. In such a process, Joseph Smith would be checking what he was hearing from the scribe against what he was viewing in the interpreters. But such agreement would not guarantee the accuracy of the manuscript. For instance, *Amalickiah* could be spelled *Ameleckiah,* but since both spellings were pronounced the same (when stress was on the first syllable), there would be no way for Joseph to detect the incorrect spelling when the scribe pronounced the name. This same difficulty applies to phonetically similar words (such as mixing up *weed* with *reed, and* with *an,* and *sons* with *son* when immediately followed by a word beginning with an *s*). Most of the undetected errors that remain in the original manuscript could not have been caught when read back because there was little if any difference in pronunciation.

Corrections in the original manuscript are also consistent with a repetition sequence. The clear majority of changes in the original manuscript were made immediately; that is, the scribe caught the error during Joseph Smith's initial dictation. Evidence for these immediate corrections include: corrections following on the same line, erasures showing ink smearing (since the ink had not yet dried), or supralinear corrections or insertions in the line with no change in the level of ink flow or difference in the quill. These immediate corrections also include numerous cases where the crossed-out word is only part of the intended word or is obviously miswritten.

On the other hand, there are also numerous changes that are consistent with a process of correcting errors found while repeating the text. In these instances, the original form is complete and the error is usually not obvious (that is, the reading is not a difficult reading); the correction is supralinear or inserted in the line, but there is no erasure, only a crossout of the error, and the level of ink flow for the correction is usually different.

We should also note that there is evidence that some corrections were done considerably later, that is, some time after the repetition sequence. In fact, a few of these later corrections in the original manuscript were apparently made when the printer's manuscript was being copied from the original or even later when sheets of the 1830 edition were being proofed. Sometimes the change was by a different scribe or in a different medium (such as pencil). In virtually every case these few corrections eliminated difficult readings in the original manuscript.

The Word Chapter *and the Corresponding Chapter Numbers Were Not Part of the Revealed Text*

Evidence from both the original and printer's manuscripts shows that Joseph Smith apparently saw some visual indication at the end of a section that the section was ending. Although this may have been a symbol of some kind, a more likely possibility is that the last words of the section were followed by blankness. Recognizing that the section was ending, Joseph Smith then told the scribe to write the word *chapter,* with the understanding that the appropriate number would be added later.

There is considerable evidence in both manuscripts to support this interpretation. First, the word *chapter* is never used by any writer in the text itself, unlike the term *book,* which is used to refer to an individual book in the Book of Mormon (such as the book of Helaman) as well as a whole set of plates (such as the book of Nephi, meaning the large plates of Nephi; see Helaman 2:13–14).

Second, chapters are assigned before the beginning of a book. For instance, in the original manuscript, we have the following at the beginning of 2 Nephi:

<Chapter <{V|I}> VIII>

second   Chapter I
The ^ Book of Nephi ^ An account of the death of Lehi . . .

Oliver Cowdery first wrote *Chapter* at the conclusion of the last section in 1 Nephi—that is, at the conclusion of Chapter VII in the original chapter system; our current chapter system dates from Orson Pratt's 1879 edition of the Book of Mormon (which has 22 chapters in 1 Nephi). At this point, Joseph Smith had no indication that a new book was beginning. All he could see was the end of Chapter VII (namely, the words "and thus it is Amen" followed probably by blankness or maybe a special symbol). Later, when Oliver Cowdery was adding the chapter numbers, he first assigned the Roman numeral *VIII* to this first chapter of 2 Nephi. But when he realized that this was actually the beginning of a new book, he crossed out the whole chapter designation and inserted (with slightly weaker ink flow) "Chapter I" after the title of the book, which originally was simply designated as "The Book of Nephi." Later he realized that there was more than one book of Nephi, which led him to also insert the word *second* (with considerably heavier ink flow).

This system of assigning chapters also explains why the two manuscripts have chapter numbers assigned to the short books found at the end of the small plates (Enos, Jarom, Omni, and the Words of Mormon) as well as 4 Nephi. These books contain only one section, but at the beginning of each of these short books, Joseph Smith apparently had no knowledge that this was the case. This fact further shows that Joseph Smith himself did not know in advance the contents or structure of the text.

Probably the strongest evidence that the word *chapter* is not original to the revealed text is that the chapter numbers are assigned later in both manuscripts. The numbers are almost always written in heavier ink and more carefully. In many cases, Oliver Cowdery added serifs to his Roman numerals. On the other hand, his *Chapter* is always written rapidly and with the same general ink flow as the surrounding text. In the printer's manuscript, at the beginning of Chapter XVII in Alma (now the beginning of Alma 36), the Roman numeral *XVII* was written in blue ink, not the normal black ink. In this part of the printer's manuscript, Oliver had been using this same blue ink to rule the manuscript sheets of P prior to copying.

Here he also used this blue ink to assign the chapter number as well
as add an *s* to the word *Commandment* in the next line. This example
clearly suggests that this part of the original manuscript itself did
not yet have chapter numbers assigned to it when Oliver Cowdery
started to copy it, perhaps six months after it had been dictated.

In addition, there is one case when the scribe got off in his
counting of the chapters. While producing the printer's manuscript,
when he came to Chapter VIII in Mosiah (now starting at chapter 13, verse 25), Oliver Cowdery accidentally assigned the Roman
numeral *IX* to this chapter, with the result that all the numbers for
the subsequent chapters in Mosiah are off by one. The compositor
for the 1830 edition caught this error and penciled in the correct
number for all but one of these later chapters.

Internal Evidence for Tight Control

The evidence for loose control seems to rely heavily upon the
notion that the nonstandard use of English in the original text could
not have come from the Lord (since he supposedly only speaks "correct" English). The use of dialectal English, in this view, is said to be
Joseph Smith's contribution; thus by inference the Lord only gave
Joseph Smith ideas, not specific words.[22] Of course, the spelling out
of names definitely suggests that a theory of loose control must be
revised in some way; Joseph Smith had some view of the specific
spelling for names, in particular, names with impossible spellings
for English literates.

In addition, there is substantial evidence within the text itself
for tight control over specific words, phrases, and sentences of
English. For instance, John W. Welch has pointed out an interesting
case where the Book of Mormon makes the same identical (nonbib-
lical) quote in widely separated parts of the text.[23] The example he
gives is based on Lehi's vision of the kingdom of God as found in
1 Nephi 1:8 and Alma 36:22:

> and he thought he saw
> *God sitting upon his throne*
> *surrounded with numberless concourses of angels*

> *in the attitude of singing and praising their God*
> (1 Nephi 1:8)

> and methought I saw
> even as our father Lehi saw
> *God sitting upon his throne*
> *surrounded with numberless concourses of angels*
> *in the attitude of singing and praising their God*
> (Alma 36:22)

This identity of quotation provides striking support for a theory of tight control over the translation.

One of the interesting complexities of the original English-language text of the Book of Mormon is that it contains expressions that appear to be uncharacteristic of English in all of its dialects and historical stages. These structures also support the notion that Joseph Smith's translation is a literal one and not simply a reflection of either his own dialect or the style of early modern English found in the King James Version of the Bible.

For instance, in the original text of the Book of Mormon we find a number of occurrences of a Hebrew-like conditional clause. In English, we have conditional clauses like "if you come, then I will come," with *then* being optional. In Hebrew this same clause is expressed as "if you come and I will come." In the original text of the Book of Mormon, there were at least fourteen occurrences of this non-English expression. One occurrence was removed in 1 Nephi 17:50 as Oliver Cowdery was producing the printer's manuscript by copying from the original manuscript:

> if he should command me that I should say unto this water be
> thou earth <u>and it shall be earth</u> (O) > <u>it should be earth</u> (P)

The remaining thirteen occurrences were all removed by Joseph Smith in his editing for the second edition of the Book of Mormon, published in 1837 in Kirtland, Ohio. One example comes from the famous passage in Moroni 10:4:

and if ye shall ask with a sincere heart with real intent having
faith in Christ <u>and</u> he will manifest the truth of it unto you by the
power of the Holy Ghost (P, 1830) > NULL (1837)

This use of *and* is not due to scribal error, especially since this *if-and* expression occurs seven times in one brief passage (Helaman 12:13–21):

13   yea and <u>if</u> he sayeth unto the earth move <u>and</u> it is moved

14   yea <u>if</u> he say unto the earth thou shalt go back that it lengthen
out the day for many hours <u>and</u> it is done . . .

16   and behold also <u>if</u> he sayeth unto the waters of the great deep
be thou dried up <u>and</u> it is done

17   behold <u>if</u> he sayeth unto this mountain be thou raised up and
come over and fall upon that city that it be buried up <u>and</u> behold
it is done . . .

19   and <u>if</u> the Lord shall say be thou accursed that no man shall
find thee from this time henceforth and forever <u>and</u> behold no
man getteth it henceforth and forever

20   and behold <u>if</u> the Lord shall say unto a man because of thine
iniquities thou shalt be accursed forever <u>and</u> it shall be done

21   and <u>if</u> the Lord shall say because of thine iniquities thou shalt
be cut off from my presence <u>and</u> he will cause that it shall be so

These examples of the *if-and* construction in the original text suggest that Joseph Smith did not simply get the idea of a conditional
construction in his mind. If that had been the case, he should have
translated that idea using the English *if-then* construction, possibly
without the *then,* but in any event, without the connective *and.* The
multiple occurrence of the non-English *if-and* construction suggests
that even the word *and* was controlled for.

Conclusion

Evidence from the original manuscript supports the traditional
belief that Joseph Smith received a revealed text through the inter-

preters. This idea of a controlled text originates with statements made by the witnesses of the translation. The evidence from the original manuscript, when joined with internal evidence from the text itself, suggests that this control was tight, but not iron-clad. The text could be "ungrammatical" from a prescriptive point of view, but the use of nonstandard English is not evidence that the text was not being tightly controlled, or that it did not come from the Lord, who apparently does not share our insistence on "proper English" (see D&C 1:24). In fact, the occurrence of non-English Hebraisms such as the *if-and* construction strongly suggests that the text was tightly controlled, down to the level of the word at least. And the spelling of names such as *Coriantumr* suggests that control could be imposed down to the very letter.

All of this evidence (from the original manuscript, witnesses' statements, and from the text itself) is thus consistent with the hypothesis that Joseph Smith could actually see (whether in the interpreters themselves or in his mind's eye) the translated English text—word for word and letter for letter—and that he read off this revealed text to his scribe. Despite Joseph's reading off of the text, one should not assume that this process was automatic or easily done. Joseph had to prepare himself spiritually for this work. Yet the evidence suggests that Joseph Smith was not the author of the Book of Mormon, not even its English language translation, although it was revealed spiritually through him and in his own language.

Part 2: The Printing

Occasionally historians and other observers of the past attempt to discredit someone's account of a past event by referring to the age of the person when the account was given. Age frequently becomes an argument against the account if the historian or observer does not agree with the implications of that account.

Yet the real issue is how an account matches up with other accounts or, even more significantly, how it matches up with the physical evidence that remains. Independent, physical evidence can

Restoration of the Grandin Print Shop, where the Book of Mormon was printed.

often be used to test the reliability of accounts. A good example of this procedure in analyzing accounts can be found in the analysis by Don Enders of numerous statements made in E. D. Howe's 1834 *Mormonism Unvailed,* in particular, claims by some of the residents around Palmyra that Joseph Smith's family were poor and lazy. Enders compared these claims against the original land and tax records and other local government papers from the 1820s and 1830s and discovered that the assessment of Joseph Smith Sr.'s property, based on the 1830 tax records, shows that the valuation of the Smith farm per acre exceeded that of nine out of ten farms owned by families who criticized the Smiths in *Mormonism Unvailed.* This finding calls into question the overall validity of these accounts in Howe's book denigrating the Smiths' work ethic.[24]

In this section, I would like to consider a statement made by John Gilbert, the compositor (or typesetter) for the 1830 edition of the Book of Mormon. Gilbert made this statement on 9 September 1892, when he was 90 years old. In his statement, a typescript located in the King's Daughters Library in Palmyra, Gilbert describes events that occurred 63 years earlier. Now of course we could dismiss his account (if we didn't like what he was saying about the early publishing history of the Book of Mormon) by simply referring to his age, or the lateness in making this statement, or even his anti-Mormon bias. But the better procedure is to test this statement against what we have been able to discover about the printing of the first edition of the Book of Mormon.

This process includes evidence from the two Book of Mormon manuscripts: the original manuscript and the printer's manuscript. The original manuscript is the dictated manuscript the scribes wrote down as Joseph Smith translated the Book of Mormon. During 1829–30, a copy of the original manuscript was made. This copy is called the printer's manuscript because, for the most part, this was the manuscript that was taken to the printer's shop in Palmyra, New York, where the type was set for the first edition of the Book of Mormon, published in 1830. About 28% of the original manuscript is extant. Most of the extant portions of the original manuscript are owned by the LDS Church. The printer's manuscript is owned by the RLDS Church and is extant except for three lines. Fragments of the original manuscript show that the original (dictated) manuscript rather than the copied printer's manuscript was used to set the 1830 edition from Helaman 13 through Mormon 9.[25]

In addition to the two manuscripts, this analysis of John Gilbert's statement has involved the examination of about one hundred copies of the 1830 edition, an original proof sheet of the 1830 title page, and a complete set of unbound sheets of the 1830 edition (sometimes called the "uncut sheets") that Gilbert had saved.

I reproduce Gilbert's entire statement (as a typographical facsimile) at the end of this article, but here I list a number of claims Gilbert made in that statement about the printing of the 1830 edition and compare those claims with the extant physical evidence dating from 1829 and 1830.

1. 500 pages of manuscript

> A few pages of the manuscript were submitted as a specimen of the whole, and it was said there would be about 500 pages.[26]

There were 466 pages in the printer's manuscript and probably a few more in the original manuscript, perhaps as many as 480 pages. In either case, the estimate that Gilbert remembered is close to the actual number of pages.

2. 5,000 copies of the 1830 edition for $3,000

> In the forepart of June 1829, Mr. E. B. Grandin, the printer of the "Wayne Sentinel," came to me and said he wanted I should assist him in estimating the cost of printing 5,000 copies of a book that Martin Harris wanted to get printed, which was called the "Mormon Bible." . . .
>
> The contract was to print and bind with leather 5,000 copies for $3,000.

The number 5,000 agrees with other accounts of the press run for the 1830 edition. For instance, these same figures are found in Joseph Smith's 1839 History, in both the draft and the final versions.[27] The final version reads:

> Mean time our translation drawing to a close, we went to Palmyra, Wayne Country, N.Y: Secured the Copyright; and agreed with Mr Egbert Grandin to print five thousand Copies, for the sum of three thousand dollars.

3. 1,000 ems per printed page

> The size of the page was agreed upon, and an estimate of the number of ems in a page, which would be 1,000.

An em is a measure of type width equal to the point size of the font being used. There are about 1,075 ems per page in the 1830 edition, with 25 ems per line and 43 lines per page (excluding the header on each page). Gilbert's recollection of the estimated number of ems is close to the actual count for an 1830 page.[28]

4. Manuscript page somewhat longer than an 1830 printed page

> A page of manuscript would make more than a page of printed matter, which proved to be correct.

As already noted, there are 466 pages of manuscript in the printer's manuscript and perhaps as many as 480 pages were in the original manuscript. The 1830 edition itself has 590 pages, which means that one manuscript page provided about one and a fourth pages in the 1830 edition.

5. A new font of small pica

> Mr. Grandin got a new font of small pica, on which the body of the work was printed.

The "small pica" of the 1830 edition is a 10-point type. The type used in the 1830 edition is called Scotch Roman, a very common type designed about 1810 by Richard Austin in Edinburgh, Scotland. This type face was widely used throughout the nineteenth century.[29]

The type used in the 1830 edition had only a few pieces of broken type. The type imprint in 1830 copies is sharp and clean and shows little wear.

6. 24 pages on foolscap paper

> When the printer was ready to commence work, [Martin] Harris was notified, and Hyrum Smith brought the first installment of manuscript, of 24 pages, closely written on common foolscap paper.

The entire printer's manuscript is a collection of gatherings of sheets. To form a gathering, Oliver Cowdery (the principal scribe for the printer's manuscript, as well as the original manuscript) would typically take 6 sheets of foolscap paper (a size of paper), line them, and fold them down the center to form a gathering of 24 pages or 12 leaves. Later, after writing the text, he would secure the gathering by producing at least 4 holes (or "stabs") along the fold (or "gutters") and weaving in yarn and then tying it to hold the gathering together. The very first gathering for the printer's manuscript starts at the beginning of 1 Nephi and goes up to 1 Nephi 14:21. Like most of the other gatherings in the printer's manuscript, this first one contains 24 pages (6 foolscap sheets folded widthwise to form 12 leaves or 24 pages).

Foolscap paper originally referred to a watermark showing a fool's cap, but by the 1800s this term was universally used to refer to a paper size. The sheets for the printer's manuscript show some variance, but range from 31.4 to 33.1 cm in width and from 38.3 to 41.5 cm in length. Published accounts (given in the *Oxford English Dictionary* under "foolscap") indicate that foolscap paper varied from 12 to 13.5 inches in width and from 15 to 17 inches in length (that is, from 30 to 34 cm in width and 38 to 43 cm in length). All the sheets in the printer's manuscript are within these bounds, as are the extant sheets of the original manuscript.

7.   Proof sheet of title page alone

> The title page was first set up, and after proof was read and corrected, several copies were printed for [Martin] Harris and his friends.

One of the individuals in the print shop that day was Stephen Selwyn Harding, who later served as territorial governor of Utah (1862–63). Harding received one of these copies of the proof sheet of the title page and in 1847 donated his copy to the LDS Church. This copy has been on display at the Church Museum in Salt Lake City. In comparing this proof sheet with the title page as actually published, we see that a number of misspellings were corrected; in addition, the spacing (or "leading") between the various lines, especially in the title and subtitle, was increased.

8.   Grammatical "errors" not corrected

> On the second day—[Martin] Harris and [Hyrum] Smith being in the office—I called their attention to a grammatical error, and asked whether I should correct it? Harris consulted with Smith

a short time, and turned to me and said: "The Old Testament is ungrammatical, set it as it is written."

For the most part, Gilbert did not edit out the grammatical "errors." The vast majority of them were copied over straight from the manuscripts into the 1830 edition. In some cases some accidental correction seems to have occurred. And in a handful of cases we have specific evidence that either John Gilbert or Oliver Cowdery consciously corrected what was perceived to be pronominal redundancies. For instance, in Ether 9:8, the printer's manuscript originally read as follows:

> & now the brother of him that suffered death & his name was Nimrah & he was angry with his father because of that which his father had done unto his brother

While punctuating the manuscript to set the type for this part of the text, Gilbert placed the intrusive "& his name was Nimrah" in parentheses and then crossed out the words "& he" that followed. This kind of conscious editing is infrequent in the text. The vast majority of "ungrammatical" expressions were left unchanged.

9. Scribes for the printer's manuscript

> Martin Harris, Hyrum Smith, and Oliver Cowdery were very frequent visitors to the office during the printing of the Mormon Bible. The manuscript was supposed to be in the handwriting of Cowdery. . . .
>
> Cowdery held and looked over the manuscript when most of the proofs were read. Martin Harris once or twice, and Hyrum Smith once, Grandin supposing these men could read their own writing as well, if not better, than anyone else; and if there are any discrepancies between the Palmyra edition and the manuscript these men should be held responsible.

The printer's manuscript is mostly in Oliver Cowdery's hand (84.6%). A not-yet-identified scribe (referred to as scribe 2) accounts for 14.9% of the printer's manuscript. This scribe basically transcribed two large portions (from Mosiah 25 to Alma 13, and from 3 Nephi 19 to the end of Mormon), but in the first portion, Hyrum

Smith briefly took over for scribe 2 on five different occasions (from Mosiah 28 to Alma 5). Hyrum's minor contribution amounts to only 0.5% of the text.

But the printer never saw the second portion done by scribe 2. Instead, the original manuscript was taken in for this portion of the typesetting. All extant fragments of the original manuscript from this part of the text (from Helaman 13 to the end of Mormon) are in Oliver Cowdery's hand, so if we presume that all this portion of the original manuscript was in Oliver's hand, the 1830 printer saw Oliver Cowdery's hand for slightly over 91% of the text. By this calculation, scribe 2 then accounts for 8.5% of the text and Hyrum the remaining 0.5%. So Gilbert's comment that the manuscript was supposed to be in Oliver's hand is probably accurate for about 91% of the text.

Gilbert's comment that Oliver Cowdery did most of the proofing, but that Martin Harris did it twice and Hyrum Smith once is intriguing, especially since these rankings are consistent with the frequency with which the printer set type from the handwriting of Oliver Cowdery, scribe 2, and Hyrum Smith. The additional statement from Grandin about proofing "their own writing" suggests that Martin Harris might have been scribe 2, although of course Gilbert's initial statement about the handwriting implies that Oliver Cowdery was the only scribe. Except for his signature, there are apparently no identified extant examples of Martin Harris's handwriting.[30]

We also have definite evidence that Oliver Cowdery was learning from his proofing of the 1830 edition. For instance, by the time he got into 3 Nephi, Oliver had learned that *exceeding(ly)* is spelled with two *e*'s after the *c*, not as *exceding(ly)*, which is how he consistently spelled the word in the original manuscript as well as in the printer's manuscript before 3 Nephi 12:12. From then on in the printer's manuscript, Oliver always spelled *exceeding(ly)* correctly.

In addition, Oliver Cowdery also learned to hyphenate at the end of lines. Earlier he had always hyphenated at the beginning of the line (in the original manuscript and the first part of the printer's manuscript). For example, in the original manuscript, if only *accord* of *according* fit at the end of a line, Oliver would have written *accord* at the end of the line and -*ing* at the beginning of the next line. But when he finally learned that hyphenation occurs at the end of the line, Oliver would have written *accord-* at the end of the line, but still he would have kept the hyphen at the beginning of the next line (that is, -*ing*), thus ending up with two hyphens.

Oliver Cowdery started this practice of double hyphenation at the beginning of 2 Nephi (page 49 in the printer's manuscript), but here he put hyphens at the end of a line only once or twice a page, so that in this part of the printer's manuscript most hyphenated words had only a single hyphen, at the beginning of a line. But by the time Oliver got through 200 pages of the printer's manuscript, he started to hyphenate more frequently at the ends of lines, so that ultimately in the last half of the manuscript we often find double hyphenation more than ten times a page.

10. Paragraphing and punctuation in the manuscript

Every chapter, if I remember correctly, was one solid paragraph, without a punctuation mark, from beginning to end.

. . . I punctuated it to make it read as I supposed the author intended, and but very little punctuation was altered in proof-reading.

Originally, very little punctuation appeared on the printer's manuscript and virtually none on the original manuscript, including that portion (from Helaman 13 to the end of Mormon) used to set the type for the 1830 edition. For the first part of the printer's manuscript, Oliver Cowdery copied the original manuscript without adding punctuation. He finally realized that he himself could add the punctuation, so beginning with page 106 of the printer's manuscript, Oliver started to add a little punctuation, but only sporadically and never systematically. Moreover, Gilbert basically ignored Oliver's punctuation.

Beginning with page 129 of the printer's manuscript, Oliver Cowdery added paragraph marks as he prepared this manuscript, but by page 145 he stopped this practice, probably because he had realized that the compositor was ignoring his suggested paragraph breaks. In any event, all the original chapters in the Book of Mormon manuscripts were written as a single paragraph. Gilbert is responsible for the actual paragraphing in the 1830 edition, although he does not mention it in this statement. While inserting punctuation, he would also use the letter *P* (not the reversed paragraph symbol ¶) whenever he wanted to show the beginning of a new paragraph.

Scribe 2, unlike Oliver Cowdery, fairly consistently punctuated the portions of the printer's manuscript that he was responsible for, although scribe 2 had only a single punctuation mark that sometimes looks like a period and sometimes like a small comma. This same mark is used interchangeably for both full and half stops. Once more, for the first portion of scribe 2's handwriting (from Mosiah 25 to Alma 13), Gilbert ignored this rather confusing punctuation mark from scribe 2.

As Gilbert indicated, he basically typeset the 1830 edition with the same punctuation marks that he had placed in the printer's manuscript. I would estimate that over 90% of Gilbert's punctuation marks in the printer's and original manuscripts were carried over without change into the 1830 edition.

11. Capitalization in the manuscript

> Names of persons and places were generally capitalized, but sentences had no end. The character & was used almost invariably where the word *and* occurred, except at the end of a chapter.

In those portions of the original manuscript in the hand of Oliver Cowdery, the first word in a chapter was systematically capitalized (as were names). If the first word was *and*, it was written as *And*. Gilbert's "end of a chapter" refers, of course, to the beginning of a new chapter, since one implies the other. But other sentence-initial words in the original manuscript were generally not capitalized by Oliver. And he wrote virtually all other examples of *and* as an ampersand (&). Oliver nearly always followed this same practice in the printer's manuscript. In a couple instances in the manuscripts, Oliver did write *and* as *and,* but in each case he had accidentally started to write some other word and he then overwrote the incorrect word by writing out the full *and* rather than using the shorter ampersand.

On the other hand, it should be noted that in the book of Helaman, Oliver Cowdery started to occasionally show the beginning of a new sentence in the middle of a chapter by capitalizing the sentence-initial word, as in Helaman 5:5–6:

> for they remembered the words which their father Helaman spake unto them & these are the words which he spake Behold my Sons I desire that . . .

Although Oliver never consistently applied this practice in the rest of the printer's manuscript, still he occasionally did capitalize a few sentence-initial words in the middle of a chapter. And eventually, there are examples of mid-chapter sentences beginning with *And* instead of &, as in 3 Nephi 13:34–14:1:

> sufficient is the day unto the evil thereof And now it came to pass that . . .

Although this sentence begins chapter 14 in our current chapter system (dating from Orson Pratt's editing for the 1879 edition), originally this sentence occurred about one-third the way through chapter VI of 3 Nephi. But since this part of the printer's manuscript was never seen by John Gilbert, he never saw this example of a mid-chapter *And*. Only in a few cases in Ether and Moroni of the printer's manuscript could Gilbert have seen in the middle of a chapter an occasional *And* instead of Oliver Cowdery's much more frequent &. In nearly all instances, Gilbert would have seen & in the printer's manuscript.

The two other scribes in the printer's manuscript (scribe 2 and Hyrum Smith) used both & and *and* interchangeably, but this variation would have occurred for only 8.9% of the text (from Mosiah 25 to Alma 13). In any event, Gilbert's recollection of the massive use of & is accurate for the vast majority of the Book of Mormon text.

12. John Gilbert works on the manuscript at home

> After working a few days, I said to [Hyrum] Smith on his
> handing me the manuscript in the morning: "Mr. Smith, if you
> would leave this manuscript with me, I would take it home with
> me at night and read and punctuate it, and I could get along faster
> in the day time, for now I have frequently to stop and read half a
> page to find how to punctuate it." His reply was, "We are com-
> manded not to leave it." A few mornings after this, when Smith
> handed me the manuscript, he said to me: "If you will give your
> word that this manuscript shall be returned to us when you get
> through with it, I will leave it with you." I assured Smith that it
> should be returned all right when I got through with it. For two
> or three nights I took it home with me and read it, and punctu-
> ated it with a lead pencil. This will account for the punctuation
> marks in pencil.

John Gilbert had to wait more than "a few mornings" after "a
few days" before getting permission to take the printer's manuscript
home to punctuate it. In the first part of the manuscript, before page
73, there are only a few minor places where Gilbert added punctuation to the manuscript. These few punctuation marks are all in pencil. When Gilbert refers to reading down half a page of manuscript
to determine the punctuation, he was apparently trying to determine the reading of the text and then adding the punctuation to the
typeset text only, not on the manuscript itself (except in those few
cases).

The first place where Gilbert began to systematically punctuate
the printer's manuscript is on page 73 (beginning with 2 Nephi 17:4).
Since this place is about one-sixth the way through the manuscript,
Gilbert's impression about when he started to take the manuscript
home is a little too early. I would estimate that he probably took the
manuscript home sometime in the last half of September 1829, after
at least one month of printing.

We do have evidence that Gilbert took the manuscript home for
two days. For these two sessions, Gilbert marked the punctuation in
heavy black ink, not in pencil. The first session covers pages 73–75 of

the printer's manuscript. The second session covers pages 77–79 and the first third of page 80.

After these two sessions, all of Gilbert's subsequent punctuation marks on the printer's manuscript (and on the original manuscript for Helaman 13 through the end of Mormon) are in pencil rather than ink. Gilbert's penciling seems to be restricted to work actually done in the printing shop, not at home, especially since his punctuation marks are interspersed with take marks (also in pencil) that were made during the actual setting of the type. (These take marks show where in the manuscript the compositor finished setting the type for a portion of the text.)

Since the clear majority of Gilbert's punctuation is in pencil, it is understandable that he might not have remembered that he used ink for the two nights he took the manuscript home to prepare it for typesetting.

13. Details about the signatures

> The [Mormon] Bible was printed 16 pages at a time, so that one sheet of paper made two copies of 16 pages each, requiring 2,500 sheets of paper for each form of 16 pages. There were 37 forms of 16 pages each, 570 pages in all.

The 1830 edition has 16 pages to a signature and has 37 signatures. Of course, Gilbert could determine this by referring to a copy of the edition (or perhaps to his set of 37 unbound folded sheets). There are, however, 592 pages in the 1830 edition (37 x 16 = 592), of which the last two are blank, thus giving 590 printed pages, not 570. Perhaps the 570 is a typo for 590.

The 2,500 sheets for each signature would thus account for 5,000 copies since they were printing all 16 pages of each signature on both sides of the sheet. This process, called half-sheet imposition (or in more modern terminology, "work and turn"), requires that each sheet be properly oriented and lined up (a process referred to as registering) before printing the opposite side. Finally, the 2,500 larger sheets were torn or cut in two—so that prior to binding, 5,000 copies of each signature were available.

Examination of the unbound sheets shows quite clearly the torn side at the top of each of the 37 signatures. Here each of the original larger sheets was folded and cut along the crease with a bone cutter (personal communication from Don Enders), which left a rough, tornlike edge. The bottom edge has always been cut mechanically, whereas the sides always show a deckle edge—that is, the original uneven edge that results from the paper-making process itself. In addition, the two pinholes resulting from pinning down the middle of the full sheet to the tympan (the frame to which the sheet is secured during the presswork) can be found about half the time near the torn upper edge of the unbound sheets. Thus the unbound sheets clearly show that Gilbert's statement about printing 2,500 sheets to produce 5,000 copies was entirely accurate.[31]

Conclusion

From these many examples, we can see that in every instance, John Gilbert's recollections regarding the printing of the 1830 edition of the Book of Mormon are either precisely correct or, where wrong, the error is easily explained. In a number of cases where he thought something held in every instance, the actual facts show that his recollection is still correct for the clear majority of cases. All in all, these examples show that Gilbert's memory is very accurate, even at 90 years of age and 63 years after the fact.[32]

Notes

Editors' note: Part 1 of this article was originally published as "Translating the Book of Mormon: Evidence from the Original Manuscript," in *Book of Mormon Authorship Revisited*, edited by Reynolds, 61–93; part 2 was originally published as "John Gilbert's 1892 Account of the 1830 Printing of the Book of Mormon," in *The Disciple as Witness*, edited by Ricks, Parry, and Hedges, 383–405.

1.   I wish to thank Richard L. Anderson and John W. Welch for their critiques of an earlier version of this section.

2.   Manuscript History of the Church, Book A-1, 121–22, cited in Richard Lloyd Anderson, "'By the Gift and Power of God,'" *Ensign* 7 (September 1977): 79–85.

3.   See the general bibliography at the end of "Translating the Book of Mormon: Evidence from the Original Manuscript," 91, for a list of sources that discuss the witnesses' statements.

4. Joseph Smith, "History, 1839," in *The Papers of Joseph Smith,* ed. Dean C. Jessee (Salt Lake City: Deseret Book, 1989), 1:284.

5. Milton V. Backman Jr., *Eyewitness Accounts of the Restoration* (Orem, UT: Grandin Book, 1983), 209–13 (quoting John A. Clark, *Gleanings By the Way* [Philadelphia: W. J. and J. K. Simon, 1842], 222–31) and 215–23 (quoting two letters of Charles Anthon, the first in E. D. Howe, *Mormonism Unvailed* [Painesville, OH: E. D. Howe, 1834], 270–2), and the second in Clark, *Gleanings By the Way,* 233, 237–38).

6. Joseph Smith III, "Last Testimony of Sister Emma," *The Saints' Herald* 26/19 (1 October 1879): 289–90.

7. Dean C. Jessee, "Joseph Knight's Recollection of Early Mormon History," *BYU Studies* 17/1 (1976): 35.

8. John W. Welch, "The Miraculous Translation of the Book of Mormon," in *Opening the Heavens,* 129 (citing Edmund C. Briggs, "A Visit to Nauvoo in 1856," *Journal of History* 9 [January 1916]: 454).

9. Edward Stevenson, "One of the Three Witnesses. Incidents in the Life of Martin Harris," *The Latter-Day Saints' Millennial Star* 44/5–6 (30 January and 6 February 1882): 78–89, 86–87.

10. Lyndon W. Cook, ed., *David Whitmer Interviews: A Restoration Witness* (Orem, UT: Grandin Book, 1991), 3.

11. Cook, *David Whitmer Interviews,* 115.

12. The original typescript signed by Samuel Richards is located in the Family and Church History Department, The Church of Jesus Christ of Latter-day Saints (Samuel Whitney Richards Collection, Ms 6576, Box 2, Folder 14); the quotes here are based on a transcript (made by Scott Faulring) of the statement.

13. Joseph Smith III, "Last Testimony of Sister Emma," 290.

14. See Dean C. Jessee, ed., *The Personal Writings of Joseph Smith* (Salt Lake City: Deseret Book, 1984), 252, 260, 285, and 427.

15. See the example *posess,* first crossed out and then rewritten the same way, in Jessee, *Personal Writings of Joseph Smith,* 21; the 1840 *possession* is found on page 468.

16. Ibid., 261.

17. For a published photograph of this respelling, see page 221 in Daniel H. Ludlow, ed., *Encyclopedia of Mormonism* (New York: Macmillan, 1992).

18. Welch, *Translation of the Book of Mormon,* 129.

19. Cook, *David Whitmer Interviews,* 174.

20. David Whitmer, *An Address to All Believers in Christ* (Richmond, MO: David Whitmer, 1887), 12.

21. Cook, *David Whitmer Interviews,* 62.

22. For further discussion of whether or not the Lord himself insists on using standard English, see the discussion in Royal Skousen, "Towards a Critical Edition of the Book of Mormon," *BYU Studies* 30/1 (1990): 54–56.

23. "Book of Mormon Translation by Joseph Smith," in *Encyclopedia of Mormonism,* 1:210–13.

24. Donald L. Enders, "The Joseph Smith, Sr., Family: Farmers of the Genesee," in *Joseph Smith: The Prophet, the Man,* ed. Susan Easton Black and Charles D. Tate Jr. (Provo, UT: BYU Religious Studies Center, 1993), 213–25; see page 220 for the nine-out-of-ten statistic.

25. For further information about the use of the original manuscript as the printer's copy, see Royal Skousen, "Piecing Together the Original Manuscript," *BYU Today* (May 1992): 18–24; or Royal Skousen, "The Book of Mormon Critical Text Project," in *Joseph Smith: The Prophet, the Man*, 65–75.

26. To enhance readability, a few changes (mostly in punctuation and grammar) have been made in the quotations from the typographical facsimile that appears at the end of this article.

27. See *The Papers of Joseph Smith*, 1:241 and 300.

28. I wish to thank Jonathan Saltzman for help in determining these figures.

29. I wish to thank Jonathan Saltzman for identifying the type face for the 1830 edition. For further information about Scotch Roman, see W. Pincus Jaspert, W. Turner Berry, and A. F. Johnson, *The Encyclopaedia of Type Faces*, 4th ed. (Poole, Dorset, England: Blandford, 1970), 203.

30. For an early discussion of this problem, see Dean C. Jessee, "New Documents and Mormon Beginnings," *BYU Studies* 24/4 (1984): 397–428.

31. I wish to thank Louis E. Crandall of the Crandall Historical Printing Museum (Provo, UT) for his valuable assistance in identifying these aspects of the unbound sheets. For further information on printing in the 1800s and earlier, see Ronald B. McKerrow, *An Introduction to Bibliography for Literary Students* (1928; reprint, New Castle, DE: Oak Knoll, 1994), 22–23 (for registering), 19 and 45–46 (for the tympan), 66–70 (for half-sheet imposition), and 103 (for deckle edge).

32. I wish to thank Richard L. Anderson and Larry C. Porter for providing copies of Gilbert's 1892 statement. Scott Faulring provided access to some related documents; Matthew Empey, my research assistant, helped collect some of the information for this section. Don Enders also provided a helpful critique of this paper as well as some additional information.

Memorandum, made by John H. Gilbert Esq, Sept
8th. I892.

Pa;myra. N. Y.

-:-:-:-:-:-:-:-:-:-:-:-:-

I am a practical printer by trade. I have been a resident
of Palmyra, N. Y. since about the year I824, and during all that
time have done some type-setting each year. I was aged ninety
years on the I3thday of April, I892., and on that day I went to
the office of the Palmyra Courier and set a stick-ful of type.

My recollection of past events, and especially of the matters
connected with the printing of the " Mormon Bible," is very accurate and faithful, and I have made the following memorandum at
request, to accompany the photographs of " Mormon Hill, " which
have been made for the purpose of exhibits at the World's Fair in
I893.

-+++++++++++++++++++++++++++++++-

In the forepart of June, 1829. Mr E. B. Grandin, the printer
of the "Wayne Sentinel," came to me and said he wanted I should
assist him in estimating the cost of printing 5000 copies of a
book that Martin Harris wanted to get printed, which was called
the " Mormon Bible. " It was the second application of Harris to
Grandin to do the job.- Harris assuring Grandin that the book
would be printed in Rochester if he declined the job again.

Harris proposed to have Grandin do the job, if he would, as
it would be quite expensive to keep a man in Rochester during the
printing of the book, who would have to visit Palmyra two or three
times a week for Manuscript, &c. Mr Grandin consented to do the
job if his terms were accepted.

A few pages of the manuscript were submitted as a specimen

of the whole, and it was said there would be about 500 pages.

The size of the page was agreed upon, and an estimate of the number of ems in a page, which would be IOOO. and that a page of manuscript would make more than a page of printed matter, which proved to be correct.

The contract was to print, and bind with leather, 5000 copies for $3.OOO. Mr Grandin got a new font of Small Pica, on which the body of the work was printed.

When the printer was ready to commence work, Harris was noti-fied, and Hyrum Smith brought the first installment of manuscript, of 24 pages, closely written on common foolscap paper,;- he had it under his vest, and vest and coat closely buttoned over it. At night Smith came and got the manuscript, and with the same precau-tion carried it away. The next morning with the same watchfulness, he brought it again, and at night took it away. This was kept up for several days. The title page was first set up, and after proof was read and corrrected, several copies were printed for Harris and his friends. On the second day - Harris and Smith being in the office - I called their attention to a grammatical error, and asked whether I should correct it ? Harris consulted with Smith a short time, and turned to me and said; "The Old Testament is un-grammatical, set it as it is written."

After working a few days, I said to Smith on his handing me the manuscript in the morning; " Mr Smith, if you would leave this manuscript with me, I would take it home with me at night and read and punctuate it, and I could get along faster in the day time, for now I have frequently to stop and read half a page to find how to punctuate it." His reply was," We are commanded not to leave it. " A few mornings after this, when Smith handed me the manu-script, he said to me;-" If you will give your word that this manuscript shall be returned to us when you get through with it, I will leave it with you." I assured Smith that it should be returned all right when I got through with it. For two or three nights I took it home with me and read it, and punctuated it with a lead pencil. This will account for the punctuation marks in pencil, which is referred to in the Mormon Report, an extract from which will be found below.

Martin Harris, Hyrum Smith and Oliver Cowdery, were very frequent visitors to the office during the printing of the Mormon Bible. The manuscript was supposed to be in the handwriting of Cowdery. Every Chapter, if I remember correctly, was one solid paragraph, without a punctuation mark, from beginning to end.

Names of persons and places were generally capitalized, but sentences had no end. The character or short &, was used almost invariably where the word and, occurred, except at the end of a chapter. I punctuated it to make it read as I supposed the Author intended, and but very little punctuation was altered in proof-reading. The Bible was printed 16 pages at a time, so that one sheet of paper made two copies of 16 pages each, requiring 2500 sheets of paper for each form of 16 pages. There were 37 forms of 16 pages each,- 570 pages in all.

The work was commenced in August 1829. , and finished in March 1830,- seven months. Mr J. H. Bortles and myself done the press work until December taking nearly three days to each form.

In December Mr Grandin hired a journeyman xxxxxxxx pressman, Thomas McAuley, or " Whistling Tom," as he was called in the office, and he and Bortles did the balance of the press-work.The Bible was printed on a " Smith " Press, single pull, and old fashioned " Balls" or " Niggerheads " were used - composition rollers not having come into use in small printing offices.

The printing was done in the third story of the west end of

" Exchange Row," and the binding by Mr Howard, in the second story
the lower story being used as a book store, by Mr Grandin, and now
- 1892- by Mr M. Story as a dry-goods store.

Cowdery held and looked over the manuscript when most of the
proofs were read. Martin Harris once or twice, and Hyrum Smith
once, Grandin supposing these men could read their own writing as
well, if not better, than anyone else; and if there are any discrepancies between the Palmyra edition and the manuscript these m
men should be held responsible.

Joseph Smith Jr had nothing to do whatever with the printing
or furnishing copy for the printers, being but once in the office
during the printing of the Bible, and then not over I5, or 20 minutes.

Hyrum Smith was a common laborer, and worked for anyone as
he was called on.

Cowdery taught school winters- so it was said - but what he
done summers, I do not know.

Martin Harris was a farmer, owning a good farm, of about I50
acres, about a mile north of Palmyra Village, and had money at
interest. Martin,- as every body called him,- was considered by
his neighbors a very honest man; but on the subject of Marmonism,
he was said to be crazy. Martin was the main spoke in the wheel
of Mormonism in its start in Palmyra, and I may say, the only
spoke. In the fall of I827. he told us what wonderful discoveries Jo Smith had made, and of his finding plates in a hill in the
town of Manchester, (three miles south of Palmyra,)- also found
with the plates a large pair of " spectacles," by putting which
on his nose and looking at the plates, the spectacles turned the
hyroglyphics into good English. The question might be asked here
whether Jo or the spectacles was the translator?

Sometime in I828. Martin Harris, who had been furnished by someone with xxxxxx what he said was a fac-simile of the hyroglyph ics of one of the plates started for New York. On his was he stopped at Albany and called on Lt Gov Bradish,- with what success I do not know. He proceeded to New York, and called on Prof C. Anthon, made known his business and presented his hyroglyphics.

This is what the Professor said in regard to them;- I834-

" The paper in question was, in fact, a singular scroll.

It consisted of all kinds of singular characters, disposed in columns, and had evidently been prepared by some person who had before him at the time a book containing various alphabets; Greek and Hebrew letters, crosses and flourishes, Roman letters inverted or placed sidewise, arranged and placed in perpendicular columns, and the whole ended in a rude delineation of a circle, divided in- to various compartments, arched with various strange marks, and evidently copied after the Mexican Calendar, given by Humboldt, but copied in such a way as not to betray the source whence it was derived. I am thus particular as to the contents of the paper, in asmuch as I have frequently conversed with my friends on the sub- ject since the Mormon excitement began, and well remember that the paper contained anything else but " Egyptian Hyroglyphics."

Martin returned from his trip east satisfied that " Joseph" was a " little smarter than Prof Anthon."

Martin was something of a prophet:--He frequently said that that " Jackson would be the last president that we would have; and that all persons who did not embrace Mormonism in two years time would be stricken off the face of the earth." He said that Palmy- ra was to be the New Jerusalem, and that her streetswere to be paved with gold.

Martin was in the office when I finished setting up the testimony of the three witnesses,- (Harris- Cowdery and Whitmer-)

I said to him,- " Martin,did you see those plates with your naked

eyes ?" Martin looked down for an instant, raised his eyes up,

and said, " No, I saw them with a spirtual eye,"

Oliver Cowdery and the
Mythical "Manuscript Found"

Matthew Roper

Author's note: For most of the nineteenth and much of the twentieth century, those who rejected Joseph Smith's account of the
coming forth of the Book of Mormon argued that the Book of
Mormon narrative was based upon an unpublished romance written by a former minister named Solomon Spalding. Proponents of
this theory argued that by some means Sidney Rigdon obtained
a copy of this manuscript to which he added additional religious
material and then had Joseph Smith publish the manuscript as
the Book of Mormon. One of the many weaknesses of this theory
is that it inadequately explained how Rigdon, who was living in
western Ohio at the time the Book of Mormon was translated and
published, could have interacted with Joseph Smith who lived
hundreds of miles away in New York. Although the Spalding
theory has largely fallen out of favor, a few zealous critics have
recently tried to resurrect this explanation. These Spalding advocates argue that Oliver Cowdery could have provided a missing
link between Sidney Rigdon in Ohio and Joseph Smith in New
York. In order to bolster this conspiracy theory these critics have
tried to place Oliver Cowdery near Palmyra New York in the early
1820s, where he could conceivably have helped the Smith family
in such an endeavor. The following, which was initially published
as part of a longer overview of the Spalding theory addresses the
evidence for these recent claims.

*I*n order to link Sidney Rigdon and Joseph Smith, Wayne L.
Cowdrey, Howard A. Davis, and Arthur Vanick claim that Oliver

Cowdery was responsible for bringing Rigdon and Joseph Smith together. They make their argument for this claim in chapters 8, 9, and 10 of their book, *Who Really Wrote the Book of Mormon?* Noting significant gaps of information or limited sources on portions of Oliver Cowdery's life, they suggest that Cowdery may have been ashamed of his past and therefore deliberately concealed much of this information (210). Those who work with historical sources, however—in family history, for example—realize that this is a common problem in tracing the history of individuals that is far from unique to Oliver Cowdery. Nonetheless, these three authors prefer to see conspiracies everywhere. For example, "One must also question why pro-Mormon historians do not seem to have been particularly concerned with uncovering who this man was," they complain. They also fault Latter-day Saint scholars for making "so slight an effort to fill the void" (210). But their complaints are misconceived. There is a substantial literature on Oliver Cowdery of which the authors show little or no awareness and with which they make little attempt to engage.[1]

The trio of Cowdrey, Davis, and Vanick paint Oliver Cowdery as a none too smart dupe of Sidney Rigdon who "was simply too credulous for his own good" and "too weak to resist the sly manipulations of Joseph Smith's overpowering personality. In short, Oliver was a convenient stooge to machinations that were, at first, largely over his head—things that, when he finally began to perceive what was really happening, he was powerless to stop or withdraw from without considerable risk" (211). While this is the proposed view, it is dramatically inconsistent with the actual Oliver, who appears to have been a man of exceptional intelligence and ability both as an elder of the church and as a non-Mormon lawyer.[2]

Mistaken Identities

In November 1830, Oliver Cowdery, Parley P. Pratt, Peter Whitmer Jr., and Ziba Peterson visited western Ohio on their way to Missouri to fulfill a mission to the Lamanites.[3] Local Ohio newspapers took note of the missionary visit and some of their activities. On 30 November 1830, the *Cleveland Herald* printed an article on Mormonism; the writer—probably the editor, John St. John—had noticed the name of Oliver Cowdery in some of the newspaper descriptions of the missionaries' activities.

> On reading the name of Oliver Cowdry, in support of the divine authenticity of the work, whatever faith we might have been inspired with on reading the certificate, was banished, for we had known Cowdry some seven or eight years ago, when he was a dabbler in the art of Printing, and principally occupied in writing and printing pamphlets, with which, as a pedestrian Pedlar he visited the towns and villages of western New-York and Canada.[4]

In what may be an echo of this earlier article, the *Lockport Balance* in New York printed another piece in 1832 on Mormonism. The author, probably the editor Orsamus Turner, portrayed the Book of Mormon witness, without further explanation, as "an itinerant pamphlet pedlar, and occasionally, a journeyman printer, named *Oliver Cowdry*."[5] In 1849, Turner published a local history of western New York in which he described early settlers and pioneers of the region. In a short sketch for the town of Albion, New York, near Lockport, he recalled, "In 1823 it ["the fine lands in the immediate neighborhood of Albion"] had sufficiently advanced to indicate the necessity of a press and newspaper, and Oliver Cowdery, (who has been the pioneer printer in at least a half dozen localities,) took a part of the old battered 'small pica' that had been used in printing the Lockport Observatory, and adding to it indifferent materials from other sources, commenced the publication of the 'Newport Patriot.'"[6]

If correct, these two newspaper articles and Turner's 1849 recollection would place Oliver in New York around 1822 or 1823, working there as a "pioneer printer" and "journeyman printer," a veteran of various publishing ventures that included commencing a paper in Albion in 1823 and writing and publishing pamphlets in western New York and Canada, which he peddled and sold in New York and Canada. The authors favor these sources because they would, if accepted, place Oliver in New York—where they could more easily connect him with their hypothetical Gold Bible conspiracy.[7]

Unfortunately for this prospect, though, there is no supporting evidence for the claim that Oliver was involved in printing before December 1829, when he provided some assistance in the preparation of the Book of Mormon for publication. In a letter to Joseph Smith in December 1829, Oliver wrote: "It may look rather strange to you to find that I have so soon become a printer."[8] The clear implication in this private letter to Joseph Smith is that printing was a new experience for him. Moreover, it can be clearly shown that it was *Franklin* Cowdery, Oliver's uncle, and not Oliver Cowdery, who began publication of the *Newport Patriot* in 1822.[9]

It is true that, during the Kirtland period and after his excommunication in 1838, Oliver engaged in a few printing ventures, but there is no support for this kind of activity before 1829. Second, a family source, Oliver's half-sister Lucy Cowdery Young, said that when Oliver, who had previously lived in Vermont, "arrived at the age of twenty he went to the State of New York where his older brothers were married and settled." This would be around 1826. During that time, she said, he clerked in a store and after two years went to Manchester, where he taught school.[10] While Cowdrey, Davis, and Vanick assert that Lucy was mistaken about this, no evidence refutes her recollection. The authors also undercut their own theory in their characterization of Oliver's health, describing him as weak, not very intelligent, and a "poor, consumptive, wheezing 'little man'" (211) with an often fragile constitution. Yet it is this same individual who is supposed to have traveled on foot across the length and breadth of western New York and Canada, writing, printing, and peddling pamphlets, all at the tender age of 16! This seems unlikely.

A better explanation is that the sources mentioned above represent a case of mistaken identity in which the two editors associated Oliver with Franklin Cowdery. Franklin *was* a pioneer printer who engaged in numerous publishing ventures in New York from 1817–48, which included the *Moscow Advertiser and Livingston Farmer* (1817), the Olean *Hamilton Recorder* (1819–20), the Angelica

Allegany Republican (1820–22), the Angelica *News Record and Allegany Patron of Industry* (1822), the *Newport Patriot* (1824–1825), the Geneva *Ontario Chronicle* (1828–29), the *Geneva Chronicle* (1829), the Albion *Orleans Mercury* (1832), the *Cuylerville Telegraph* (1847–48), the Rochester *Genesee Olio* (1847), and, in Ohio, the *Oberlin Evangelist* (1847). In 1852, Turner quoted an old resident of Allegany who remembered that, in 1820, "the *pioneer printer* in so many different localities—Franklin Cowdery—had moved a rude press, and a few fonts of battered type, from Olean, where he had published the Hamilton Recorder, and had started the first paper in Allegany county, the Angelica Republican."[11] "It was a pretty hard place for newspaper publishing," Franklin recalled,

> I had to take my pay in all manner of traps—just what I could get. I feasted upon fat venison; it hung around my domicil in the shape of saddles, quarters, and hams; and I had maple sugar in profusion; the great trouble was to get something the paper and ink maker would take in payment ... To print for a livelihood there, was up-hill work—rather less lucrative than hunting and trapping. And so little intercourse was there with the business world, that the highways were often so bad getting over, that paper had to be carried on horseback; and ink manufactories so distant, that typo made his own printing ink, composed mostly of linseed oil, lamp black, and rosin; during the three years he *luminated* the woods of Cattaraugus and Allegany.[12]

One historian of New York printers noted that there was a "general opinion" that "Franklin Cowdery, was poorly qualified to speak for the printers. ... He had complained constantly about the public patronage and his own meager support."[13] With Oliver's notoriety as one of the three witnesses of the Book of Mormon and as one of the early missionaries to Ohio, it would have been easy to mistake one Cowdery for the other. The authors speculate that on occasion from 1822 to 1827 Oliver may have *worked for* Franklin in several of these printing ventures, but there is no evidence for this.

It is not enough, though, to get Oliver Cowdery to New York in 1822. The authors also want to place him in or near Palmyra where he can conspire with the Smith family in the early 1820s. In order to bolster this claim, they cite an 1869 history of Vermont by Robert Parks and an 1849 history of New York by Orsamus Turner. In 1869, Parks recalled, "'We well remember this same Oliver Cowdery when in our boyhood. . . . He attended school in the District where we reside[d] in 1821 and 1822. He then went to Palmyra, N.Y.'" (237). Cowdrey, Davis, and Vanick take this rather dogmatically to mean that Oliver left Wells, Vermont, and arrived in Palmyra in late 1822 or 1823, but there is no reason to interpret Parks's statement so narrowly. Oliver *did* go to Palmyra *after* he left Vermont. Writing almost fifty years after the event, Parks could easily mean by "then" any time from 1823 to 1829.

In another mid-nineteenth-century history of New York, Orsamus Turner wrote a brief sketch of early Mormonism. As a young man, Turner began his apprenticeship in late 1818 with Timothy Strong at the *Palmyra Register*. He appears to have spent 1821 and 1822 in Canandaigua, where he finished his apprenticeship working for James Beamis. After this, during a brief return to Palmyra, Turner heard of a printer position in Lockport about one hundred miles away. He then moved there and purchased the *Lockport Observatory* in August 1822. Turner's brief discussion of early Mormonism is a mixture of hearsay and personal recollection and is filled with sarcasm and permeated with a tone of ridicule. Turner admitted that he did not take Mormonism seriously, treating it "lightly—with a seeming levity."[14] Still, his own personal recollections, where they can be shown to be such, are valuable in that they tend to confirm and flesh out details about the Smith family residence in Palmyra. As Richard L. Anderson explains, however, "Turner's personal recollections of Joseph Smith of necessity refer to the period *prior to* the late summer of 1822 and are probably no later than 1820, the latest date of Palmyra memoirs in his writings."[15] Dan Vogel, while admitting that it was possible for Turner to have occasionally visited Palmyra after that time, claims that "much of what Turner writes, particularly about events subsequent to his departure from the area, is from the standpoint of a distant observer."[16]

Eager to put Cowdery in Palmyra by 1822, Cowdrey, Davis, and Vanick uncritically accept all of Turner's statements, including passing remarks about Cowdery, as events observed. But this is obviously problematic. For example, Turner said that after the death of Alvin Smith, "the mantle of the Prophet which Mrs. and Mr. Joseph Smith and one Oliver Cowdery, had wove of themselves—every thread of it—fell upon their next eldest son, Joseph Smith, Jr."[17] *The Spalding Enigma* transfigures this comment, along with Turner's 1832 *Lockport Balance* article, into firsthand testimony for Oliver being in Palmyra in 1823 (243). But Turner was living in Lockport in 1823 when Alvin died—approximately a hundred miles away—and there is simply no evidence that he was present in Palmyra, even less that he was lurking at Alvin's deathbed when Alvin passed away. There is no basis upon which to assert that Turner's comments on Alvin's death were based upon anything more than distant hearsay. The same can be said of his comments about Oliver. In fact, while Turner describes firsthand experiences with Joseph Smith, he never gives any indication that he had so much as met the Book of Mormon scribe.

Based upon this dubious foundation, Cowdrey, Davis, and Vanick then embark on a series of bewildering speculations and irrelevancies as they opine where Oliver *may* have been and what he *might* have been doing. *Maybe* he was dousing with Walters the magician over in Sodus or Palmyra or wherever. *Maybe* he was scribing for William Morgan on his exposé of Freemasonry. This kind of thing can be fun, of course. Stacking each unproven assumption upon the previous unproven assumption, the authors construct an ugly theoretical caricature of Cowdery, a veritable castle in the clouds, but it has no foundation and the picture is a mirage. It is their wish list, not history. Those seeking to know the historical Oliver Cowdery will have to look elsewhere.

Notes

Editors' note: This article is an excerpt of a review of *Who Really Wrote the Book of Mormon? The Spalding Enigma*, by Wayne L. Cowdrey, Howard A. Davis, and Arthur Vanick, *FARMS Review* 17/2 (2005): 7–140.

1.   See "Further Reading" at the end of this book for additional bibliographic sources on Oliver Cowdery.

2.   See, for example, Richard Lloyd Anderson, *Investigating the Book of Mormon Witnesses* (Salt Lake City: Deseret Book, 1981), 37–65, 170–75, 178–79; Scott H. Faulring, "The Return of Oliver Cowdery," in *The Disciple as Witness: Essays on Latter-day Saint History and Doctrine in Honor of Richard Lloyd Anderson,* ed. Stephen D. Ricks, Donald W. Parry, and Andrew H. Hedges (Provo, UT: FARMS, 2000), 117–73. W. Lang—a lawyer who read and studied law with Oliver Cowdery in Tiffin, Ohio, before passing the bar and who had a distinguished career as an attorney, mayor, and state senator—said,

> Mr Cowdery was an able lawyer and a great advocate. His manners were easy and gentlemanly; he was polite, dignified, yet courteous. He had an open countenance, high forehead, dark brown eyes, Roman nose, clenched lips and prominent lower jaw. He shaved smooth and was neat and cleanly in his person. He was of light stature, about five feet, five inches high, and had a loose, easy walk. With all his kind and friendly disposition, there was a certain degree of sadness that seemed to pervade his whole being. His association with others was marked by the great amount of information his conversation conveyed and the beauty of his musical voice. His addresses to the court and jury were characterized by a high order of oratory, with brilliant and forensic force. He was modest and reserved, never spoke ill of any one, never complained. He left Tiffin with his family for Elkhorn, in Wisconsin, in 1847, where he remained but a short time, and then moved to Missouri, where he died in 1848 [1850]. The writer read law with Mr. Cowdery in Tiffin, and was intimately acquainted with him from the time he came here until he left, which afforded me every opportunity to study and love his noble and true manhood. (W. Lang, *History of Seneca County* [Springfield, OH: Transcript, 1880], 365)

3.   For an overview, see Richard Lloyd Anderson, "The Impact of the First Preaching in Ohio," *BYU Studies* 11 (summer 1971): 474–96, and reprinted in this volume.

4.   "The Golden Bible," *Cleveland Herald,* 25 November 1830.

5.   "Mormonism," *Lockport Balance,* ca. September 1832; reprinted in the *Boston Recorder,* 10 October 1832.

6.   Orsamus Turner, *Pioneer History of the Holland Purchase of Western New York . . .* (Buffalo: Jewett, Thomas, 1849), 658.

7.   Cowdery, who was born in October 1806, could scarcely have been a veteran of anything in 1822–23.

8.   Oliver Cowdery to Joseph Smith, 28 December 1829, in Richard L. Anderson and Scott H. Faulring, eds., *Witness of the Second Elder: The Documentary History of Oliver Cowdery* (Provo, UT: FARMS, 1999), 1:80.

9.   Milton W. Hamilton, *The Country Printer: New York State, 1785–1830* (Port Washington, NY: Friedman, 1936), 266. Turner's 1849 recollection seems to have been off by a year.

10.   Lucy Cowdery Young to Brigham H. Young, 7 March 1887, Milo, Ms 842, Family and Church History Department Archives, The Church of Jesus Christ of Latter-day Saints, Salt Lake City; see Anderson and Faulring, *Witness of the Second Elder,* 4.

11.   Orsamus Turner, *History of the Pioneer Settlement of Phelps & Gorham's Purchase, and Morris' Reserve* (Rochester, NY: Alling, 1852), 554.

12. Turner, *History of the Pioneer Settlement,* 554, emphasis in original.

13. Hamilton, *Country Printer,* 92. On Franklin's publishing ventures, see 265–66.

14. In Turner's opinion, Mormonism was a "bald, clumsy cheat" that only "an enthusiast, a monomaniac or a knave" could believe in. It could only be treated with ridicule

> because it will admit of no other treatment. There is no dignity about the whole thing; nothing to entitle it to mild treatment. It deserves none of the charity extended to ordinary religious fanaticism, for knavery and fraud has been with it incipiently and progressively. It has not even the poor merit of ingenuity. Its success is a slur upon the age. Fanaticism promoted it at first; then ill advised persecution; then the designs of demagogues who wished to command the suffrages of its followers; until finally an American Congress has abetted the fraud and imposition by its acts, and we are to have a state of our proud Union—in this boasted era of light and knowledge—the very name of which will sanction and dignify the fraud and falsehood of Mormon Hill, the gold plates, and the spurious revelation. (Turner, *History of the Pioneer Settlement,* 217)

According to Cowdrey, Davis, and Vanick, though, Turner "had no particular religious axe to grind" (242).

15. Richard Lloyd Anderson, "Circumstantial Confirmation of the First Vision through Reminiscences," *BYU Studies* 9, no. 3 (1969): 378, emphasis added.

16. Vogel, *Early Mormon Documents,* 3:47.

17. Turner, *History of the Pioneer Settlement,* 213.

Oliver Cowdery and the
Restoration of the Priesthood

Brian Q. Cannon and the BYU Studies Staff

*F*ew events in the history of the restoration of the gospel are as consequential as the bestowal of the priesthood upon Joseph Smith and Oliver Cowdery.

Long before he received the priesthood, Joseph Smith learned of it from Moroni. According to an Oliver Cowdery account published in 1835, Moroni appeared to Joseph in September 1823 and informed him, "When they [the golden plates] are interpreted the Lord will give the holy priesthood to some, and they shall begin to proclaim this gospel and baptize by water, and after that they shall have power to give the Holy Ghost by the laying on of their hands."[1] While it is unclear to what extent this retrospective account may contain details that were actually learned after 1823, Joseph definitely learned more about the priesthood as he translated the Book of Mormon in 1829. From the golden plates, Joseph learned that power was necessary to perform ordinances including baptism (3 Ne. 11:22), the sacrament (3 Ne. 18:5), and conferring the Holy Ghost (3 Ne. 18:37; Moro. 2:1–3); that this power was conferred by the laying on of hands (3 Ne. 18:38; Moro. 2:1; 3:2); that one could be ordained to the calling of disciple or elder, who in turn could ordain priests and teachers (Moro. 3:1); and that elders or disciples, unlike priests and teachers, could confer the gift of the Holy Ghost by the laying on of hands (Moro. 2:1–2). Additionally, a passage in Alma 13 discussed the calling and ordination of high priests including Melchizedek to the "high priest-hood of the holy order of God" (Alma 13:6, 14, 18).

Having learned through the writings of ancient prophets that baptism by proper authority was necessary, Joseph Smith and Oliver Cowdery sought that ordinance. In response to their supplication, John the Baptist appeared and conferred the priesthood of Aaron upon them. At a later date, Peter, James, and John appeared and bestowed what is known today as the Melchizedek Priesthood.[2]

The Restoration of the Aaronic Priesthood

The historical record clearly identifies the circumstances sur-rounding the restoration of the Aaronic Priesthood, including the date that it occurred, and unambiguous evidence links Joseph and Oliver's quest for that priesthood to knowledge they gained while translating the Book of Mormon. An 1829 document in Oliver Cowdery's handwriting entitled "Articles of the Church of Christ" testified that Cowdery had been given power to baptize "of Jesus Christ," and Cowdery made similar statements in 1830.

Details regarding the restoration of the Aaronic Priesthood, including John the Baptist's role in that event, however, were sel-dom if ever shared prior to 1832 "owing to a spirit of persecution," as Joseph Smith indicated in 1838.[3] Two of Joseph and Oliver's close associates, David Whitmer and William McLellin, recalled in 1885 and 1878, respectively, that they first learned of John the Baptist's 1829 appearance two to four years after the Church's organiza-tion.[4] In writing, Joseph Smith first referred to this event in 1832, describing "the reception of the holy Priesthood by the ministring of Aangels to adminster the letter of the Gospel." Oliver Cowdery offered the first detailed, recorded account of the restoration of the priesthood in 1834. The following year, Cowdery specified the date and location of the restoration of the Aaronic Priesthood. Joseph Smith's fullest account of the event corroborated Oliver's record and added new details: for instance, Joseph recorded words used by John regarding the nature of the keys that he bestowed; explained that John had acted under the direction of Peter, James, and John;

and indicated that John promised them that later they would receive power to bestow the gift of the Holy Ghost. In 1844, Joseph Smith referred to the preparatory priesthood as "the power of Elias" and indicated that John the Baptist, the forerunner of the Savior, was "the Spirit of Elias."[5]

Early members read Joseph's and Oliver's testimonies regarding the restoration of the Aaronic Priesthood and used the information in their missionary work. For instance, Orson Hyde quoted directly from Oliver Cowdery's 1834 account, while Reuben Miller in an 1847 publication relied on Joseph Smith's accounts of John's visitation. Many accounts mention John the Baptist by name; others call him "the angel John," "the angel of the Lord," simply "the angel," or some other similar appellation.

Despite detailed accounts by Joseph and Oliver, some errors crept into the record: William Appleby, for instance, erroneously indicated in a tract published in 1844 that the power to baptize had been restored in 1830. Additionally, ambiguity and imprecision arose through leaders' and members' frequent use of the phrase "the holy priesthood" to refer to the Aaronic Priesthood on some occasions, to the Melchizedek Priesthood on others, and to the priesthood in general on yet other occasions. Still, the documentary record demonstrates that detailed accounts of the restoration of the Aaronic Priesthood were available to members of the Church as early as 1834 and that early members used those accounts in teaching others about the Aaronic Priesthood's restoration.

The Events of the Restoration of the Melchizedek Priesthood

The written record regarding the restoration of the Melchizedek Priesthood is less complete. Although repeatedly testifying that Peter, James, and John had appeared to them and restored this high priesthood authority, or referring alternatively to "apostles," "Peter," "angels," or "those who had been held in reserve," neither Joseph Smith nor Oliver Cowdery specified the date of that restoration or reported the words used by Peter in ordaining them to this priesthood beyond "declaring themselves as possessing the keys," Oliver

Cowdery's accounts concerning the restoration of the Melchizedek Priesthood corroborate the accounts of Joseph; whereas Oliver Cowdery provided the earliest detailed report of the visit of John the Baptist, his accounts of the visit of Peter, James, and John seldom add new information.

Significant evidence suggests that the Melchizedek Priesthood may have been restored in connection with the translation of the Book of Mormon. A revelation dated June 1829 referred to the apostolic calling of David Whitmer and Oliver Cowdery, likening their calling to the apostle Paul's, although the revelation did not detail the restoration of priesthood authority or any ordination in connection with that calling. Additionally, David Whitmer recalled in 1887 that he was "baptized, confirmed, and ordained an Elder" in June 1829 and that "previous to this, Joseph Smith and Oliver Cowdery had baptized, confirmed and ordained each other to the office of an Elder."[6] The Book of Mormon, which was being translated at that time, described the ancient ordination of disciples, known as elders, who had power to confer the gift of the Holy Ghost (3 Ne. 18; Moro. 2–3). Inasmuch as the translation of 3 Nephi 11 had made Joseph and Oliver sensitive to their lack of power to baptize and impelled them to seek that power, it is possible that the translation of 3 Nephi 18 and Moroni 2–3 had a similar effect upon them, motivating them to pray to receive by the laying on of hands the additional power to bestow the gift of the Holy Ghost.

The first printed reference to Joseph's and Oliver's ordination as apostles appeared in 1831. It indicated that Joseph and Oliver were each "called of God and ordained an apostle of Jesus Christ." In 1833, Joseph Smith discussed the restoration of apostolic authority in greater detail. Thereafter, most of his and Oliver's written accounts expressly mentioned that angels played a role in the restoration of apostolic authority and of the power to bestow the gift of the Holy Ghost. In 1833, Joseph Smith testified that he had seen "the Apostles" and could perform miracles. The following year, Joseph met with the Kirtland Stake High Council. On February 12, 1834, he discussed "the dignity of the office which has been conferred

The Restoration of the Priesthood, by Minerva Teichert, oil on canvas, 1934. Courtesy Museum of Church History and Art.

upon me by the ministring of the Angel of God." While this might have been a reference to John the Baptist, it is also possible that Joseph was referring to Peter's role in conferring the Melchizedek Priesthood upon him. Five days later he instructed the same group that anciently "the apostle Peter was the president of the Council and held the keys of the Kingdom of God."[7] In a blessing which Oliver Cowdery dated 1833 and copied in 1835, Joseph Smith referred to the reception of "the holy priesthood under the hands of those who ... received it under the hand of the Messiah."

In 1835 the original edition of the Doctrine and Covenants gave the first precise published account of the appearance of Peter, James, and John to Joseph and Oliver.[8] This edition indicated that the three ancient apostles had "ordained" and "confirmed" Joseph and Oliver as "apostles" and granted them "the keys of your ministry." In subsequent statements, Joseph reiterated the role of Peter, James, and John in the restoration of the "priesthood" and "the keys" of the kingdom and indicated that the angelic ministrants' voices had come to them "in the wilderness" between Harmony, Pennsylvania, and Colesville, New York.[9] Following the Prophet's death, Oliver Cowdery testified repeatedly and fervently that he had received the higher priesthood under the hands of angelic ministrants.[10] In 1846 he mentioned only Peter's role in the restoration of the Melchizedek Priesthood, but in 1849 he confirmed that James and John had also been present.

Supplementing Joseph's and Oliver's own accounts in several respects are Addison Everett's recollections, written in 1881, 1882, and 1883, of statements he had heard Joseph Smith make in a conversation in 1844. According to Everett's longest account, Joseph Smith indicated that while translating the Book of Mormon in Harmony, Pennsylvania, he and Oliver had been arrested; after escaping from a courtroom, they spent the night in the woods eluding their enemies. At daybreak, Peter, James, and John appeared to them and "ordained us to the Holy Apostleship and gave unto us the Keys of the Dispensation of the fullness of times."[11]

The foregoing accounts all seem to describe a single event: a restoration between Harmony and Colesville of (what came to be known as) the Melchizedek Priesthood under the Savior's direction by Peter with the assistance of James and John. However, the draft and final version of an 1839 account by Joseph Smith may describe a separate set of events connected with the restoration of "the Melchesidec Priesthood, which holds the authority of the laying on of hands for the gift of the Holy Ghost." Those documents indicate that after Joseph and Oliver had prayed for this authority, "the word of the Lord" came to them in a second location, the Whitmer home in Fayette, commanding them to ordain one another to the office of elder once they had "called together our brethren and had their sanction" and then to "attend to the laying on of hands for the Gift of the Holy Ghost."[12]

No single document written by the principals discusses both the appearance of Peter, James, and John and the revelation received in the Whitmer home, specifying the chronological order of these revelations, but the revelation received in the Whitmer home was definitely received prior to the organization of the Church, since Joseph Smith carried out its instructions on April 6, 1830. Joseph Smith's history indicates that he and Oliver ordained each other on April 6 "according to previous commandment."[13]

In their written accounts, most of which were produced for didactic purposes, many early members compressed all the events of priesthood restoration into a general reference to a visitation by a holy messenger or angel. Although a published revelation referring to separate ministrations by John the Baptist and by Peter, James, and John was widely disseminated and readily available beginning in 1835, more details were circulated about the restoration of the Aaronic Priesthood, probably because that authority was more immediately relevant to the issue of conversion and baptism. Under these circumstances, it is possible that some members regarded the restoration of the authority to baptize as the primary facet of priesthood restoration and therefore focused on that restoration in their teachings.

It is also likely that some writers focused on a single messenger's role in the restoration of the priesthood in order to simplify the restoration of the gospel for hymns or missionary work, particularly when they desired to draw a parallel between the other angel mentioned in Revelation 14:6 and the restoration of the gospel. Charles Thompson, for instance, borrowed heavily from John's prophecy in Revelation when he wrote, "God sent an holy angel from the midst of heaven, with the Priesthood and authority of Jesus Christ, to preach the everlasting Gospel unto them who dwell on the earth, and to every nation, kindred, tongue and people."

Statements by William McLellin and David Patten demonstrate that some members who had studied Doctrine and Covenants 27 understood clearly that the Aaronic and Melchizedek Priesthoods were restored on separate occasions. Similarly, other leaders and missionaries, including Brigham Young and Reuben Miller, referred to two separate appearances in their sermons and writings.

The accounts by Joseph's and Oliver's contemporaries show that early members arrived at different conclusions regarding the timing of the restoration of the Melchizedek Priesthood. In the 1880s, Everett calculated that it probably occurred in August 1829. Although William McLellin recognized the importance of Peter, James, and John's visitation, he seems to trace the reception of the Melchizedek Priesthood to the ordination of Joseph and Oliver as elders on April 6. Hiram Page, one of the Eight Witnesses to the Book of Mormon, was convinced that Joseph and Oliver received the Melchizedek Priesthood from Peter, James, and John "before the 6th of april 1830." Agreeing with Hiram Page, in 1853 and again in 1874, Brigham Young emphasized that Joseph Smith received apostolic power from Peter, James, and John prior to the organization of the Church. Independent historian D. Michael Quinn's reading of Brigham Young's comment that "Peter, James, and John came to him [Joseph Smith] in Kirtland" led Quinn to conclude that key words and contextual information found in that discussion by President Young concerning several revelations regarding the priesthood were omitted.[14]

Modern readers have also arrived at divergent conclusions regarding the timing of the Melchizedek Priesthood restoration and Joseph Smith's early understanding of the distinction between the Aaronic and Melchizedek Priesthoods. Two recent interpretations are illustrative. Larry C. Porter, Professor Emeritus of Church History at Brigham Young University, maintains that "the evidence suggests a date near the end of May 1829" and "certainly before the organization of the Church on 6 April 1830."[15] In support of this conclusion, Porter highlights the revelation received prior to June 14, 1829, and first printed in the "Articles of the Church of Christ" that identifies Oliver Cowdery and David Whitmer as apostles who are "called even with that same calling" as "Paul mine apostle." As evidence that this call to the apostleship included priesthood authority, Porter highlights the Prophet's preface to a later publication of this revelation: "The following commandment will further illustrate the nature of our calling to this Priesthood as well as that of others who were yet to be sought after." Porter also notes that Joseph and Oliver conferred the gift of the Holy Ghost upon members of the Church on April 6, 1830, and assumes that they used the priesthood that they had received from Peter, James, and John to do so. Based on Joseph Smith's later recollections of instructions he had received in 1829 from John the Baptist, Porter infers that by April 1830 "Joseph Smith recognized the limitations of John's power"[16] and thus would not have conferred the Holy Ghost on members unless he had already received the power to do so from Peter, James, and John. To support this view, Porter cites Joseph Smith's 1844 statement:

> John's mission was limited to preaching and baptizing; but what he did was legal; and when Jesus Christ came to any of John's disciples, He baptized them with fire and the Holy Ghost.
>
> We find the Apostles endowed with greater power than John. . . . John did not transcend his bounds, but faithfully performed that part belonging to his office.[17]

Whereas Porter identifies spring 1829 as the time for the restoration of the Melchizedek Priesthood, D. Michael Quinn concludes that Joseph Smith did not receive the higher priesthood from Peter, James, and John until July 1830.[18] He acknowledges the 1829 reference to the calling of apostles, but he argues that the revelation merely likens Oliver Cowdery and David Whitmer to Paul. Then, overlooking Paul's assertion in 1 Timothy 2:7, "I am ordained a preacher, and an apostle, (I speak the truth in Christ, and lie not)," Quinn follows Dan Vogel's interpretation and suggests that Paul may have been an unordained "charismatic apostle and special witness"[19] rather than an ordained apostle, citing the LDS Bible Dictionary for general support. Quinn argues that Cowdery and Whitmer as witnesses of the Book of Mormon were called apostles in that sense prior to 1830.[20] Quinn admits that elders were ordained as early as mid-1829, but he suggests that those ordinations and all confirmations prior to that time might have been performed solely on the basis of the revelation received in June 1829 instructing Joseph and Oliver to ordain each other. He suggests further that the ordinations carried out on April 6, 1830, were reordinations.[21]

Quinn looks mainly to documents from Joseph Smith[22] and to the 1881 and1882 Addison Everett accounts to support his conclusion that the Melchizedek Priesthood was formally restored by Peter, James, and John in July 1830. Joseph Smith mentions the restoration of the Melchizedek Priesthood and the pouring out of "the gift of the Holy Spirit" upon the Church after referring to the Church's organization.[23] Quinn infers that this document and another document[24] (also found in D&C 128:20) are a chronological listing of events. But the second document helps Quinn's case only if one assumes that one can date to June 1830 the event referred to as "the voice of Michael on the banks of the Susquehanna, detecting the devil when he appeared as an angel of light."[25] While he acknowledges that the date specified by Everett for the restoration of the higher priesthood is 1829, Quinn notes that this date does not match the events that occurred in June and July 1830. Thus, for Quinn, Everett's account "seems to confirm the July 1830 date."[26]

While Porter acknowledges the statements by Everett and believes that "Addison Everett was a man of veracity," he is more skeptical of Everett's statements because thirty-seven years had passed between the time that Everett heard the Prophet's statements and the time that he recorded them, and because Everett admitted his limitations and "lack of technical skills" as a historian. Porter concludes that "portions of his [Everett's] remembrance are inconsistent enough to warrant some obvious cautions when attempting to reconstruct the sequence of events surrounding the restoration process from his citations."[27]

Conclusion

The fact that the historical record can be used to support different interpretations demonstrates how puzzling any fragmentary record of the past can be. Because Joseph and Oliver never identified a date for the restoration of the Melchizedek Priesthood, they left room for speculation about the date of that priesthood's restoration. Further complicating the task is our inability using extant documents to determine with certainty Joseph Smith's full understanding of the nature of the priesthood at the time of the Church's organization.

While the documentary record is fragmentary regarding the date for the restoration of the Melchizedek Priesthood, and further work remains to be done in analyzing and interpreting these documents, the record is extensive and rich in many respects. It strongly shows that Joseph Smith and Oliver Cowdery repeatedly testified that they received power from on high to perform ordinances, first from John the Baptist and then from Peter, James, and John. Their testimonies began early in Church documents and intensified as these first and second elders drew closer to their own impending deaths. The powerful thrust of these accounts, corroborated by numerous statements from other early members of the Church, is intellectually challenging and spiritually invigorating.

Oliver Cowdery's Accounts of the Restoration of the Priesthood

Oliver Cowdery (November 16, 1830)

> About two weeks since some persons came along here with the book, one of whom pretends to have seen Angels, and assisted in translating the plates. He proclaims destruction upon the world within a few years,—holds forth that the ordinances of the gospel, have not been regularly administered since the days of the Apostles, till the said Smith and himself commenced the work. . . . The name of the person here, who pretends to have a

divine mission, and to have seen and conversed with Angels, is *Cowdray*.[28]

Oliver Cowdery (December 7, 1830)

Those who are the friends and advocates of this wonderful book [Book of Mormon], state that Mr. Oliver Cowdry has his commission directly from the God of Heaven, and that he has credentials, written and signed by the hand of Jesus Christ, with whom he has personally conversed, and as such, said Cowdry claims that he and his associates are the only persons on earth who are qualified to administer in his name. By this authority, they proclaim to the world, that all who do not believe *their* testimony, and be baptised by them for the remission of sins, and come under the imposition of *their* hands for the gift of the Holy Ghost . . . must be forever miserable.[29]

Oliver Cowdery (December 5, 1834)

The reader may further understand, that the reason why High Counsellor Cowdery was not previously ordained to the Presidency, was, in consequence of his necessary attendance in Zion, to assist Wm. W. Phelps in conducting the printing business; but that this promise was made by the angel while in company with President Smith, at the time they received the office of the lesser priesthood.[30]

Oliver Cowdery (1834)

From *his* [Joseph Smith's] hand I received baptism, by the direction of the angel of God—the first received into this church, in this day. . . . On a sudden, as from the midst of eternity, the voice of the Redeemer spake peace to us, while the vail was parted and the angel of God came down clothed with glory, and delivered the anxiously looked for message, and the keys of the gospel of repentance! . . . [O]ur eyes beheld—our ears heard. . . . We listened—we gazed—we admired! 'Twas the voice of the angel from glory. . . . [W]e were rapt in the vision of the Almighty! . . . [W]e received under [the angel's] hand the holy priesthood, as he said, "upon you my fellow servants, in the name of Messiah I confer this priesthood and this authority, which shall remain

upon earth, that the sons of Levi may yet offer an offering unto
the Lord in righteousness!" . . . The assurance that we were in
the presence of an angel; the certainty that we heard the voice of
Jesus, and the truth unsullied as it flowed from a pure personage,
dictated by the will of God, is to me, past description.[31]

Oliver Cowdery (February 1835)

Brethren, you have your duty presented in this revelation.
You have been ordained to the Holy Priesthood. You have received it from those who had their power and authority from an
angel. You are to preach the gospel to every nation.[32]

Oliver Cowdery (October 2, 1835)

The following blessings by the spirit of prophecy, were pronounced by Joseph Smith, jr. the first elder, and first patriarch of
the church: for although his father laid hands upon, and blessed
the fatherless, thereby securing the blessings of the Lord unto
them and their posterity, he was not the first elder, because God
called upon his son Joseph and ordained him to this power and
delivered to him the keys of the kingdom, that is, of authority and
spiritual blessings upon the Church, and through him the Lord
revealed his will to the Church: he [Joseph Smith] was ministered
unto by the angel, and by his direction he obtained the Records
of the Nephites, and translated by the gift and power of God:
he was ordained by the angel John, unto the lesser or Aaronic
priesthood, in company with myself, in the town of Harmony,
Susquehannah County, Pennsylvania, on Fryday, the 15th day
of May, 1829, after which we repaired to the water, even to the
Susquehannah River, and were baptized, he first ministering unto
me and after I to him. But before baptism, our souls were drawn
out in mighty prayer to know how we might obtain the blessings of baptism and of the Holy Spirit, according to the order of
God, and we diligently sought for the right of the fathers and the
authority of the holy priesthood, and the power to admin[ister]
in the same: for we desired to be followers of righteousness and
the possessors of greater knowledge, even the knowledge of the
mysteries of the kingdom of God. Therefore, we repaired to the
woods, even as our father Joseph said we should, that is to the

bush, and called upon the name of the Lord, and he answered us out of the heavens, and while we were in the heavenly vision the angel came down and bestowed upon us this priesthood: and then, as I have said, we repaired to the water and were baptized. After this we received the high and holy priesthood: but an account of this will be given elsewhere, or in another place. Let it suffice, that others had authority to bless, but after these blessings were given, of which I am about to write, Joseph Smith, Sen. was ordained a president and patriarch, under the hands of his son Joseph, myself, Sidney Rigdon, and Frederick G. Williams, presidents of the Church. These blessings were given by vision and the spirit of prophecy, on the 18th of December, 1833, and written by my own hand at the time; and I know them to be correct and according to the mind of the Lord.[33]

Oliver Cowdery (October 1835, relating Moroni's instructions to Joseph Smith on September 22, 1823)

When they [the golden plates] are interpreted the Lord will give the holy priesthood to some, and they shall begin to proclaim this gospel and baptize by water, and after that they shall have power to give the Holy Ghost by the laying on of their hands.[34]

Oliver Cowdery (April 1836)

The least among us values more highly his profession, and holds too sacredly that heavenly communication bestowed by the laying on of the hands of those who were clothed with authority, than all that frail, worse than thread-bare hypocritical pretention, which came down through the mother of abominations, of which himself [a reverend] and all others of his profession can boast.[35]

Oliver Cowdery (March 23, 1846)

I have cherished a hope, and that one of my fondest, that I might leave such a character as those who might believe in my testimony, after I shall be called hence, might do so, not only for the sake of the truth, but might not blush for the private character of the man who bore that testimony. I have been sensitive on this subject, I admit; but I ought to be so—you would be, under the circumstances, had you stood in the presence of John, with our departed brother Joseph, to receive the Lesser Priesthood—and in the presence of Peter, to receive the Greater, and look down through time, and witness the effects these two must produce.[36]

Oliver Cowdery (October 21, 1848)

The priesthood is here. I was present with Joseph when an holy angle from god came down from heaven and confered or restored the Aronic priesthood. And said at the same time that it should remain upon the earth while the earth stands. I was also present with Joseph when the Melchesideck priesthood was confered by the holy angles of god—this was the more necessary in order that by which we then confirmed on each other by the will and commandment of god. This priesthood is also to remain upon the earth until, the Last remnant of time.[37]

Oliver Cowdery, as Reported by George A. Smith (October 31, 1848)

Oliver Cowdery, who had just arrived from Wisconsin with his family, on being invited, addressed the meeting. He bore testimony in the most positive terms of the truth of the Book of Mormon—the restoration of the priesthood to the earth, and the mission of Joseph Smith as the prophet of the last days; and told the people if they wanted to follow the right path, to keep the main channel of the stream—where the body of the Church goes, there is the authority; and all these lo here's and lo there's, have no authority; but this people have the true and holy priesthood; "for the angel said unto Joseph Smith Jr., in my hearing, that this priesthood shall remain on earth unto the end." His [Oliver Cowdery's] testimony produced quite a sensation among the gentlemen present who did not belong to the Church, and it was gratefully received by all the saints.[38]

Oliver Cowdery (January 13, 1849)

While darkness covered the earth and gross darkness the people; long after the authority to administer in holy things had been taken away, the Lord opened the heavens and sent forth his word for the salvation of Israel. In fulfilment of the sacred Scripture the everlasting Gospel was proclaimed by the mighty angel, (Moroni) who, clothed with the authority of his mission, gave glory to God in the highest. This Gospel is the "stone taken from the mountain without hands." John the Baptist, holding the keys of the Aaronic Priesthood; Peter, James and John, holding the keys of the Melchisedek Priesthood, have also ministered for those who shall be heirs of salvation, and with these ministrations ordained men to the same Priesthoods. These Priesthoods, with their authority, are now, and must continue to be, in the body of the Church of Jesus Christ of Latter-day Saints. Blessed is the Elder who has received the same, and thrice blessed and holy is he who shall endure to the end. Accept assurances, dear Brother, of the unfeigned prayer of him, who, in connection with Joseph the Seer, was blessed with the above ministrations, and who earnestly and devoutly hopes to meet you in the celestial glory.[39]

Notes

Editors' Note: This article is an excerpt of a longer article originally published in *BYU Studies* 35/4 (1995–96): 162–207, and reprinted in *Opening the Heavens*, eds. John W. Welch and Erick B. Carlson (Provo, UT: Brigham Young University Press, 2005), 215–33.

1.   *Messenger and Advocate*, October 1835, 199. Further words given by Moroni at that time, now found in Doctrine and Covenants 2, were provided by Joseph Smith in 1838: "Behold, I will reveal unto you the Priesthood, by the hand of Elijah" (D&C 2:1).

2.   As Gregory Prince has observed, the earliest occurrences of the word *priesthood*, in written Mormon sources outside the Book of Mormon, begin in 1831 (27). Moreover, although priesthood authority had been restored prior to that time, the terms *Aaronic Priesthood* and *Melchizedek Priesthood* "were not adopted until 1835" (p. 14). Gregory A. Prince, *Having Authority: The Origins and Development of Priesthood during the Ministry of Joseph Smith* (Independence, MO: Independence, 1993). William E. McLellin's journal entry for October 25, 1831, speaks of "the High-Priesthood" and "the lesser Priest-Hood." Jan Shipps and John W. Welch, eds., *The Journals of William E. McLellin, 1831–1836* (Provo, UT: BYU Studies; Urbana: University of Illinois Press, 1994), 45, 283.

3.   Joseph Smith Jr., *History of The Church of Jesus Christ of Latter-day Saints*, ed. B. H. Roberts, 2nd ed., rev. (Salt Lake City: Deseret Book, 1971), 1:43 (hereafter cited as *History of the Church*).

4.   While remaining true to his testimony as a witness to the Book of Mormon, David Whitmer rejected any aspect of the restoration of the gospel that recognized or promoted central Church authority. In 1885, Whitmer stated:

I moved Joseph Smith and Oliver Cowdery to my fathers house in Fayette Seneca County New York, from Harmony, Penn. in the year 1829, on our way I conversed freely with them upon this great work they were bringing about, and Oliver stated to me in Josephs presence that they had baptized each other seeking by that to fulfill the command—And after our arrival at fathers sometime in June 1829, Joseph ordained Oliver Cowdery to be an Elder, and Oliver ordained Joseph to be an Elder in the church of Christ and during that year Joseph both baptized and ordained me an elder in the church of Christ. . . . I never heard that an Angel had ordained Joseph and Oliver to the Aaronic priesthood until the year 1834 5. or 6—in Ohio.

Notwithstanding numerous attestations to the contrary by Joseph Smith and Oliver Cowdery, David Whitmer in 1885 maintained, "I do not believe that John the Baptist ever ordained Joseph and Oliver as stated and believed by some." Zenas H. Gurley, interview, January 14, 1885, Gurley Collection, Family and Church History Department Archives, The Church of Jesus Christ of Latter-day Saints, Salt Lake City (hereafter Church Archives), quoted in Lyndon W. Cook, ed., *David Whitmer Interviews: A Restoration Witness* (Orem, UT: Grandin Book, 1991), 154–55. Earlier, Whitmer had been very impressed, however, by Oliver Cowdery's testimony regarding the visitation of Peter, James, and John; see note 10 below.

In 1878, William E. McLellin wrote:

In 1831 I heard Joseph tell his experience about angel visits many times, and about finding the plates, and their contents coming to light. . . . But I never heard one word of John the baptist, or of Peter, James, and John's visit and ordination till I was told some year or ~~two~~ afterward [that is, in 1832] in Ohio. (William E. McLellin statement, 10, numbered item 28, quoted in D. Michael Quinn, *The Mormon Hierarchy: Origins of Power* [Salt Lake City: Signature Books, 1994], 19).

5. Part of a revelation dated August and September 1830 (D&C 27) and published for the first time in 1835 stated that Elias had informed Zacharias, the father of John the Baptist, that John would "be filled with the spirit of Elias" (D&C 27:7).

6. David Whitmer, *An Address to All Believers in Christ: By a Witness to the Divine Authenticity of the Book of Mormon* (Richmond, MO: By the author, 1887), 32.

7. Kirtland High Council Minutes, February 17, 1834, Church Archives.

8. These verses did not appear in the earlier text of the revelation printed in the Book of Commandments, 1833. Joseph Smith recalled in 1839 that all of section 27 was received as a revelation in August 1830 but that most of the revelation, including these words, was not recorded until September 1830. Dean C. Jessee, ed., *The Papers of Joseph Smith* (Salt Lake City: Deseret Book, 1989–1992), 1:320–21.

9. This passage mentions "the voice of Peter, James, and John" but does not discuss a physical ordination. The reason is that this is part of a response to the preceding question, "What do we *hear*?" (emphasis added).

10. During an 1861 visit with David Whitmer, David H. Cannon reported that Whitmer recalled yet another testimony given by Cowdery regarding the appearance of Peter, James, and John:

The thing which impressed me most of all was, as we stood beside the grave of Oliver Cowdery the other Witness, who had come back into the Church before his death, and in describing Olivers action, when bearing his testimony, said to the people in his room, placing his hands like this upon his head, saying "I know the Gospel to be true and upon this head has Peter James and John laid their hands and confered the Holy Melchesdic Priestood," the manner in which this tall grey headed man went through the exhibition of what Oliver had done was prophetic. I shall never forget the impression that the testimony of . . . David Whitmer made upon me.

David H. Cannon, autobiography, March 13, 1917, 5, photocopy of holograph in possession of Richard L. Anderson, quoted in Larry C. Porter, "The Restoration of the Priesthood," *Religious Studies Center Newsletter* 9, no. 3 (May 3, 1995): 10.

11. Addison Everett wrote:

A few days Before Br Joseph & Hiram ware calld to Carthage By Gov. Ford I wus Passing the Mansheon House I observed Bro Joseph & Hiram & some five or six Brethren in earnest conversation Before the Door of the House. I opened the gate and steped in. . . . Br Joseph Ex[p]resed Greate simpathy for Br Oliver saying Poor Boy[,] Poor Boy[,] casting his eyes to the ground. And then Said as they Ware Tran[s]lating the Book of Mormon at His Father In Laws in Susquhanah County Penny. T[h]ey ware thretned By a Mob and in the same time Father Kn<i>ghts came Down from Cole[s]vill[e] Broom[e] County New York and Desired them to go home with him and preach to them in his Neighbourhood And on Account of the Mob Spirit prevailing they concluded to goe. And they ware teachi[n]g And preaching the Gospele they ware taken with <a> writ and Before a Judge as fals[e] Prophets. And the Prossecuting Atorny had conceived in his own Mind That A few simple qu[e]stions would Convince the Court By the Answers Bro Joseph would giv[e] <to> that <the> charge was Correct. So he calls out Jo which was the first Merical Jesus raught [wrought.] Why <said Br Joseph> we read He Created the worlds And what He done previous to that I have not as yet Learned. This answer completly con-founded the Prossicuting Atorny that he requested the Judge to Dismis the case. and went out To Organ<ize> the Mob that was on the Out Side. At about this time a Lawyer By the Name of Reede I think was his name came in to the court and Stated He was Mr Smiths Atorney and wished to see him <in> a Private room And was <put> in to <a> Back room and when in he hoisted a window and told Br Joseph & Oliver to flee in to the forest which was close at hand. And they wandered in a dense Forest all Night and often times in Mud and water up to thare Knees. And Brother Oliver got quite exausted in the After Part of the Night and Brother Joseph had to put his arm arround him and allmost carry him. And Just as the day Broke in the East Brother Oliver gave out Entirely and he[,] Br Joseph[,] leaned him against an Oake tree Just out side a field fenc[e] Br Oliver Crying out how long O Lord O how Long Br Joseph hav[e] we got to suffer these things[?] Just this moment Peter James & John came to us and Ordained to<us to> the Holy Apostelship and gave <unto> us the Keys of the Disp<e>nsation of the fullness of times. And we had some 16 or 17 miles to goe to reach our place of residence and Brother Oliver could travel as well as I could <after the Endowment>. Now as to *time* and *Place*. I heard the Name of the Banks of the Susquehanah river spoken <of> But whare it was pla[c]ed I cannot till. No doubt the Oake tree and the field fence was ajacent to the river. As to time I cannot Be Very Explsit. But as the Mob spirit had not abated when they returned they had to remove to Father Whitmores <at Fayet[te] Seneca Co> to finish the Translation. I should <jud[g]e> it to <Be> the Latter part of August.

> Now Beloved Brother I am Not Writing as wone of the Lords Historians But as your friend reproduc<i>ng the last words I heard our Beloved and Gods Holy Prophet Speake before his depart[ure] Into the Eternal Heavens to Dwell with the Holy & Eternal gods forever & Ever!

Addison Everett to Joseph F. Smith, January 16, 1882, Joseph F. Smith Collection, Personal Papers, Church Archives (underlining in the original), quoted in Porter, "Restoration of the Priesthood," 8. Angle brackets < > designate material inserted by Everett above the line. See also Addison Everett to Oliver B. Huntington, February 17, 1881, recorded in "Oliver Boardman Huntington Journal no. 14," under backdate of January 31, 1881; and "Oliver Boardman Huntington Journal no. 15," entry for February 18, 1883, L. Tom Perry Special Collections, Harold B. Lee Library, Brigham Young University, Provo, UT, quoted in Porter, "Restoration of the Priesthood," 7. The 1881 entry reads as follows:

> Joseph went on to state that "at Coalville he & Oliver were under arrest on charge of Deceiving the people & in court he stated that the first miracle done was to create this earth. About that time his attorney told the court that he wanted to see Mr. Smith alone a few moments. When alone Mr. Reid said that there was a mob in front of the house, & ho[i]sting the window, Joseph & Oliver went to the woods in a few rods, it being night, and they traveled until Oliver was exhausted & Joseph almost carried him through mud and water. They traveled all night and just at the break of day Olive[r] gave out entirely and exclaimed "O! Lord! How long Brother Joseph have we got to endure this thing,"
>
> Brother Joseph said that at that very time Peter, James, & John came to them and ordained them to the Apostleship.
>
> They had 16 or 17 miles to travel to get back to Mr. Hales his father in law and Oliver did not complain anymore of fatigue."

Compare these comments with the early history of Joseph Smith by Joseph Knight, "Joseph Knight's Recollection of Early Mormon History," ed. Dean Jesse, *BYU Studies* 17, no. 1 (1976): 37–38.

12. The first ordinations to the office of elder occurred in 1829. On April 6, 1830, Joseph and Oliver reordained one another as First and Second Elder and then "laid our hands on each individual member of the Church present, that they might receive the gift of the Holy Ghost, and be confirmed members of the Church of Christ." *History of the Church*, 1:78. Both Joseph and Oliver were elders prior to this time. See Porter, "Restoration of the Priesthood," 3.

13. *History of the Church*, 1:77–78.

14. On April 6, 1853, President Young said, "I know that Joseph received his Apostleship from Peter, James, and John, before a revelation on the subject was printed, and he never had a right to organize a Church before he was an Apostle." Brigham Young and others, in *Journal of Discourses*, 1:137. On June 23, 1874, Brigham Young indicated:

> [Joseph Smith] received the Aaronic Priesthood, and then he received the keys of the Melchisedek Priesthood, and organized the Church. He first received the power to baptise, and still did not know that he was to receive any more until the Lord told him there was more for him. Then he received the keys of the Melchisedek Priesthood, and had power to confirm after he had baptized, which he had not before. He would have stood precisely as John the Baptist

stood, had not the Lord sent his other messengers, Peter, James and John, to ordain Joseph to the Melchisedek Priesthood. (*Journal of Discourses*, 18:240)

In 1861, in a discourse on the priesthood, President Young said:

How came these Apostles, these Seventies, these High Priests, and all this organization we now enjoy? It came by revelation. Father Cahoon, who lately died in your neighbourhood, was one of the first men ordained to the office of High Priest in this kingdom. In the year 1831 the Prophet Joseph went to Ohio. He left the State of New York on the last of April, if my memory serves me, and arrived in Kirtland sometime in May. They held a General Conference, which was the first General Conference ever called or held in Ohio. Joseph then received a revelation, and ordained High Priests. You read in the Book of Doctrine and Covenants how he received the Priesthood in the first place. It is there stated how Joseph received the Aaronic Priesthood. John the Baptist came to Joseph Smith and Oliver Cowdery. When a person passes behind the vail, he can only officiate in the spirit-world; but when he is resurrected he officiates as a resurrected being, and not as a mortal being. You read in the revelation that Joseph was ordained, as it is written. When he received the Melchisedek Priesthood, he had another revelation. Peter, James, and John came to him. You can read the revelation at your leisure. When he received this revelation in Kirtland, the Lord revealed to him that he should begin and ordain High Priests; and he then ordained quite a number, all whose names I do not now recollect; but Lyman Wight was one; Fathers Cahoon and Morley, John Murdock, Sidney Rigdon, and others were also then ordained. These were the first that were ordained to this office in the Church. I relate this to show you how Joseph proceeded step by step in organizing the Church. At that time there were no Seventies nor Twelve Apostles. (*Journal of Discourses*, 9:88–89)

Readers may judge for themselves if the Kirtland revelation referred to here was the visit of Peter, James, and John or the revelation instructing Joseph Smith to begin ordaining high priests. Likewise, when Brigham Young said that Joseph Smith "was taken in the spirit to the 3d heavens & all this with the aronic priesthood" before he was ordained an apostle, Brigham need not have been referring to the vision of the three degrees of glory received by Joseph Smith and Sidney Rigdon in February 1832, as Quinn argues (Quinn, *Mormon Hierarchy*, 26). It was common for people to use the phrase "third heaven" from 2 Corinthians 12:2 in connection with Paul's gift of vision in general, as in *History of the Church*, 5:30, but this phrase is ambiguous.

15. Porter, "Restoration of the Priesthood," 3, 6–7.

16. Porter, "Restoration of the Priesthood," 3.

17. Joseph Fielding Smith, comp., *Teachings of the Prophet Joseph Smith* (Salt Lake City: Deseret Book, 1976), 336, quoted in Porter, "Restoration of the Priesthood," 3.

18. Quinn, *Mormon Hierarchy*, 22.

19. Dan Vogel, *Religious Seekers and the Advent of Mormonism* (Salt Lake City: Signature Books, 1988), 144–45; Quinn, *Mormon Hierarchy*, 10, 22.

20. Quinn, *Mormon Hierarchy*, 10; "Bible Dictionary," in Holy Bible (Salt Lake City: The Church of Jesus Christ of Latter-day Saints, 1983), 612, s.v. "*Apostle.*"

21. Quinn, *Mormon Hierarchy*, 10, 27–30. Quinn argues that Joseph and Oliver could have felt justified in ordaining elders using the authority that they received from

John the Baptist because they did not at that time associate the office of elder exclusively with the Melchizedek Priesthood. In support of this position, Quinn indicates that Joseph Smith conferred the Melchizedek Priesthood upon several who had previously been ordained elders in June 1831. At the October 1831 conference in Kirtland, "the authority of the Melchizedek Priesthood was manifested and conferred for the first time upon several of the Elders." *History of the Church*, 1:175–76. A September 1832 revelation specified that "elder and bishop are necessary appendages belonging unto the high priesthood" (D&C 84:29). Editor's note: We have deleted a paragraph dealing with the complete collection of documents reprinted in *Opening the Heavens*.

22. Document 10, Joseph Smith (April 21, 1834) and document 16, Joseph Smith (September 6, 1842) in *Opening the Heavens*, 237, 240.

23. Document 10.

24. Document 16.

25. Quinn dates this event only by indirect association with two other events. Quinn, *Mormon Hierarchy*, 23.

26. Quinn, *Mormon Hierarchy*, 25. Quinn also cites a discourse by Erastus Snow in 1882. See *Journal of Discourses* 23:183 and *Opening the Heavens*, pp. 232-33 n. 23.

27. Porter, "Restoration of the Priesthood," 8–9.

28. "The Golden Bible," *Painesville (Ohio) Telegraph*, November 16, 1830, 3.

29. *Painesville Telegraph*, December 7, 1830.

30. Joseph Smith, History, 1834–36, in Jessee, *Papers of Joseph Smith*, 1:21.

31. Oliver Cowdery to W. W. Phelps, September 7, 1834, Norton, Ohio, in *Messenger and Advocate*, October 1834, 14–16.

32. Kirtland High Council Minutes, under heading of February 21, 1835, 159. The occasion was the blessing of several new members of the Twelve Apostles. Following their blessings, Oliver Cowdery gave them this charge.

33. Patriarchal Blessings, Book 1 (1835): 8–9. The end of this blessing contains this information about its origin: "Oliver Cowdery, Clerk and Recorder. Given in Kirtland, December 18, 1833, and recorded September 1835."

34. *Messenger and Advocate*, October 1835, 199.

35. Oliver Cowdery, "The Atlas Article," *Messenger and Advocate*, April 1836, 303.

36. Oliver Cowdery to Phineas Young, March 23, 1846, Tiffin, Seneca County, OH. Quoted in Stanley R. Gunn, *Oliver Cowdery: Second Elder and Scribe* (Salt Lake City: Bookcraft, 1962), 161.

37. Reuben Miller, journal, October 21, 1848, microfilm of holograph, 14, Church Archives. Report of "Conference held on Misqueto Creek Council Bluffs October 21st ["21st" may have been added later, as it was written in a different color ink] 1848."

38. George A. Smith to Orson Pratt, October 20 and 31, 1848, Carbonca, Council Bluffs, IA, photocopy of typescript; reprinted, with a few minor differences, in Manuscript History of Brigham Young, October 31, 1848, 78, Church Archives.

39. Oliver Cowdery to Elder Samuel W. Richards, January 13, 1849, in *Deseret Evening News*, March 22, 1884, 2. The location of the original letter is unknown, but scholars find little reason to doubt the authenticity of this piece and its 1849 date.

An Examination of the 1829 "Articles of the Church of Christ" in Relation to Section 20 of the Doctrine and Covenants

Scott H. Faulring

Section 20 of the Doctrine and Covenants was originally labeled the "Articles and Covenants." It was the first revelation canonized by the restored Church and the most lengthy revelation given before the first priesthood conference was held in June 1830. Scriptural commentators in recent years have described the inspired set of instructions in section 20 as "a constitution for the restored church."[1] In many respects, the Articles and Covenants was the Church's earliest *General Handbook of Instructions.* Although Latter-day Saints typically associate the Articles and Covenants with the organization of the Church on April 6, 1830, this regulatory document had roots in earlier events: in the earliest latter-day revelations, in statements on Church ordinances and organization from the Book of Mormon, and in the preliminary set of Articles written by Oliver Cowdery in the last half of 1829.

This article will review those early revelations to show how the organization of the Church was prophetically foreshadowed and instituted. It will then identify certain prescriptions in the Book of Mormon that influenced the steps taken and pronouncements issued as the Church was organized on April 6, 1830. In particular, the contents of the 1829 Articles of the Church of Christ (figs. 1, 2, 3) and the 1830 Articles and Covenants of the Church of Christ will be summarized and contrasted. From this, the process through which Doctrine and Covenants 20 came into being will be explored in order to explain more fully how it came to be accepted as scripture.

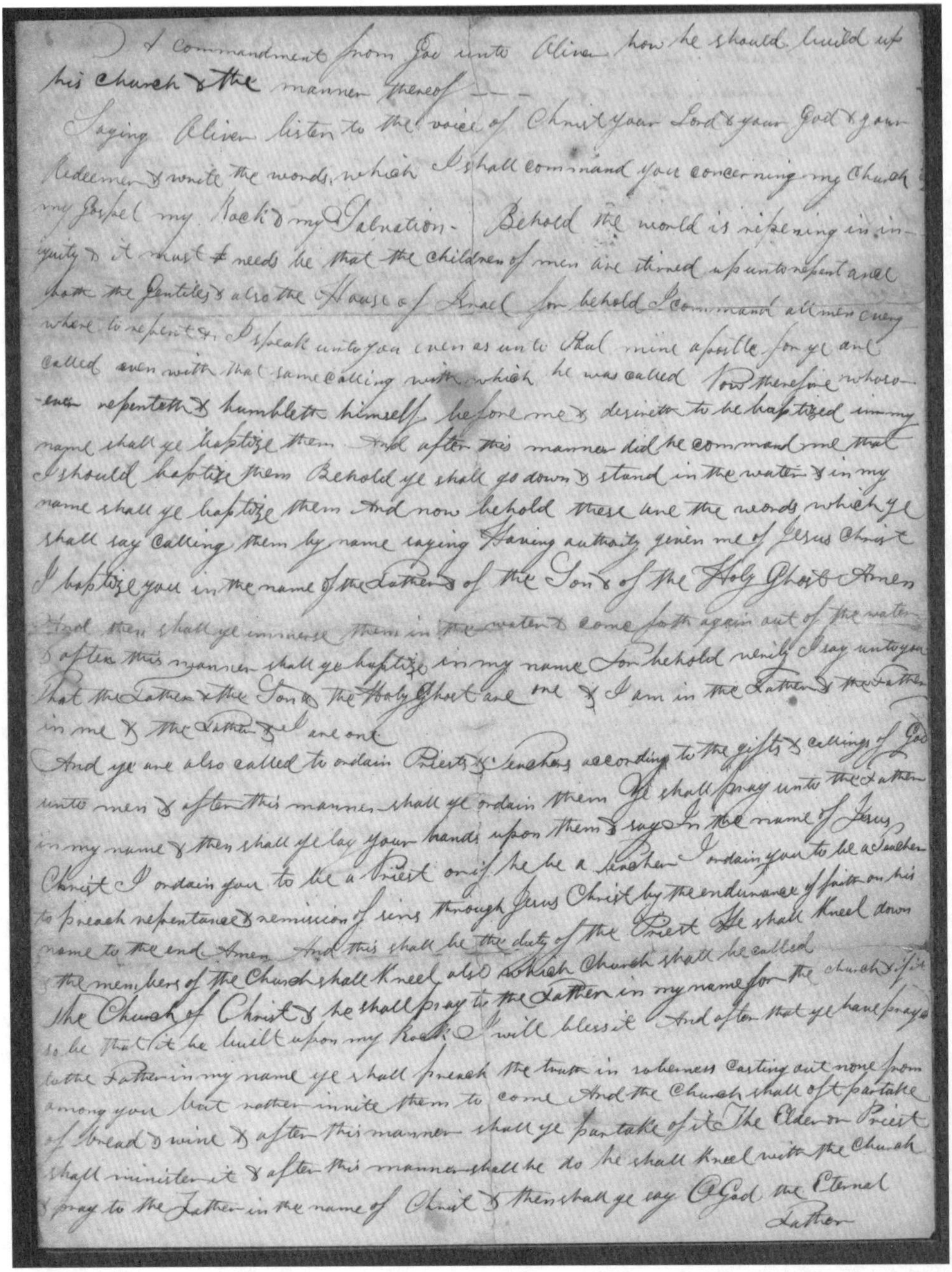

Fig. 1. 1829 "Articles of the Church of Christ," page 1. In anticipation of the organization of the Church, Oliver Cowdery prepared the Articles, describing how the Church should be governed. The entire two-and-a-half page document is written in Oliver Cowdery's distinct handwriting. Priesthood authority and baptism by immersion are first discussed. All images in this chapter courtesy of the Church Archives, The Church of Jesus Christ of Latter-day Saints.

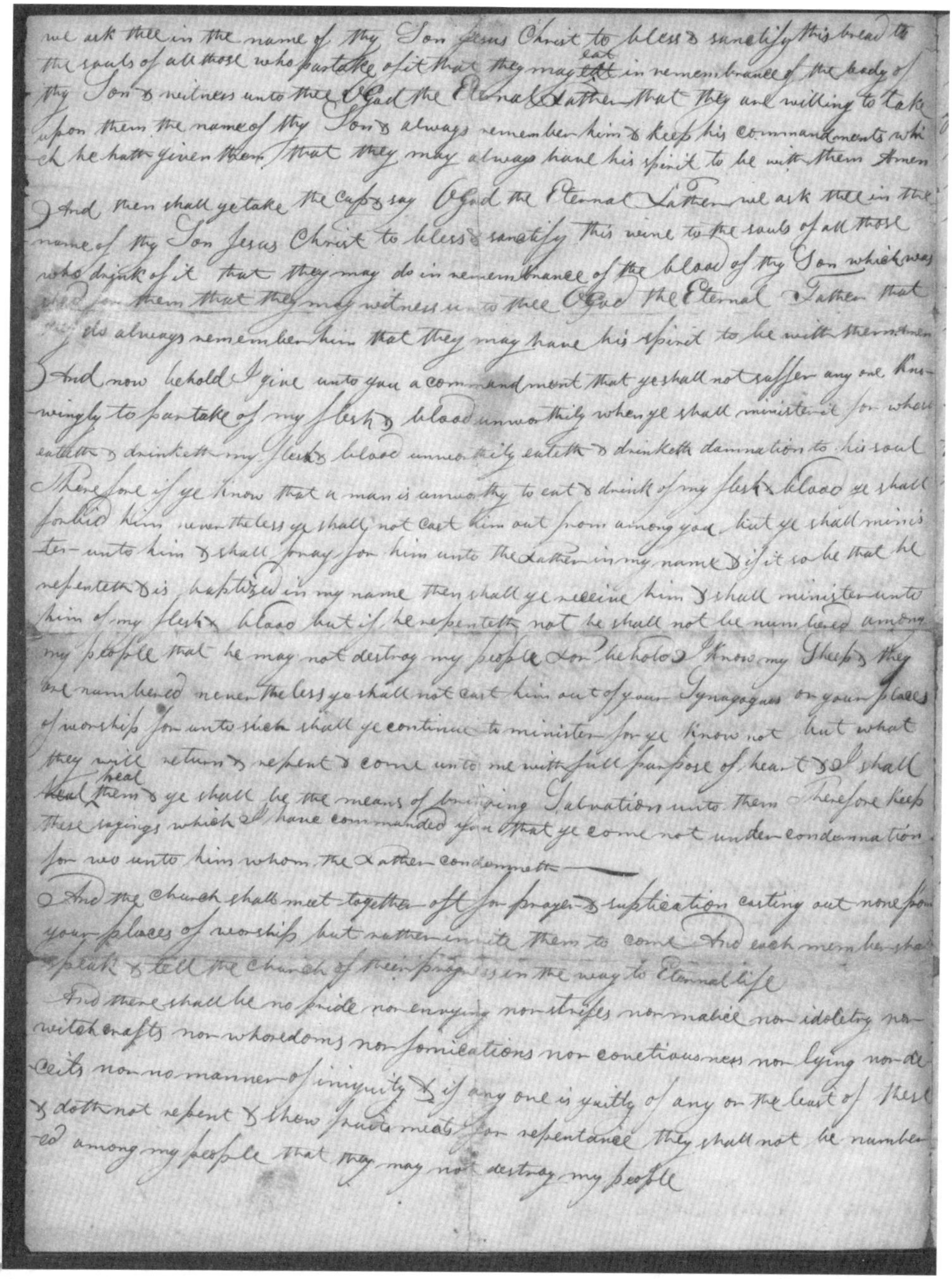

we ask thee in the name of thy Son Jesus Christ to bless & sanctify this bread to the souls of all those who partake of it that they may eat in remembrance of the body of thy Son & witness unto thee O God the Eternal Father that they are willing to take upon them the name of thy Son & always remember him & keep his commandments which he hath given them that they may always have his spirit to be with them Amen

And then shall ye take the cup & say O God the Eternal Father we ask thee in the name of thy Son Jesus Christ to bless & sanctify this wine to the souls of all those who drink of it that they may do in remembrance of the blood of thy Son which was shed for them that they may witness unto thee O God the Eternal Father that they do always remember him that they may have his spirit to be with them Amen

And now behold I give unto you a commandment that ye shall not suffer any one knowingly to partake of my flesh & blood unworthily when ye shall minister for whoso eateth & drinketh my flesh & blood unworthily eateth & drinketh damnation to his soul Therefore if ye know that a man is unworthy to eat & drink of my flesh & blood ye shall forbid him nevertheless ye shall not cast him out from among you but ye shall minister unto him & shall pray for him unto the Father in my name & if it so be that he repenteth & is baptized in my name then shall ye receive him & shall minister unto him of my flesh & blood but if he repenteth not he shall not be numbered among my people that he may not destroy my people for behold I know my sheep & they are numbered nevertheless ye shall not cast him out of your synagogues or your places of worship for unto such shall ye continue to minister for ye know not but what they will return & repent & come unto me with full purpose of heart & I shall heal them & ye shall be the means of bringing salvation unto them Therefore keep these sayings which I have commanded you that ye come not under condemnation for wo unto him whom the Father condemneth ——

And my church shall meet together oft for prayer & supplication casting out none from your places of worship but rather invite them to come And each member shall speak & tell the church of their prayers is in the way to Eternal life

And there shall be no pride nor envying nor strifes nor malice nor idolatry nor witchcrafts nor whoredoms nor fornications nor covetousness nor lying nor deceits nor no manner of iniquity & if any one is guilty of any or the least of these & doth not repent & shew fruits meet for repentance they shall not be numbered among my people that they may not destroy my people

Fig. 2. 1829 "Articles of the Church of Christ," page 2. In building up the Church, Oliver Cowdery was commanded to rely "upon the things which are written" (D&C 18:3). On this page, the words of the sacrament prayers parallel Moroni chapters 4 and 5.

And now I speak unto the Church Repent all ye ends of the Earth & come
unto me & be baptized in my name which is Jesus Christ & endure to the end &
ye shall be saved Behold Jesus Christ is the name which is given of the Father &
there is none other name given whereby man can be saved Therefore all men must
take upon them the name which is given of the Father for in that name shall they
be called at the last day & Therefore if they know not the name by which they are
called they cannot have place in the Kingdom of my Father Behold ye must walk
uprightly before me & sin not & if ye do walk uprightly before me & sin not my grace
is sufficient for you that ye shall be lifted up at the last day Behold I am
Jesus Christ the Son of the living God I am the same which came unto my own
& my own received me not I am the light which shineth in darkness & the darkness comprehendeth it not these words are not of men nor of man but of me Now remember the words of him who is the first & the last the light & the life of the world
And I Jesus Christ your Lord & your God & your Redeemer by the power of my
Spirit hath spoken it Amen ——— And now if I have not authority to write
these things judge ye behold ye shall know that I have authority when you &
shall be brought to stand before the judgment seat of Christ Now may the
of God the Father & our Lord Jesus Christ be & abide with you all & fi
lly save you Eternally in his Kingdom through the Infinite atonement which is
in Jesus Christ Amen ——— Behold I am Oliver I am an Apostle
of Jesus Christ by the will of God the Father & the Lord Jesus Christ
Behold I have written the things which he hath commanded me for behold
his word was unto me as a burning fire shut up in my bones & I was weary with
forbearing & I could forbear no longer Amen ———

Written in the year of our Lord & Saviour 1829 ——— A true Copy
of the articles of the Church of Christ

Prophetic Anticipation of the Organization of the Church

Joseph Smith's first responsibility as the latter-day prophet was to translate the Book of Mormon plates, which were entrusted to him by the angel Moroni on September 22, 1827. Only later would restoring and organizing the Lord's Church become an obvious extension of his prophetic mission, for that aspect of the restoration had to wait until the Prophet had finished translating the Book of Mormon in 1829.[2] But as the work of translation unfolded, the way was simultaneously being prepared for the imminent restoration and organization of the Church.

The earliest revelation that specifically mentions the impending establishment of the Church was given in late summer 1828. It was received shortly after Martin Harris had carelessly lost the initial 116 pages (containing the book of Lehi) from the Book of Mormon translation. In the revelation that followed, the Lord told Joseph Smith that in reestablishing His Church, this modern generation should be openhearted and spiritually prepared. The Lord admonished: "And for this cause have I said, if this generation harden not their hearts, I will establish my church among them. Now I do not say this to destroy my church, but I say this to build up my church: therefore, whosoever belongeth to my church need not fear, for such shall inherit the kingdom of heaven."[3]

A few months later, in March 1829, the Lord spoke again on this subject, telling Joseph Smith and Martin Harris that the restored Church would be patterned after the New Testament-era organization. Expanding the earlier precondition, the Savior declared, "And thus, if the people of this generation harden not their hearts,[4] I will work a reformation among them, . . . and I will establish my church, like unto the church which was taught by my disciples in the days of old."[5] The Lord explained to his latter-day disciples that this reformation marked "the beginning of the rising up, and the coming forth of my church out of the wilderness—clear as the moon and fair as the sun, and terrible as an army with banners."[6]

After Martin Harris was dismissed as scribe over the loss of the 116-page manuscript of the book of Lehi, Joseph Smith prayed fervently for another assistant to help him complete the work. His prayers were answered when Oliver Cowdery, the district school teacher from Manchester, New York, came to Harmony, Pennsylvania, in early April 1829. As part of his teaching remuneration, Cowdery had boarded with Joseph's parents, who eventually confided in Oliver about Joseph Jr.'s possession of the Book of Mormon record. After receiving profound spiritual confirmation of Joseph's calling, Oliver traveled to Harmony with the intention to be Joseph Smith's scribe. With Cowdery's assistance, the Book of Mormon translation made substantial progress. Inside of an amazingly productive three-month stretch, from early April to late June 1829, Joseph translated and Oliver, as the main scribe, wrote more than four hundred closely written foolscap pages—almost the entire unsealed portion of the Nephite plates. Also during these months, Joseph Smith received at least a dozen revelations and accomplished several other important tasks.[7]

The Nature of Oliver's Authority

Soon after they met, Oliver asked Joseph to inquire of the Lord to know his (Oliver's) duty. In response the Lord told Oliver—not once, but twice—to "give heed unto my words."[8] Cowdery was also counseled, "Now as you have asked, behold, I say unto you, keep my commandments, and seek to bring forth and establish the cause of Zion."[9] The Lord reminded the young schoolmaster, "For thou hast inquired of me, and behold as often as thou hast inquired, thou hast received instruction of my Spirit."[10] Oliver was assured that he would "receive a knowledge of whatsoever things [he] shall ask in faith, with an honest heart."[11]

Fascinated by Joseph's ability to translate the ancient record, Oliver sought for the same blessing. Weeks earlier, the Lord had promised Oliver the gift "to translate even as my servant Joseph."[12] Few details are known about the scribe's attempt to translate, but, after Cowdery "did not translate according to that which [he] desired" of the Lord, he went back to writing for the Prophet. The Lord told Oliver to continue as scribe until the translation was completed.[13]

By May 1829, the Prophet Joseph was hard at work translating the book of 3 Nephi. As the work progressed, Joseph and Oliver became inspired by the Savior's teachings to his disciples in ancient Bountiful. Years later, Cowdery reflected on how the translation spiritually motivated them. He wrote:

> No men in their sober senses, could translate and write the directions given to the Nephites, from the mouth of the Savior, of the precise manner in which men should build up his church, . . . without desiring a privilege of showing the willingness of the heart by being buried in the liquid grave, to answer a "good conscience by the resurrection of Jesus Christ."

As the pure, undiluted gospel of Christ in 3 Nephi unfolded before them, Joseph and Oliver wanted to know more about priesthood authority and baptism for the remission of sins mentioned particularly in 3 Nephi 11:18–27. Oliver explained that in reflecting on 3 Nephi they realized that "none had authority from God to administer the ordinances of the gospel."[14] The Prophet's history confirms that a desire for baptism for the remission of sins influenced their subsequent inquiry.[15]

On May 15, 1829, Joseph and Oliver adjourned to the nearby woods where they prayed for guidance. There along the tree-lined bank of the Susquehanna River, the heavens opened and the Lord's faithful servant John the Baptist came to Joseph Smith and Oliver Cowdery to lay his hands upon their heads and bestow upon them the Aaronic Priesthood.[16] As Oliver later explained, John the Baptist delivered the keys of the gospel of repentance, which included authority to baptize. The Aaronic Priesthood did not include the power of the laying on of hands for the gift of the Holy Ghost (as is made clear in 3 Nephi 18:37), but Joseph and Oliver were promised that they would receive higher priesthood authority in due time. The heavenly minister directed Joseph to baptize Oliver, and Oliver to do the same for Joseph. After these baptisms were performed in the Susquehanna River, the Holy Ghost was manifested. Joseph Smith recounted:

> No sooner had I baptized Oliver Cowdery than the Holy Ghost fell upon him and he stood up and prophecied many things which should shortly come to pass. And again so soon as I had been baptized by him, I also had the Spirit of prophecy when standing up I prophecied concerning the rise of this Church and many other things connected with the Church and this generation of the children of men.[17]

After their baptisms, Joseph and Oliver laid hands on each other's head and conferred the Aaronic Priesthood. Thus Joseph Smith and Oliver Cowdery, as companions, received a transcendent understanding of the preparatory events connected to the "rise of this Church" almost a year before the Church was organized on April 6, 1830.

Shortly after John the Baptist's appearance, the Savior's three presiding apostles during the meridian of time—Peter, James, and John—came to Joseph and Oliver and bestowed the Melchizedek Priesthood and the associated keys, including the apostleship.[18] Although Joseph and Oliver were given the keys and powers necessary to reestablish Christ's Church upon the earth, they did not exercise these keys or bestow the Holy Ghost by the laying on of hands until the Church was organized in early April 1830. Shortly after receiving the essential gospel ordinances and priesthood authority, Joseph and Oliver moved, in early June 1829, to Peter Whitmer Sr.'s farmhouse in Fayette, New York. There they could work on the remainder of the Book of Mormon translation without concern for provisions or persecution.

As the translation proceeded, Joseph, Oliver, and Peter Whitmer's son, David, prayed to the Lord in mid-June 1829 for further "instructions relative to building up the church of Christ, according to the fullness of the gospel."[19] The first part of the revelation that came in answer to their prayer implies that Oliver, in particular, wanted to know how to organize the Church. The Lord told Oliver to "rely upon the things which are written, for in them are all things written concerning [the foundation of][20] my church, my gospel, and my rock. Wherefore if you shall build up my church, upon the foundation of[21] my gospel and my rock, the gates of hell shall not prevail against you" (D&C 18:3–5).

Later in the summer of 1829, the Prophet and his closest associates gathered at Peter Whitmer Sr.'s farmhouse and eagerly petitioned the Lord for permission to exercise the Melchizedek Priesthood keys by laying on hands for the gift of the Holy Ghost.[22] Responding to their solemn and fervent request, the Lord gave a revelation describing the manner in which they should hold the organizational meeting of the Church. This revelation called for Joseph to ordain Oliver an elder in the Church and for Oliver to then ordain Joseph to the same office. Joseph would be called the First Elder, and Oliver the Second Elder. Together they would select and ordain other men to either the Aaronic or Melchizedek Priesthood as directed by the Spirit. The assemblage would then vote, by the rule of common consent, to sustain Joseph and Oliver as their presiding officers and spiritual teachers. The sacrament would be administered by priesthood authority, and then Joseph and Oliver would be permitted to lay on hands for the gift of the Holy Ghost.

Joseph explained that these actions were to be deferred until "such times, as it should be practicable to have our brethren, who had been and who should be baptized, assembled together."[23] Months before the organization of the Church, a separate revelation given "by the Spirit of Prophecy" revealed "the precise day upon which, according to his [the Lord's] will and commandment, we should proceed to organize his Church once again, here upon the earth."[24] The date revealed was April 6, 1830, half a year in the future.

During the second half of 1829, Oliver Cowdery set about to use the as-yet-unpublished manuscript of the Book of Mormon, along with several early manuscript revelations, to compose the statement on Church procedure and organization that he called the "Articles of the Church of Christ." In doing so, he literally fulfilled the command given to him the previous June when the Lord told him to "build up my church" by "rely[ing] upon the things which are written."[25] Oliver's Articles are an example of how closely he worked with the Prophet in laying the foundation of the Church. Years later, perhaps reflecting on these early events, Oliver confided to Phineas Young, his brother-in-law, how the Church, "the foundation of which my own hands helped to lay, is constantly near my thoughts."[26]

The authoritative tone is what first strikes the reader of the Articles. It is written so that the Lord speaks in the first person, just as many of the revelations to Joseph. It may seem odd that Oliver was the actual compiler of revelation when his role as scribe for the Prophet seems so commonplace. Nevertheless, in the context of the pre-Church organization, Cowdery's actions were legitimate. Not until a year later, in the summer of 1830, months after the Church was organized, did the Lord specify that Joseph Smith, and Joseph Smith alone, was the Lord's appointed mouthpiece (D&C 28:1–7). Oliver Cowdery, as a bipartite holder of the restored keys of the Melchizedek Priesthood, was entitled to certain gifts of the Spirit. Elder Joseph Fielding Smith, who served for many years as Church historian and, later, as Church President, described Oliver's unique position: "Oliver Cowdery's standing in the beginning was as the 'Second Elder' of the Church, holding the keys jointly with the Prophet Joseph Smith."[27] Heber C. Kimball, a contemporary of Oliver Cowdery and later a counselor to Brigham Young in the First Presidency, noted that "Oliver Cowdery received revelations and wrote them."[28] However, it should not be automatically assumed that God's word to Oliver is precisely the same in nature as Joseph's revelations. The following two sections will highlight many differences.

Still, in his calling as the Second Elder, Oliver apparently held sufficient authority to write the first articles in anticipation of the Church's organization. Oliver testified that the Spirit of the Lord guided him throughout: "Behold I have written the things which [the Lord] hath commanded me for behold his word was unto me as a burning fire shut up in my bones and I was weary with forbearing and I could forbear no longer."[29]

The Contents of Cowdery's 1829 Articles

The surviving copy of Cowdery's "Articles of the Church of Christ" is transcribed and printed in full as an appendix at the end of this article. A brief synopsis of its contents shows that Oliver selected doctrinal or essential ordinance passages from the unpublished Book of Mormon manuscript, integrated those passages with material from several of the Prophet's 1829 revelations, and added a few lines of his own commentary.

The Articles begin simply with the words "A commandment from God unto Oliver how he [Oliver] should build up his [the Lord's] church and the manner thereof." The Spirit tells Oliver to "listen to the voice of Christ . . . and write the words which I [the Lord] shall command you concerning my Church my Gospel my Rock and my Salvation."

The Church is then warned, "Behold the world is ripening in iniquity and it must needs be that the children of men are stirred up unto repentance both the Gentiles and also the House of Israel." Thus, a call to repentance is issued and the apostolic calling of Oliver is affirmed: "For behold I [the Lord] command all men every where to repent and I speak unto you [Oliver] even as unto Paul mine apostle for ye are called even with that same calling with which he was called."

Next, the manner and form of baptism are defined (reflecting 3 Nephi 11 and Mosiah 18). The procedure to be used by Church elders in ordaining priests and teachers is then explained (following Moroni 3), duties of the priests are specified, and the manner and form of administering the sacrament are defined (complete with the words of the sacrament prayers from Moroni 4–5). A commandment is given to refuse to allow the unworthy (unrepentant) to partake of the sacrament (echoing 3 Nephi 18:28).

Church members are counseled to meet together often for prayer and fasting and to report their personal progress toward eternal life (as the people are commanded in 3 Nephi 18:22 and Moroni 6). A warning is given against a dozen evils and iniquities (along the lines of Alma 1:32), and instructions are given to dismiss those who will not repent. The Lord calls all to repentance and invites them to come unto him, be baptized, endure to the end, and be saved, using language reminiscent of the words spoken by Jesus Christ as recorded in 3 Nephi 11.

The next sentence reads, "Behold ye must walk uprightly before me and sin not and if ye do walk uprightly before me and sin not my grace is sufficient for you that ye shall be lifted up at the last day." This is followed by a direct quotation from the earliest revelation given to Oliver Cowdery by the Prophet Joseph Smith in April 1829, found in D&C 6:21: "Behold I am Jesus Christ the Son of the liveing God I am the same which came unto my own and my own received me not I am the light which shineth in darkness and the darkness comprehendeth it not."

Finally, the Lord bears testimony that "these words are not of men nor of man but of me," and the closing statement reads, "Now remember the words of him who is the first and the last the light and the life of the world And I, Jesus Christ, your Lord and your God and your Redeemer, by the power of my Spirit hath spoken it Amen[.]"

Oliver appends an assertion of the authority by which this statement is issued: "And now if I have not authority to write these things judge ye behold ye shall know that I have authority when you and I shall be brought to stand before the judgment seat of Christ[.]" Cowdery then bears his apostolic testimony: "Behold I am Oliver I am an Apostle of Jesus Christ by the will of God the Father and the Lord Jesus Christ."

As is further confirmed by the notes to the transcription that follows in the appendix below, Oliver incorporated procedures and ordinances gleaned from the Book of Mormon, supplemented by modern revelation or commentary of his own origination, to write his Articles of the Church of Christ.[30]

A Brief Comparison of Cowdery's 1829 Articles with the 1830 Articles and Covenants

In the last twenty years, several Mormon writers have described Cowdery's 1829 Articles as the source or as a draft of the later Articles and Covenants (D&C 20).[31] By this they imply that Joseph Smith revised and expanded Cowdery's earlier Articles. For the following reasons, such an interpretation is both inaccurate and misleading.

Comparison of Oliver Cowdery's 1829 Articles with an original 1830 version manuscript of the Articles and Covenants (D&C 20) is impossible since no surviving copy of the latter predates early 1831. The earliest extant manuscript of Doctrine and Covenants 20 is cited herein as Watters-Daily.[32] This early copy was made by an unidentified scribe sometime between February 9 and June 19, 1831.[33] Careful textual comparison of Cowdery's 1829 Articles against this early copy of Doctrine and Covenants 20 reveals that Oliver Cowdery's document is far more dependent on the Book of Mormon text than is the latter. Roughly one-fifth of section 20[34] relies on the Book of Mormon for its text, while more than half of Cowdery's Articles are either direct quotations or paraphrases with slight deviations from the Book of Mormon.[35]

Since the Prophet Joseph Smith left only a brief, general description of the reception of Doctrine and Covenants 20, we are left to wonder exactly how the Articles and Covenants information was received.[36] Apparently a large percentage of the Articles and Covenants came by direct revelation to the Prophet. While the wording of the baptismal and sacramental ordinances in both documents is similar (as one would expect, given that the restored Church's use of baptismal and sacramental prayers are derived from the Book of Mormon),[37] significant differences exist. Cowdery's manuscript quotes or paraphrases almost double the amount of words from the Book of Mormon as does the Watters-Daily copy of Doctrine and Covenants 20.[38] The Articles and Covenants, given through the Prophet Joseph Smith, is a richer, more comprehensive doctrinal and procedural document that in fact bears little or no resemblance to the earlier Cowdery Articles. More than a decade ago, Richard Lloyd Anderson described Cowdery's Articles not as a draft, but as a "forerunner" of section 20.[39] Analysis and comparison of these two early regulatory documents bears this description out. Cowdery's 1829 document came before the 1830 Articles and Covenants, but Cowdery's document was not revised, corrected, expanded, or specifically used to create section 20.

As shown in the next section, the more comprehensive Articles and Covenants, which was received during the second quarter of 1830, quickly eclipsed Cowdery's less complex version of the Church articles. Oliver's 1829 document should be read and understood simply as a preliminary step taken by the Second Elder to assist in laying the administrative groundwork for the organization of the restored Church.

Writing the Articles and Covenants of the Church

The historical heading of section 20 in the current edition of the Doctrine and Covenants says that the Articles and Covenants was received in April 1830, but does not say where it was received. No explanation or source is given to support this dating. When the Articles and Covenants was published in the 1833 edition of the Book of Commandments, the date and location were given as June 1830 at Fayette, New York.[40] Regrettably, we do not have an original manuscript or even a pre-1831 copy of the Articles and Covenants. The two earliest copies are the Watters-Daily manuscript and a version printed in an Ohio newspaper. Both of these items preserve the text as it read in early 1831.[41] In analyzing these copies, one needs to remember that the Articles and Covenants was a practical religious text that the Prophet revised and expanded as the Church organization developed.[42]

Reliable sources provide enlightening details that allow us to approximate the time period for the reception of section 20. It appears that Joseph Smith dictated Doctrine and Covenants 20 between late March and the first week of June 1830.[43] This dating is derived from the earliest time period in 1830 that Joseph Smith was in western New

York for a sustained visit (not a brief visit such as those mentioned by Mother Lucy Mack Smith[44]) and the June 9, 1830, church conference at Fayette, where the Articles and Covenants was first read in public. A manuscript history written by Joseph Knight, a close friend and supporter of Joseph Smith, describes how he transported the Prophet in his wagon from Harmony to Manchester at the time E. B. Grandin was completing the printing of the Book of Mormon, just before the Church's organization. Mother Lucy Mack Smith, in her family memoir, recalled that Joseph returned from Pennsylvania "about the first of April of the same year in which the Book of Mormon was published."[45]

Additional historical evidence suggests that Joseph Smith and Oliver Cowdery were together when the Articles and Covenants was written. Oliver was living in the Palmyra-Manchester area during spring 1830 as he, along with Joseph's brother Hyrum, personally supervised the publication of the Book of Mormon. In late March or early April 1830, Cowdery traveled along with Joseph Smith and others to Fayette, New York, where they participated in the organization of the restored Church of Christ on April 6, 1830.

Though Oliver Cowdery was probably involved in writing section 20, this time it was only in the mechanical sense—as the Prophet's scribe. Years later, Brigham Young described how Joseph had to struggle with Oliver as the Prophet dictated a revelation on priesthood—evidently the 1830 Articles and Covenants. President Young said, "You read that Oliver Cowdery was the Second Elder and you remember the Revelation on the Priesthood [section 20];[46] . . . Joseph was two hours laboring with O[liver] C[owdery] to get him to write the Revelation in humility."[47] The fact that Oliver Cowdery had compiled an earlier set of Articles could at least partially explain his reluctance or difficulty. The Second Elder may have felt that his earlier composition of the Articles was being overlooked or was already sufficient.

It is uncertain whether Joseph Smith had either received or committed the Articles and Covenants to paper by the time the Church was organized at Fayette on April 6, 1830. Since there are no contemporary minutes for the meeting that day, it is not known if Doctrine and Covenants 20 was presented or discussed. None of those present in Fayette on that memorable day mentioned the Articles and Covenants in connection with the formal organization of the Church.

On the other hand, during the first quarterly conference of elders held in Fayette on June 9, 1830, Joseph Smith read the Articles and Covenants and then called for a sustaining vote.[48] The conference minutes reported that the revelation was "recieved [*sic*] by the unanimous voice of the whole congregation, which consisted of most of the male members of the Church."[49] At this inaugural conference, the priesthood holders were given licenses showing their priesthood office (fig. 4) and certifying that they had been "baptized and received into the Church according to the Articles and Covenants of the Church." Alongside his official Church leadership title, the Prophet signed his name to these simple handwritten certificates as First Elder, and Oliver Cowdery signed as Second Elder.[50]

A Brief Overview of the Contents of the 1830 Articles and Covenants

An examination of the contents and structure of the Articles and Covenants (fig. 5) discovers that the revelation has two sections. The first part, verses 1–36 in the current edition of the Doctrine and Covenants, has five subsections or paragraphs that all end with "Amen" and that are beautifully succinct historical and doctrinal statements. The second part, comprising verses 37–84, details the procedural requirements and ordinances of the restored Church of Christ. A brief outline of the contents, referenced by the modern versification, follows.

The five "Amen" sections are:

Verses 1–4: The Church of Jesus Christ of Latter-day Saints was founded according to civil law and "by the will and commandments of God" on April 6, 1830. The Lord gave these commandments to "Joseph the Seer,"[51] whom he called and ordained an Apostle of the Savior "to be the first elder"[52] of the Church and to Oliver Cowdery, whom the Savior called and ordained an Apostle and "the second elder."

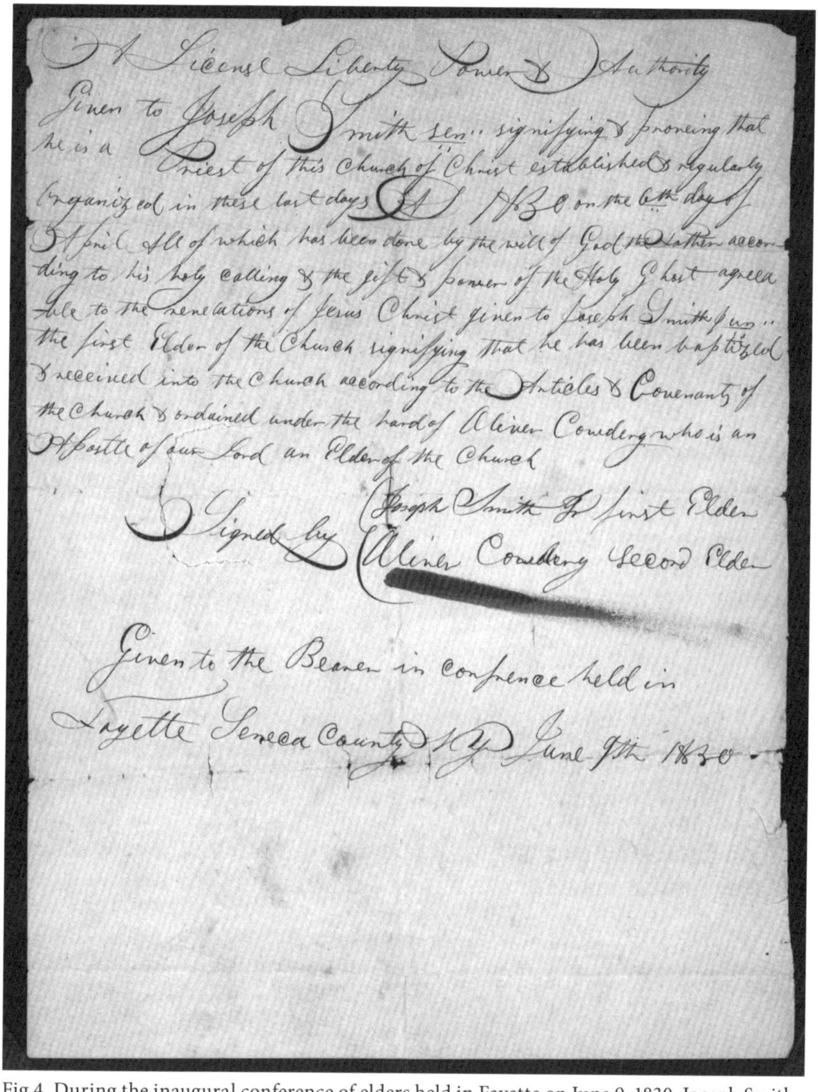

A License Liberty Power & Authority
Given to Joseph Smith sen.. signifying & proveing that
he is a Priest of this Church of Christ established & regularly
Organized in these last days AD 1830 on the 6th day of
April All of which has been done by the will of God the Father according to his holy calling & the gift & power of the Holy Ghost agreeable to the revelations of Jesus Christ given to Joseph Smith Jun..
the first Elder of the Church signifying that he has been baptized
& received into the church according to the Articles & Covenants of
the Church & ordained under the hand of Oliver Cowdery who is an
Apostle of our Lord an Elder of the Church

Signed by Joseph Smith Jr first Elder
Oliver Cowdery Second Elder

Given to the Bearer in conference held in
Fayette Seneca County NY June 9th 1830

Fig.4. During the inaugural conference of elders held in Fayette on June 9, 1830, Joseph Smith read the Articles and Covenants and then called for a sustaining vote. Ten handwritten priesthood licenses were then given to the priesthood holders present. This license given to Joseph Smith Sr. is signed by the Prophet as First Elder and Oliver Cowdery as Second Elder. All of the licenses issued that day were written out by Oliver Cowdery. The long ink splotch under Cowdery's signature was a crude seal added to prevent anyone else from signing their names to the licenses.

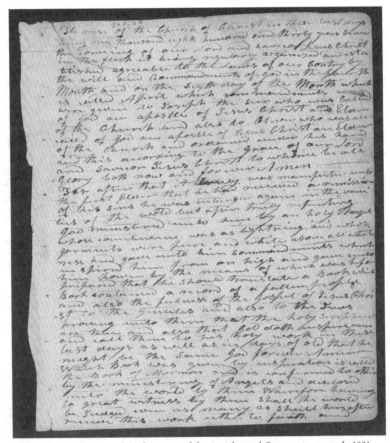

Fig. 5. Manuscript copy of the first page of the Articles and Covenants, ca. early 1831, referred to as the Watters-Daily copy in this essay and written in the hand of an unknown scribe. This is the earliest known manuscript of what would become D&C 20.

Verses 5–12: After Joseph Smith received forgiveness for his youthful sins (during the First Vision), he became "entangled again in the vanities of the world." But Joseph repented, and God sent a "holy angel [Moroni], whose countenance was as lightning and whose garments were pure," to the Prophet multiple times from 1823 to 1827. In due time, the Lord "inspired him and gave him power from on high" to translate the Book of Mormon plates, "proving to the world that the holy scriptures are true" and that the Book of Mormon is a second witness of Jesus Christ and his eternal gospel.

Verses 13–16: The world will be judged by the testimony of the Three Witnesses. Those who accept the Book of Mormon will "receive a crown of eternal life; but those who harden their hearts and reject it" will be damned.

Verses 17–28: The doctrine of the unchangeable God and the creation, fall, and atonement are explained.

Verses 29–36: The Lord explains the doctrines of repentance, faith, justification, and sanctification. Verse 36 concludes the historical and doctrinal section of the Articles and Covenants.

The remainder of Doctrine and Covenants section 20 contains the core administrative procedures and ordinances by which the priesthood and general Church membership are to abide. The Prophet organized the final section of the Church's constitution in the following order:

Verse 37: The prerequisites for baptism are explained.

Verses 38–67: Duties of the elders, priests, teachers, deacons, and members of the Church of Christ are detailed.

Verses 68–71: Duties of baptized members are explained.

Verses 72–74: The mode of baptism is specified (that is, immersion), and the baptismal prayer is given (compare 3 Nephi 11:25).

Verses 75–79: The Church is commanded to "meet together often" to partake of the sacrament in the "remembrance of Jesus Christ." The sacramental prayers on the bread and wine of the Lord's Supper are specified (compare Moroni 4–6).[53]

Verse 80: The procedure for dealing with members in transgression is explained.

Verses 81–84: Finally, Church regulations governing membership lists and recommends are given.

Acceptance of the Articles and Covenants

An interesting episode directly connected with the acceptance of the Articles and Covenants occurred a short time after the Church was organized. The Prophet's manuscript history preserves some of the details of the incident.[54] Sometime in July or August 1830, while Oliver Cowdery was living with the Whitmers at Fayette, he discovered what he thought was an error in the Articles and Covenants. Oliver became alarmed when he read "and truly manifest by their works that they have received of the Spirit of Christ unto the remission of their sins."[55] Cowdery wrote an angry letter to Joseph, who was working his farm in Harmony, pointing out the alleged doctrinal mistake. It is possible that Oliver associated the requirement of "manifest by their works" as being too closely akin to the requirement that a believer must prove before the congregation that he or she has received God's grace before being admitted into full fellowship,[56] but the basis of his objection remains unstated and obscure. Oliver simply demanded "in the name of God" that Joseph make the deletion so that, as he warned, "no priestcraft be amongst us."[57]

In a prompt reply to his assistant, Joseph Smith asked Oliver "by what authority he took upon him to command [the Prophet] to alter or erase, to add or diminish to or from a revelation or commandment from the Almighty God."[58] A short time later, Joseph visited Oliver and the Whitmer family, and, as the Prophet describes, "with great difficulty, and much labour" he reasoned with and convinced them that Oliver Cowdery's "rash judgment" did not accord with the Spirit of God and that the challenged religious doctrine in the Articles and Covenants was "in accordance with the rest of the commandment."[59] The evidence indicates that after all they had been through—their shared revelatory experiences in the restoration of the Aaronic and Melchizedek priesthood and the inspired translation of the Book of Mormon—Cowdery evidently viewed himself as Joseph Smith's coequal—a position that was not his to claim.

When the Church met for the second quarterly conference on September 26, 1830, at Fayette, conference attendees appointed the Prophet to preside. The minutes show that the first item of business voted upon was the appointment of Joseph Smith as the one "to receive and write Revelations & Commandments for this Church," and the "voice of the Conference" sanctioned the resolution.[60] Oliver Cowdery was not the only prominent individual who had challenged the Prophet's authority; Hiram Page had attempted to receive revelation "concerning the upbuilding of Zion [and] the order of the Church."[61] Acknowledging Joseph Smith as the only revelator for the Church clarified, for leaders and members alike, that he alone was charged with the prophetic governance of the Church.[62]

During the conference, Oliver Cowdery read the Articles and Covenants to the congregation, and the Prophet commented upon them.[63] Evidently, by autumn 1830, Oliver had become reconciled to and sustained the Articles and Covenants as the procedural authority of the Church, as did all other members at that time.

Conclusion

The Articles and Covenants of the Church of Christ began to take shape shortly after Joseph Smith and Oliver Cowdery first met in April 1829. The Lord commanded Oliver to "rely upon the things which are written" in shaping the forthcoming Church's earliest policies and procedures (D&C 18:3). Cowdery's Articles of the Church of Christ, prepared sometime in the second half of 1829, was a relatively short procedural statement that depended heavily on excerpts from the Book of Mormon and early revelations to the Prophet. Thus it can be concluded that even though Oliver's Articles were written in the first person of Christ's voice, it does not rise to the same stature of original and authoritative revelation. At some point between late March and early June 1830, the Prophet Joseph Smith, assisted by Oliver Cowdery as scribe, wrote the revelation known as the Article and Covenants, which superceded Cowdery's earlier Articles. In the more comprehensive and longer Articles and Covenants, the Lord gave to Joseph, Oliver, and the Church a constitutional and procedural guide to regulate Church affairs. Oliver's 1829 document was simply a preliminary attempt to compile a governing document, but it lacked the organizational details needed to administer to the needs of the Church. The material in Doctrine and Covenants section 20 was read in the first two conferences of the Church and was cited authoritatively in official Church documents, such as priesthood licenses and member recommends, from the earliest years of the Church.

Appendix: Oliver Cowdery's 1829
"Articles of the Church of Christ"

In the early 1970s, while conducting research on the historical and textual development of the revelations in the Doctrine and
Covenants, Robert J. Woodford analyzed all extant manuscript
copies of Joseph Smith's revelations, most of which are in the LDS
Church Archives.[64] Woodford's analysis of Doctrine and Covenants
section 20 includes the earliest verbatim transcription of Oliver
Cowdery's Articles of the Church of Christ.[65] Woodford's was the
first public presentation of Cowdery's 1829 document.

The only surviving copy of Cowdery's Articles was written on a
large sheet of paper folded in half, creating a four-page manuscript.
Oliver wrote on the first three pages and left the fourth page blank.[66]
The document's concluding notation, written by Oliver, indicates that
this manuscript is a "true copy" of the Articles of the Church as they
existed in 1829. This suggests that an earlier, original Articles manuscript must have once existed. From mid-1831 until the late 1950s, this
three-page "true copy" was hidden away and unknown to anyone.

What is unique about Cowdery's manuscript is that it was
once part of the official Church records but was lost (probably stolen) from the Church in summer 1831. Almost 130 years later, in
1960, the Church unexpectedly received Cowdery's Articles document as part of a larger donation of early church manuscripts. The
unsolicited donation came from a non-Mormon descendant of an
individual briefly noticed in the Ohio period of Latter-day Saint history. Many readers of early Mormon history will recall the name
Symonds Ryder. He had joined the Church by June 1831, but his conversion was short-lived and he apostatized after only a few months.
In addition, the official Church history identifies Symonds Ryder as
the notorious ringleader of the Hiram, Ohio, mob that tarred and
feathered Joseph Smith and Sidney Rigdon in March 1832.[67] Earlier,
prior to his apostasy, Ryder was mentioned in a revelation (D&C
52:37), when the Lord called him to replace an unfaithful missionary. Unfortunately, in writing the revelation and letter of appoint-

ment, the Prophet's scribe misspelled Symonds Ryder's name by writing an *i* rather than a *y*. This innocent mistake allegedly gave Ryder reason to doubt Joseph Smith's source of inspiration. Even though Ryder himself was not very consistent, his preferred spelling of the name is Symonds Ryder. Strangely, and with perhaps a touch of humorous irony, the current edition of the Doctrine and Covenants still misspells Ryder's first name.

There is a potential link, recently discovered, between Symonds Ryder's apostasy and the disappearance of the manuscript of Oliver Cowdery's Articles of the Church in 1831. Ryder was in Kirtland on June 6, 1831, when he was ordained an elder by Joseph Smith.[68] Two weeks after Symonds's ordination, the Prophet, accompanied by many of the leading brethren in Ohio, departed from Kirtland on their first visit to Independence, Jackson County, Missouri—the site of the prophesied city of the New Jerusalem and the land designated as Zion. Allegedly, with the Church leaders away, Symonds Ryder traveled north from his farm in Hiram, Ohio, up to the Church headquarters in Kirtland. Somehow, without being discovered, he accessed the Church records. Symonds apparently knew what he was looking for. He secured a certain group of manuscript revelations. The documents he took detailed, in one way or another, the organization, procedures, or laws of the Church. Included in these materials was Oliver Cowdery's 1829 Articles.[69] Ironically, also among the manuscripts was a copy of the revelation in which Ryder's name was misspelled. More than 125 years later, in 1958, Symonds Ryder's descendants discovered these manuscript revelations tightly rolled up in a linen handkerchief inside the drawer of a dresser that had been in the Ryder family for many years. The family believes that Ryder himself hid these documents for unknown reasons and they remained untouched until being discovered in 1958. It was his great-great-granddaughter who unrolled the precious old documents and flattened them in books. Two years later, the Ryder family, assisted by a Latter-day Saint family living in the community of Ravenna, Ohio, forwarded these priceless historical revelation documents to the Church historian in Salt Lake City.[70]

The following is a verbatim transcription of the original manuscript now in the LDS Church Archives. Spelling, punctuation, capitalization, and paragraphing are reproduced as in the handwritten document. Angle brackets (as in <eat>) are used to show letters or words inserted in the text by Oliver Cowdery. Editorial additions are indicated with square brackets (as in [it]). Bracketed page numbers (as in [p. 1]) denote the end of a page in the original. Cowdery's frequent use of the ampersand has been silently replaced with "and." The entire document is in Oliver's handwriting.

Transcription of the 1829 Articles of the Church of Christ:

A commandment from God unto Oliver how he should build up his church[71] and the manner thereof—

Saying Oliver listen to the voice of Christ your Lord and your God and your Redeemer and write the words which I shall command you concerning my Church my Gospel my Rock[72] and my Salvation. Behold the world is ripening in iniquity and it must needs be that the children of men are stirred up unto repentance both the Gentiles and also the House of Israel[73] for behold I command all men every where to repent and I speak unto you even as unto Paul mine apostle for ye are called even with that same calling with which he was called[74] Now therefore whosoever repenteth and humbleth himself before me and desireth to be baptized in my name shall ye baptize them[75] And after this manner did he command me that I should baptize them Behold ye shall go down and stand in the water and in my name shall ye baptize them And now behold these are the words which ye shall say calling them by name saying Having authority given me of Jesus Christ[76] I baptize you in the name of the Father and of the Son and of the Holy Ghost Amen And then shall ye immerse them in the water and come forth again out of the water and after this manner shall ye baptize in my name For behold verily I say unto you that the Father and the Son and the Holy Ghost are one and I am in the Father and the Father in me and the Father and I are one.

And ye are also called to ordain Priests and Teachers according to the gifts and callings of God unto men[77] and after this manner shall ye ordain them Ye shall pray unto the Father in my name and then shall ye lay your hands upon them and say In the name of Jesus Christ I ordain you to be a Priest or if he be a Teacher[78] I ordain you to be a Teacher to preach repentance and remission of sins through Jesus Christ by the endurance of faith on his name to the end Amen[79] And this shall be the duty of the Priest He shall kneel down and the members of the Church shall kneel also which Church shall be called The Church of Christ and he shall pray to the Father in my name for the church and if it so be that it be built upon my Rock I will bless it And after that ye have prayed to the Father in my name ye shall preach the truth in soberness casting out none from among you[80] but rather invite them to come And the Church shall oft partake of bread and wine[81] and after this manner shall ye partake of it The Elder or Priest shall minister it and after this manner shall he do he shall kneel with the Church and pray to the Father in the name of Christ and then shall ye say O God the Eternal Father [p. 1] we ask thee in the name of thy Son Jesus Christ to bless and sanctify this bread to the souls of all those who partake of it that they may et <eat> in remembrance of the body of thy Son and witness unto thee O God the Eternal Father that they are willing to take upon them the name of thy Son and always remember him and keep his commandments which he hath[82] given them that they may always have his spirit to be with them Amen[83] And then shall ye take the cup and say O God the Eternal Father we ask thee in the name of thy Son Jesus Christ to bless and sanctify this wine to the souls of all those who drink of it that they may do [it] in remembrance of the blood of thy Son which was shed for them that they may witness unto thee O God the Eternal Father that they do always remember him that they may have his spirit to be with them Amen[84] And now behold I give unto you a commandment[85] that ye shall not suffer any one knowingly to partake of my flesh and blood unworthily when ye shall minister it for whoso eateth and drinketh my flesh and blood unworthily eateth and drinketh damnation to his soul Therefore if

ye know that a man is unworthy to eat and drink of my flesh and
blood ye shall forbid him nevertheless ye shall not cast him out from
among you but ye shall minister unto him and shall pray for him
unto the Father in my name and if it so be that he repenteth and is
baptized in my name then shall ye receive him and shall minister
unto him of my flesh and blood but if he repenteth not he shall not
be numbered among my people that he may not destroy my people
For behold I know my sheep and they are numbered nevertheless
ye shall not cast him out of your Synagogues or your places of worship for unto such shall ye continue to minister for ye know not
but what they will return and repent and come unto me with full
purpose of heart and I shall heal <heal> them and ye shall be the
means of bringing Salvation unto them Therefore keep these sayings which I have commanded you that ye come not under condemnation for wo unto him whom the Father condemneth—[86]

And the church shall meet together oft for prayer and
sup[p]lication casting out none from your places of worship but
rather invite them to come And each member shall speak and tell
the church of their progress in the way to Eternal life

And there shall be no pride nor envying nor strifes nor malice
nor idoletry nor witchcrafts nor whoredoms nor fornications nor cov-
etiousness nor lying nor deceits nor no manner of iniquity[87] and if
any one is guilty of any or the least of these and doth not repent and
show fruits mee<a>ts [meets] for repentance they shall not be numbered among my people that they may not destroy my people [p. 2]

And now I speak unto the Church Repent all ye ends of the
Earth and come unto me and be baptized in my name[88] which is
Jesus Christ and endure to the end and ye shall be saved Behold
Jesus Christ is the name which is given of the Father and there is
none other name given whereby men can be saved Wherefore all
men must take upon them the name which is given of the Father for
in that name shall they be called at the last at <day> Wherefore if
they know not the name by which they are called they cannot have
place in the Kingdom of my Father[89] Behold ye must walk uprightly
before me and sin not and if ye do walk uprightly before me and sin

not[90] my grace is sufficient for you that ye shall be lifted up at the last day[91] Behold I am Jesus Christ the Son of the liveing God I am the same which came unto my own and my own received me not I am the light which shineth in darkness and the darkness comprehendeth it not[92] these words are not of men nor of man but of me[93] Now remember the words of him who is the first and the last the light and the life of the world[94] And I Jesus Christ your Lord and your God and your Redeemer by the power of my Spirit hath spoken it Amen[95]

And now if I have not authority to write these things judge ye behold ye shall know that I have authority when you and I shall be brought to stand before the judgment seat of Christ[96] Now may the [*manuscript torn*] [grace] of God the Father and our Lord Jesus Christ be and abide with you all[97] and [*manuscript torn*] [finally] save you Eternally in his Kingdom through the Infinite atonement which is in Jesus Christ Amen—

Behold I am Oliver I am an Apostle of Jesus Christ by the will of God the Father and the Lord Jesus Christ Behold I have written the things which he hath commanded me for behold his word was unto me as a burning fire shut up in my bones and I was weary with forbearing and I could forbear no longer[98] Amen—

Written in the year of our Lord and Saviour 1829—

A true Copy of the articles of the Church of Christ &c.[99]

Notes

Editors' note: This article was originally published in *BYU Studies* 43/4 (2004): 57–91.

1. Lyndon W. Cook, *The Revelations of the Prophet Joseph Smith* (Provo, UT: Seventy's Mission Bookstore, 1981), 31. See also Robert John Woodford, "The Historical Development of the Doctrine and Covenants," 3 vols. (PhD diss., Brigham Young University, 1974; CD version, Joseph Fielding Smith Institute for Latter-day Saint History and BYU Studies, 2001), 1:286–93.

2. Oliver Cowdery, in the final installment of his history of the "rise of the church," stated that Moroni told Joseph Smith in 1823 that "when they [the Book of Mormon plates] are interpreted the Lord will give the holy priesthood to some, and they shall begin to proclaim this gospel and baptize by water, and after that they shall have power to give the Holy Ghost by the laying on of their hands." Oliver Cowdery to W. W. Phelps, Letter 8, undated, ca. September–October 1835, printed in *Messenger and Advocate* 2

(October 1835): 199. All primary sources, both published and unpublished, will be cited as in the original documents, with no attempt to correct spelling, capitalization, and so forth.

3. *A Book of Commandments, For the Government of the Church of Christ Organized According to Law, on the 6th of April, 1830* (Zion [Independence, MO]: W. W. Phelps, 1833), 9:14 (hereafter cited as Book of Commandments); current D&C 10:53–55.

4. Joseph Smith read a similar statement sometime in May or June 1829, while translating the Savior's teachings to the Nephites. Speaking about the latter-day Gentiles, the Lord said, "But if they will repent, and hearken unto my words, and harden not their hearts, I will establish my church among them." *The Book of Mormon* (Palmyra, NY: E. B. Grandin, 1830), [3rd] Nephi, chapter 10 (p. 501) (hereafter cited as 1830 Book of Mormon); current 3 Nephi 21:22.

5. Book of Commandments 4:5. When the revelation was prepared for publication in the 1835 Doctrine and Covenants, verses 5 and 6 of the Book of Commandments were replaced by the material in the latter half of verse 3 in the 1835 edition. Current D&C 5:18–20 reads the same as the 1835 D&C. The only extant manuscript copy of Doctrine and Covenants 5 is worded slightly differently: "And I will establish my Church yea even the church which was taught by my Disciples." D&C 5 manuscript, undated, 1, Newel K. Whitney Collection, L. Tom Perry Special Collections, Harold B. Lee Library, Brigham Young University, Provo, Utah (hereafter cited as Perry Special Collections).

6. 1835 D&C 32:3; current D&C 5:14. This phrase was first included in the revelation when it was published in the 1835 D&C.

7. These revelations are found in current D&C 6–9, 11–18. Current D&C 10, received in summer 1828, is chronologically out of order due to the 1833 Book of Commandments editors incorrectly assigning a later date of May 1829 (see Book of Commandments, chapter 9, heading). While compiling the Prophet's official history in 1839, James Mulholland, one of Joseph Smith's clerks, inserted a copy of this revelation into the Prophet's manuscript history immediately following section 3 (dated July 1828). Mulholland used the 1835 D&C as his source text for this revelation. See Manuscript History of the Church, Book A-1, 10–11, Church Archives, The Church of Jesus Christ of Latter-day Saints, Salt Lake City (hereafter cited as LDS Church Archives), published in Dean C. Jessee, ed., *The Papers of Joseph Smith*, 2 vols. (Salt Lake City: Deseret Book, 1989–92), 1:287–88. For an in-depth discussion of the dating of D&C 10, see Max H. Parkin, "A Preliminary Analysis of the Dating of Section 10," *Sidney B. Sperry Symposium, January 27, 1979, The Doctrine and Covenants* (Provo, UT: Brigham Young University Press, 1979), 68–84. For a convenient listing of the activities of that eventful spring, see John W. Welch, "How Long Did It Take to Translate the Book of Mormon?" in *Reexploring the Book of Mormon*, ed. John W. Welch (Salt Lake City: Deseret Book and FARMS, 1992), 1–8.

8. Book of Commandments 5:1; current D&C 6:2.

9. Book of Commandments 5:3; current D&C 6:6.

10. Book of Commandments 5:6; current D&C 6:14.

11. Book of Commandments 7:1; current D&C 8:1. See also Book of Commandments 5:2, 5, 6–7 (current D&C 6:5, 10–11, 14–15); Book of Commandments 7:1–2, 3–4 (current D&C 8:1–4, 9–11).

12. Book of Commandments 5:11; current D&C 6:25.

13. Book of Commandments 8:1; current D&C 9:1. The Lord told Oliver that after completing this sacred assignment he would be given power to help translate other records. In verse two of the current D&C 9, the superscript letter *a* on the word *other* is keyed to the phrase *other records*. The corresponding footnote describes Oliver Cowdery's later participation in the "New Translation" of the Bible (the Joseph Smith Translation, or JST) and a similar revelatory translation called the Book of Abraham, which was derived from Egyptian papyrus purchased by Church members at Kirtland in July 1835. Oliver Cowdery was the first of several scribes who helped the Prophet Joseph Smith with the translation of the Bible. Working from June through mid-October 1830, Oliver Cowdery wrote the first installment of the Old Testament, Manuscript One (Joseph Smith Translation, Old Testament 1), starting on page one and ending on page ten, line five (Moses 1:1–5:43). For a typographical facsimile of Oliver Cowdery's contribution to the Bible translation, see *Joseph Smith's New Translation of the Bible: Original Manuscripts*, ed. Scott H. Faulring, Kent P. Jackson, and Robert J. Matthews (Provo, UT: Religious Studies Center, Brigham Young University, 2004), 83–95. In 1866, Emma Smith, the Prophet's widow, gave the original JST manuscripts to her son, Joseph Smith III, the leader of the Reorganized Church of Jesus Christ of Latter Day Saints (RLDS Church). These manuscripts are in the library-archives of the Community of Christ (formerly RLDS Church), headquartered in Independence, Missouri. Since October 1880, The Church of Jesus Christ of Latter-day Saints has canonized the vision of Moses (Moses 1) and the first eight chapters of the JST in the Pearl of Great Price. Oliver Cowdery's involvement with the translation of the Book of Abraham (also in the Pearl of Great Price) occurred in the latter half of 1835. The surviving Kirtland Egyptian manuscripts, very little of which are in Oliver's handwriting, are in LDS Church Archives. Before Cowdery was involved in either of these scriptural undertakings, he lent a hand in laying the foundation of the latter-day Church of Christ.

14. Oliver Cowdery to William W. Phelps, Letter 1, September 7, 1834, published in *Messenger and Advocate* 1 (October 1834): 15.

15. Manuscript History of the Church, Book A-1, 17–18, published in Jessee, *Papers of Joseph Smith*, 1:290; Joseph Smith Jr., *History of The Church of Jesus Christ of Latter-day Saints*, ed. B. H. Roberts, 2d ed., rev., 7 vols. (Salt Lake City: Deseret Book, 1971), 1:39 (hereafter cited as *History of the Church*); Joseph Smith—History 1:68–70.

16. The official account of the Aaronic Priesthood restoration is in Manuscript History of the Church, Book A-1, 17–18; Jessee, *Papers of Joseph Smith* 1:290–91; *History of the Church,* 1:39–41; and Joseph Smith—History 1:68–72.

17. 1839 Draft History, first unnumbered page, Archive of the First Presidency, published in Jessee, *Papers of Joseph Smith*, 1:231. This draft was the source of the material copied into Manuscript History of the Church, Book A-1, 18; and published in Jessee, *Papers of Joseph Smith*, 1:291; *History of the Church,* 1:42; and Joseph Smith—History 1:73.

18. For a complete set and analysis of all known accounts of the restoration of the Melchizedek Priesthood, see Brian Q. Cannon and BYU Studies Staff, "Priesthood Restoration Documents," *BYU Studies* 35, no. 4 (1995–96): 163–207. Although many details were given, neither Joseph Smith nor Oliver Cowdery revealed the precise date on which Peter, James, and John restored the Melchizedek Priesthood. In the last twenty-five years, Mormon historians have written many articles attempting to identify the time frame for the bestowal of the Melchizedek Priesthood and the accompanying

apostleship. After carefully studying the known facts and different views of this issue, I accept Larry Porter's findings (see his 1996 *Ensign* article listed below) that this event most likely occurred in late May 1829. For further, sometimes divergent, interpretations, see Larry C. Porter, "Dating the Restoration of the Melchizedek Priesthood," *Ensign* 9 (June 1979): 5–10; Larry C. Porter, "The Priesthood Restored," in *Studies in Scripture, Volume Two: The Pearl of Great Price*, ed. Robert L. Millet and Kent P. Jackson (Salt Lake City: Randall Book, 1985), 2:389–409; William G. Hartley, "'Upon You My Fellow Servants': Restoration of the Priesthood," in *The Prophet Joseph: Essays on the Life and Mission of Joseph Smith*, ed. Larry C. Porter and Susan Easton Black (Salt Lake City: Deseret Book, 1988), 49–72; Gregory A. Prince, *Having Authority: The Origins and Development of Priesthood During the Ministry of Joseph Smith* (Independence, MO: John Whitmer Historical Association Monograph Series, 1993), 16–32, updated and expanded in Gregory A. Prince, *Power from on High: The Development of Mormon Priesthood* (Salt Lake City: Signature Books, 1995), 3–15, 47–57; Larry C. Porter, "The Restoration of the Priesthood," *Religious Studies Center Newsletter* 9 (May 1995): 1–12; D. Michael Quinn, *The Mormon Hierarchy: Origins of Power* (Salt Lake City: Signature Books, 1994), 1–38; and Larry C. Porter, "The Restoration of the Aaronic and Melchizedek Priesthoods," *Ensign* 26 (December 1996): 30–47.

19. Book of Commandments, chapter 15, heading.

20. Book of Commandments 15:3–4. The material in square brackets was added to this revelation when it was published in the 1835 D&C (43:1). See current D&C 18:3–5.

21. 1835 D&C replaced *and* with *upon the foundation of*. See current D&C 18:3–5.

22. The historical evidence is ambiguous as to whether just Joseph Smith and Oliver Cowdery, or whether they and others (such as Martin Harris, Hyrum Smith, or any of the five Whitmer brothers), joined in asking the Lord for further revelation on the issue of receiving permission to bestow the gift of the Holy Ghost. See 1839 Draft History, 7–8; Jessee, *Papers of Joseph Smith*, 1:238–39. This draft was the source for the material copied into Manuscript History of the Church, Book A-1, 26–27; and published in Jessee, *Papers of Joseph Smith*, 1:299–300; and *History of the Church*, 1:60–62.

23. 1839 Draft History, 7–8. See also Jessee, *Papers of Joseph Smith*, 1:238–39, 299. Those helping compile the Prophet's history copied this part of the draft, with some editing, into the Manuscript History of the Church, Book A-1, 26–27. See Jessee, *Papers of Joseph Smith*, 1:298–300. In both the 1839 Draft History and Manuscript History of the Church, Book A-1, the revelation given in June 1829 to Joseph Smith, Oliver Cowdery, and David Whitmer (current D&C 18) *comes after* the narrative about the revelation received at Father Whitmer's log home. However, the correct historical sequence is the reverse. The other revelations, telling in detail the order of the Church organizational meeting and specifying the date when they should restore the Church, were given after mid-June 1829 (the latest possible date on which Joseph Smith could have received the revelation in D&C 18) and following completion of the Book of Mormon translation at the end of June. Joseph Smith received these revelations before his departure from western New York for his farm in Harmony in late August 1829, soon after contracting with E. B. Grandin to print the Book of Mormon.

24. Manuscript History of the Church, Book A-1, 29; Jessee, *Papers of Joseph Smith*, 1:300. This material was original to the Manuscript History of the Church. The 1839 Draft History reads, "We continued to receive instruction concerning our duties from

time to time, and among many things the fol[l]owing directions, fixing the time of our anticipated meeting together for the purpose of being organized were given by the Spirit of prophecy and revelation." 1839 Draft History, 8; and Jessee, *Papers of Joseph Smith*, 1:239.

25. Book of Commandments 15:3–4. See current D&C 18:3–4.

26. Oliver Cowdery to Phineas H. Young, November 12, 1846, Brigham Young Collection, LDS Church Archives.

27. Joseph Fielding Smith, *Doctrines of Salvation*, 3 vols., comp. Bruce R. McConkie (Salt Lake City: Bookcraft, 1954), 1:212. President Smith was an Apostle and the Church historian at the time he expressed this view.

28. Heber C. Kimball, in *Journal of Discourses*, 26 vols. (Liverpool: F. D. Richards, 1855–86), 5:28, July 12, 1857. These remarks were delivered in a public discourse in Salt Lake City.

29. Oliver Cowdery, "Articles of the Church of Christ," 3, LDS Church Archives. Oliver Cowdery's spiritual reaction, which he described "as a burning fire shut up in my bones, and I was weary with forbearing and I could forbear no longer," is a close paraphrase of Jeremiah 20:9.

30. A detailed discussion of the use of the Book of Mormon in Cowdery's 1829 Articles is presented in Scott H. Faulring, "The Book of Mormon: A Blueprint for Organizing the Church," *Journal of Book of Mormon Studies* 7, no. 1 (1998): 60–69, 71.

31. See, for example, Woodford, "Historical Development," 1:287; Richard L. Bushman, *Joseph Smith and the Beginnings of Mormonism* (Urbana: University of Illinois Press, 1984), 157; David J. Whittaker, "The 'Articles of Faith' in Early Mormon Literature and Thought," in *New Views of Mormon History,* ed. Davis Bitton and Maureen Ursenbach Beecher (Salt Lake City: University of Utah Press, 1987), 64–65; Stephen E. Robinson and H. Dean Garrett, *A Commentary on the Doctrine and Covenants*, 2 vols. (Salt Lake City: Deseret Book, 2000), 1:126; and Joseph Fielding McConkie and Craig J. Ostler, *Revelations of the Restoration: A Commentary on the Doctrine and Covenants and Other Modern Revelations* (Salt Lake City: Deseret Book, 2000), 155.

32. Named after the donor-facilitator who returned this manuscript to the Church in 1960. See additional details on this transaction later in this paper.

33. This copy was made about the same time as the reception of D&C 42 (which occurred early February 1831), a copy of which is in the same "manuscript gathering" containing this copy of D&C 20. At the latest, this copy was in existence in mid-June 1831, when Joseph Smith left Kirtland for Missouri and Symonds Ryder searched among the records the Church leaders had left behind. See note 67.

34. Because it is the earliest manuscript, the Watters-Daily copy of D&C 20 at the LDS Church Archives is used in this study for textual comparison. Of its 2,119 words, only 443 are derived from the Book of Mormon text.

35. Approximately 746 words (52 percent) of the total 1,444 words included in Cowdery's Articles are directly dependent on the Book of Mormon text.

36. The Prophet's manuscript history suggests that the Articles and Covenants was written in mid- to late-1829, which is actually a more accurate historical context for the writing of Cowdery's 1829 Articles. See 1839 Draft History, 8; and Jessee, *Papers of Joseph Smith,* 1:239, 241. This draft material, with some editing, was copied into the Manuscript History of the Church, Book A-1, 29–30.

37. The Savior instituted the sacrament among the Nephites during his personal ministrations in AD 34 (see 3 Nephi 18), but specific wording for administering the sacrament is not recorded there. The manner of administering the sacrament along with the specific sacramental prayers are found in Moroni, chapters 4–5.

38. The Watters-Daily copy of D&C 20 has 392 words dealing with baptism or sacrament, while Oliver Cowdery's Articles has 650 words on these same subjects.

39. Richard Lloyd Anderson, "The Organization Revelations (D&C 20, 21, and 22)," in *Studies in Scripture, Volume One: Doctrine and Covenants,* ed. Robert L. Millet and Kent P. Jackson (Salt Lake City: Deseret Book, 1984), 1:114.

40. See Book of Commandments, chapter 24, heading. The Book of Commandments was the Church's first, though unsuccessful, attempt to publish Joseph Smith's revelations in book form. The earliest publication of the Articles and Covenants by the Latter-day Saints was on the front page of the Church's first periodical, *The Evening and the Morning Star* (June 1832). No date or location for the reception of the Articles and Covenants was given in *The Evening and the Morning Star.*

41. See manuscript copy of D&C 20 from the Watters-Daily acquisition (described in note 70), Revelations Collection, LDS Church Archives; and "The Mormon Creed," *Painesville Telegraph,* April 19, 1831, 4. In this last reference, E. D. Howe, the antagonistic editor of the *Telegraph,* claimed that the copy he printed in his *Telegraph* newspaper was "obtained from the hand of Martin Harris" and was titled "The articles and covenants of the Church of Christ agreeable to the will and commandments of God."

42. A detailed analysis of the textual differences in the Articles and Covenants is in Woodford, "Historical Development," 1:303–51.

43. It is assumed from the earliest sources that the Articles and Covenants was written in western New York, either at Manchester or Fayette.

44. Mother Smith's narrative mentions at least two brief return trips made by Joseph during the winter of early 1830. The first was for Joseph to enforce his copyright on the Book of Mormon against Abner Cole for his (Cole's) unauthorized publication of Book of Mormon excerpts in the Palmyra *Reflector* in January 1830. The second return trip was when E. B. Grandin, fearful that he would not be paid for printing the Book of Mormon, stopped printing after being notified of a local boycott against the sale of the Book of Mormon. See Lucy Mack Smith, *Biographical Sketches,* 149–51.

45. See Dean C. Jessee, ed., "Joseph Knight's Recollection of Early Mormon History," *BYU Studies* 17, no. 1 (1976): 36–37; and Lucy Mack Smith, *Biographical Sketches,* 151. The first edition Book of Mormon was available for purchase by the last week of March 1830. The book was first advertised for sale in the *Wayne Sentinel,* March 26, 1830, 3.

46. The priesthood revelation mentioned here by Brigham Young, during which Oliver was present, can only be the "Articles and Covenants" (D&C 20). In the Latter-day Saint scriptures, there are only two other revelations given to the Prophet Joseph Smith that overwhelmingly focus on priesthood: D&C 84 and 107. When D&C 84 was received in September 1832, Cowdery was serving as the presiding priesthood leader in Zion (Jackson County, Missouri) and was not present in Kirtland, Ohio, for the reception of this revelation. Also, there is no evidence to suggest that Cowdery was in conflict with Joseph Smith over the contents of, or involved in the writing (scribal or otherwise) of, D&C 107, parts of which were given in 1831 and 1835.

47. Brigham Young, Provo School of the Prophets Minutes, April 15, 1868, 1, published in Elden J. Watson, ed., *Brigham Young Addresses, 1865–1869*, vol. 5 (Salt Lake City: Elden J. Watson, 1982). It should be pointed out that in 1830 Brigham Young was not yet affiliated with the restored Church of Christ (he joined in 1832), so he was probably relating information he heard from Joseph Smith or someone else present in 1830.

48. The official minutes note that this first conference was convened "according to the Church Articles and Covenants." Far West Record, 1, published in Donald Q. Cannon and Lyndon W. Cook, eds., *Far West Record: Minutes of The Church of Jesus Christ of Latter-day Saints, 1830–1844* (Salt Lake City: Deseret Book, 1983), 1.

49. Oliver Cowdery took the minutes of the June 1830 conference because he was serving as Church recorder at the time. A retained copy is in the Far West Record, 1. See Cannon and Cook, *Far West Record*, 2.

50. At least three of the ten licenses issued on June 9, 1830, still exist, and they all refer to the authority of the Articles and Covenants. See Joseph Smith Sr. priest license, June 9, 1830, Joseph Smith Papers, LDS Church Archives (fig. 4 herein); John Whitmer elder license, June 9, 1830, Western Americana Collection, Beinecke Rare Book and Manuscript Library, Yale University; and Christian Whitmer teacher license, June 9, 1830, Western Americana Collection, Beinecke Rare Book and Manuscript Library.

51. Both of the earliest manuscript copies of D&C 20 (the Watters-Daily document and a copy made by John Whitmer for Zebedee Coltrin) refer to the Prophet Joseph Smith as "Joseph the Seer."

52. Earlier versions (both manuscript and published) read simply "an elder." Joseph Smith's unique position and calling as "first elder" was clarified in the 1835 D&C. It should be noted that the priesthood licenses issued at the first conference of elders, held June 9, 1830, specifically designated that Joseph was the First Elder and Oliver Cowdery was the Second. See Joseph Smith Sr. (fig. 4), John Whitmer, and Christian Whitmer priesthood licenses, as cited in note 50 above.

53. The dependence of D&C 20:75–79 on Moroni 4–6 is apparent. In the first printing of D&C 20 in the 1831 *Painesville Telegraph*, the text explicitly states: "And the manner of baptism and the manner of administering the Sacrament are to be done *as is written in the Book of Mormon*" (emphasis added). See Anderson, "The Organization Revelations," 121 n. 26. As in the 1830 edition, other early sources for D&C 20 simply refer the reader to "Book of Mormon, 575," in lieu of quoting the wording of the Book of Mormon prayers, or they place the material from Moroni 4–5 and 3 Nephi 11 in quotation marks. See Woodford, "The Historical Development of the Doctrine & Covenants," 343. These factors confirm that D&C 20:75–79 was composed intentionally as a reiteration of Moroni 4–5. See further, John W. Welch, "From Presence to Practice: Jesus, the Sacrament Prayers, the Priesthood, and Church Discipline in 3 Nephi 18 and Moroni 2–6," *Journal of Book of Mormon Studies* 5, no. 1 (1996): 119–39.

54. See 1839 Draft History, 23; and Jessee, *Papers of Joseph Smith*, 1:259–60. This draft material, with some editing, was copied into the Manuscript History of the Church, Book A-1, 50–51. See Jessee, *Papers of Joseph Smith*, 1:319–20. It also appears in a slightly edited version in *History of the Church*, 1:104–5.

55. See Daniel G. Reid, ed., *Dictionary of Christianity in America* (Downer's Grove, IL: InterVarsity Press, 1990), s.v. "Conversion Narratives." See also Edmund S. Morgan, *Visible Saints: The History of a Puritan Idea* (Ithaca and London: Cornell Paperbacks,

Cornell University Press, 1965), 88–92; and Patricia Caldwell, *The Puritan Conversion Narrative: The Beginnings of American Expression* (Cambridge: Cambridge University Press, 1983).

56. 1833 Book of Commandments 24:30; current D&C 20:37. The Watters-Daily manuscript reads, "and truly manifest by their works that they have received the Spirit unto the remission of their sins."

57. Manuscript History of the Church, Book A–1, 50–51; published in *History of the Church,* 1:105. Oliver was obviously concerned that the offending phrase legitimized a form of priestcraft in the restored Church and that it was not in harmony with the restored gospel. Cowdery's passionate misinterpretation was unwarranted given that the Book of Mormon presents a similar doctrinal statement concerning baptism. See the prophet Moroni's teachings on baptism in the 1830 Book of Mormon, Moroni 6 (p. 576); current Moroni 6:1–4.

58. The Prophet's letter to Oliver Cowdery is not presently located, but was summarized in his 1839 Draft History, 23; and Jessee, *Papers of Joseph Smith,* 1:260. This draft material, with some editing, was used in the Manuscript History of the Church, Book A–1, 51. See Jessee, *Papers of Joseph Smith,* 1:320. It also appears in a slightly edited version in *History of the Church,* 1:105.

59. 1839 Draft History, 23, and Manuscript History of the Church, Book A–1, 51. Published in Jessee, *Papers of Joseph Smith,* 1:260, 320.

60. As with the June conference, Oliver Cowdery, serving as Church recorder, took the minutes for the second conference. A retained copy of the minutes is in Far West Record, 2. See Cannon and Cook, *Far West Record,* 3.

61. 1839 Draft History, 25; and Jessee, *Papers of Joseph Smith,* 1:263. This draft material, with some editing, was copied into the Manuscript History of the Church, Book A–1, 53–58. See Jessee, *Papers of Joseph Smith,* 1:322–23. It also appears in a slightly edited version in *History of the Church,* 1:109–15.

62. More than four years later, in December 1834, after being set apart as Assistant President of the Church, Oliver Cowdery elaborated on the "power and authority" of the office of Church President. Oliver explained, "The office of the President [of the Church] is to preside over the whole Church; to be considered as at the head; to receive revelations for the Church; to be a Seer, Revelator and Prophet, having all the gifts of God:—taking Moses for an ensample." See Oliver Cowdery, "Unfinished Manuscript History," December 5–6, 1834, in Manuscript History of the Church, Book A–1, 17 (first numbering); and Jessee, *Papers of Joseph Smith,* 1:21.

63. Far West Record, 2; Cannon and Cook, *Far West Record,* 3.

64. In April 1974, Woodford, a Church Educational System instructor, completed his massive 1,900-page dissertation at Brigham Young University entitled "The Historical Development of the Doctrine and Covenants." Woodford later privately published a limited edition of this three-volume work. At the core of his meticulous study was a section-by-section examination of the textual variants in each revelation in the Doctrine and Covenants. Woodford compared all known manuscripts, early Church publications, and English language editions of the Book of Commandments and Doctrine and Covenants.

65. Portions of Cowdery's Articles were either direct revelation to Oliver, quoted or paraphrased material from the Book of Mormon manuscript, or ideas influenced

by modern revelation given to the Prophet Joseph Smith. Citations to the 1829–1830 printer's manuscript (Community of Christ Archives) are used here for comparison, since the relevant parts of the original (LDS Church Archives) are no longer extant. The transcription presented herein corrects Woodford's transcription errors and adds extensive textual annotations. Additional articles dealing with the relationship of this manuscript to the organization of the Church and D&C 20 are Woodford, "Historical Development," 1:287–93; Bushman, *Beginnings of Mormonism,* 156–57, 166–67; Whittaker, "Articles of Faith," 64–66; Anderson, "The Organizational Revelations," 109–23; and Robert J. Woodford, "The Articles and Covenants of the Church of Christ and the Book of Mormon," in *Sperry Symposium Classics: The Doctrine and Covenants* (Provo, UT: Religious Studies Center, Brigham Young University; Salt Lake City: Deseret Book, 2004), 103–16. Appreciation is given to Robert J. Woodford, Ronald O. Barney, and Steven R. Sorensen for their assistance in understanding this important document and its historical background.

66. There are 1,444 words in Cowdery's Articles; page one has 522 words, page two has 521 words, and page three has 401 words.

67. Manuscript History of the Church, Book A-1, 205–8; Jessee, *Papers of Joseph Smith,* 1:374–78; *History of the Church,* 1:260–64.

68. Ryder's ordination was recorded in the Far West Record, 6. See Cannon and Cook, *Far West Record,* 9.

69. Later in life, Symonds Ryder explained that when Joseph Smith and the other Church authorities went up to Zion (Jackson County, Missouri) in 1831, they "left their papers behind." Without directly identifying himself as one of the "new converts," Symonds described how the "new converts [took] an opportunity to become acquainted with the internal arrangement of their church." Symonds Ryder to A. S. Hayden, February 1, 1868, published in A. S. Hayden, *Early History of the Disciples in the Western Reserve, Ohio* (Cincinnati: Chase & Hall Publishers, 1876), 221. In addition to Oliver Cowdery's 1829 articles, Symonds Ryder had in his possession copies of the following manuscript revelations: D&C 20, 35, 36, 42, 52, and 56. This listing was noted by Church archivist Earl Olson in his May 27, 1964, typewritten notation on William D. Daily's September 27, 1960, statement.

70. These documents are now at the LDS Church Archives. Further information on the finding and subsequent donation of these documents is in William D. Daily, Statement, September 27, 1960, in author's possession (see note 70); Woodford, "Articles and Covenants," 262–63; and Scott H. Faulring, "Symonds Ryder," *Mormon History Association Newsletter,* no. 103 (fall 1996): 3–5. The specific details about the documents being found by the Ryder family tightly rolled up in a linen handkerchief in a dresser drawer is from a personal telephone conversation between the author and Mr. Wayne E. Watters and his wife, Virginia (she is the descendant of Symonds Ryder), on October 2, 1996. Notes of conversation in author's possession.

Oliver composed these articles either at the Joseph Smith Sr. residence in Manchester, New York, or at the Peter Whitmer Sr. home in Fayette, New York. The Church acquired the document in 1960. On September 27, 1960, William D. Daily, a Latter-day Saint serviceman stationed at the Ravenna Arsenal, made the following statement:

> The enclosed writings were given to William D. Daily and his family on
> the night of 26 September 1960 by Mr. Wayne E. Watters, the principal of the

Ravenna City High School, Ravenna, Ohio. Mr. Watters lives at 7101 State Rt. 44, Ravenna Ohio.

Mrs. Watters' great-great grandfather was Symonds Ryder. It was in his belongings that these writings were found. They were found about 2 years ago rolled in a linen cloth. The Watters pressed them in books and have held them in a pressed condition until they were delivered to me on the above date. . . .

[*signature over typed name*]

William D. Daily

(Elder)

Quarters "Q" RD2

Ravenna, Ohio

Later in the 1960s, after Cowdery's three-page Articles manuscript was returned to the Church by Symonds Ryder's descendants, the archivists filed it in the LDS Church Archives' Revelations Collection. Earl Olson, a Church archivist, mistakenly cataloged the Articles as two separate documents. In a typewritten note appended to William D. Daily's September 1960 statement, Olson described the first two pages of the Articles as "A supposed revelation to Oliver Cowdery, beginning: 'A commandment from God unto Oliver how he should build up his Church.'" This manuscript leaf, written on both sides, had become separated from the other half of the sheet and did not identify Cowdery as the author. The first two pages of the Articles were filed in the "Unpublished Revelations" section of the Revelations Collection and assigned a "ca. 1830" date. The other half, the third page with a blank reverse side, had the year 1829 written on it, but it was not included in the Revelations Collection. Olson described this page as simply "A supposed revelation to Oliver Cowdery, 1829, beginning: 'And now I speak unto the Church.'" Cowdery's Articles document, recently deacidified and reattached, has since been moved to a collection of Oliver Cowdery's personal papers. A photocopy of William D. Daily's statement is in the author's possession.

71. Compare with Book of Commandments 15:4. See also 1835 D&C 43:1 and current D&C 18:5.

72. The phrase "my church, my gospel, and my rock" is in Book of Commandments 15:3. See also 1835 D&C 43:1 and current D&C 18:4–5.

73. First published in Book of Commandments 15:5. A descriptive summary of the revelation's contents is included in the chapter heading to Book of Commandments 15 and reads in part "and also, instructions relative to building up the church of Christ, according to the fulness of the gospel." This revelation was received by June 14, 1829, as evidenced by Oliver Cowdery using excerpts of the revelation in a letter written that day to Hyrum Smith from Fayette, New York. A retained copy of the letter is found in Joseph Smith Letterbook 1:5–6, Joseph Smith Collection, LDS Church Archives. See also 1835 D&C 43:2 and current D&C 18:6.

74. Compare with Book of Commandments 15:11. See also 1835 D&C 43:3 and current D&C 18:9.

75. Compare with Book of Mormon Printer's Manuscript, 381; published in *The Printer's Manuscript of the Book of Mormon*, ed. Royal Skousen, 2 vols. (Provo, UT: Foundation for Ancient Research and Mormon Studies, Brigham Young University, 2001), 2:813; and 1830 Book of Mormon, [3rd] Nephi, chapter 5 (p. 478). See current 3 Nephi 11:23 and D&C 20:37.

76. Compare with Printer's Manuscript, 381; published in Skousen, *Printer's Manuscript*, 2:813; 1830 Book of Mormon, [3ʳᵈ] Nephi, chapter 5 (p. 478); current 3 Nephi 11:23–27. The Printer's Manuscript that corresponds to 3 Nephi 11:25 reads: "~~having authority~~ <Having authority> given me of Jesus Christ." This change, which only adds capitalization, is in Oliver Cowdery's handwriting; it appears from the similar ink color to be contemporary (ca. second half of 1829). It is not known whether the capitalization of *having* first occurred with Cowdery's Articles or the Printer's Manuscript or the no longer extant original Book of Mormon dictation manuscript. Compare Alma's prior usage of "having authority" (second century BC) in his earlier form of the baptismal prayer: Printer's Manuscript, 145; published in Skousen, *Printer's Manuscript*, 1:341; 1830 Book of Mormon, Mosiah, chapter 4 (p. 192); and current Mosiah 18:13. All of the earliest manuscript copies of the Articles and Covenants use the Book of Mormon phraseology, "Having authority given me of Jesus Christ," from the baptismal prayer form given by the Savior when he appeared to the Nephites in Bountiful. Printer's Manuscript, 381; published in Skousen, *Printer's Manuscript*, 2:813; 1830 Book of Mormon, [3ʳᵈ] Nephi, chapter 5 (p. 478); current 3 Nephi 11:25. The wording was modified by the Prophet Joseph Smith when the Articles and Covenants was published in the 1835 D&C (2:22) and reads "Having been commissioned of Jesus Christ." The wording in the current D&C 20:73 is the same as in the 1835 D&C.

77. Compare with Printer's Manuscript, 454; published in Skousen, *Printer's Manuscript*, 2:959; 1830 Book of Mormon, Moroni, chapter 3 (p. 575); and current Moroni 3:4. Similar wording is used in the current D&C 20:60.

78. Parentheses enclose "or if he be a teacher" in 1830 Book of Mormon, Moroni, chapter 3 (p. 575); the same words are also enclosed in the current Moroni 3:3. The Printer's Manuscript, 454, does not use parentheses for this phrase. Published in Skousen, *Printer's Manuscript*, 2:959.

79. This part of the paragraph is also based upon material found in Printer's Manuscript, 454; published in Skousen, *Printer's Manuscript*, 2:959; 1830 Book of Mormon, Moroni, chapter 3 (p. 575); and current Moroni 3:3. Joseph Smith, in composing the Articles and Covenants for the Church in mid-1830, did not give defined wording for priesthood ordinations. This direction of the Prophet harmonized with the last sentence of the 1830 Book of Mormon, Moroni, chapter 3 (p. 575), indicating that priesthood ordinations were to be given "by the power of the Holy Ghost, which was in them." See current D&C 20:60 and Moroni 3:4.

80. Printer's Manuscript, 392–93; published in Skousen, *Printer's Manuscript*, 2:835–36; 1830 Book of Mormon, [3ʳᵈ] Nephi, chapter 8 (p. 492); and current 3 Nephi 18:22, 30, 32 describe the Savior teaching the Nephites that Church members should not cast out the weak in faith unless those lacking in testimony refuse to repent.

81. The phrase "And the Church shall oft partake of bread and wine" is paraphrased from Printer's Manuscript, 455; published in Skousen, *Printer's Manuscript*, 2:960; 1830 Book of Mormon, Moroni, chapter 6 (p. 576); and current Moroni 6:6. See also current D&C 20:75.

82. The wording varies slightly between the current editions of the Book of Mormon and the Doctrine and Covenants. The current Moroni 4:3 reads "hath," while D&C 20:77 reads "has."

83. Compare with Printer's Manuscript, 454; published in Skousen, *Printer's Manuscript*, 2:959; 1830 Book of Mormon, Moroni, chapter 4 (p. 575); and current Moroni 4:3. See also current D&C 20:77.

84. Compare with Printer's Manuscript, 454; published in Skousen, *Printer's Manuscript*, 2:959; 1830 Book of Mormon, Moroni, chapter 4 (pp. 575–76); and current Moroni 5:1–2. See also current D&C 20:78–79.

85. The phrase "I give unto you a commandment" appears to be a paraphrase by Oliver. Printer's Manuscript, 392 (published in Skousen, *Printer's Manuscript*, 2:835) reads: "& now behold this is the commandment which I give unto you." All published sources follow the printer's manuscript wording.

86. Compare with Printer's Manuscript, 392–93; published in Skousen, *Printer's Manuscript*, 2:835–36; 1830 Book of Mormon, [3rd] Nephi, chapter 8 (p. 492); and current 3 Nephi 18:28–33.

87. A similar warning, given to the latter-day Gentiles by the Lord through the prophet Mormon, is in Printer's Manuscript, 410; published in Skousen, *Printer's Manuscript*, 2:870; 1830 Book of Mormon, [3rd] Nephi, chapter 14 (p. 513); and current 3 Nephi 30:2.

88. Identical wording of the phrase "Repent all ye ends of the Earth and come unto me and be baptized in my name" is found in Printer's Manuscript, 406; published in Skousen, *Printer's Manuscript*, 2:862; 1830 Book of Mormon, [3rd] Nephi, chapter 12 (p. 508); and current 3 Nephi 27:20. See also current Ether 4:18 and Moroni 7:34.

89. The block beginning "which is Jesus Christ" is from Book of Commandments 15:23–26. See 1835 D&C 43:4 and current D&C 18:22–25.

90. This material is paraphrased from Book of Commandments 15:34. See 1835 D&C 43:5 and current D&C 18:31.

91. The wording here is from another modern revelation also received in June 1829 and first published in the 1835 D&C 42:3; see current D&C 17:8. The phrase "my grace is sufficient for you" is actually found in both June 1829 revelations; see current D&C 17:8 and 18:31.

92. This material is nearly verbatim from the earliest revelation given on Oliver's behalf through the Prophet Joseph Smith in April 1829. See Book of Commandments 5:10; 1835 D&C 8:10; and current D&C 6:21. The phrase "Behold I am Jesus Christ the Son of the liveing God I am the same which came unto my own and my own received me not" is also a direct quote of Printer's Manuscript, 378; published in Skousen, *Printer's Manuscript*, 2:807; 1830 Book of Mormon, [3rd] Nephi, chapter 4 (p. 473); and current 3 Nephi 9:15, 16.

93. This phrase is from material later published in Book of Commandments 15:37; 1835 D&C 43:5; and current D&C 18:34.

94. This phrase is an expanded form of Book of Commandments 9:19; 1835 D&C 36:18; and current D&C 10:70. The Savior's voice, just prior to his postmortal ministry to the people of Nephi in the land Bountiful, testified that he was "the light and the life of the world" similar to the phrase quoted here. See Printer's Manuscript, 378; published in Skousen, *Printer's Manuscript*, 2:807; 1830 Book of Mormon, [3rd] Nephi, chapter 4 (p. 473); and current 3 Nephi 9:18. This description of the Savior is also found in other places in the Book of Mormon (Mosiah 16:9, Alma 38:9, 3 Nephi 11:11, and Ether 4:12).

95. This material is paraphrased from Book of Commandments 15:50; 1835 D&C 43:7; and current D&C 18:47.

96. Paraphrased from Printer's Manuscript, 436; published in Skousen, *Printer's Manuscript*, 2:922; 1830 Book of Mormon, Ether, chapter 2 (p. 548); and current Ether 5:6.

97. The same phrase "Now may the grace of God the Father and of our Lord Jesus Christ be and abide with you all" is used by Oliver Cowdery in his June 14, 1829, letter to Hyrum Smith. See retained copy in Joseph Smith Letterbook 1:6 (5–6), Joseph Smith Collection, LDS Church Archives.

98. The wording here about "a burning fire shut up in my bones" and so forth is paraphrased from Jeremiah 20:9. Ezra Booth, who apostatized from the Church in fall 1831, was shown this document (presumably by fellow dissident Symonds Ryder who allegedly took it from Church headquarters during summer 1831), and he (Booth) quoted this paraphrase of Jeremiah in one of his letters critical of Mormonism that was published in an Ohio newspaper. See Ezra Booth to Rev. I. Eddy, Letter 8, November 29, 1831, "Mormonism," *The Ohio Star*, December 8, 1831, 1.

99. The "&c." (for "etc.") has been misread as being "O.C.", Oliver Cowdery's initials, but careful examination of the original manuscript confirms the reading of "&c."

The Impact of the First Preaching in Ohio

Richard Lloyd Anderson

Specific plans to preach the restored gospel in the West matured during the second conference after Church organization, held late September 1830. Members gathered near Waterloo, New York, to transact business for an essentially New York Church of fewer than a hundred members. Even before the conference assembled at the Whitmer home in Fayette township, a revelation was given to the "second elder" regarding a proposed mission to Indian territory just west of Missouri:

> Thou shalt take thy journey among the Lamanites. And it shall be given thee from the time that thou shalt go, until the time that thou shalt return, what thou shalt do. And thou must open thy mouth at all times, declaring my gospel with the sound of rejoicing.[1]

During the conference a revelation formally designated Peter Whitmer Jr. as junior companion to Oliver Cowdery in this mission.[2] Oliver Cowdery was then Mormonism's most eloquent spokesman, standing next to Joseph Smith in Church government and in prominence as a witness of the early visions. The importance of the Western mission is evident from the fact that he headed it.

This conference set significant precedents for Church administration. However, the missionary theme was prominent during its three days duration. The official minutes not only give the date of convening as September 26, 1830, but also summarize what was probably the first missionary farewell in LDS history: "Singing and prayer in behalf of Brother Oliver Cowdery and Peter Whitmer, Jr., who were previously appointed to go to the Lamanites."[3]

Two companions were soon added, Ziba Peterson and the dynamic Parley P. Pratt, neither of whom are mentioned in the September conference minutes. Pratt had been converted by reading the Book of Mormon and talking at length with Hyrum Smith and other Book of Mormon witnesses. After Oliver Cowdery baptized him "about the first of September, A.D. 1830," Parley P. Pratt then traveled some 200 miles east to Columbia County, New York, where he baptized his brother Orson on September 19 and soon left to return to Church headquarters.[4] Pratt later recalled details:

> Returning to western New York the same autumn, I saw for the first time Joseph Smith, the Prophet, at his father's house in Manchester, heard him preach, and preached in his house, at the close of which meeting we baptized seven persons. After this he inquired of the Lord, and received a Revelation appointing me a mission to the west, in company with Oliver Cowdery, Peter Whitmer, Jr., and Ziba Peterson. We started this mission in October, 1830.[5]

The first printing of the revelation calling Pratt and Peterson confirms the October 1830 date and promises, "I myself will go with them and be in their midst—and I am their advocate with the Father, and nothing shall prevail."[6] Such words do not overstate the power of their preaching in Ohio. The October departure appears in another source, Peter Whitmer's unsophisticated but tersely eloquent survey of their mission: "The word of the Lord came unto me by the Prophet Joseph Smith on the tenth month, saying, "Peter, thou shalt go with thy brother Oliver to the Lamanites. We started on the same month to the west."[7]

In outfitting these men for their long journey, the women of the Church played an unpublicized role. Joseph Smith mentioned that "preparations were made for the journey of the brethren"; his mother was more specific:

As soon as this revelation was received, Emma Smith and several other sisters began to make arrangements to furnish those who were set apart for this mission with the necessary clothing, which was no easy task, as the most of it had to be manufactured out of the raw material. Emma's health at this time was quite delicate; yet she did not favor herself on this account. But whatever her hands found to do, she did with her might, until she went so far beyond her strength that she brought upon herself a heavy fit of sickness, which lasted four weeks.[8]

Loved ones were left behind. Thankful Halsey Pratt lived in the Peter Whitmer Sr. household while her husband filled his missionary call.

Pratt's autobiography sets departure as "late in October."[9] This harmonizes with a remarkable document from an unusual source. The Methodist preacher Ezra Booth was converted after the first missionaries left Ohio; in his short career as a skeptical Mormon he gathered information to expose the Church. His "inside story" was printed in the *Ohio Star* during the last three months of 1831 and principally contained his many complaints and doubts concerning his mission to Missouri earlier that year. The source is filled with hearsay and sarcastic narrative (a technique certain to distort history); however, the Booth letters are the first printed source for the revelation of Joseph Smith, mostly reproduced in short extracts. Booth obviously could quote documents without eroding them with his acrid bias. His quotations are generally accurate, particularly the fairly long revelations calling Oliver Cowdery on the Lamanite mission.[10] (Revelations were circulated in private copies before the first printed edition in 1833; Joseph Smith recalled one presented to the Western missionaries: "a copy of the Revelation was given them.")[11] Since Booth responsibly copied the Oliver Cowdery revelation, an associated document very probably originated from a manuscript source. It is a covenant of cooperation among the four missionaries, filled with faith and humility in the face of their challenging task:

Manchester, Oct. 17, 1830

I, Oliver, being commanded of the Lord God to go forth unto
the Lamanites to proclaim glad tidings of great joy unto them by
presenting unto them the fulness of the gospel of the only begot-
ten son of God, and also to rear up a pillar as a witness where
the temple of God shall be built in the glorious New Jerusalem;
and having certain brothers with me who are called of God to
assist me, whose names are Parley, Peter, and Ziba, do therefore
most solemnly covenant before God that I will walk humbly before him and do this business and this glorious work according as
he shall direct me by the Holy Ghost, ever praying for mine and
their prosperity and deliverance from bonds and from imprisonments and whatsoever may befall us, with all patience and faith.
Amen.

OLIVER COWDERY

We, the undersigned, being called and commanded of the Lord
God, to accompany our brother Oliver Cowdery to go to the
Lamanites and to assist in the above mentioned glorious work
and business; we do therefore most solemnly covenant before
God that we will assist him faithfully in this thing by giving heed
unto all his words and advice which [are] or shall be given him
by the spirit of truth, ever praying with all prayer and supplication for our and his prosperity and our deliverance from bonds
and imprisonments and whatsoever may come upon us, with all
patience and faith. Amen.

Signed in presence of

P. P. PRATT

JOSEPH SMITH, Jr.   ZIBA PETERSON

DAVID WHITMER   PETER WHITMER[12]

Paul-like, the four missionaries walked eighty miles west to
Buffalo, where they spoke to an Indian group about the Book of
Mormon as a record of their ancestors and left copies with those who
could read. But the most dramatic scene of the mission opened 200
miles further west near Cleveland, Ohio. Parley P. Pratt earlier had
been converted to the Disciples' movement when the noted Sidney

Rigdon had come into Pratt's neighborhood west of Cleveland (Lorain Co.) in 1829. Now the tables were turned as Pratt sought out Sidney Rigdon with a more thoroughgoing restorationism than Rigdon had once presented Pratt. The Mormon elders arrived in Rigdon's locality to declare new revelation, and the re-creation of the spiritual power enshrined as a dead letter in the Bible. Rigdon and scores of careful Bible readers were affected.[13]

In a few short weeks the restored Church of Christ had as many members in Ohio as in New York. The earliest sources agree on the number of conversions. The short "journal" of eyewitness Peter Whitmer Jr. was written in 1831 and summarizes the Ohio phase of the mission: "there we declared the fulness of the gospel and had much success. We baptized 130 members." Written the same year, the opening lines of John Whitmer's history are similar:

> They journeyed as far west as the state of Ohio, and through the divine influences of the Holy Spirit, by the assistance of the Lord they built a branch of the church in Geauga County, state of Ohio, which consisted of about 130 members.[14]

The most spectacular conversion was Sidney Rigdon, and no source captures his recollections more authentically than the "History of Joseph Smith," written and published while Rigdon was available for consultation and criticism.[15] There were searching expectations in the circles about Sidney Rigdon, but his was "the first house at which they called." The noted preacher was polite but "very much prejudiced" to hear that the Book of Mormon was an additional revelation to the Bible. Pressed in discussion, the seasoned minister declined to argue but promised: "I will read your book . . . and will endeavor to ascertain whether it be a revelation from God or not." During the next "fortnight" the missionaries returned "occasionally" to find an earnest searcher reading the Book of Mormon, "meditating on the things he heard and read," and also "praying to the Lord for direction." Finally convinced, he counted the cost (which was considerable) and fearlessly submitted to baptism.[16]

Of Parley P. Pratt's statements recounting this notable conversion, the most specific supplements the Rigdon history just
summarized:

> About the 15th of Oct., 1830, I took my journey, in company
> with Elder O. Cowdery and Peter Whitmer to Ohio. We called
> on Elder S. Rigdon, and *then* for the *first* time, his eyes beheld the
> Book of Mormon; I myself had the happiness to present it to him
> in person. He was much surprised, and it was with much persua-
> sion and argument that he was prevailed on to read it. And after
> he had read it, he had a great struggle of mind before he fully
> believed and embraced it.[17]

In later life the conversion force was still powerful in the mind
of a man who had known more than his share of disillusionment.
President A. W. Cowles of Elmira College visited Sidney Rigdon in
1868 and soon after reported the interview, though with the conde-
scending style of the religious journalist. The former Mormon leader
remembered receiving the Book of Mormon and his impressions on
investigating it:

> Rigdon solemnly affirms that this was his first personal knowl-
> edge of Joe Smith and the Mormons. After a few days Cowdery
> returned and held a long interview with Rigdon. Rigdon had read
> a considerable portion of the book. He questioned Cowdery about
> Smith and found that he was entirely illiterate. Rigdon expressed
> the utmost amazement that such a man should write a book which
> seemed to shed a flood of light on all the old scriptures, open all
> their profoundest mysteries, and give them perfect consistency
> and complete system. In his fresh enthusiasm he exclaimed that if
> God ever gave a revelation, surely this must be divine.[18]

Rigdon's respect for the Book of Mormon message is confirmed
by family traditions from his son, John W. Rigdon. When informed
that Joseph Smith was a young man with "hardly a common school
education," the well-read minister replied: "if that is all the education he has got, he never wrote this book."[19] Other issues besides the
message of the Book of Mormon are prominent in Sidney Rigdon's
conversion, apparent from a detailed contemporary account pub-

lished in early 1831 over the initials M.S.C. The author was probably Matthew S. Clapp, a young and capable convert of Sidney Rigdon to the Disciples' movement in Mentor—the article reveals the Mentor congregation's experience in the conversion of their pastor.[20] Here the testimony of the Book of Mormon witnesses is stressed, for the missionaries "related the manner in which they obtained faith"— through prayer, "and an angel was shown unto them," an apparent reference to Oliver Cowdery's vision.[21] Beyond the Book of Mormon, another great issue was the source of authority to teach and baptize. "M.S.C." relates that the missionaries insisted upon rebaptizing their converts—and after "seventeen persons were immersed by them in one night," the missionaries "came next day to his house" to find a "much displeased" Sidney Rigdon, negative because he had already immersed his followers in a covenant of remission of sins.[22] Pratt recalled the resolution of the problem:

> At length Mr. Rigdon and many others became convinced that they had no authority to minister in the ordinances of God, and that they had not been legally baptized and ordained. They therefore came forward and were baptized by us, and received the gift of the Holy Ghost by the laying on of hands and prayer in the name of Jesus Christ.[23]

The conversion of Sidney Rigdon rested upon the double thrust of new revelation and restored authority, a combination quite evident in the contemporary newspaper reports. For instance, the first *Painesville Telegraph* story of the mission specifically named "Cowdray" and his teaching:

> About two weeks since some persons came along here with the book [of Mormon], one of whom pretends to have seen angels and assisted in translating the plates. He proclaims destruction upon the world within a few years, holds forth that the ordinances of the gospel have not been regularly administered since the days of the apostles till the said Smith and himself commenced the work. ... In the neighboring township of Kirtland, we understand that twenty or thirty have been immersed into the new order of things, many of whom had been previously baptized.[24]

At their first interview the missionaries had requested Rigdon's permission to speak to the Mentor church. The open-minded leader agreed, with the following result:

> The appointment was accordingly published, and a large and re-spectable congregation assembled. Oliver Cowdery and Parley P. Pratt severally addressed the meeting. At the conclusion Elder Rigdon arose and stated to the congregation that the information they had that evening received was of an extraordinary character and certainly demanded their most serious consideration. [H]e would exhort his brethren to . . . give the matter a careful investigation and not turn against it without being fully convinced of its being an imposition, lest they should possibly resist the truth.[25]

The Mentor congregation had been created under the leadership of Rigdon, whose vigorous views of the restoration of the primitive gifts went beyond Campbellite concepts. John Murdock, brother-in-law of the Clapps in the Mentor congregation, shared these views. A Campbellite minister living near Warrensville (southwest of Kirtland), he heard of Rigdon's investigation and other Mormon conversions as he was on his way to fill a Sunday preaching appointment. An initial angry reaction turned to curiosity, and by the following Thursday he traveled twenty miles to Kirtland to hear the new message for himself. Pratt's *Autobiography* mentions the general excitement "in Kirtland, and in all the region round about" at the news of the Book of Mormon and revelation surrounding its origin: "The people thronged us night and day, insomuch that we had no time for rest or retirement." Some came "for curiosity, some to obey the gospel, and some to dispute or resist it."[26] Murdock's more detailed autobiography portrays these situations: constant news about "the new preachers," his own journey to Kirtland, with opponents of the Mormons determined to keep him from reaching Kirtland or dissuading his interest when there, and the intense day and night conversations with the missionaries. John Murdock already believed in the literal restoration of primitive Christianity, so the essential question was whether the Mormon missionaries were imposters or authentic servants of God:

> I said, if it be so, their walk will agree with their profession, and the Holy Ghost will attend their ministration of the ordinances, and the Book of Mormon will contain the same plan of salvation as the Bible. . . . I did not ask a sign of them by working a miracle. . . . For I did not believe that the spirit would attend their ministration if the Book of Mormon was not true, neither if they were not sent forth of God.[27]

Murdock remembered that night as "the first confirmation meeting that was held in Ohio."[28] Although he did not attend, he carefully questioned a half dozen who had been confirmed: "I found their testimony agreed on the subject that there was a manifestation of the spirit attended the ministration of the ordinance of laying on hands."[29] In the meantime he formed a first impression of the motives of Oliver Cowdery and a Campbellite opposer:

> And I watched the spirit of each one of them in their conversation, and I found that Goodwell bore down with warmth, whereas Cowdery wished not for contention and endeavored to evade controversy.[30]

While the confirmation meeting was held, Murdock read the Book of Mormon; when the group returned, "the spirit of the Lord rested on me, witnessing to me of the truth of the work."[31] The next morning he requested baptism, which was performed by Parley P. Pratt in the Chagrin River:

> And the spirit of the Lord sensibly attended the ministration, and I came out of the water rejoicing and singing praises to God and the Lamb. An impression sensibly rested on my mind that cannot by me be forgotten. This was the third time that I had been immersed, but I never before felt the authority of the ordinance. But I felt it this time and felt as though my sins were forgiven. I continued with the brethren till Sunday, at which time they preached in Mayfield and baptized a number. And on Sunday evening they confirmed about thirty. I was one of the number.[32]

Murdock gave the date of his baptism as November 5, so the Mayfield meeting just mentioned was Sunday, November 7, and Levi Hancock was probably there. Single and twenty-seven years of age, he heard the news of the four men with the revealed book from his brother, who mentioned a Sunday meeting and reported their practice of baptizing and bestowing the Holy Ghost:

> At these last words I gathered faith, and there seemed to fall on me something pleasant and delightful. It seemed like a wash of something warm took me in the face and ran over my body, which gave me that feeling I cannot describe. The first word I said was, "It is the truth—I feel it I will go and hear for myself tomorrow."[33]

The next morning Hancock accompanied his family to Mayfield, taking his mother on the horse behind him. A crowd assembled there at the Jackson home:

> I got in the chamber where there had been a few boards pulled up (which had been laid down loose before) to give the spectators a fair chance to hearing. In the chamber I took a seat beside a lawyer by the name of Card. He sat with his pencil and paper and commenced to scribble as the speaker arose and began to talk.

This first speaker was Parley P. Pratt, who told of Christ's ministry in the Book of Mormon, and afterwards stressed "that there must be something sent from God in order to prepare the people for the glorious reign of Christ."[34] Sidney Rigdon spoke next, apparently prior to his baptism, for he expressed doubt that he should preach again "and advised the people not to contend against what they had heard." The final speaker was undoubtedly Oliver Cowdery:

> There arose another young man whose countenance bespoke a spirit of peace and love. He said he had been an eye witness to the things declared, and the book reported to be a revelation was truth, however strange it may appear to the people.[35]

Levi Hancock's father and sister were baptized that day, and the first of the week Levi followed the missionaries to Kirtland and requested baptism of Parley P. Pratt. Pratt's *Autobiography* recalls that "meetings were convened in different neighborhoods," and the Hancock record illustrates this. He returned to Mayfield with Oliver Cowdery's promise to follow. Hancock and Lyman Wight spoke there on one evening, followed the next day by Cowdery, Peterson, and Whitmer. "They held meetings and baptized some, and in the evening they confirmed many members in the church."[36]

At this time Lyman Wight was in the midst of his own investigation of the Mormon claims, and his story illustrates how fully prepared for conversion a number in his circle were. Filled with a desire to comply strictly with the early Christian order, Wight, Isaac Morley, and others had entered into a covenant to hold "all things common."

> In conformity to this covenant I moved the next February [1830] to Kirtland, into the house with Bro. Morley. We commenced our labors together with great peace and union. We were soon joined by eight other families. Our labors were united both in farming and mechanism, all of which was prosecuted with great vigor. We truly began to feel as if the millennium was close at hand.[37]

About the beginning of November, Wight had been appointed to move seven miles from Kirtland to Mayfield and take charge of five families who would become a branch of this society:

> When I had my goods about half loaded, there came along four men (namely P. Pratt, O. Cowdery, P. Whitmer, and Ziba Peterson) and brought with them the Book of Mormon, which they wished to introduce to us. I desired they would hold on till I got away, as my business was of vital importance, and I did not wish to be troubled with romances nor idle speculations. But nothing daunted, they were not to be put off, but were as good-natured as you please. Curiosity got uppermost, and I concluded to stop for a short time. We called meeting, and one testified that he had seen angels, and another that he had seen the plates, and that the gifts were back in the church again, etc. The meeting became so interesting withal that I did not get away till the sun was about an hour high at night, and it was dark before I arrived at my new home.[38]

With pressing duties, Wight dismissed the episode by assuming that the missionaries would immediately travel on to Missouri. As discussed, however, they followed him to his new home of Mayfield.

Wight despaired of giving full details of the elders' stay on the
Western Reserve, but summarized: "I shall therefore content myself
by saying that they brought the Book of Mormon to bear upon us,
and the whole of the common stock family was baptized."[39]

The four missionaries were not the only ones "who brought the
Book of Mormon to bear." After his conversion trip to Kirtland and
Mayfield, John Murdock returned to his home (Orange Township)
to ignite interest in a new area:

> I endeavored to bear testimony to my neighbors whom I met by
> the way, but they would not believe. At length I arrived home. My
> family gladly received me and my words, thank the Lord. And my
> wife and Brother Covey both believed the Book of Mormon, for I
> brought it home with me and read it to them, and I was filled with
> the spirit as I read. At length the first day of the next week ar-
> rived, and the New York brethren held meeting in Warrensville,
> four miles west of my house, and I bore testimony to the truth.
> My wife, Brother Covey, and three others were baptized. Brother
> Ziba Peterson held meeting in my house the evening before, and I
> bore testimony to my neighbors.[40]

Kirtland was base of operations for the New York missionaries after their initial contact with Rigdon at Mentor. As Wight
indicated, Kirtland was headquarters for Isaac Morley's "family,"
which attempted to live the early Christian economic order. Those
who already believed in the experiences and programs of the book
of Acts were obviously ripe for a restored gospel. Through the New
Testament they knew vividly of eyewitnesses of revelation, of religious leaders called by God and authorized by the laying on of
hands, of baptism by immersion for the remission of sins, and of the
laying on of hands for the gift of the Holy Ghost (neglected by even
Christian restorationists). The Rigdon-oriented official history gives
an overview of the success with the Kirtland "family":

> About two miles from Elder Rigdon's, at the town of Kirtland,
> were a number of the members of his church, who lived together
> and had all things common ... to which place they immedi-
> ately repaired, and proclaimed the gospel to them, with some

considerable success. For their testimony was received by many of the people, and seventeen came forward in obedience to the gospel.[41]

This number corresponds to the seventeen baptisms that "M.S.C." claimed had at first offended Rigdon. In fact, by November 16, the *Painesville Telegraph* editor had heard of "twenty or thirty" baptisms at Kirtland.[42]

Rigdon's influence and presence was significant at Kirtland in the "fortnight" of his investigation. As a matter of fact, he was baptized there about November 15, and his public profession at Kirtland touched many. "M.S.C." set his baptism on a Monday and reported the surrounding events with a tone of irony:

> The Monday following he was baptized. On the morning of the preceding day he had an appointment to preach in the Methodist chapel at Kirtland. He arose to address the congregation *apparently* much affected and deeply impressed. He seemed exceedingly humble, confessed the sins of his former life, his great pride, ambition, vainglory, etc., etc. After he was baptized, he professed to be exceedingly joyful, and said he would not be where he was three days ago for the universe.[43]

Parley P. Pratt evidently describes the same sermon in giving other details of Sidney Rigdon's baptism:

> And when finally convinced of its truth, he called together a large congregation of his friends, neighbors, and brethren, and then addressed them very affectionately for near two hours, during most of which time both himself and nearly all the congregation were melted into tears. He asked forgiveness of everybody who might have had occasion to be offended with any part of his former life. He forgave all who had persecuted or injured him in any manner. And the next morning, himself and wife were baptized by Elder O. Cowdery. I was present—it was a solemn scene. Most of the people were greatly affected. They came out of the water overwhelmed in tears.[44]

The firstfruits in Ohio were by no means confined to the Rigdon circle of disciples. An example of an outsider to these connections

is Philo Dibble, newly married and 24, who had recently settled on
land five miles east of Kirtland. By way of ridicule he was told "that
four men had come to Kirtland with a golden Bible, and one of them
had seen an angel." Dibble "did not feel inclined to make light of
such a subject," however, but "thought that if angels had administered to the children of men again, I was glad of it; I was afraid,
however, it was not true." The next morning he and his wife drove
the carriage to "hunt up those strange men in Kirtland."[45] Since the
missionaries were in Mayfield that day, Dibble and his wife returned
the next day, accompanied by a neighboring family. They met the
four New York missionaries:

> I remained with them all day, and became convinced that they
> were sincere in their professions. I asked Oliver what repentance
> consisted of, and he replied, "Forsaking sin and yielding obedi-
> ence to the gospel." That evening he preached at Brother Isaac
> Morley's and bore his testimony to the administration of an angel
> at noonday. He then dwelt upon the subjects of repentance and
> baptism and the bestowal of the Holy Ghost, and promised that
> all who embraced these principles with honesty of heart should
> receive a testimony.[46]

The meeting closed with Dibble, William Cahoon, and three
other persons standing in response to Cowdery's invitation to
indicate willingness for baptism. Against his wife's cautions, Philo
Dibble was baptized and describes his elation afterward:

> When I came out of the water I knew that I had been born of wa-
> ter and of the spirit, for my mind was illuminated with the Holy
> Ghost. I spent that evening at Dr. F. G. Williams. While in bed
> that night I felt what appeared to be a hand upon my left shoulder,
> and a sensation like fibers of fire immediately enveloped my body.
> . . . I was enveloped in a heavenly influence and could not sleep
> for joy. The next morning I started home a happy man.[47]

Dibble's conversion is typical in beginning with Oliver
Cowdery's testimony and ending with a personal witness. The
man whose name headed the Testimony of Three Witnesses in the
Book of Mormon insisted on the reality of seeing angels in his Ohio

preaching in 1830, evidenced by Mormon and non-Mormon alike, including several newspaper articles reporting the same thing. If a supernatural experience is easy to allege, it is more difficult to give the personal impression of sincerity. The sources on Cowdery's Ohio preaching in 1830 furnish the means of measuring the man who claimed to have stood in the presence of angels. This Book of Mormon witness was no fanatic, but a man of firm and quiet assurance. Edward Partridge was a mature businessman who was skeptical of the claims of Christian ministers when the four New York missionaries called at his hatter's shop in Painesville and presented the Book of Mormon. Lydia Partridge remembered the confrontation:

> He told them he did not believe what they said, but believed them to be imposters. Oliver Cowdery said he was thankful there was a God in heaven who knew the hearts of all men. After the men were gone my husband sent a man to follow them and get one of their books.[48]

Similarly, the reception at the Shaker community at North Union was cool, but their iron-willed leader nevertheless considered Cowdery's deportment consistent with his claim. Ashbel Kitchell's journal noted that the missionaries caused "a good deal of excitement" in the Kirtland area, followed by their visit of "two nights and one day" at the Shaker community of North Union:

> Late in the fall a member of that society came to our house to visit the Believers. His name was Oliver Cowdrey. He stated that he had been one who assisted in the translation of the golden Bible, and had seen the angel, and also had been commissioned by him to go out and bear testimony that God would destroy this generation. By his request we gave liberty for him to bear his testimony in our meeting. But finding he had nothing for us, we treated him kindly and labored to find out their manner of spirit. He appeared meek and mild.[49]

This impression of Cowdery is generally found in the records of the Kirtland preaching. John Corrill, shocked at the effrontery of Mormon claims and worried about the conversion of his

Campbellite friends, traveled thirty miles to challenge the missionaries personally at Mentor: "I felt indignant and sought an argument with Oliver Cowdery, who refused."[50] The appraisals of several converts have already been mentioned. The blunt Lyman Wight sought to avoid hearing the new message, but the missionaries "were not to be put off, but were as good-natured as you please." John Murdock observed an antagonist bear down "with warmth" upon Cowdery, who "wished not for contention and endeavored to evade controversy." Levi Hancock reported that the speaker who "had been an eye witness to the things declared" was a "young man whose countenance bespoke a spirit of peace and love."

Such experiences show clearly why Philo Dibble could travel to Kirtland to find out whether an angel had really appeared, and conclude that the four missionaries "were sincere in their professions." Their conviction overshadowed a clear lack of polish. Orson Hyde was a young Campbellite preacher of some education and promise. The elders traveled west from the Cleveland area to his station near Elyria, and he could not easily dismiss their declarations:

> I encountered them, but perceiving that they were mostly illiterate men, and at the same time observing some examples of superior wisdom and truth in their teaching, I resolved to read the famed "golden Bible," as it was called.[51]

The religious integrity of the first Ohio Mormons is clear. Irresponsible emotionalism does not characterize their beginnings on the Western Reserve. Excesses came later, but these were criticized by Mormon leaders and also by the first converts studied here. On the whole these pioneer Mormons had an impressive background of Bible study. Lydia Partridge probably speaks for the majority of the 1830 converts: "I was induced to believe for the reason that I saw the gospel in its plainness as it was taught in the New Testament, and I also knew that none of the sects of the day taught those things."[52] In her own terms, she had joined "the Campbellite Church," but she was in reality a "Rigdonite," baptized by him and having faith in some form of modern revelation and spiritual gifts.

The missionaries brought not only the Book of Mormon but full faith in the book of Acts, with the laying on of hands for the gift of the Holy Ghost and its accompanying spirituality. Spiritual out-pourings which followed duplicated early Christian experiences.

These "gifts" were not automatic but came from intense inquiry, in which reading the Book of Mormon was stressed. Ashbel Kitchell explained why Oliver Cowdery left seven copies at the Shaker community:

> This Mormon appeared to have full faith in their books, that whosoever would read them, would feel so thoroughly convinced of the truth of what they contained, that they would be unable to resist and would finally be obliged to unite with them. He then thought it prudent to wait for us a while for the leaven to work.[53]

In this case the challenge was rather weakly accepted. The seven copies of the Book of Mormon were distributed, but "they were soon returned as not interesting enough to keep one awake while read-ing."[54] Conversions through the Book of Mormon were of varied duration. Some knew immediately, some in weeks, and some only after long months of considering. Orson Hyde obtained a Book of Mormon "and read a portion of it, but came to the conclusion that it was all fiction." After preaching against it, he honestly assessed his lack of knowledge of the book, and moved to Kirtland for serious investigation: "After about three months of careful and prayerful investigation. . . . I came to the conclusion that the Mormons had more light and a better spirit than their opponents."[55]

Early Ohio conversions that did not last are consistent with those that have been examined. A noted instance of semi-conversion is illuminating. In his first Mormon meeting (at Mayfield) Levi Hancock sat by the young lawyer Card, who was taking notes. Apparently at a later Sunday, after Rigdon's baptism and ordination, Varnum J. Card came to Mayfield accompanied by his friend John Barr. Cowdery and Rigdon spoke at a morning meeting, and Rigdon baptized in mid-afternoon. In the midst of a moving service, "Mr. Card suddenly seized my arm and said, 'Take me away.'" Card's face was "pale," and "his frame trembled as we walked away and mounted our horses." Regaining his composure, Varnum Card evaluated his experience: "'Mr. Barr, if you had not been there, I certainly should have gone into the water.' He said the impulse was irresistible."[56]

John Corrill investigated Mormonism while Oliver Cowdery and Peter Whitmer Jr. were first in Kirtland—and was baptized some six weeks later. Disillusioned at the Mormon persecutions in Missouri, he left the Church and wrote a careful appraisal of his LDS career. His conversion contained both rational and spiritual elements; on renouncing Mormonism, Corrill explained away neither approach. He had "made very diligent inquiry" concerning the origin of the Book of Mormon and was certain that Smith was the author:

> As to its being a revelation from God, eleven persons besides Smith bore positive testimony of its truth. After getting acquainted with them, I was unable to impeach their testimony.[57]

Corrill attended a Kirtland confirmation meeting in which he sought "to detect their hypocrisy" with "a jealous eye." The ordinances of the sacrament of the Lord's supper and the laying on of hands were followed by a testimony meeting in which prophecy and speaking in tongues were prominent:

> I watched closely and examined carefully every movement of the meeting, and after exhausting all my powers to find the deception, I was obliged to acknowledge in my own mind that the meeting had been inspired by some supernatural agency.[58]

During the ensuing winter Ezra Booth and Symonds Ryder were converted, only to be deconverted within a short time. Ryder's attitude on leaving is known, and Booth's long exposé (as earlier discussed) was printed. They both lapsed because of human qualities in a divine organization. Yet neither convincingly dismisses the spirituality of their conversions. Booth wrote:

> When I embraced Mormonism, I conscientiously believed it to be of God. The impressions of my mind were deep and powerful, and my feelings were exerted to a degree to which I had been a

stranger. Like a ghost, it haunted me by night and day, until I was mysteriously hurried, as it were, by a kind of necessity, into the vortex of delusion.[59]

Booth's friend Ryder assessed the apparent integrity of those who founded the new religion, an issue that began for the Ohio converts with Oliver Cowdery and Peter Whitmer Jr. but immediately included Joseph Smith himself. Almost three decades later Ryder recalled his first impressions:

> In the winter of 1831 Joseph Smith with others had an appointment in the south school house in Hiram. Such was the apparent piety, sincerity and humility of the speakers, that many of the hearers were greatly affected and thought it impossible that such preachers should lie in wait to deceive.[60]

The possibility of deception dictated the countermission of Sidney Rigdon and Edward Partridge to the New York neighborhood of Joseph Smith. "M.S.C." wrote contemporaneously that Rigdon left for New York "about three weeks after" his baptism. By then the four New York missionaries had resumed their journey to Missouri, taking the Kirtland convert Frederick G. Williams as an ordained companion, and leaving the Ohio saints under the new elders Sidney Rigdon, John Murdock, and Lyman Wight. In the words of Lydia Partridge, at this time "my husband partly believed, but he had to take a journey to New York State and see the Prophet."[61] Several sources establish the trip as a fact-finding mission. John Corrill perhaps confuses personalities but gives his understanding of the visit's purpose: "After Rigdon had joined the Church in Kirtland, he was afraid that he had been deceived, so he and Edward Partridge went to the state of New York to inquire further into it."[62] According to Philo Dibble, Partridge also went on behalf of several others. A skeptical neighbor identified Partridge and his business: "We have sent a man down to York State to find out the truth of this work, and he is a man who will not lie."[63] John Whitmer's contemporary history indicates the openness of Partridge's inquiries: "he being desirous to know the truth of these things, but not having confidence enough to inquire at the hand of God; therefore, he sought testimony of man, and he obtained it."[64] Lucy Mack Smith recalled the arrival of Rigdon and Partridge while a meeting was in progress at Waterloo, New York. When Joseph Smith finished speaking, he extended an opportunity for spontaneous remarks:

> Upon this Mr. Partridge arose and stated that he had been to Manchester, with the view of obtaining further information respecting the doctrine which we preached. But not finding us, he had made some inquiry of our neighbors concerning our characters, which they stated had been unimpeachable until Joseph deceived us relative to the Book of Mormon. . . . [H]aving heard that our veracity was not questioned upon any other point than that of our religion, he believed our testimony and was ready to be baptized.[65]

Partridge wrote a letter from New York disclosing his belief and baptism to his nonmember friends—perhaps with dubious results, for it only caused Philo Dibble's neighbor to avoid him.[66] Rigdon and Partridge were back in Ohio by February 1, and Rigdon confirmed their findings:

> [He] commenced a long detail of his researches after the character of Joseph Smith. He declared that even his enemies had nothing to say against his character. He had brought a transcript from the docket of two magistrates, where Smith had been tried as a disturber of the peace, which testified that he was honorably acquitted.[67]

The above episode illustrates the continuing effect of the preaching of the Cowdery-Pratt mission in Ohio, for growth was just beginning as they left. The hundred converts on the Western Reserve in November 1830 were a thousand by the next summer. The missionaries, according to the contemporary "M.S.C.," had arrived "about the last of October.[68] On November 16 the *Painesville Telegraph* indicated that they had come "about two weeks since"—and John Murdock's autobiography pinpoints a report of the Mentor preaching by October 31.[69] Lyman Wight remembered the missionaries coming to him at Kirtland, "about the first of November,"[70] an episode following the first Mentor preaching. Wight also thought that they stayed "seven weeks," but this is inaccurate. The "two or three weeks" of Pratt's *Autobiography* is a corrective, but "less than four weeks" from Cowdery corresponds better with precise facts.[71] The latest dates at which the New York elders were in the Kirtland vicinity are November 18 (Wight's confirmation date) and November 20 (Wight's ordination as elder).[72] The missionaries immediately left, for by November 26 a news story had been written regarding these "deluded mortals" and the arrest of Pratt near Amherst, some fifty miles west of Kirtland.[73]

In four action-packed weeks, missionaries of the restored gospel had preached intensively in Mentor, Kirtland, and Mayfield, and they had held important meetings in North Union (in Cleveland's Shaker Heights), Warrensville, and Painesville.[74] They had saturated the Kirtland area with their message and testimony. Their newspaper valedictory reported that "the four persons . . . have proceeded on their mission to the Indians"—and accorded them a grudging tribute:

> There are rising of 100 in this and an adjoining county who have embraced the ideas and assertions of Joseph Smith, Jr., many of them respectable for intelligence and piety.[75]

Although the Missouri phase deserves to be fully narrated, the Lamanite Mission achieved its main success among those prepared for the message on the Western Reserve, not among Indian peoples, where political and cultural conditions were not yet ripe. The Ohio labors of Oliver Cowdery, Parley P. Pratt, and their companions doubled the membership of the Church and created a solid nucleus for rapid growth and a secure, if temporary, gathering location. One assesses the impact of four men in four weeks with a certain awe. The fields were ripe, and the hands of the harvesters sure. The documents of the rise of the Church in New York do not furnish personal records that so visibly re-create the events and emotions of the first yield in Ohio. More than any other segment of LDS history, early Kirtland reveals why the restored gospel reached independent minds and induced powerful action. In fact, a study of the conversions on the Western Reserve in 1830 has more than a little relevance for the spread of Mormonism today.

Notes

Editors' note: This article was originally published in *BYU Studies* 11/4 (1971): 474–96.

1. Book of Commandments 30; also D&C 28. The mission was inspired by Book of Mormon promises to the Indian descendants of the Lamanite race.

2. Book of Commandments 32; also D&C 30.

3. Far West Record, typescript, p. 2.

4. "History of Parley P. Pratt," *Deseret News*, May 19, 1858. For Orson Pratt's recollection of his brother's visit and his baptismal date (Orson's birthday), see "History of Orson Pratt," *Deseret News*, June 2, 1858.

5. "History of Parley P. Pratt," *Deseret News*, May 19, 1858.

6. D&C 54 (1935 ed.) also D&C 32:3 (present ed.).

7. Journal of Peter Whitmer Jr. The quoted revelation paraphrases both the September and October revelations referring to him.

8. Lucy Smith, *Biographical Sketches of Joseph Smith the Prophet, and His Progenitors for Many Generations* (Liverpool: Richards, 1853), 169. Minor editorial modifications are made in this quotation and others in the article, restricted to spelling, capitalization, and punctuation.

9. *The Autobiography of Parley Parker Pratt* (New York: Russell Brothers, 1874), 49.

10. Book of Commandments 30; also D&C 28.

11. "History of Joseph Smith, " *Times and Seasons* 4 (1843): 172; also *History of the Church*, 1:120.

12. Letter of Ezra Booth to Reverend Ira Eddy, November 24, 1831, Nelson, Ohio, cited in *Ohio Star* [Ravenna], December 8, 1831. The bracketed "are" is an editorial replacement of "is" and the names of witnesses have been placed in a separate column.

13. For Rigdon's pre-Mormon convictions of restorationism, see A. S. Hayden, *Early History of the Disciples in the Western Reserve* (Cincinnati: Chase and Hall, 1875), 191–95, 209–10, and also F. Mark McKiernan, "The Conversion of Sidney Rigdon to Mormonism," *Dialogue* 5/2 (1970): 71–78.

14. The Book of John Whitmer, ms. p. 1. The same figure was given in the *Evening and the Morning Star*, April 1833, a newspaper of which Oliver Cowdery was coeditor; see n. 71 below. Lyman Wight's Journal, discussed later in the article, also gives "130 members"; see n. 37 below. Pratt, *Autobiography*, 50, gives the number of baptisms as "127 souls." John Whitmer's location of Kirtland in Geauga County was correct at the time he wrote, though it is now in Lake County.

15. Compare the prefacing remark to the very detailed biography and conversion account: because of irresponsible beliefs about Rigdon, a "correct account" of his life will be given "from authentic sources." The most accessible authentic source was Rigdon himself. *Times and Seasons* 4 (1843): 172.

16. Ibid., 289–90; also *History of the Church*, 1:122–25.

17. Parley P. Pratt, *Mormonism Unveiled* (New York, 1838), 41.

18. A. W. Cowles, "The Mormons," *Moore's Rural New Yorker,* January 23, 1869, 61. "Entirely illiterate" is likely Cowles's phraseology, not Rigdon's.

19. John W. Rigdon, Lecture on the Early History of the Mormon Church, ms. at the LDS Historian's Office. Compare the similar lecture notes held by the Rigdon family and published by Karl Keller, "'I Never Knew a Time When I Did Not Know Joseph Smith,'" *Dialogue* 1/4 (1966): 24; compare 41–42.

20. Orson Hyde mistakes the middle initial but identifies locality in writing of the year 1829, when he "returned to Mentor and spent one season with a young man by the name of Matthew J. Clapp, at his father's house where the public library was kept. "History of Orson Hyde," *Deseret News,* May 5, 1858. Sidney Rigdon and Orris Clapp, Matthew's father, were neighbors, according to the 1830 census. For the education and religious zeal of young Clapp, see Hayden, *Early History of the Disciples,* 193, 195, 197, etc.

21. "Mormonism," *Painesville Telegraph,* February 15, 1831. This article is the source behind E. D. Howe's account in *Mormonism Unveiled* and also the main source for Hayden's account in *Early History of the Disciples.* A convenient copy of the "M.S.C." source is in Francis W. Kirkham's valuable *A New Witness for Christ in America: The Book of Mormon,* rev. ed. (Salt Lake City: Utah Printing, 1959), 2:80–87. Other articles cited are at 2:41–49.

22. *Painesville Telegraph,* February 15, 1831.

23. Pratt, *Autobiography,* 50.

24. *Painesville Telegraph,* November 16, 1830.

25. *Times and Seasons* 4 (1843): 289–90; also *History of the Church,* 1:124.

26. Pratt, *Autobiography,* 50.

27. John Murdock, Journal and Autobiography, ms. p. 12.

28. Ibid., 13.

29. Ibid., 16.

30. Ibid., 13.

31. Ibid., 15.

32. Ibid., 16.

33. Clara E. H. Lloyd, ed., *The Life of Levi W. Hancock* (n.d., n.p.), 23. Since Hancock described further preaching at Mayfield, November 7 is the Sunday that best fits the circumstances of his journal.

34. Ibid.

35. Ibid., 24.

36. Ibid.

37. Journal of Lyman Wight, cited by the careful historian-grandson Heman C. Smith, *History of the Reorganized Church of Jesus Christ of Latter Day Saints* (Independence, MO, 1951 reprint), 1:153. Competent RLDS historians think that the original has perished. The passage also mentions [Titus] Billings as making the covenant, though the 1830 census places him in Mentor, not Kirtland. Wight and Morley both appear in Kirtland on this census.

38. Ibid. "Speculators" of the second sentence has been replaced with the "speculations" of the printing of this extract in the *Saints' Herald* 29 (1882): 192. The *History* printing has been followed in retaining "withal" in the last sentence.

39. Ibid. "Of the" was probably accurately transcribed in the *History* and accidentally deleted in the *Saints' Herald* version.

40. Murdock, Journal and Autobiography, 17.

41. *Times and Seasons* 4 (1843): 290; also *History of the Church*, 1:124. "Two miles,"
made more open in the *History*, might be accurate. Adjoining townships may be meant,
not villages.

42. "The Golden Bible," *Painesville Telegraph*, November 16, 1830.

43. "M.S.C." seems to eclipse Rigdon's investigation into a week but may be quite
correct in setting a Monday baptism, which fits into Pratt's recollection of a two-day
sequence. The official narrative of Rigdon's conversion specifies conviction a "fortnight"
after receiving the Book of Mormon and baptism shortly afterward. *Times and Seasons*
4 (1843): 290; also *History of the Church*, 1:125. In 1882 Heman C. Smith reported that
his grandmother (widow of Lyman Wight) "told me a few days ago that she remembers distinctly that Sidney Rigdon was baptized the same day herself and husband were;
but perhaps not by the same person, as there were several baptizing at the same time."
Saints' Herald 29 (1882): 192. The Wight journal sets the date of baptism of the Wights:
"Myself and family were baptized by P. Pratt on the 14th of November, 1830, in Chagrin
River, at Kirtland, Ohio." *History of the Reorganized Church*, 1:154. A Monday baptism
would make the actual date November 15 and Mrs. Wight's recollection very significant
but off by one day. Some personal histories imply a Rigdon baptism very early in the
short stay of the missionaries, but none of these are firsthand and are only reporting the
rumors that attended his first Mormon investigations. Compare n. 21 above and *Comprehensive History of the Church*, 1:231–35.

44. Pratt, *Mormonism Unveiled*, 41. The quote is a direct continuation of that cited
in n. 17 above.

45. "Philo Dibble's Narrative," in *Early Scenes in Church History* (Salt Lake City: Juvenile Instructor Office, 1882), 75.

46. Ibid., 75–76.

47. Ibid., 76. William F. Cahoon's published baptism date (October 16, 1830) is an
obvious error. Compare Andrew Jenson, *Latter-day Saint Biographical Encyclopedia*
(Salt Lake City: Jenson History, 1936), 4:687.

48. Extracts from Lydia Partridge's Writings, Family History of Edward Partridge,
Jr., p. 5. This episode did not occur at Kirtland, since Lydia Partridge says that the elders
next "went to Kirtland to Isaac Morley's." Partridge's residence at Painesville is shown
by his enumeration there on the 1830 census; advertisements in the *Painesville Telegraph* during 1830 for his business accounts and "hat factory" at Painesville; his August
31, 1833, letter from Independence, Missouri: "When I left Painesville two years ago
last June, I expected to have returned again to that place the same season." *Latter-day
Saints Messenger and Advocate* 1 (January 1835): 56. Compare Cowdery's comment in
the same issue that Partridge "formerly resided" at Painesville (p. 63).

49. Journal of Ashbel Kitchell, copied by Henry C. Blinn, held by the Shaker Museum, Old Chatham, New York. A second copy exists, made by Elisha D. Blakeman,
but in this Cowdery incident the Blinn copy seems superior. I am very grateful for the
assistance of Director Robert F. W. Meader, who agrees with the above judgment. I have
spelled Cowdery's name as it apparently read in the original, assuming that the final "y"
was not correctly copied by Blinn.

50. John Corrill, *Brief History of the Church of Christ of Latter Day Saints* (St. Louis, 1839), 8.

51. "History of Orson Hyde," *Deseret News*, May 5, 1858.

52. Extracts, History of Edward Partridge, Jr., 5.

53. Journal of Kitchell, copied by Blinn.

54. Ibid.

55. "History of Orson Hyde," *Deseret News*, May 5, 1858.

56. Statement of John Barr, cited in Frederic G. Mather, *Lippincott's Magazine* 36 (1880): 206–7. Card's first name follows the spelling of the Cleveland publications and the *Directory, Cleveland and Ohio City, for the Years 1837–8* (Cleveland, 1837), in which both Card and Barr are listed as practicing attorneys.

57. Corrill, *Brief History*, 11.

58. Ibid., 9.

59. Letter of Ezra Booth to Rev. Ira Eddy, September 12, 1831, Nelson, Ohio, cited in *(Ravenna) Ohio Star*, October 13, 1831.

60. Letter of Symonds Ryder to A. S. Hayden, February 1, 1868, Hiram, Ohio, cited in Hayden, *Early History of the Disciples*, 220.

61. Extracts, History of Edward Partridge, Jr., 5.

62. Corrill, *Brief History*, 17.

63. "Philo Dibble's Narrative," 77.

64. The Book of John Whitmer, ms. p. 2.

65. Lucy Mack Smith, *Biographical Sketches*, 170.

66. "Philo Dibble's Narrative," 77.

67. "M.S.C.," *Painesville Telegraph*, February 15, 1831.

68. Ibid.

69. Murdock's journal gives his baptism as November 5 and reports his hearing of the Mormon elders on the previous Sunday. This was October 31.

70. Wight's Journal, cited in *History of the Reorganized Church*, 153.

71. Cowdery was coeditor and presumably the source of information for this historical summary in the *Evening and the Morning Star* 1 (April 1833), which summarized the Ohio preaching: "These first four, having added one to their number, proceeded to the west, after having baptized one hundred and thirty disciples in less than four weeks and ordained four of them elders."

72. Wight's Journal, cited in *History of the Reorganized Church*, 154. After a Sunday meeting, apparently held November 14 at Warrensville, John Murdock relates: "On Monday morning the York brethren, accompanied by F. G. Williams, a late convert, took leave of us and started for upper Missouri." But the missionaries appear to be in the midst of their ministry at Kirtland on November 14 and 15, judging by the data of Wight and Rigdon. It is possible that November 15 was simply a farewell to the Warrensville area, but it is more likely that Murdock gives a wrong impression of meeting in his area on Sunday, November 14—that in reality these were on Sunday, November 21, and that he is correct on the day of departure as Monday, November 22.

73. On December 14, 1830, the *Painesville Telegraph* copied this story "from the Milan (Huron County [Ohio]) Free Press," in the form of a letter to the editor dated "Amherst, Lorain County, Ohio, Nov. 26, 1830." Compare n. 75 below.

74. The missionaries personally contacted Edward Partridge at Painesville (see n. 48 above). Evidence of their public preaching there comes from a source to be used with great care, A. B. Deming's melodramatic newspaper, *Naked Truths about Mormonism.* In January 1888 an affidavit of May 6, 1885 from K. A. E. Bell was printed. Filled with hearsay, the statement contains some personal experience: "I attended the first Mormon meeting Pratt and Cowdery held in Painesville. . . . They told about Prophet Jo Smith finding the gold plates, and said they saw them." Bell might have confused Kirtland with Painesville, but Ketchel E. Bell is enumerated in Painesville on the 1830 census.

75. "The Book of Mormon," *Painesville Telegraph*, November 30, 1830.

Oliver Cowdery's 1835 Response to Alexander Campbell's 1831 "Delusions"

John W. Welch

*T*he present study deals with a little-known editorial written by Oliver Cowdery in the 1830s.[1] Oliver's insightful article responds to the first substantive attack on the Book of Mormon, which had been published four years earlier by the formidable Alexander Campbell. Cowdery's response is articulate, well-conceived, and quite effective, as it focuses only on a few crucial issues. A lesser mind or a disingenuous fabricator would have been more inclined to defend himself and his book on the smaller issues. The fact that Cowdery sees the big picture and cuts to the chase reveals as much about his analytic skills as about his truthful testimony.

The First Substantive Attack on the Book of Mormon

As early as February 1831, a barrage of incendiary criticisms against the Book of Mormon was published by a Baptist minister, greeting the first of the Saints as they moved into the Kirtland, Ohio, area. The author of that onslaught was Alexander Campbell (1788–1866), a potent preacher, lecturer, and philosopher who took part in contemporary debates; ran two newspapers (*Christian Baptist* and *Millennial Harbinger*); organized and led the largest indigenous Protestant group in the New World (the Campbellites); became the founder, first president, and professor of Bethany College; and crusaded for a new basis of Christian unity.[2] "During his life he sought

Alexander Campbell. Courtesy Kenyon College, Ohio.

to bring essential religious beliefs and the philosophically novel ideas
of his contemporaries into some kind of intellectual harmony."[3]

The *Millennial Harbinger*, launched on 4 January 1830, was the
second and larger of the two papers published and contributed to by
Campbell. On its masthead was the text of Revelation 14:6–7. Living
and working in northern Ohio, Campbell indicated that the comprehensive object of the magazine was to be "devoted to the destruc-

tion of sectarianism, infidelity, and antichristian doctrine and practice. It shall have for its object the development and introduction of that political and religious order of society called The Millennium, which will be the consummation of that ultimate amelioration of society proposed in the Christian Scriptures."[4] Campbell then listed nine objectives of the magazine that were based on an interest in proclaiming fundamental gospel truth and discrediting those organizations that wandered from that path.[5]

On 10 February 1831, the *Millennial Harbinger* carried a lengthy article by Campbell entitled "Delusions." The piece reviewed the Book of Mormon and proceeded to develop a number of arguments against its authenticity. This article was published less than a year after the Book of Mormon first appeared in March 1830, and it ran only a few weeks after the conversion of Sidney Rigdon, a Campbellite minister also living near the soon-to-become-Mormon Kirtland, Ohio. Though Campbell probably had only a few weeks to read the Book of Mormon and to write his response, he covered most of the areas of criticism still in use by anti-Mormons against the Book of Mormon today.

Campbell began his article by taking insulting jabs at the Book of Mormon as he rehearsed the history of the Nephites: He called the book a romance: "This romance—but this is for it a name too innocent" (p. 86). This label still pops up from time to time in anti-Mormon literature. Campbell exaggerated the claims made by the Book of Mormon. According to Campbell, "Lehi was a greater prophet than any of the Jewish prophets, and uttered *all the events* of the Christian era, and developed the records of Matthew, Luke and John 600 years before John the Baptist was born" (p. 87, emphasis added). He glibly affixed oversimplified classifications: "The Nephites were good Christians, believers in the doctrines of the Calvinists and Methodists" (p. 87). And so on: Nephi preached "every thing which is now preached in the state of New York" (p. 87); Mormon was no Quaker—he commanded 42,000 men (see p. 89); God is the same—"consequently, must always create suns, moons, and stars, every day!!" (p. 90)—not such a bad idea. After his cursory overview of the Book of Mormon, Campbell presented a number of evidences that he thought worked against Joseph Smith's story: "Admitting the Bible now received to have come from God," Campbell asserted, "it is impossible that the book of Mormon came from the same Author" as the Bible (p. 91)—which conclusion at least ignores the fact that the Bible was actually written by many authors.

Despite the sarcasm and occasional misunderstanding, Campbell gave a fairly accurate synopsis and detailed overview of the historical contents of the Book of Mormon. Though the book was quite new, Campbell obviously had read much of it in a very short time.

The body of his attack presents a parade of evidences that he thought invalidated Joseph Smith's story. Campbell argued that because the following "internal evidences" were contrary to his understanding of the Bible, the claim of the Book of Mormon to have come from the same God as the Bible had to be false:

1.   According to scripture, God gave Levi all rights to the priesthood and Aaron all rights to the high priesthood, forever. Even Jesus, said Campbell, "were he on earth, could not be a priest; for he was of a tribe concerning which Moses spake nothing of priesthood" (p. 91). The result of Korah's rebellion against the priesthood in Numbers 16, Campbell asserted, was that no one except Levites can ever hold the priesthood. Campbell was disturbed that Lehi offered sacrifices and that Nephi was a priest and consecrated others as priests, built a temple, and made "a new priesthood which God approbates" (p. 91). Campbell was concerned that the tribe of Joseph, which supposedly followed the law of Moses, could have a new priesthood. He held that such a development would make God a liar—effectively repudiating his promises to the tribe of Levi (see p. 92).

2.   Campbell saw a problem in the existence of a second promised land. If reprobate Jews had departed from the Holy Land on their own initiative and had gone off to another land and built another temple, that would be tolerable because it would not implicate God in the process. But to think that God would command Lehi to depart from the land which God himself had sworn to their

fathers was their promised land was a "monstrous" error (p. 92), in Campbell's mind.

3.   He also believed Lehi violated the law by separating a family from the nation of Israel (see Deuteronomy 29:21), and he concluded incredulously that the Book of Mormon depicts Lehi as doing better out in the desert than the best Israelite ever did living "under the best of all governments!!!" (p. 92).

4.   Campbell criticized the Book of Mormon for seeming to claim there were more Jews in the New World than in Judah, that the scepter had departed from Judah, and that King Benjamin in the Book of Mormon was wiser than Solomon in the Bible (see p. 92).

5.   The Book of Mormon, contrary to every precept of the law of Moses, told of temple worship in the new land. Campbell accused the Nephites of never being sad about being cut off from the main group and never having looked back to Jerusalem and to God's temple. Even Jews in captivity looked to Jerusalem, but the Nephites, in their "wig wam temple" enjoyed God's presence in a foreign land—even though God's only house of prayer stood in Jerusalem (see p. 92). Campbell claimed that the Book of Mormon portrayed the Nephites as subverting the law of Moses, even though Malachi and Moses commanded the Jews to keep the law until the Messiah should come (see pp. 92–93).

6.   The Book of Mormon, according to Campbell, besides distorting God's laws and commandments, also proved to be ignorant of the New Testament (see p. 93). In Ephesians 3:5, Paul reserved for the apostles the first right of announcing certain secrets that were disclosed by Nephi regarding the blessing of gentiles. Paul said that those things were "not made known unto the sons of men, as it is now revealed to his holy apostles and prophets" (Ephesians 3:5). Campbell also concluded that the Book of Mormon was betrayed by its portrayal of the geography of Judea (see p. 93). It claimed that John baptized in the village of Bethabara (see 1 Nephi 10:9; John 1:28 is not so clear) and—Campbell misstates—that Jesus was born in Jerusalem (see Alma 7:10).

7. Campbell was surprised that the Book of Mormon contained sections that discussed—according to his topic headings—infant baptism, ordination, the Trinity, regeneration, repentance, justification, the fall of man, the atonement, transubstantiation, fasting, penance, church government, religious experience, the call to the ministry, general resurrection, eternal punishment, who may baptize, the right of man, and apostasy. He claimed that phrases such as "your own eternal welfare," "salvation is free," "everlasting salvation of your souls," "an infinite atonement," "flesh must go to mother earth," and "death must deliver up its dead" (p. 94) reflected the New York background of Joseph Smith and confirmed the book's falseness. He concluded that it must have been easy for Joseph Smith to "prophecy [sic] of the past or of the present time" (p. 93).

8. Pre-Christian Jewish-Christianity was claimed by the Book of Mormon. Campbell observed that the Nephite-Jews were called Christians (see Alma 46:14–15), that the resurrection of Jesus was known to them, that they believed the Great Creator would die for all men, and that they knew his name would be called Jesus Christ (see 2 Nephi 10:3).

9. "I could swear that this book was written by one man," said Campbell (p. 93). He criticized its uniform style, calling Joseph Smith, who names himself the author on the title page, a very ignorant man (see p. 93). He said the phrase *of which hath been spoken* appears in other writings by Joseph Smith, words of Oliver Cowdery, as well as in the Book of Mormon (see p. 94), and he pointed out several other often-used phrases.

10. Campbell also took delight in singling out mistakes of grammar in the first edition of the Book of Mormon: "we are a descendant," "virgin which," "ye are like unto they," "I saith," "arrive to the promised land," "made mention upon the first plate," "the righteous ... shall be confounded," "I had spake," "for a more history part," "do not anger again," and "Lord remembereth all they" (p. 94).

11. He alleged the presence of anachronisms in the Book of Mormon. He was the first to cite such examples as "the God of

Nature suffers" (a pagan concept), and Shakespeare's idea of death being a silent grave (see p. 94).

12. Campbell also criticized those who were associated with the Book of Mormon, starting with Joseph Smith, claiming that this "New York imposter" (p. 85) was "as ignorant and impudent a knave as ever wrote a book" (p. 91); he also included many other disparaging opinions about Smith's intellect and practices.

I have reviewed many of Campbell's arguments, not because they are particularly insightful or compelling, but because he charted the course that has been followed almost routinely by anti-Mormon writers ever since. It is interesting that from the 1830s, virtually all the criticisms raised against the Book of Mormon by numerous detractors can be classified into five general assertions. In the 1980s, I organized a project to identify anything that anyone had ever claimed was wrong with the Book of Mormon. With the help of many people (initially Ara Norwood, Joe Zwick, and subsequently Matthew Roper, Donald Parry, William Hamblin, Daniel Peterson, and others), we found that the claimed errors could be classified into five categories: (1) supposed contradictions between the Book of Mormon and such other things as the Bible, Israelite culture, or even the subsequent teachings of Joseph Smith; (2) alleged absurdities and anachronisms—including internal inconsistencies, erroneous quotations from the Bible, mistakes in geography, or other incomprehensible details; (3) asserted environmental influences from nineteenth-century sources, culture, or ideas; (4) claims that significant people involved with the coming forth of the Book of Mormon were untrustworthy, unreliable, or generally evil; and (5) discrepancies and changes in the subsequently published editions of the Book of Mormon from one printing to the next. Even a cursory glance shows that Campbell's arguments cover the first four categories in considerable detail and the only reason he did not claim any problems in the fifth category was because only one edition of the Book of Mormon had been published at the time. Campbell covered many of the main types of arguments ever raised in opposition to the Book of Mormon.

Many of Campbell's arguments continue to lead the recurring parade of Book of Mormon criticisms. These five areas are still the main areas of attack pursued by anti-Mormons today, many of whom merely rehash the same points or questions Campbell raised. Moreover, many of his specific attacks are still found among the most familiar and often repeated accusations. For example, Campbell's criticism that the Nephites and Lamanites took upon themselves the name of Christ before the time of Christ is often brought up by critics.[6] Many authors still bring up the questions of whether the Nephites and Lamanites really kept the law of Moses,[7] offered sacrifices,[8] or had anything like a compass.[9] To those familiar with the routine fare of Book of Mormon criticism, reading Campbell's parade of horribles is like seeing yet another rerun of an old TV show.

The Published LDS Response to Campbell

When Latter-day Saints settle in an area, they often begin distributing official Church publications or start unofficial Church-oriented papers to share local news and to keep posted on the international Church.[10] The early Saints took advantage of the news media popular in their day: "The period from 1800 to 1865 saw the printing of religious literature in America reach a high point—the result of the Second Great Awakening and the activities of various interdenominational Bible and tract societies. It was in this environment of vigorous printing activity that the [LDS] Church emerged and grew."[11]

The *Latter Day Saints' Messenger and Advocate* succeeded the *Evening and the Morning Star* in October 1834 as a publication of the Church.[12] It was published in Kirtland, Ohio, from October 1834 to September 1837, in the form of thirty-six sixteen-page, two-column issues. Its name described its purpose: to be the messenger and advocate of the Church of Jesus Christ of Latter-day Saints, thus to help the Saints better understand its doctrine and principles.[13] "Main doctrinal contributions came from Joseph Smith, Sidney Rigdon, Oliver Cowdery, W. W. Phelps, and John Whitmer. . . . Oliver Cowdery edited the *Messenger and Advocate* from October 1834 to May 1835. He was succeeded by John Whitmer from June

1835 to March 1836, but returned as editor from April 1836 to January 1837."[14]

The members of the Church at this time had had many encounters with Campbellites.[15] A response to Alexander Campbell's article was therefore important to clarify the Church's stand. Accordingly, an article entitled "Delusions" was printed in March 1835 during Oliver Cowdery's first term as editor. It ran with the byline "ed.," presumably indicating that Oliver Cowdery was the author. This little-known article is a classic early Mormon testimony of the truthfulness and importance of the Book of Mormon and is one of the most impressive responses to an anti-Mormon publication ever printed in an official Church magazine.

As interesting as what Cowdery said in this editorial is what he did not say. Of all the many trivial and scurrilous barbs thrown at the Book of Mormon by Campbell, Cowdery responded only to three points. By focusing his rebuttal on these three points—the priesthood, the promised land, and temple worship—Oliver managed to answer his critic by affirming and preaching important principles of the restored gospel of Jesus Christ.

Cowdery avoided the temptation of responding point by point to insignificant criticisms hardly worth mentioning; instead, he turned the tables by basing his response on key concepts of the restoration. By grounding his rebuttal in these ultimate declarations, Cowdery rested his case, as a good lawyer would, on firm ground and did not allow Campbell to set the ground rules or to prescribe the boundaries of their debate. Instead, Cowdery took the upper hand by answering with solid arguments that not only responded defensively, but also established affirmatively his three most meaningful points.

Because of its obscurity, Cowdery's 1835 document will be quoted here in full, interspersed with a few brief remarks. Cowdery, like Campbell, began his editorial with mild sarcasm, discounting the effect of Campbell's publication and viewing it as a mere distraction:

Said Mr. A. Campbell, in 1831, soon after the church of the Saints
began to be established in this place; but unfortunately for his
purpose, if a purpose he had, his cry was unheard, the cause still
progressed, and *continues* to progress. As this gentlemen [sic]
makes high professions as a Reformer, and is some tenacious
that his sentiments are to pervade the earth before the final end
of darkness, we think, or at least hope, our readers will pardon
our digress from ordinary matters, to give this modern apostle a
passing notice. (p. 90)

The Priesthood

Cowdery then got serious with the first of his three points. He
quoted Campbell's claim that God had given the priesthood only to
the tribe of Levi:

In his [not] far-famed pamphlet, of Feb. 10, 1831, this grave
Reformer, while examining the book of Mormon, says:

"Internal Evidences: It admits the Old and New Testaments
to contain the revelations, institutions, and commandments of
God to Patriarchs, Jews and Gentiles, down to the year 1830—
and always, as such, speaks of them and quotes them. This admission at once blasts its pretensions to credibility. For no man with
his eyes open can admit both books to have come from God.
Admitting the Bible now received to have come from God, it is
impossible that the Book of Mormon came from the same Author.
For the following reasons:—

1. Smith, its real author, as ignorant and impudent a knave
as ever wrote a book, betrays the cloven foot in basing his whole
book upon a false fact, or a pretended fact, which makes God a
liar. It is this:—With the Jews God made a covenant at Mount
Sinai, and instituted a priesthood, and a high priesthood. The
priesthood he gave to the tribe of Levi, and the high priesthood to
Aaron and his sons for an everlasting priesthood.— He separated
Levi, and covenanted to give him this office irrevocably while
ever the temple stood, or till the Messiah came." (pp. 90–91)

It is significant that Cowdery began his defense of the Book
of Mormon by defending the restoration's knowledge of the doc-

trines of the priesthood. After all, Oliver Cowdery was present with Joseph Smith when the Aaronic and Melchizedek Priesthoods were restored. This topic would have been close to Oliver Cowdery's heart; on this matter he could speak from firsthand knowledge. Indirectly, his answer to Campbell becomes one of the earliest testimonies for the restoration of the Aaronic and Melchizedek Priesthoods.

Cowdery answered Campbell by making four points: that God takes a longer view of things, that God can bestow or restore the priesthood anew on any people he wishes, that the temple itself did not stand when Aaron was given the priesthood (and so Campbell's picky argument on this point collapses), and that modern revelation has clarified how Moses received his priesthood, which allows for others holding the Melchizedek Priesthood to officiate as did Lehi and his posterity:

> Mr. Campbell attempts by a single stroke, to overthrow the validity of the book of Mormon, by bringing forward the institution of the priesthood, conferred upon Aaron and his sons, but we are willing to go the whole length in this matter of priesthood, and say that it was conferred upon Aaron and his seed throughout their generations. Ex. 40:15. And thou shalt anoint them, as thou didst anoint their father, that they minister unto me in the priest's office: for their anointing shall surely be an everlasting priesthood throughout their generations. We quote this passage because Mr. C. says, that it was only "while ever the temple stood, or till the Messiah came." Israel's God takes a longer stretch than this Rev. gentleman. He says "throughout their generations." If the literal descendants of Aaron are no more, then this priesthood is lost from Israel, unless God bestows it upon another family; but if not, not.
>
> But Mr. C. says "while ever the temple stood, or till the Messiah came."— By-the-by the temple was not reared when this covenant was made, it, nor the Messiah at the time: it is only one of this Reformer's new fashioned spiritualizing systems—we have not yet learned it.
>
> This is not all: He says that the scripture teaches, that a person of another family who should come near, when this holy

ordinance [sacrifice] was being performed should be put to death. We know that, "the stranger, who cometh nigh, shall be put to death," and that the heathens were called strangers, but not the children of Israel.

Again: Lehi and his sons, who were descendants of Joseph, offered sacrifice, and this is enough to "blast the pretensions of the book of Mormon, to credibility."

Now, as it is, and very correctly too, Lehi and his sons were blessed with the high priesthood—the Melchesedek priesthood. They never made any pretense that they were descendants of Aaron or ever received that priesthood which was conferred upon him by the hand of Moses, at the direction of the Lord.

How did it happen that Moses had authority to consecrate Aaron a priest? Where did he get his authority to arrange the tabernacle, ark, &c.? Who laid hands upon him? Had he authority to "come near" when the Lord was entreated by sacrifice? He was Aaron's brother, to be sure, but Aaron was the high priest.

Should Mr. C. finally learn, that Moses received the holy priesthood, after the order of Melchisedek, under the hand of Jethro, his father-in-law [see D&C 84:6], that clothed with this authority he set Israel in order, and by commandment ordained Aaron to a priesthood less than that, and that Lehi was a priest after this same order, perhaps he will not raise so flimsy a criterion as he does when he says the validity of the book of Mormon is destroyed because Lehi offered sacrifice; and perhaps, also, he may not be quite so lavish with his familiar titles as he was when he called brother Smith "as impudent a knave as ever wrote a book!!" (p. 91)

The Land of Zion

Second, Oliver Cowdery turned to Campbell's claim that only one land of promise could ever exist—namely, the land of Canaan. But the early Saints knew that not only had a land of promise been given to Lehi and his people, but that Zion was being gathered for the New Jerusalem in the Western Hemisphere. The concept of a promised land was a critical doctrine of the restoration in the 1830s, and

Cowdery defended it by making early and novel uses of Genesis 49:26 (in which Jacob declared that Joseph's blessings prevailed above those of his progenitors unto the utmost bounds of the everlasting hills; Jacob conferred those blessings on the head of his son Joseph, from whom Lehi descended) and Deuteronomy 33:13 (in which Moses promised land to Joseph) in support of the Book of Mormon and of the gathering of Zion from all the corners of the earth:

> This is a mere specimen: "This ignorant and impudent liar, [bro. Smith] in the next place, makes the God of Abraham, Isaac and Jacob, violate his covenants with Israel and Judah concerning the land of Canaan, by promising a new land to a pious Jew."
>
> We know that God promised to give the land of Canaan to Abraham and his seed, but we have yet to learn where he said that he would not give them any more. Mr. C. will find, in the 49th of Genesis, where Jacob declared that his blessings had prevailed above those of his progenitors unto the utmost bounds of the everlasting hills, and that he confers them upon the head of his son Joseph, of whom Lehi was a descendant.
>
> If the reader will also look into the 33d chap. of Deut. he will find that Moses promises Joseph a land; for he says, "blessed of the Lord be his land, for the precious things of heaven, for the dew, and the deep that crouches beneath, and for the precious fruits bro't forth by the sun, and for the precious things put forth by the moon, and for the chief things of the ancient mountains, and for the precious things of the lasting hills.
>
> Why all this parade about the blessing of Joseph, if he were only to inherit an equal proportion of the land of Canaan? Surely the Messiah was never promised through his lineage, or descendants: then why say so much about Joseph? But we quote another verse from the same chap which makes the subject sufficiently plain only to a man who has been crying Millennium! Millennium!! some four or five years, without ever giving his hearers one solitary scroll to point them to the word of God for a preparatory guide to be prepared for that august period!
>
> "His [Joseph's] glory is like the firstling of his bullock, and his horns are like the horns of unicorns: with them he shall push the

people together to the ends of the earth: and they are the ten thousands of Ephraim, and they are the thousands of Manasseh."

Now, if some friend of ours, or even the editor of the *Millennial Harbinger,* will be so kind as to solve one mystery on the subject of Joseph's blessing, he will do us a favor. Place Joseph in the land of Canaan and never suffer his descendants to go out, and then set him to push the *people together to [from] the ends of the earth,* and if you do not see a new thing under the sun, it will be because the Millennial Harbinger has gathered Israel from the four winds, and left them all standing where they now are!

If the Lord promised, (which he did,) the land of Canaan to Abraham, and Jacob's blessing had prevailed above that, to the utmost bounds of the everlasting hills, where could he find it? Not in the land of Canaan, merely, though Mr. C. has the daring effrontery to say that if God should take any of the seed of Jacob to any other part of the earth, he would violate his covenant which he had previously made!—How does he know it? (pp. 91–92)

The Temple

Third, Oliver Cowdery defended the idea that God's people in all dispensations are temple-building people. The construction of the Kirtland Temple was well under way when his answer to Campbell went to press, and dreams were still alive for a temple in Independence, Missouri. Cowdery rightly rejected Campbell's interpretation of the Bible to the effect that it permitted the building of a temple only in Jerusalem, and he boldly declared the right of men, namely Joseph Smith and himself, who were "endowed with the holy priesthood, after the order of Melchizedek," to construct a house of glory acceptable to God:

> With his boasted knowledge he will not be disturbed if we give our readers another specimen:
>
> "The pious Jews in the captivity turned their faces to Jerusalem and the holy place, and remembered God's promises concerning the place where he recorded his name. They hung their harps upon the willow trees, and could not sing the songs of Zion in a foreign land; but the Nephites have not a single wish for

Jerusalem, for they can, in their wig wam temple, in the America, enjoy more of God's presence than the most righteous Jew could enjoy in that house of which David had rather be a door-keeper than to dwell in the tabernacles of men. And all this too, when God's only house of prayer, according to his covenant with Israel, stood in Jerusalem."

Here are further secrets unfolded.—We remember to have read, in the 137th Ps. either a history of what had taken place, or a prophecy concerning something to come, and which, in the days of David was yet to transpire;—but the lamentation was uttered by those who were in distress and mocked by the heathen. The reader will also remember that Solomon, the son of David, built the Temple, and how, we ask, could David be a door-keeper in the same, when it was not reared until his earthly tabernacle was crumbling to dust? But it does very well for Mr. C.—he can get him up there with songs of thanksgiving, waiting before God, and keeping the doors of his sacred Temple, and not a stone of it yet laid!!

We remember also to have read a sublime sentence uttered by the mouth of a prophet, in the name of the Lord, something like this: "Thus saith the Lord, the heaven is my throne, and the earth is my footstool: Where is the house that ye build unto me? And where is the place of my rest? For all those things that my hand has made." Solomon, who built the Temple, of which Mr. C. says David desired to be a door-keeper, after he was gathered to his fathers, says: "But will God indeed dwell on the earth? Behold, the heaven, and heavens of heavens cannot contain thee."

Now, if God's presence and glory fill the heavens, is he not sufficient to fill more than one small house like that built at Jerusalem? and has not a man, endowed with the holy priesthood, after the order of Melchisedek, authority to build a house to the honor of HIS name, and especially, when the worship of that at Jerusalem was corrupted, or it thrown down? We have yet to be informed *when* the Lord said that he would *not* fill another house with his glory, if he did that at Jerusalem, or when he ever said that the descendants of Joseph should be cursed, if they should build another like that, when enjoying the promised blessing, made to them by the mouth of God, through Moses, that they should possess the ends of the earth.

Our readers will understand that these extracts are taken from Mr. C.'s writings of 1831, and if occasion requires, we shall give them a specimen of his writings since, in a future number, and then close with this gentleman forever.—[Editor.] (pp. 92–93)

Conclusion

Oliver Cowdery's reply was logically persuasive and forensically compelling. Displaying his aptitude for lawyering, he showed keen ability to mount a strong response. He argued effectively on technical grounds: for example, he incisively showed that the priesthood was conferred by Moses upon Aaron and his seed throughout *their* generations (see Exodus 40:15) and that if the literal descendants of Aaron are no more, then God is not limited but can bestow it on another. He skillfully exposed logical inconsistencies in his opponent's position: for instance, in response to the claim that only Levi was to have the priesthood "while ever the temple stood, or till the Messiah came," Cowdery pointed out that the temple was not reared nor the Messiah come in the days of Moses at the time the covenant was made. Cowdery accurately interpreted authoritative texts: for example, he rightly observed that when the scriptures require that if any foreigners were to come near when sacrifices were being performed, they should be put to death ("the stranger that cometh nigh shall be put to death," Numbers 18:7), this refers to heathens, not the children of Israel. In several ways, Cowdery exposed defects in Campbell's position and showed ways in which Campbell had not carried his burden of persuasion. Moreover, he showed how modern revelation had clarified how Moses received his priesthood as did Lehi and his posterity.

Moreover, a good debater knows that the best defense is a strong offense. Cowdery offered affirmative arguments: for example, he asked how Jacob's blessing to Joseph was to be fulfilled that he should reach to the ends of the earth and prevail to the "utmost bounds of the everlasting hills" (Genesis 49:26), and how Moses's promise to the tribe of Joseph would come to pass that he "shall push the people together to the ends of the earth" (Deuteronomy 33:13), if Joseph was to be found only in the land of Canaan.

But even more than that, Cowdery was effective in singling out a few key points and focusing his attention on those issues while simply ignoring the dozens of other sometimes flippant and even silly arguments that Campbell had tossed into his stew. Many papers have been published by others over the years that have more than amply answered virtually all of Campbell's detailed concerns; but instead of responding line by line or word by word, Cowdery took the tack of building his response on three points—only those that were most important and that were points of strength for the restoration: the restoration of the priesthood, the gathering of Zion from the ends of the earth, and the reinstitution of temple ordinances. By turning his attention to the strengths of his own position, Cowdery was able to reclaim the higher ground in the debate and, in the process, to proclaim affirmatively the main messages of the restoration.

Oliver Cowdery's strategy offers modern defenders of the Book of Mormon an interesting model to keep in mind. Although Campbell may not have conceded the victory to Cowdery and may have felt that Cowdery failed to address his numerous sparring jabs, I think that Cowdery won the exchange going away, by showing, in effect, that Campbell had neither discredited nor even hit upon the real issues of the restoration.

Notes

Editors' note: This article was originally published in *The Disciple as Witness: Essays on Latter-day Saint History and Doctrine in Honor of Richard Lloyd Anderson*, ed. Stephen D. Ricks, Donald W. Parry, and Andrew H. Hedges (Provo, UT: FARMS, 2000), 435–58.

The author thanks Claire Foley for her work on this article.

1.   Oliver Cowdery, "'Delusions,'" *Messenger and Advocate* 1/6 (March 1835): 90–93, which responds to Alexander Campbell, "Delusions," *Millennial Harbinger* 2/2 (7 February 1831): 84–96.

2.   See S. Morris Eames, *The Philosophy of Alexander Campbell* (New Brunswick, NJ: Standard, 1966), 16.

3.   Ibid., 17.

4. *Millennial Harbinger* 1/1 (4 January 1830), quoted in Robert-F. West, *Alexander Campbell and Natural Religion* (New Haven: Yale University Press, 1948), 165.

5. See West, *Alexander Campbell*, 165–66.

6. See H. Stevenson, *Lecture on Mormonism* (1839), 11; Tyler Parsons, *Mormon Fanaticism Exposed* (Boston, 1841), 75; Edmund Clay, *The Book of Mormon Proved to Be a Blasphemous and Impudent Forgery* (London: Wertheim and Macintosh, 1850), 14; John Bowes, *Mormonism Exposed* (1850), 31; J. M. Burgess, *The Book of Mormon Contradictory* (Liverpool: Blevin, 1850), 25; Josiah B. Lowe, *Mormonism Exposed* (Liverpool: Howell, 1852), 14; John Haynes, *The Book of Mormon Examined* (London: Seely, 1853), 15; William Sheldon, *Mormonism Examined* (Broadhead, WI: by the author, 1876), 20; A. G. Hobbs, *Did the Book of Mormon Come from God?* (Fort Worth, TX: Hobbs, 1954), 17; Jack Free, *Mormonism and Inspiration* (Concord, CA: Pacific, 1962); Marvin W. Cowan, *Mormon Claims Answered* (Salt Lake City: Cowan, 1975), 35; W. N. Jackson, *Is the Book of Mormon from God?* (Tupelo, MS: Barber, 1977), 5–6; James M. Tolle, *Is the Book of Mormon from God?* (San Fernando, CA: Tolle, 1977); William J. Mitchell, *A Christian Looks at Mormonism* (Mesa, AZ: by the author, 1977), 11; Walter-R. Martin, *The Maze of Mormonism* (Santa Ana, CA: Vision House, 1978), 327; Latayne C. Scott, *The Mormon Mirage* (Grand Rapids, MI: Zondervan, 1979), 87; Weldon Langfield, *The Truth about Mormonism: A Former Adherent Analyzes the LDS Faith* (Bakersfield, CA: Langfield, 1991), 46; John Ankerberg and John Weldon, *Everything You Ever Wanted to Know about Mormonism* (Eugene, OR: Harvest House, 1992), 322.

7. See James H. Hunt, *Mormonism* (St. Louis: Ustick and Davies, 1844), 27, 36; Sheldon, *Mormonism Examined* (1876), 13–14; Charles J. Sundberg, *The Mysterious Book of Mormon* (Sandy, Utah: by the author, 1917), 11; Bales, *The Book of Mormon?* (Fort Worth, TX: Manney, 1958), 148–56; Michael H. Marquardt, *The Use of the Bible in the Book of Mormon* (Salt Lake City: Utah Lighthouse Ministry, 1979), 116–17; Wesley P. Walters, "The Use of the Old Testament in the Book of Mormon" (master's thesis, Covenant Theological Seminary, 1981), 15–17; Jerald and Sandra Tanner, *Covering Up the Black Hole in the Book of Mormon* (Salt Lake City: Utah Lighthouse Ministry, 1990), 56–59.

8. See Eber D. Howe, *Mormonism Unvailed* (Painesville, Ohio: by the author, 1834), 47, 61–62; Origen Bacheler, *Mormonism Exposed Internally and Externally* (New York, 1838), 30–32; Parsons, *Mormon Fanaticism Exposed* (1841), 70–71; Jonathan B. Turner, *Mormonism in All Ages* (New York: Platt & Peters, 1842), 192; Hunt, *Mormonism* (1844), 85–86; William Palmer, *Mormonism Briefly Examined* (London: Hall, 1849), 4–5; Clay, *The Book of Mormon Proved* (1850), 11–12; Lowe, *Mormonism Exposed* (1852), 13–14; Haynes, *The Book of Mormon Examined* (1853), 13; John Hyde, *Mormonism: Its Leaders and Designs* (New York: Fetridge, 1857), 229–30; Martin T. Lamb, *The Golden Bible* (New York: Ward & Drummond, 1887), 98–99; Golman B. Hancock, *Mormonism Exposed* (Marianville, MO: Doggett, 1902), 38; Free, *Mormonism and Inspiration* (1962), 126–27; Martin, *The Maze of Mormonism* (1978), 327; Cary Trivanovich, *Speaking the Truth in Love* (Orange, CA: Promise, 1988), 10.

9. See Howe, *Mormonism Unvailed* (1834), 32; Anonymous, "The Book of Mormon and the Mormonites," *Athenaeum, Museum of Foreign Literature, Science, and Art* 42 (July 1841): 372; Parsons, *Mormon Fanaticism Exposed* (1841), 11, 66; Turner, *Mormonism in All Ages* (1842), 192; Hunt, *Mormonism* (1844), 30–31; Daniel P. Kidder, *Mormonism and the Mormons* (New York: Lane and Tippett, 1844), 259; Charles S. Smith, *The Mormonites: The Origin, History and Their Pretensions* (Bristol, 1849), 3; R. Clarke, *Mormonism Unmasked*

(London: G. J. & R. Books, 1849), 26; Palmer, *Mormonism Briefly Examined* (1949), 6; Edmund Clay, *The Book of Mormon: Its History and an Analysis of Its Contents* (1850), 9–10; Bowes, *Mormonism Exposed* (1850), 31–32; Andrew B. Hepburn, *An Exposition of the Blasphemous Doctrines and Delusions* (London: Marshall, 1852), 12; Haynes, *The Book of Mormon Examined* (1853), 14–15; Dawson Burns, *Mormonism Explained and Exposed* (London: Houlston & Stoneman, 1853), 19n; W. Sparrow Simpson, *Mormonism: Its History, Doctrines and Practices* (London: Pigott, 1853), 3; Andrew B. Hepburn, *Mormonism Exploded* (Sheffield: Thomas, 1855), 38–39; Samuel Hawthornthwaite, *Adventures among the Mormons* (Manchester, England: by the author, 1857), 69; Hyde, *Mormonism: Its Leaders and Designs* (1857), 222– 23; Thomas B. H. Stenhouse, *The Rocky Mountain Saints* (New York: Appleton, 1873), 530–31; Sheldon, *Mormonism Examined* (1876), 138–40; Joseph Johnson, *The Great Mormon Fraud* (Manchester: Butterworth & Nodal, 1885), 81; Enos T. Hall, *The Mormon Bible* (Columbus, Ohio: Heer, 1899), 8; Henry C. Sheldon, *A Fourfold Test of Mormonism* (New York: Abingdon, 1914), 49– 50;-Sundberg, *The Mysterious Book of Mormon* (1917), 10; Stuart Martin, *The Mystery of Mormonism* (London: Odhams, 1920), 44; Frank Ballard, *Why Not Mormonism?* (London: Epworth, 1922), 12; James H. Snowden, *The Truth about Mormonism* (New York: Dunn, 1926), 104; George B. Arbaugh, *Revelation in Mormonism* (Chicago: University of Chicago Press, 1932), 55; William E. Biederwolf, *Mormonism under the Searchlight* (Grand Rapids, MI: Eerdmans, 1947), 16; Hobbs, *Did the Book of Mormon Come from God?* (1954), 9; George B. Arbaugh, *Gods, Sex and Saints* (Rock Island, IL: Augustana, 1957), 22; Tolle, *Is the Book of Mormon from God?* (1957), 13; Leslie Rumble, "The Book of Mormon," *The Homiletic and Pastoral Review* 60/4 (January 1960): 344; Anthony A. Hoekema, *Mormonism* (Grand Rapids, MI: Eerdmans, 1963), 28; Ben M. Bogard, *An Exposure of Mormonism* (Little Rock, AR: Missionary Baptist Seminary, 1965), 33; Gordon R. Lewis, *The Bible, the Christian, and Latter-day Saints* (Grand Rapids, MI: Presbyterian and Reformed, 1966), 17; Mitchell, *A Christian Looks at Mormonism* (1977), 11; Martin, *The Maze of Mormonism* (1978), 48; Rick Branch, "A Few Problems," *The Director* (Marlow, Oklahoma) 3/5 (January–February 1983): 3; Thomas Key, "A Biologist Looks at the Book of Mormon," *Journal of the American Scientific Affiliation* 37/2 (1985): 98–99; James R. White, *Letters to a Mormon Elder* (Southbridge, MD: Crowne, 1990), 175; Langfield, *The Truth about Mormonism* (1991), 45–46.

10. See Jack A. Nelson, "LDS Newspapers," in *Encyclopedia of Mormonism*, 3:1011. In 1831 a revelation was given to Joseph Smith, recorded in section 57 of the Doctrine and Covenants, which includes a command to W. W. Phelps to be a printer, and to Oliver Cowdery to edit material for publication. See also Doctrine and Covenants 112:6.

11. Larry W. Draper, "Publications," in *Encyclopedia of Mormonism*, 3:1173.

12. See Ronald D. Dennis, "The Evening and Morning Star," in *Encyclopedia of Mormonism*, 2:477.

13. See David B. Galbraith, "Messenger and Advocate," in *Encyclopedia of Mormonism*, 2:892.

14. Ibid.

15. See, for example, *The Journals of William E. McLellin: 1831–1836*, ed. Jan Shipps and John W. Welch (Provo, Utah: BYU-Studies, 1994), 65–66, 124, 152, 160, 167–68, 224, 225; *Times and-Seasons* 1 (1840): 135–36; John Murdock Journal, typescript, BYU-A, 8–11; and Milton V. Backman Jr., "The Quest for a Restoration: The Birth of Mormonism in Ohio," *BYU Studies* 12/4 (1972): 346–64.

Oliver Cowdery's Kirtland, Ohio, "Sketch Book"

Leonard J. Arrington

$\mathcal{A}$s a witness of significant events in the rise of The Church of Jesus Christ of Latter-day Saints, Oliver Cowdery's importance is superseded only by that of the Prophet Joseph Smith. With the exception of Joseph's First Vision and the appearances of Moroni, Cowdery participated with the Prophet in the key events of the Restoration. The scope of his experiences include the translation of the Book of Mormon, the restoration of the priesthood, the organization of the Church, the first extensive missionary work of the Church, and divine manifestations in the Kirtland Temple.

The youngest of eight children, Oliver Cowdery[1] was born 3 October 1806 in Wells, Rutland County, Vermont. In 1825 he moved to New York, where he worked successively as a clerk in a general store, as a blacksmith, and as a farmer. In 1828 he entered the teaching profession in Manchester, New York, where he first became acquainted with the religious claims of Joseph Smith. His entry into the mainstream of Mormon history occurred in April 1829 when he traveled to Harmony, Pennsylvania, to meet Joseph Smith, who was engaged in the translation of the Book of Mormon. Cowdery assisted Joseph as a scribe during the translation of the major part of that work, and his name appears in the Book of Mormon as one of the witnesses to the reliability of the claims of Joseph Smith regarding its origin and method of translation.

Oliver Cowdery testified that he was with Joseph Smith in the
spring of 1829 when they "called upon the Lord, and he answered
us out of the heavens, and while we were in the heavenly vision
the angel came down and bestowed upon us this priesthood; and
. . . after this we received the high and holy priesthood."[2] Oliver's
description of the events he witnessed is more than a colorless statement of facts:

> Earth, nor men, with the eloquence of time, cannot begin to clothe
> lanquage in as interesting and sublime a manner as this holy per-
> sonage The assurance that we were in the presence of an Angel; the
> certainty that we heard the voice of Jesus, and the truth unsullied
> as it flowed from a pure personage, dictated by the will of God, is to
> me past description, and I shall ever look upon this expression of
> the Savior's goodness with wonder and thanksgiving.[3]

Oliver Cowdery held many positions of importance and was
engaged in a variety of experiences during the initial eight years of his
Church activity. He was present at the meeting that marked the official beginning of the Church on 6 April 1830 and delivered the first
public discourse to members of the new organization five days later.
In the fall of 1830 he traveled west from New York with three companions on one of the most portentous missionary journeys in the
annals of Church history. After baptizing 130 disciples in Ohio in less
than four weeks and traveling some 1500 miles to western Missouri,
in what has been described as "a journey perhaps as spectacular as
any of the apostle Paul,"[4] Cowdery and his associates taught the message of the restoration to Indians along America's western frontier.
He was one of eight men with Joseph Smith who participated in the
dedication of the temple site at Independence, Missouri, on 3 August
1831. As one of the presidents of the Church in Missouri, Oliver
saw the expulsion of the Latter-day Saint community from Jackson
County in 1833. In February 1834 he was named to the High Council
in Kirtland, Ohio, acting first as clerk, and later, as president of that
body. In December of that year he was ordained Assistant President of
the Church—second only to Joseph Smith. In February 1835 he officiated, with fellow witnesses to the Book of Mormon, in the selection,

instruction, and ordination of the Quorum of Twelve Apostles. And although he served as Church Historian and Recorder in 1830–31, he was again appointed to that office in Kirtland in 1835.

Oliver Cowdery also performed a variety of activities as a printer and publisher for the Church. In June 1831 he was named in a revelation to direct the selection, writing, and printing of books for the instruction of children in the Church schools. After returning to Kirtland from Missouri in the summer of 1831, he was called to a committee to review and prepare Church revelation for publication. Then, in company with John Whitmer, Elder Cowdery was sent back to Missouri with the revelation for publication by the Church press in Independence. After the destruction of the press in 1833, Cowdery was directed to republish the Church paper, *The Evening and the Morning Star,* in Kirtland. He later edited two other Church papers—the *Northern Times* and the *Messenger and Advocate.*

After allying himself with dissenters from the Church, Oliver Cowdery was excommunicated in Missouri on 12 April 1838. During the following ten years that he remained out of the Church, Oliver resided in Kirtland and Tiffin, Ohio, and Elkhorn, Wisconsin. He practiced law in all three communities, participated in local political and civic affairs, and edited two newspapers.

In October 1848, through the instrumentality of his brother-in-law, Phinehas Young, Oliver returned to the Church at the time Latter-day Saints were encamped at Council Bluffs, Iowa, during their trek across the Plains to Salt Lake Valley. He was initiated into his former faith by Orson Hyde, who baptized him in the Missouri River on 12 November 1848. Less than two years later, on 3 March 1850, Cowdery succumbed to tuberculosis while visiting relatives in Richmond, Missouri.

The words of an ex-law partner, William Lang, give a vivid description of Oliver Cowdery, typical of the esteem in which he was held among his associates:

> Mr. Cowdery was an able lawyer and a great advocate. His manners were easy and gentlemanly; he was polite, dignified,

yet courteous. He had an open countenance, high forehead, dark brown eyes, Roman nose, clenched lips and prominent lower jaw. He shaved smooth and was neat and cleanly in his person. He was of light stature, about five feet, five inches high, and had a loose, easy walk. With all his kind and friendly disposition, there was a certain degree of sadness that seemed to pervade his whole being. His association with others was marked by the great amount of information his conversation conveyed and the beauty of his musical voice. His addresses to the court and jury were characterized by a high order of oratory, with brilliant and forensic force. He was modest and reserved, never spoke ill of any one, never complained.[5]

Oliver Cowdery's involvement in the beginning events of Church history establishes his writings as essential to any study of the claims of Joseph Smith and Mormon beginnings. In light of the role he played in early Church history, the recent finding of a Cowdery diary covering three months in 1836 is of more than passing significance. The diary is written in Cowdery's own hand, and in the back of it is a volume of the Nauvoo High Council minutes. Filed in the Church Archives, the twenty-two page "Sketch Book" contains valuable insight into the life and character of the Second Elder of the Church, and gives a detailed account of his activities immediately preceding the dedication of the Kirtland Temple. The diary provides a view of persons and events in Kirtland from a significant perspective. It is reproduced here in its entirety without editorial corrections.

OLIVER COWDERY'S SKETCH BOOK,

January 1836

January 1, 1836.

This year came in on Friday: the Lord having spared me another year, and my family also enjoying health, I pray that I may be spared from the temptations of the adversary, and that I and my family may have health.

The man that keeps the commandments of the Lord will never be forsaken: his soul shall be filled with the Holy Spirit, his days shall be many, and his seed shall inherit the earth.

Saturday, the 2nd.

Presided with Presidents F. G. Williams and David Whitmer in a high council, in the case of elder Wm. Smith, was was brought before the same for unchristianlike conduct. He acknowledged the charges to be correct, and was forgiven.

Sunday the 3rd

This morning I left for Columbus, the capital of this State, to attend a Convention to nominate a candidate for Governor,[6] in company with Benj. Adams, Lyman Root[7] and Simeon Wright. I did not like to start a journey on Sunday, but was obliged to do so, or go in the stage: this I could not do for want of means. From the 3rd to the morning of the 8th I was on the road, a part of the way being very muddy. My company used me with perfect respect, and spoke favorably of the cause of truth.

Friday & Saturday, the 8th & 9th

Sat in Convention in the Theatre: a great many men assembled from different parts of the State. Here the delegation from this section treated me with deference, and appointed me on an important committee in preference to others.

While in Columbus I had several interviews with Mr. John A. Byan [Bryan],[8] the Auditor of State, from whom I received expressions of the most perfect friendship and confidence. My only wish in forming acquaintances with the great men of the nation, is, that I may be of service to my fellow beings and benefit the cause of truth and righteousness. I would that all these were men of God, walking in the path of holiness. While in Columbus I also visited the house of Cyprian Rudd,[9] a member of the Church of Christ: his wife was very low of a fever.

Sunday the 10th

Left for home in company with Mr. Root and Wright. On my way I called on Silas Austin,[10] the son of my present mother: he received me with a smile, and wished me to remember him.

Monday the 11th

Left Newark, Licking Co. and left Mr. Wright, who is to come home another way. Nothing of importance occurred from this till I arrived home of importance.

Thursday the 14th

Arrived home this evening, and found my family all alive, though my child was some unwell.[11] My heart was truly greatful to God for extending his mercy, and suffering me to behold them once more, after fateaguing my body so long. My soul also rejoiced to meet my brethren of the Church, with whom I have lived since the organization of the same.

Friday the 15th.

The several Quorams of the authorities of the Church met today, and transacted important business preparatory to the endowment.[12] The Spirit of the Lord was in our midst.

Saturday the 16th

Wrote a letter to my brother Warren[13] on the subject of a difficulty which exists between him and the Twelve.[14] Wrote another to John A. Bryan, of Columbus, Auditor of State, on the subject of the Post Office.[15] See Post Script below.

Sabbath the 17th

The quorums of the Church were organized in the presence of the Church, and commenced confessing their faults and asking forgiveness. The Holy Spirit rested upon us. O may we be prepared for the endowment,—being sanctified and cleansed from all sin.

Post Script to Saturday the 16th.

Met in the evening with bro. Joseph Smith, jr. at his house, in company with bro. John Corrill,[16] and after pure water was prepared, called upon the Lord and proceeded to wash each other's bodies, and bathe the same with whiskey, perfumed with cinnamon. This we did that we might be clearn before the Lord for the Sabbath, confessing our sins and covenanting to be faithful to God. While performing this washing unto the Lord with solemnity, our minds were filled with many reflections upon the propriety of the same, and how the priests anciently used to wash always before ministering before the Lord. As we had nearly finished this purification, bro. Martin Harris[17] came in and was also washed.

Monday the 18th

Recorded blessings until evening,[18] when a man came in by the name of Lee Reed, and said he had been sued for an assault, and that his opponent had sought thus to destry him: he urged me to go before the court and plead his cause. On examining the same before the court, I saw the man was guilty of a misdemeanor, and could not say but little in his behalf. He was finally bound over to await his trial before the court of common Please: this descission was just, for he was guilty of throwing a stick against a little child.

Tuesday the 19th

Wrote blessings: this day I felt more like dedicating my self to the Lord than usual. O my God, my soul desires to see thee as thy favored ones in days of old. Received a letter from Joel Sweetland, of East Evans, Erie County, N.Y. and answered the same.[19] Peace be to my soul forever.

Wednesday the 20th

Copied blessings until evening, at which time I went, in company with my wife, to Elder John F. Boynton's[20] wedding: a large company assembled, and after the services we were treated with wine and cake very sumptuously. While these things were passing, and joy filled each heart, I reflected back to the seasons in my life when I, like a stranger, was cast out of society of men, without the common blessings of nature; and also did I think upon the afflictions of the Saints, in being driven from their homes; and further, upon the time when the righteous will enjoy peace and plenty, aside from the society of the Gentile. Then, as when Israel walked in favor with God, will our sons and daughters be united in marriage, and joy will possess each bosom, there being nothing to molest or make afraid. O my [may] the Lord my God roll on the day of peace and rest!

Thursday, the 21st

This morning, at 15 minutes past nine, my little daughter is 5 months old.[21] O Lord, I thank thee that thou hast thus been merciful and spared my only child. At about three o'clock P.M. I assembled in our office garret, having all things prepared for the occasion, with presidents Joseph Smith, jr. F. G. Williams,[22] Sidney Rigdon[23] Hyrum Smith,[24] David Whitmer,[25] John Whitmer[26] and elder John Corrill, and washed our bodies with pure water before the Lord, preparatory to the annointing with the holy oil. After we were washed, our bodies were perfumed with a sweet smelling oderous wash. At evening the presidents of the Church, with the two bishop and their counsellors, and elder Warren Parrish,[27] met in the presidents' room, the high councils of Kirtland and Zion in their rooms. Those named in the first room were annointed with the same kind of oil and in the man[ner] that were Moses and Aaron, and those who stood before the Lord in ancient days, and those in the other rooms with annointing oil prepared for them. The glorious scene is too great to be described in this book, therefore, I only say, that the heavens were opened to many, and great and marvelous things were shown.[28]

Friday, the 22nd.

Copied blessings. At evening met in the president's room where were the presidents, the twelve, the presidents of the 70, the high councils of Kirtland and Zion, and the bishops and their counsellors. The presidents proceeded and annointed Thomas B. Marsh,[29] the president of the twelve, and he annointed the other eleven. The twelve then proceeded, president Marsh taking the lead, and annointed the presidents of the Seventy. Elder Don Carlos Smith[30] was ordained and annointed president of the high priesthood of the Melchisedek priesthood, by the presidents of the Church. Near the close of the meeting, 2 o'clock in the morning, almost all present broke out in tongues and songs of Zion.[31]

Saturday, the 23rd.

Was, most of the time, in the office, though I did not write much. Conversed considerable time with president Rigdon on the subject of his vision concerning the return of the Ten Tribes. In the evening Elder Marsh called at my house: we talked much upon the subject of visions: he greatly desired to see the Lord. Brother Marsh is a good man, and I pray that his faith may be strengthed to behold the heavens open.

Sunday, the 24th.

The quorums met today: we had a good season. At evening met the presidency in the upper room in the printing office, and conversed upon the time of, and preperation and sanctification for the endowment.

Monday the 25th. Wrote a little: settled with James M. Carrel,[32] who left the office. I gave him a reproof for urging himself into the society of a young female while he yet had a wife living, but he disliked my admonition: he however confessed his impropriety.

Tuesday, the 26th. This day commenced the Hebrew language under the tuition of Mr. J. Seixas,[33] besides making selections for the Northern Times.[34] My family are well.

P. S. To Monday: In the evening the high priests and elders, all who did not belong to the quorums, met in the Lord's house, and also the Lesser priesthood, with the bishop at their head, to receive instructions relative to washing and annointing a large number of elders convened; more than I had supposed resided in Kirtland.

Wednesday, the 27th. Attended the Hebrew School.

Thursday, the 28th. Attended Hebrew School: at evening met many brethren in the Lord's house, who assembled to receive annointing.

Friday, the 29th. Attended Hebrew School.

Saturday, 30. Attended Hebrew School: at evening met in the upper rooms with the 70, elders & priests, who were anointing.

Sunday, 31. Attended meeting in the forenoon: the quorums met as before. In the afternoon went, but the house being full did not go in.

February 1836

Monday, February 1. Met with the remaining committee of the School and assisted to make up the other Hebrew class of 30, or 31.

Tuesday, 2. Attended Hebrew School, At 11 o'clock the new class of 31 members took *their* first lesson. In the evening I finished the selections for this week's Times, and wrote a short article on the present agitating question of slavery and antislavery. There is a hostile spirit exhibited between the North and South, and ere long must make disturbances of a serious nature. If the North says that Slavery is unjust the South says, you are endangering our lives, and we *will* not endure it.

Wednesday, 3. Attended school. At evening went to a wedding at bishop Whitney's:[35] elder Joseph C. Kingsbury[36] was married to Caroline Whitney, sister of bishop Whitney. This day a man arrived, as he said, from Jackson County, Mo. and wished to join the Church: Suspicions are entertained that he is not an honest man. Time will tell.

Thursday, 4. Attended school. After our class had recition the committee selected a new class of 15 who are to receive lessons in the Hebrew. In the evening wrote two editorial articles for the Times, one on the subject of our difficulties with France and another upon the subject of Slavery. Our country is agitated, & many look with anxious eyes for coming events. May the Lord preserve his people. Amen.

Friday, 5. Attended Hebrew School.

Saturday, 6. Attended Hebrew School. In the afternoon wrote a letter in the name of the committee containing a request to Professor Seixa's wife, for a valuable Lexicon.[37] In the evening met with the presidency any [and] quorums in the Lord's house, when their anointing blessings were sealed by uplifted hands and praises to God. Many saw visions, many prophesied, and many spoke in tongues. Closed a little before 12 o'clock.

Sunday, 7. Copied the committee's letter to Mrs. Seixas, as her husband was urging for it. The quorums met in the room below the printing office and proceeded as previous. In the afternoon assisted Pres. Phelps[38] in keeping the door, seating the congregation, and keeping order out at the door. Met the presidency and presidents of the 70 soon after meeting in No. 2 printing office, blessed one of the sons of Zion, and also selected another quorum of 70 from among the elders. Previously to the close of the afternoon services I asked for a letter from the Church for bro. James M. Carrel, now abscent:—the church directed me to send him one.

Monday, 8. Att. Heb. School. In the evening visited Profess. Seixas in company with Pres. J. Smith, jr. & S. Rigdon.

Tuesday, 9. Att. Heb. School. Also wrote a letter to my Mother,[39] now in Ellery, Chautauque County, N.Y. Received a letter from my brother Stephen F. Cowdery,[40] of Buffalo, N.Y. Also wrote a letter to James M. Carrel, informing him that I could not send him a certificate of fellowship, as I heard that he had been intoxicated since he left. Wrote another letter to Gen. Joseph Thompson,[41] now a Member of Congress, for the Congressional Globe, and also upon the Post Office business.

Wednesday, 10. Attended Heb. School. In the evening took supper, in company with pres. Phelps, at my father's table, with my wife. My sister Lucy[42] was also there.

Thursday, 11. Received a letter from my bro. Warren, from Freedom, N.Y. accompanying a letter to the High Counsil, and one to the Twelve. Read them to pres. Rigdon, who thought that they would be satisfactory—I hope they may. In the evening met bro. Phelps and J. Whitmer in the upper room of the office and studied our Heb. lessons.

Friday, 12. Att. Heb. School. Met the quorums in the presidents'
room in the evening to transact some church business.—regulating
the manner and power to ordain.

Saturday, 13. Att. Heb. School. Engaged a cutter for pro. Seixas to go
to Hudson in the afternoon.

Sunday, 14. At home—the weather cold & house crowded, was the
reason why I did not go to meeting.

Monday, 15. Att. Heb. School. The profess. being abscent, our class
appointed myself to look over them for the time. After, assisted pres.
Smith to overlook the 11 o'clock. In the afternoon met Pres's. J. Smith,
jr. S. Rigdon, W. W. Phelps John Whitmer and elder S. James[43] in the
office study and united in prayer for Professor Seixas and his family,
pres. Smith taking the lead: The items asked for were in substance as
follows: That the Lord will have mercy upon the man whom we have
employed to teach us the Hebrew language; that all evil prejudice
may be taken from his heart, and that the Spirit of God may visit
him continually by night and by day, that he may be lead to embrace
the gospel and believe the book of Mormon; that he will give him
the spirit of humility and meekness that we may become his teachers in the things of salvation, that he may come forth and be baptized into the Church of Christ, that we may be benefitted with the
knowledge he has of languages: and that the Lord will have mercy
upon his family, and visit them with his Holy Spirit and cause them
to embrace the fulness of the gospel, that they may be saved with
him. We do not ask to become his teachers only that he may become
our brother in the faith of the gospel, that his soul may be saved: all
of which are asked in the name of the Lord Jesus Christ. Amen.

Tuesday, 16. Att. Heb. School.

Wed. 17 Att. Heb. School.

Thursday, 18 Att. Heb. School.

Friday, 19. Att. Heb. School. Visited profess. Seixas in the evening, with pres. J. Smith, jr. & S. Rigdon. We found him weary with his labors in teaching the school.

Saturday, 20. Att. Heb. School. Received a letter from James M. Carrel, and also wrote him an answer—in which I enclosed a certificate from the Church, having learned that the accusation was untrue charging him with intoxication since he left this place. Received another letter from my brother Lyman Cowdery,[44] of Manchester, N.Y. Wrote a letter to Mr. S. Burnett, of Orange, Ohio, on the subject of the Post Office in this place.

Sunday, 21. Attended meeting in the afternoon.

Monday, 22. At the school (Heb.)

Tuesday, 23. At school. (Heb.)

Wednesday, 24. Attended Heb. school. In the evening met the quorums of the Church in the Lord's house, and heard the petitions of several brethren, who wished to be ordained. Was appointed by the council, in company with pres. Orson Hyde[45] and Sylvester Smith,[46] to draft resolutions to be adopted as a rule of Church, regulating the recording of licenses, and conference minutes.

Thursday, 25. My brother Warren and family arrived this morning from Freedom, N.Y. I was glad to see them—they were well. Att. Heb. School. This evening conversed with a brother-in-law of mine, upon the subject of religion, and found him very stubborn, and ignorent, and withal far from God. His name is Winslow Wilber:[47] he married my sister Olive.

Friday, 26. Attended Hebrew School

Saturday, 27. Professor Seixas left this morning to visit his family at Hudson, Ohio. I was called to lay hands upon pres. T. B. Marsh, in company with pres. J. Smith, jr. and also upon my brother-in-law, Peter Whitmer, jr.[48] the latter was very sick of a Typhus fever, and was immediately heald and arose from his bed. I heard the other was better. In the afternoon and evening met pres. Orson Hyde and Sylvester Smith in committee and dictated resolutions to be introduced Thursday evening for the consideration of the quorums.

Sunday, 28. Attended meeting on the flats, and preached in the forenoon. In the afternoon broke bread and administered the Sacrament.

Monday, 29. Professor Seixas not being in town my class met and studied together.

March, 1836.

Tuesday, 1. Attended Heb. School.

Wednesday, 2. Att. Heb. School.

Thursday, 3. Att. Heb. School. met the quorums in the evening in the Lord's house, and read the committee's report previously drawn, which was adopted without amendment, except a small addition in the last article, extending the power of certain conference further, in signing licenses. I confess the hand of God in this matter, in giving me his Holy Spirit, to indite this valuable article, as by it the elders will enjoy their privileges as citizens, and the churches be freed from imposition.

Friday 4. Attended Heb. School.

Saturday, 5. Attended Heb. School. In the evening met the Twelve, pres. J. Smith, jr. & S. Rigdon, and my brother Warren, in the upper room of the printing office. The Twelve had prefered a charge against my brother for a letter he wrote last summer upon the subject of their teaching while at the Freedom conference. My brother confessed his mistake, upon the testimony of the Twelve, and said he was willing to publish that they were not in the fault, but that he was satisified they delivered those instructions which he had supposed they had not.[49]

Sunday, 6. Did not attend meeting in consequence of there not being sufficient room for so many in the small houses occupied for meetings.

Monday, 7. Attended Heb. School.

Tuesday 8. Attended Heb. School.

Wednesday 9. Attended Heb. School.

Thursday 10. Attended Heb. School.

Friday 11. Attended Heb. School.

From this time to Saturday the 19th attended Hebrew School, without anything of note's transpiring.

From Saturday 19th attended Heb. School, up to Saturday the 26. Nothing of note's transpiring. This day our school did not keep, we prepared for the dedication of the Lord's house.[50] I met in the president's room, pres. J. Smith, jr. S. Rigdon, my brother W. A. Cowdery & Elder W. Parrish, and assisted in writing a prayer for the dedication of the house.[51]

Sunday, the 27the attended on the dedication of the Lord's house. For the particulars of this great event see my account written by myself, and printed in the March No. of The Messenger and Advocate, signed C. In the evening I met with the officers of the church in the Lord's house. The Spirit was poured out—I saw the glory of God, like a great cloud, come down and rest upon the house, and fill the same like a mighty rushing wind. I also saw cloven tongues, like as of fire rest upon many, (for there were 316 present,) while they spake with other tongues and prophesied.

Notes

Editors' note: This article was originally published in *BYU Studies* 12/4 (1972): 410–26.

1.   The most significant works on Oliver Cowdery are Stanley R. Gunn, *Oliver Cowdery* (Salt Lake City, 1962); an essay by Richard L. Anderson, "Oliver Cowdery, Esq.: His Non-Church Decade," *To the Glory of God*, ed. Truman G. Madsen and Charles D.

Tate, Jr. (Salt Lake City, 1972), pp. 199–216; and four articles by Dr. Anderson in *The Improvement Era:* "Oliver Cowdery's Non-Mormon Reputation," 71 (August 1968), 18–26; "The Second Witness of Priesthood Restoration," 71 (September 1968), 15–24; "The Second Witness on Priesthood Succession," 71 (November1968), 14–20; and "The Scribe as a Witness," 72 (January 1969), 53–59.

2. Part of an introduction to some blessings given by Joseph Smith, Junior, written by Oliver Cowdery in "The Book of Patriarchal Blessings, 1834," pp. 8–9, MS, Family and Church History Department Archives, The Church of Jesus Christ of Latter-day Saints (hereafter Church Archives). This volume consists mainly of patriarchal blessings given by Joseph Smith, Senior.

3. *Latter Day Saints' Messenger and Advocate* (Kirtland, Ohio), 1 (October 1834), 16.

4. Anderson, "The Scribe as a Witness," p. 54.

5. William Lang, *History of Seneca County* (Springfield, OH: Transcript Printing Co., 1880), p. 365. For a fuller treatment of Cowdery's ten years out of the Church see Anderson, "Oliver Cowdery, Esq.: His Non-Church Decade."

6. Oliver Cowdery had been elected by the Geauga County Democratic Convention on 10 October 1835 as a delegate to the State Convention to be held at Columbus on 8 January 1836.

7. Lyman Root was one of the original settlers of Ridgeville, Lorain County, Ohio, in 1810.

8. John A. Bryan, a Democratic editor of the Columbus *Sentinel*, was a native New Yorker and an opponent of excessive state banking privileges. In 1835 he was being mentioned in the public press as a candidate for governor of Ohio. In a letter dated 15 October 1835 Oliver pledged his support for Bryan in the up-coming state convention. See "Cowdery Letterbook," pp. 51–52, MS, Henry E. Huntington Library and Art Gallery, San Marino, California.

9. Cyprian Rudd was born in Bennington, Vermont, and was fifty-three years of age in 1836.

10. Oliver Cowdery's mother, Rebecca Fuller Cowdery, died on 3 September 1809 when Oliver was two years old. The following year his father, William, married Mrs. Keziah Pearce Austin. Silas Austin was a son of Oliver's stepmother by a former marriage.

11. Reference is made here to Maria Louise, the first of six children born to Oliver and Elizabeth Ann Whitmer Cowdery. Born on 11 August 1835, Maria was the only one of the Cowdery children who grew to maturity.

12. The "endowment" referred to was not the ordinance performed in later Latter-day Saint temples, but a preliminary ordinance of washing and anointing. At this meeting Oliver's father, William, was appointed to preside over the Priest's Quorum in Kirtland. See Joseph Smith, "Diary," 1835–1836, 114–119, MS, Church Archives.

13. Warren A. Cowdery (1788–1851), an older brother of Oliver, was born in Poultney, Vermont, in October 1788. He practiced medicine in Vermont and in Freedom, New York, between 1816 and 1831, and was also the first postmaster of Freedom, beginning in 1824. He joined the LDS Church about 1830 and moved to Kirtland, where he remained until his death on 23 February 1851. Warren succeeded his brother, Oliver, as editor of the *Latter Day Saints' Messenger and Advocate,* and assisted Joseph Smith as a scribe.

14. The difficulty that existed between Warren A. Cowdery and the Twelve is summarized in a published notice at the time the problem was concluded in March 1836:

"NOTICE is hereby given to all whom it may concern, that Messrs. T. B. Marsh and others, denominated the 'Twelve' while on their mission to the East, last season, received a letter from the Presidency of the church in which they were censured for neglecting to teach the Church in Freedom Cattaraugus County, N.Y., the necessity of contributing of their earthly substance for the building of the House of the Lord in this place. The rebuke from the Presidency, (as the undersigned has been informed) was predicated upon a letter addressed by him, to the Presidents or some one of them, stating that they, the Twelve taught no such thing. The undersigned although actuated by the purest motives at the time he wrote believing he had stated nothing but the truth, has since become satisfied from the best of evidence, that, that particular item in their instructions was not omitted as he had represented, he, therefore, most deeply regrets it, being sensible as he now is, that he was the cause (although innocent) of wounding the best of feelings, and depressing spirits buoyant with hope, while in a field of useful labor at a distance from home. W. A. COWDERY. Kirtland, March 7th 1836." *Messenger and Advocate* 2 (February 1836), 263.

15. James M. Carrel describes the post office difficulty that existed in Kirtland at this time which no doubt explains Oliver's correspondence on the subject. In a letter to R. M. Williams, Post Master of Potter, New York dated 29 October 1835, Carrel charges the Whig postmaster of Kirtland with "gross neglect of duty, and disqualified for the office," on the grounds that when absent from his office he "leaves it in care of a *woman!*" and when he is in the office "he is entirely destitute of that spirit of accommodation, and gentlemanly deportment towards those having business in the office, that should characterize the conduct of every man who is living in the bounty of the government." Carrel charges further that the Whig postmaster treats those of an opposite political sentiment "with marked indignity and contempt." Furthermore, instead of publishing his lists of letters in the *Northern Times* where everyone in town "could see when there was a letter for him," and which was published "almost at his own door," the postmaster posted the lists in the local tavern, to the inconvenience of the town's people. Carrel concluded his letter by giving reasons "that lead us to petition for the appointment of Mr. Oliver Cowdery" as postmaster at Kirtland. See "Cowdery Letterbook," pp. 58–60.

16. John Corrill (1794–?) was born 17 September 1794 in Worcester, Massachusetts. He was living in Ashtabula, Ohio, in the fall of 1830 when Oliver Cowdery and fellow missionaries passed through Ohio and baptized him. In June 1831 he was ordained a high priest and set apart as second counselor to Bishop Edward Partridge. Soon after this, he was sent to Missouri, where he presided over branches of the Church in Jackson County. At the time of the difficulties in Jackson County in 1833, Corrill was imprisoned for a time in Independence, where he had been engaged in terminating the business of the Church. He returned to Ohio with Joseph Smith following the Zion's Camp march in 1834 and was appointed to take charge of the final construction of the Kirtland Temple. After dedication of the Temple in March 1836, Corrill returned to Missouri, where he participated in building up the Church center at Far West. He was appointed as a Church historian along with Elias Higbee in 1838, but soon afterward left the Church. See John Corrill, *A Brief History of the Church* . . . (St. Louis: printed for the author, 1839).

17. Martin Harris (1783–1875) was born in Easttown, Saratoga County, New York. With Oliver Cowdery and David Whitmer, he was one of the witnesses to the divine

origin of the Book of Mormon. Nine years after his birth his family moved to Palmyra, New York, where, in 1827, he became acquainted with Joseph Smith. Harris assisted the Prophet financially and clerically during the translation and publication of the Book of Mormon. He was appointed as a member of the High Council of the Church in Kirtland in 1834 and assisted Oliver Cowdery and David Whitmer in instructing and ordaining the Twelve Apostles at the time of the calling of that Quorum in February 1835. Three years later he became dissatisfied and remained in Kirtland after the Church moved west. He did not return to the Church until he came to Utah in 1870.

18.   Thirty-five pages of the patriarchal blessing book kept by Joseph Smith Sr. are in the handwriting of Oliver Cowdery. Several of the blessings were written during the first months of 1836.

19.   A copy of Cowdery's letter to Joel Sweetland, in which he suggests reasons Sweetland did not receive his *Messenger and Advocate* subscription, is found in the "Cowdery Letterbook," p. 76.

20.   John F. Boynton (1811–1890), who married Susan Lowell on this date, was a native of Bradford, Essex County, Massachusetts. He was baptized by Joseph Smith at Kirtland in September 1832. He engaged in proselyting activity for the Church in Pennsylvania in 1832 and in Maine in 1833–34. He was ordained an Apostle under the hands of the Three Witnesses in February 1935. Boynton left the Church in 1837 and took up residence in New York, but in 1872 he visited Brigham Young and his former associates in Utah. He was engaged as an engineer in the invention of weapons systems during the Civil War, and at least thirty-six patents were issued under his name. He died in Syracuse, New York, 20 October 1890.

21.   See note 11 above.

22.   Frederick G.Williams (1787–1842) was born 28 October 1787 in Suffield, Hartford County, Connecticut. He was baptized in Kirtland by Oliver Cowdery during Oliver's mission to Missouri in 1830–31. Williams became second counselor to Joseph Smith in the Church presidency on 18 March 1833. In Kirtland he was the owner of the F.G. Williams and Company printing establishment, and was a member of the committee to arrange the interior of the Kirtland Temple. In 1834 he served as paymaster in Zion's Camp. Williams was excommunicated from the Church at a conference in Quincy, Illinois, on 17 March 1839, but was reinstated in April 1840. He died in Quincy on 10 October 1842. See Nancy Clement Williams, *After 100 Years* (Independence, MO, 1951). and Frederick G. Williams, "Frederick Granger Williams of the First Presidency of the Church," *BYU Studies* 12 (Spring 1972), 243–61.

23.   Sidney Rigdon (1793–1876) was born in St. Clair, Alleghany County, Pennsylvania, on 19 February 1793. He was a popular Campbellite minister in Mentor, Ohio, when Oliver Cowdery converted him to Mormonism in the fall of 1830. In 1831 Rigdon accompanied Joseph Smith to Missouri and was present at the dedication of the land of Zion. After returning to Kirtland, Sidney assisted Joseph as a clerk, and in March 1833 he was appointed as a counselor to the Prophet in the First Presidency. During Joseph Smith's absence with Zion's Camp in 1834, Sidney assisted Oliver Cowdery in directing the affairs of the Church in Kirtland. Rigdon taught penmanship, arithmetic, English grammar, and geography in the Kirtland School, and assisted in the publication of the *Doctrine and Covenants of the Church* in 1835. He left Kirtland with Joseph Smith in 1838 and in the following year was imprisoned during the Mormon difficulties in Mis-

souri. After the death of Joseph Smith in 1844, Rigdon left the main body of the Church. He died at his home in Friendship, New York, in 1876. See F. Mark McKiernan, *The Voice of One Crying in the Wilderness: Sidney Rigdon, Religious Reformer* (Lawrence, KS: Coronado Press, 1971).

24. Hyrum Smith (1800–1844), an older brother of Joseph Smith, was born in Tunbridge, Vermont, on 9 February 1800. He was a faithful supporter of his brother and the cause of the Latter-day Saints from the beginning. His name is among the witnesses of the Gold Plates from which the Book of Mormon was translated. He was a leader of Zion's Camp in 1834 and was chosen to serve on the Kirtland High Council that same year. In September 1837 Hyrum was appointed as assistant counselor to the First Presidency of the Church and two months later replaced Frederick G. Williams as second counselor in the Presidency. He was appointed Patriarch to the Church in 1841. Hyrum lost his life by the side of his brother, Joseph, in Carthage, Illinois, on 27 June 1844. Pearson H. Corbett, *Hyrum Smith, Patriarch* (Salt Lake City: Deseret Book, 1963).

25. David Whitmer (1805–1888) was born 7 January 1805 near Harrisburg, Pennsylvania. He met Oliver Cowdery in Palmyra, New York, while on a business trip in 1828. Whitmer was associated with Joseph Smith during the translation of the Book of Mormon at the Whitmer residence in Fayette, New York, and became one of the Three Witnesses of that work. He was ordained a High Priest by Oliver Cowdery in October 1831, and went to Missouri, where he settled in Jackson County. After the Mormon expulsion from that county in 1833, David Whitmer settled in Clay County, where he was appointed president of the High Council on 3 July 1834. Whitmer then became dissatisfied and was rejected by the Church in 1838. After leaving the Church he resided in Richmond, Missouri, some fifty years, until his death on 25 January 1888.

26. John Whitmer (1802–1878) first met Oliver Cowdery in 1829 during the translation of the Book of Mormon. He was born 27 August 1802 in Fayette, New York. In March 1831 he was appointed Church Historian and later that year accompanied Oliver Cowdery to Missouri to prepare the Church revelations for printing. He was a presiding officer of the Church in Missouri and Ohio. John Whitmer left the Church in 1838 and settled in Far West, where he died in 1878.

27. Warren Parrish was an officer in the Kirtland Bank and a member of the Quorum of Seventy in Kirtland. He had accompanied Zion's Camp to Missouri in 1834 and was a scribe to Joseph Smith. Charged with conduct injurious to the Church, Parrish denounced his membership in 1837 and associated with others in open dissent. See also D. Paul Sampson and Larry T. Wimmer, "The Kirtland Safety Society: the Stock Ledger Book and the Bank Failure," *BYU Studies* 12/4 (1972): 427-36.

28. Joseph Smith's description of events on 21 January was recorded extensively in his diary. Among other things he noted that "the heavens were opened upon us and I beheld the celestial Kingdom of God, and the glory thereof, whether in the body or out I cannot tell,—I saw the transcendant beauty of the gate through which the heirs of that Kingdom will enter, which was like unto circling flames of fire, also the blasing throne of God, whereon was seated the Father and the Son,—I saw the beautiful streets of that Kingdom, which had the appearance of being paved with gold . . ." Joseph Smith, "Diary," 1835–1836, pp. 134–38.

29. Thomas Baldwin Marsh (1799–1866) was born in Acton, Massachusetts, on 1 November 1799. He first met Oliver Cowdery in 1829 after traveling to Palmyra, New

York, to investigate rumors he had heard about Joseph Smith. He moved to Palmyra from Massachusetts in the fall of 1830 and was baptized. In the spring of 1831 he went to Kirtland, Ohio, and the following year settled in Missouri. He was driven from his home in the 1833 Mormon expulsion from Jackson County. After returning to Kirtland in 1835 he was appointed as one of the Twelve Apostles and ordained by Oliver Cowdery. Marsh left the Church during the Missouri difficulties of 1838, but was reunited with the Latter-day Saints in Nebraska in 1857 and settled in Ogden, Utah, where he died in 1866.

30. Don Carlos Smith (1816–1841) was the youngest of Joseph Smith's brothers. In 1833 he was employed by Oliver Cowdery who taught him the business of printing. He published the *Elder's Journal* in Kirtland prior to the fire that destroyed the printing office in 1837 and later edited thirty-two issues of the *Times and Seasons* in Nauvoo, where he also served on the City Council. He died of tuberculosis in Nauvoo on 7 August 1841. Don Carlos was the father of California's first poet laureate, Ina Coolbrith.

31. Joseph Smith described this occasion in these words: ". . . the gift of toungs fell upon us in mighty pour, angels mingled their voices with ours, while their presence was in our midst, and unseasing prases swelled our bosoms for the space of half an hour. . . ." Joseph Smith, "Diary," 1835–1836, p. 141.

32. James M. Carrel was a member of the Kirtland Safety Society. He was also the recorder of several of the letters in the "Cowdery Letterbook" at the Huntington Library.

33. Joshua Seixas, a resident of Hudson, Ohio, taught Hebrew in the Kirtland School for two months beginning 26 January 1836. He was held in high esteem by Joseph Smith, and the School was attended by many of the leading men of the Church in Kirtland.

34. The *Northern Times* was a political newspaper edited by Oliver Cowdery and published by Frederick G. Williams in Kirtland beginning in February 1835. A Democratic sheet, the *Times*, supported the candidacy of Martin Van Buren in 1835–36.

35. Newel Kimball Whitney (1795–1850) was born in Marlborough, Vermont, on 5 February 1795. He served in the War of 1812 before moving to Ohio about 1817. He was a partner in the mercantile firm of Gilbert and Whitney in Kirtland, Ohio, when he met Oliver Cowdery and the Indian missionaries in November 1830 and was converted. Newel was appointed bishop of the Church at Kirtland in December 1831, and was identified with the mercantile affairs of the Church during the Kirtland years. After the Latter-day Saints were driven from Missouri in 1839, Bishop Whitney assisted in locating and settling them on newly purchased land in Illinois. He officiated as bishop and was Trustee-in-trust of the Church in the years prior to his death in Salt Lake City in September 1850.

36. Joseph C. Kingsbury (1812–1898) was born 2 May 1812 in Endfield, Connecticut, and was baptized in January 1832 in Kirtland. On 13 January 1836 he was appointed to the High Council in Kirtland in the place of Orson Hyde who had been ordained an Apostle. Kingsbury migrated to Utah in 1847 and served as a bishop of the Salt Lake City Second Ward.

37. Signed by the First Presidency and Oliver Cowdery, the letter to Madam Seixas expresses a belief that her husband "has been sent to this institution through the immediate directions of God," and solicits the purchase of the valuable lexicon "as our only object is to do good to lay aside error when we discover it forsake evil and follow righteousness and truly be the better prepared and qualified to render assistance to our fel-

low men and glorify the name of the Lord. . . ." Dated 13 February, the letter is recorded in the "Cowdery Letterbook," pp. 77–78.

38. William W. Phelps (1792–1872) was born on 17 February 1792 in Hanover, New Jersey. Arriving in Kirtland in 1831, he was called to assist Oliver Cowdery in printing and writing books for the schools of the Church. He was the editor of *The Evening and the Morning Star* (Zion [Independence, Mo.]), and published the *Book of Commandments* in Missouri prior to the destruction of the press in 1833. In Kirtland he assisted the committee appointed to compile the *Doctrine and Covenants* and was appointed to revise and arrange the hymns of the Church for printing. In July 1834 Phelps was appointed as a counselor to David Whitmer in the presidency of the stake in Missouri. As a scribe for Joseph Smith he drafted and signed numerous Church documents. In 1838 he became embittered toward the Church and was excommunicated. In 1841, however, he returned to the Church and was prominent in literary and agricultural affairs in pioneer Utah. See Walter D. Bowen, "The Versatile W. W. Phelps: Mormon Writer, Educator, and Pioneer" (master's thesis, Brigham Young University, 1958).

39. See note 10 above.

40. Stephen Fuller Cowdery (1791–?), an older brother of Oliver, was living with his family in Buffalo, New York, in 1835 when Oliver traveled east to purchase books and equipment for the Church. A letter to Warren Cowdery from Oliver on 22 November 1835 reveals that at the time of Oliver's visit in Buffalo, Stephen's home had been demolished by "wind and water," but they escaped injury. "Cowdery Letterbook," p. 63.

41. A Democrat, John Thompson was a member of the U.S. House of Representatives from the Chillicothe District of Ohio.

42. Lucy was Oliver's half sister, the second of three girls born after their father married Keziah Pearce Austin in 1810. Lucy later married Phinehas H. Young, the brother of Brigham Young.

43. Samuel James was appointed to the High Council in Kirtland on 13 January 1836 in the place of Joseph Smith, Senior. In the following years he undertook extensive missionary labor for the Church in the East.

44. Lyman Cowdery (1802–?), an older brother of Oliver, resided in Freedom, New York, and later became a prominent lawyer and judge in Wisconsin.

45. Orson Hyde (1805–1878) was born in Oxford, Connecticut, on 8 January 1805. At the age of fourteen he walked from Connecticut to Ohio, and was a clerk in the Gilbert and Whitney store in Kirtland. He joined the Campbellites under Sidney Rigdon in 1827 and became a pastor. He was converted to Mormonism in 1831 and ordained a high priest by Oliver Cowdery in October of that year. During the next four years he performed lengthy missionary journeys to the East. On 15 February 1835 he was chosen one of the Twelve Apostles in Kirtland and ordained by Oliver Cowdery. He was prominently involved in Church affairs until the time of his death in Spring City, Utah, on 28 November 1878. See Marvin S. Hill, "An Historical Study of the Life of Orson Hyde, Early Mormon Missionary and Apostle" (master's thesis, Brigham Young University, 1955).

46. Sylvester Smith was a president of the Seventy in Kirtland from 1835–1837. He had been ordained a high priest by Oliver Cowdery in 1831 and was a member of the High Council organized in Kirtland in February 1834. He also accompanied Zion's Camp in 1834.

47. Winslow Shepherd Wilbur was a member of the Seventy in 1837 and accompanied the Kirtland Camp to Missouri in 1838.

48. Peter Whitmer Jr. (1809–1836) was born in Fayette, New York, on 27 September 1809. He first met Oliver Cowdery in the summer of 1829 during the final stages of the translation of the Book of Mormon, of which Whitmer was one of the witnesses. He was a companion of Oliver Cowdery on the Indian Mission in 1830–31. Employed as a tailor in Independence, Whitmer was among the Saints driven from Jackson County, Missouri, in 1833. He died of tuberculosis near Liberty, Missouri, on 22 September 1836.

49. See note 14 above.

50. Construction of the Kirtland Temple began 23 July 1833. The building was dedicated 27 March 1836. See Lauritz G. Petersen, "The Kirtland Temple," *BYU Studies* 12/4 (1972): 400–9.

51. The dedicatory prayer of the Kirtland Temple is published as section 109 in the Doctrine and Covenants.

Oliver Cowdery and the Kirtland Temple Experience

Steven C. Harper

$\mathcal{M}$ankind's knowledge and power from God expanded exponentially in the temple at Kirtland, Ohio, from January through April 1836. This promised outpouring served as a reward for early obedience and a catalyst for further blessings described finally as "an infinity of fulness" (D&C 38:32–33; 105:9–12; 109:77). An abundant historical record affirms and embodies this remarkable endowment of divine power.[1]

The Religious and Historical Context of the Kirtland Manifestations

The Saints regarded their experiences as a continuation of the pentecostal experience recorded in the Acts of the Apostles. What occurred in the Kirtland Temple was, as Benjamin Brown writes in his account, "even greater than at the day of Pente[cost]."[2] We can say, at least, that the historical record of the Kirtland manifestations is greater than the biblical record of the day of Pentecost (Acts 2). A non–Latter-day Saint living in Kirtland reported specifically on the manifestations in a letter to his sister. Writing on April 10, 1836, a week after the Savior appeared to Joseph Smith and Oliver Cowdery, Lucius Pomeroy Parsons noted,

> They have lately had what they term a solemn assembly. This was at the completion of the lower story of the Temple which is finished in a very singular order having four Pulpits on each end of

Jesus Christ Appears to the Prophet Joseph Smith and Oliver Cowdery, by Walter Rane, oil on canvas, 2003. Courtesy Museum of Church History and Art.

the House and curtains between each. Also, curtains dividing the house in the center. They have had wonderful manifestations there of late behind the curtains. This was in the night. Their meeting held for several nights in succession. None but the Prophets and Elders were admitted. The number of Prophets now amounts to twelve. Some can see angels and others cannot. They report that the Savior appeared personally with angels and endowed the Elders with powers to work Miracles.[3]

Even hostile observers seemed to testify of the relationship between the pentecostal manifestations of first-century Jerusalem and nineteenth-century Kirtland. John Corrill wrote of a meeting in the Kirtland Temple, "The sacrament was then administered, in which they partook of the bread and wine freely, and a report went abroad that some of them got drunk: as to that every man must answer for himself. A similar report, the reader will recollect, went out concerning the disciples, at Jerusalem, on the day of pentecost."[4]

Historians tend to situate these accounts of the "many Miraculous Experiences" and "Many Visions told" as examples of a visionary subculture in the early American republic.[5] The experiences of these eyewitnesses can partly be understood as a believing response to skepticism, confirmed by intense personal experience with God. The renewal of biblical revelation solidified faith in the Bible. As many increasingly doubted the possibility of biblical miracles in modernity and, finally, even in antiquity, the Saints believed in the gifts of the Spirit and pentecostal outpourings because they experienced them. The Kirtland Temple made these witnesses heirs of the Israelite Patriarchs and the Apostolic Church.

Those who recorded events surrounding the Kirtland Temple dedication did not overtly try to explain them. They assumed, instead, an affinity of understanding with the few who shared their experiences. Benjamin Brown wrote in 1853, for example, "Such a chain of testimonies, and an interweaving of evidences, accompanied with that perception and comprehension which the Holy Ghost alone can give, none can realize, but those who have received that Spirit and revelations unto themselves. Such persons know just how it is."[6] In the first months of 1836, Benjamin Brown, Oliver Cowdery, Edward Partridge, William Phelps, Stephen Post, and Joseph Smith were among those who gathered in solemn meetings with other Saints in the Kirtland Temple.[7] Thanks to their lengthy, detailed, contemporaneous documents, modern readers have the benefit of several independent eyewitness accounts of these events, the power and significance of which prompted each immediately to commit their experiences to writing.

Revelations had promised the Saints that if they sacrificed to build the temple as commanded, they would be endowed with divine power to transcend the temporal and mortal.[8] They anticipated an endowment of power through communion with heaven.[9] The documents that follow largely capture the effulgence of that endowment. Though some documents have suffered frustrating damage and are subject to other limitations, each confirms the general and specific testimonies of other participants of the Kirtland Pentecost. Some eyewitnesses captured more of the experience than Joseph Smith recorded in his characteristically understated journal entries. Where Joseph's entry for the evening of March 29, 1836, says, for instance, "The Holy Spirit rested down upon us and we continued in the Lord's house all night prophesying and giving glory to God," Benjamin Brown both confirms and enhances Joseph's record by noting the ministering of angels, prophesying in tongues, and visions of the Savior and eternity as part of the "many Miraculous Experiences told [and] Many Visions told."

Priesthood leaders began meeting in the Kirtland Temple January 21, 1836. In a series of meetings leading up to the March 27 dedication, members of the priesthood quorums washed and were anointed with oil consecrated for the sacred purpose of designating them clean from the sinfulness of their world. William Phelps wrote to his wife, Sally, in January 1836, "Our meeting[s] will grow more and more solemn, and will continue till the great solemn assembly when the house is finished! We are preparing to make ourselves clean, by first cleansing our hearts, forsaking our sins, forgiving every body; putting on clean decent clothes, by anointing our heads and by keeping all the commandments. As we come nearer to God we see our imperfections and nothingness plainer and plainer."[10] In the temple meetings in January brethren sang, prayed, testified, prophesied, beheld visions, received ministering angels, spoke in and interpreted tongues, and shouted hosannas.

Then, on March 27, Joseph dedicated the temple. That night he and those who had been anointed tarried all night in the temple, where spiritual gifts were richly bestowed. On March 29 the first presidency met in the temple with the stake presidencies and bishoprics of Kirtland and Missouri and washed their feet, following the pattern of Jesus as recorded in John 13. The next night, March 30, the other elders who had been anointed earlier received the same culminating ordinance, which Joseph had previously described as "calculated to unite our hearts, that we may be one in feeling and sentiment and that our faith may be strong, so that satan cannot over throw us, nor have any power over us."[11] On March 31 the dedicatory services were repeated for those unable to attend on March 27. On Sunday April 3, 1836, the Lord Jesus Christ appeared to Joseph

Smith and Oliver Cowdery and accepted the Temple, as recorded in Joseph Smith's journal entry for that day. Ministering angels followed. Elias, Moses, and Elijah each committed priesthood keys needed to gather Israel, endow the Saints with power, and seal the human family together in anticipation of the "great and dreadful day of the Lord" (D&C 110:16). Thus was accomplished the endowment of priesthood power Moroni foretold when he appeared to Joseph Smith on September 21, 1823 (D&C 2). As Joseph Smith's March 30, 1836, journal entry reports, "it was a penticost and enduement [endowment] indeed, long to be remembered for the sound shall go forth from this place into all the world, and the occurrences of this day shall be hande[d] down upon the pages of sacred history to all generations, as the day of Pentecost."[12]

Oliver Cowdery's Accounts of the Kirtland Experiences

Along with Joseph Smith, Oliver Cowdery (1806–50) received power and authority in each of the landmark events in the restoration of holy priesthood powers and keys. On May 15, 1829, John the Baptist conferred the Aaronic Priesthood on their heads (D&C 13). Soon thereafter, Peter, James, and John ordained Joseph and Oliver to the Melchizedek Priesthood and conferred the keys of the holy apostleship (D&C 7:7; 27:12–13). Then on April 3, 1836, these two witnesses envisioned the Savior and received an endowment of priesthood keys from Elias, Moses, and Elijah. Oliver Cowdery kept a private "Sketch Book"[13] in which he included more details of his involvement in the solemn meetings leading up to the March 27, 1836, dedication. (See "Oliver Cowdery's Kirtland, Ohio, 'Sketch Book,'" 241–62, in this volume.) He also penned the Church's official news account of the Kirtland Temple dedication, published in the *Messenger & Advocate* immediately after the occasion, and that account is as follows:

Messenger & Advocate

Previous notice having been given, the Church of the Latter Day Saints met this day in the House of the Lord to dedicate it to

him. The congregation began to assemble before 8 o'clock A.M. and
thronged the doors until 9, when the Presidents of the church who
assisted in seating the congregation, were reluctantly compelled to
order the door keepers to close the doors; every seat and aisle were
crowded. — One thousand persons were now silently and solemnly
waiting to hear the word of the Lord from the mouth of his servants
in the sacred desk. President S. Rigdon began the services of the day,
by reading the 96th and 24th Psalms. An excellent choir of singers,
led by M.C. Davis sung the following Hymn: ["Ere Long the Vail
Will Rend in Twain."]

President Rigdon then in an able, devout and appropriate manner, addressed the throne of Grace. The following Hymn was then
sung: ["O Happy Souls Who Pray."]

The speaker (S. Rigdon,) selected the 8th chapter of Matthew, the
18, 19 and 20th verses from which, he proposed to address the congregation, continuing himself more closely to the 20th verse — He
spoke two hours and a half in his usual, forcible and logical manner.
At one time in the course of his remarks he was rather pathetic, than
otherwise, which drew tears from many eyes. He was then taking a
retrospective view of the toils, privations and anxieties of those who
had labored upon the walls of the house to erect them. And added,
there were those who had wet them with their tears, in the silent
shades of night, while they were praying to the God of heaven, to
protect them, and stay the unhallowed hands of ruthless spoilers,
who had uttered a prophecy when the foundation was laid, that the
walls would never be reared. This was only a short digression from
the main thread of his discourse, which he soon resumed.

Here it may be not improper to give a synopsis of the discourse
for the satisfaction of our readers who were not privileged as we
were with hearing it. The speaker assumed as a postulate, what
we presume no one was disposed to deny, (viz:) that in the days of
the Savior there were Synagogues, where the Jews worshipped God,
and in addition to them, the splendid Temple at jerusalem. Yet,
when on a certain occasion, one proposed to follow him whither-
soever he went, he though heir of all things cried out like on in the

bitterness of his soul in abject poverty, The Foxes have holes, &c. This, said the speaker, was evidence to his mind, that the Most High did not put his name there, and that he did not accept the worship of those who payed their vows and adorations there. This was evident from the fact that they would not receive him, but thrust him from them, saying, away with him, crucify him! crucify him! It was therefore abundantly evident that his spirit did not dwell in them. They were the degenerate sons of noble sires: but they had long since slain the Prophets and Seers through whom the Lord revealed himself to the children of men. They were not led by revelation, This, said the speaker, was the grand difficulty among them. Their unbelieve in present revelation. He further remarked, that, their unbelief in present revelation was the means of dividing that generation into the various sects and parties that existed. They were sincere worshipers, but their worship was not required of them, nor was it acceptable to God. — The Redeemer himself who knew the hearts of all men, called them generation of vipers. It was proof positive to his mind, that there being Pharisees, Sadducees, Herodians and Essens, and all differing from each other, that they were led by the precepts and commandments of men. Each had something peculiar to himself. But all agreed in one point, (viz:) to oppose the Redeemer. So that we discover he would with the utmost propriety, exclaim, notwithstanding their synagogue and Temple worship, The foxes have holes, the birds of the air have nests, but the Son of man hath not where to lay his head. He took occasion here to remark that such diversity of sentiment ever had, and ever would obtain when people were not led by present revelation. This brought him to the inevitable conclusion that the various sects of the present day, from their manifesting the same spirit, rested under the same condemnation with those who were coeval with the Savior. He admitted there were many houses; many sufficiently great, built for the worship of God, but not one except his, on the face of the whole earth, that was built by divine revelation, and were it not for this, the dear Redeemer might in this day of science, this day of intelligence, this day of religion, say to those who would follow him, The foxes have holes, the birds of the air have nests, but the Son of man hath not where to lay his head.

Here his whole soul appeared to be fired with his subject. Arguments, strong and conclusive seemed almost to vie with each other for utterance. Indeed, there was no sophistry in his reasoning, no plausible hypothesis on which the whole rested, but on the contrary plain scripture facts. Therefore his deductions and inferences were logical and conclusive.

The comparison drawn between the different religious sects of ancient and modern times, was perfectly natural, and simple yet it was done in that confident, masterly manner, accompanied with those incontrovertable proofs of his position, that was directly calculated to cheer and gladden the hearts of the Saints, but to draw down the indignation of the sectarian world upon him and we have no doubt had our speaker uttered the same sentiments, with the same proof of their correctness, had there been those present that we might name, his voice would doubtless have been drowned as was that of the ancient apostle in the Athenian Temple, when his auditors cried incessantly for about two hours "Great is Diana of the Ephesians."

But to conclude, we can truly say no one unacquainted with the manner of delivery and style of our speaker can, from reading form any adequate idea of the powerful effect he is capable of producing in the minds of his hearers.: And to say on this occasion he showed himself mater of his subject and did well, would be doing him injustice; to say he acquitted himself with honor or did very well, would be detracting from him real merit; and to say that he did exceeding well; would be only halting praise.

After closing his discourse he presented Joseph Smith jr. to the church as a Prophet and Seer. The Presidents of the church then all in their seats, acknowledged him as such by rising. The vote was unanimous in the affirmative.

The question was then put, and carried without a manifest dissenting sentiment to each of the different grades or quorums of church officers respectively and then to the congregation. The following hymn was then sung: ["Now Let Us Rejoice."]

Services closed for the forenoon.

Intermission was about 15 minutes during which none left their seats except a few females, who from having left their infants with their friends, were compelled to do so to take care of them. The P.M. services commenced by singing the following hymn: ["Adam-ondi-Ahman."]

President J. Smith jr. then rose, and after a few preliminary remarks, presented the several Presidents of the church, then present, to the several quorums respectively, and then to the church as being equal with himself, acknowledging them to be Prophets and Seers. The vote was unanimous in the affirmative in every instance. — Each of the different quorums was presented in its turn to all the rest, and then to the church, and received and acknowledged by all the rest, in their several stations without a manifest dissenting sentiment.

President J. Smith jr. then addressed the congregation in a manner calculated to instruct the understanding, rather than please the ear, and at or about the close of his remarks, he prophesied to all that inasmuch as they would uphold these men in their several stations, alluding to the different quorums in the church, the Lord would bless them; yea, in the name of Christ, the blessings of Heaven shall be yours. And when the Lord's anointed go forth to proclaim the word, bearing testimony to this generation, if they receive it, they shall be blessed, but if not, the judgments of God will follow close upon them, until that city of that house, that rejects them, shall be left desolate. The following hymn was then sung: ["How Pleased and Blest I Was."]

He then offered the dedication prayer, which was as follows: [See D&C 109.]

The choir then sung a hymn. ["The Spirit of God."]

President Smith then asked the several quorums separately and then the congregation, if they accepted the prayer. The vote was, in every instance, unanimous in the affirmative.

The Eucharist was administered. D[on]. C[arlos]. Smith blessed the bread and wine and they were distributed by several Elders present, to the church.

President J. Smith jr. then arose and bore record of his mission. D. C. Smith bore record of the truth of the work of the Lord in which we are engaged.

President O. Cowdery spoke and testified of the truth of the book of Mormon, and of the work of the Lord in these last days.

President F. G. Williams bore record that a Holy Angel of God, came and set between him and J. Smith sen. while the house was being dedicated.

President Hyrum Smith, (one of the building committee) made some appropriate remarks concerning the house, congratulating those who had endured so many toils and privations to erect it, that it was the Lord's house built by his commandment and he would bless them.

President S. Rigdon then made a few appropriate closing remarks; and a short prayer which was ended with loud acclamations of Hosanna! Hosanna! Hosanna to God and the Lamb, Amen, Amen and Amen! Three times. Elder B. Young, one of the Twelve, gave a short address in tongues; Elder D. W. Patten interpreted and gave a short exhortation in tongues himself; after which, President J. Smith jr. blessed the congregation in the name of the Lord, and at a little past four P.M. the whole exercise closed and the congregation dispersed.

We further add that we should do violence to our own feelings and injustice to the real merit of our brethren and friends who attended the meeting, were we here to withhold a meed of praise, which we think is their just due; not only for their qui[e]t demeanor during the whole exercise, which lasted more than eight hours, but for their great liberality in contributing of their earthly substance for the relief of the building committee, who were yet somewhat involved. As this was to be a day of sacrifice, as well as of fasting, There was a man placed at each door in the morning to receive the voluntary donations of those who entered. On counting the collection it amounted to nine hundred and sixty three dollars.
Kirtland, Ohio, March, 1836.[14]

Notes

Editors' note: This article contains excerpts from a longer article originally published in *Opening the Heavens*, by Welch and Carlson.

1. See Milton V. Backman Jr., *The Heavens Resound: A History of the Latter-day Saints in Ohio 1830–1838* (Salt Lake City: Deseret Book, 1983), 285–309; Karl Ricks Anderson, *Joseph Smith's Kirtland: Eyewitness Accounts* (Salt Lake City: Deseret Book, 1989), 169–91; Gregory Prince, *Power from on High: The Development of Mormon Priesthood* (Salt Lake City: Signature Books, 1995), 184–85, 160.

2. Benjamin Brown, *Testimonies for the Truth: A record of Manifestations of the Power of God, miraculous and providential, witnessed in the travels and experience of Benjamin Brown, high priest in the Church of Jesus Christ of Latter Day Saints, Pastor of the London, Reading, Kent, and Essex Conferences* (Liverpool: S. W. Richards, 1853), 5.

3. Lucius Pomeroy Parsons to Pamelia Parsons, April 10, 1836, Family and Church History Department Archives, The Church of Jesus Christ of Latter-day Saints (hereafter Church Archives). For Joseph Smith's explanation of the power the endowment would give to perform miracles, see Jessee, *Papers of Joseph Smith*, 2:77–78.

4. John Corrill, *A Brief History of the Church of Christ of Latter Day Saints (Commonly Called Mormons; Including an Account of Their Doctrine and Discipline; with the Reasons of the Author for Leaving the Church)* (St. Louis: By the author, 1839), 23. In Acts 2:13, mockers explained the spiritual manifestations simply: "These men are full of new wine." See William McLellin to M. H. Forscutt, October 1870, Library-Archives, Community of Christ, Independence, Missouri; William Harris, *Mormonism Portrayed* (Warsaw, IL: Sharp and Gamble, 1841), 136, for perpetuated rumors of similar drunkenness in the Kirtland Temple.

5. Richard L. Bushman, "The Visionary World of Joseph Smith," *BYU Studies* 37/1 (1997–98): 183–204, outlines this culture and lists several primary documents that might comprise a genre with which the eyewitness accounts of the Kirtland experience share similarities. Similarly, see Larry C. Porter, "Solomon Chamberlin's Missing Pamphlet: Dreams, Visions, and Angelic Ministrants," *BYU Studies* 37/2 (1997–98): 113–40; Ann Taves, *Fits, Trances, and Visions: Experiencing Religion and Explaining Experience from Wesley to James* (Princeton: Princeton University Press, 1999). See also Leigh Eric Schmidt, *Hearing Things: Religion, Illusion, and the American Enlightenment* (Cambridge, MA: Harvard University Press, 2000).

6. Brown, *Testimonies for the Truth*, 5.

7. Brown, *Testimonies for the Truth*, 10–11. Joseph Smith's account of the events of March 27, 1836, which is reprinted later in this article, is in Jessee, *Papers of Joseph Smith*, 2:191–203.

8. Doctrine and Covenants 38:32; 88:67–76; 95:2–8.

9. Doctrine and Covenants 88:68–69; see also Joseph Smith to William Phelps, Kirtland, Ohio, January 11, 1833, in Dean C. Jessee, ed. and comp., *The Personal Writings of Joseph Smith*, rev. ed. (Salt Lake City: Deseret Book; Provo, UT: Brigham Young University Press, 2002), 292–93.

10. William Phelps to Sally Phelps, January 1836, in Bruce A. Van Orden, ed., "Writing to Zion: The William W. Phelps Kirtland Letters (1835–1836)," *BYU Studies* 33/3 (1993): 574.

11. Jessee, *Papers of Joseph Smith*, 2:77. Members of the School of the Prophets were "received by the ordinance of the washing of the feet" in January and February 1833 (D&C 88:139). That ordinance was next performed March 30, 1836, as the culminating ordinance of the Kirtland endowment. See Prince, *Power from on High*, 172–73.

12. Jessee, Papers of Joseph Smith, 207.

13. Oliver Cowdery, "Sketch Book," Church Archives, and published in Arrington, "Oliver Cowdery's Kirtland, Ohio, 'Sketch Book,'" 410–26.

14. This account was originally published in *Messenger and Advocate*, March 1836, 274–81. The words of the revealed prayer (now D&C 109) and the words of the hymns have been omitted here.

James H. Hart's
Contribution to Our Knowledge
of Oliver Cowdery and David Whitmer

Edward L. Hart

$\mathcal{M}$ost Latter-day Saints take for granted the existence of portraits of the Three Witnesses, but in fact no likeness of Oliver Cowdery was available to the Church until 1883, and then it was touch-and-go whether one would be obtained. Had it not been for the faith and tenacity of James H. Hart, who pursued the portrait when others had failed, we might never have known just what Oliver Cowdery looked like. In the course of following the trail of the portrait, Hart was also able to conduct important interviews with David Whitmer.

Junius F. Wells, editor of the *Contributor,* a Church publication, could find no picture of Cowdery when he planned to publish portraits of the Three Witnesses in the October 1883 issue. He knew that an oil portrait and a daguerreotype photograph, taken of Cowdery four years before his death, were in Missouri in the hands of Cowdery's daughter, whose husband, Dr. Charles Johnson, was adamant about not letting the likenesses go. Wells, with the aid of others, had tried unsuccessfully to obtain the daguerreotype and as a last resort turned to James H. Hart for assistance.[1] "As it is my special mission to obtain it," wrote Hart, "I shall no doubt be successful."[2]

At the time Wells called upon him for help, Hart was immigration agent for the Church in New York[3] and was on one of his regular visits West between immigrant ship arrivals. He immediately made plans to stop over in Missouri on his return trip to New York. He went first to see David Whitmer in Richmond, expecting to find the Johnsons there also. Whitmer informed him that the Johnsons, along with Whitmer's sister (Oliver Cowdery's widow), were in the extreme southwest corner of the state, South West City. Whitmer was not optimistic that Dr. Johnson would permit the portrait or the daguerreotype to be taken away.[4]

The railway stop nearest to South West City was Seneca, twenty-eight miles away. At Seneca, Hart hired a buggy and driver.[5] The month was August, and the heat, dust, and flies assailed the horses, the driver, and Hart—always the immaculate English gentleman, with a full beard, top hat, and cane. Undeterred, Hart continued to the Johnson home.

"The doctor was at first quite hostile," Hart wrote, "but after laboring with him several hours, during which his wife and Mrs. Cowdery warmly seconded my pleading, some kind spirit came upon him and he gave me the choice between the oil painting and the daguerreotype."[6] Hart wisely chose the daguerreotype and returned to Seneca the way he had come. He continued on to New York, where he placed the picture in the hands of H. B. Hall and Son, engravers. Since the engravers already had the likenesses of the other two Witnesses, they were able to complete the frontispiece in time for the October 1883 issue of the *Contributor.*

On a subsequent trip West, Hart repeated his journey to South West City to return the daguerreotype to its owners. Hart's acceptance of the assignment to procure the likeness as a "special mission" made him willing to expend a great deal of effort, which, along with his determination, conversational skill, and charm, resulted in the procurement of the portrait of Oliver Cowdery now familiar to virtually all Latter-day Saints.

During his journeys to obtain the daguerreotype and return it, James Hart had two opportunities to interview David Whitmer in Richmond, Missouri. Hart was one among several who reported that Whitmer remained firm to the end in his testimony of the truthfulness of the Book of Mormon. However, even though others also reported on Whitmer's testimony, some distinctive features of Hart's interviews lend a credibility that make them worth examining.

The first LDS publication of Oliver Cowdery's portrait. This frontispiece for the October 1883 *Contributor* shows the Three Witnesses over an engraving of the Hill Cumorah. The angel on the left holds a scroll that reads, "Rev. XIV-6." At the top right is a heavenly being showing the golden plates to three men. Under Cowdery's portrait are the sticks or scrolls of Joseph and Judah brought together. Courtesy Edward L. Hart.

To begin with, Hart, sometime editor of the *Bear Lake Democrat,*
which changed its name later to the *Southern Idaho Independent,*
and associate editor of the *Paris Post,* was a skilled journalist and
employed a form of Pitman shorthand to take down verbatim his
interviews with Whitmer, often putting portions in quotation marks.
Immediately after the interviews while his memory was still fresh, he
next transcribed his shorthand notes into his journal. Subsequently,
Hart expanded the interviews by providing background and setting
and then sent the write-ups to his hometown newspapers and to the
Deseret News.

On his return visit to David Whitmer, Hart showed him what he
had written, and Whitmer "fully endorsed [it] as a correct expression
of his sentiments."[7] The final stage for Hart was the transformation
of the prose versions of the interviews into a long poem divided into
iambic pentameter quatrains composed of two couplets. In this final
form, called appropriately "An Interview with David Whitmer,"[8]
Hart was able to be even more expansive with details "recollected
in tranquility."[9]

To show how the first David Whitmer interview progressed
from journal entry to *Deseret News* account to poetry, I give one
example by way of illustration, beginning with the opening sentence
of the journal entry:

> August 21st 1883
> Richmond Mo.
>
> I met David Whitmer and his son David and had a pleasant
> conversation with them.[10]

For the *Deseret News* account, Hart provided a setting and details
about the weather:

> Seneca, Newton County
> Missouri, Aug. 23d, 1883
> Having some business in Richmond, Ray County, I took
> occasion to call on Mr. David Whitmer, who was suffering con-
> siderably from the intense heat, but I had, notwithstanding,

a long and pleasant conversation with him and his son, David Whitmer, Jr.[11]

The first stanza of Hart's poem adds further detail about the age and personal appearance of David Whitmer:

> I met an aged man the other day,
> In Richmond, Missouri, in County Ray.
> His step was feeble, but his eye was bright,
> And in it beamed intelligence and light.

This poetic version allows us a personal glimpse of Whitmer that we do not get in the two previous versions: his age, the feebleness of his step, and the "intelligence and light" that beamed in his eye. The imagery makes it possible for the reader to visualize the scene, and the straightforward colloquial tone together with the versification adds force and dynamism to the statement, thus sharpening considerably the focus of the interview.

And so through the entire text of the journal entry, the full news dispatches, and the complete poem, the reader finds no alteration of substantive facts, but rather a fullness in the strengthening and vivifying enhancement of their statement. When the poem was privately printed in blue ink on a parchment broadside, James H. Hart wrote in a footnote:

> It is worthy of historical mention that the above poem was read and approved by David Whitmer. At a subsequent visit by the author, shortly before David's death, in the presence of his grandson, now the custodian of the manuscript of the Book of Mormon, and other relics, he expressed much pleasure in the receipt and reading of said poem, and acknowledged it as authentic in its entirety.[12]

James H. Hart's "special mission" proved to be successful not only in obtaining a portrait of Oliver Cowdery, but also in making a lasting contribution to our knowledge of another Book of Mormon witness, David Whitmer.

Notes

Editors' note: This article was originally published in *BYU Studies* 36/4 (1996–97): 118–24.

1. For a full account of Wells's attempts to obtain Cowdery's likeness, see Junius F. Wells, "Editorial," *Contributor* 5 (October 1883): 34–35. Other background information throughout is from Edward L. Hart, *Mormon in Motion: The Life and Journals of James H. Hart, 1825–1906* (Salt Lake City: Windsor Books, 1978).

2. James H. Hart to *Deseret News* (dispatch from Seneca, Newton County, Missouri), August 23, 1883, published in *Deseret News*, September 4, 1883.

3. Hart also served as first counselor to William Budge in the Bear Lake Stake presidency.

4. Hart to *Deseret News*, September 4, 1883.

5. Hart to *Deseret News*, September 4, 1883.

6. James H. Hart to the *Bear Lake Democrat* (dispatch from New York), August 29, 1883, published in *Contributor* 5 (October 1883): 35.

7. James H. Hart to the *Bear Lake Democrat*, March 18, 1884, published March 28, 1884. The complete texts of Hart's interviews with Whitmer are also reproduced in Lyndon W. Cook, *David Whitmer Interviews: A Restoration Witness* (Orem, UT: Grandin Book, 1991).

8. This poem has been reprinted many times. The full text of the poem can be found in *Contributor* 5 (October 1883), the same issue that carried the frontispiece of the Three Witnesses.

9. From William Wordsworth's "Observations Prefixed to Lyrical Ballads," in *The Great Critics: An Anthology of Literary Criticism*, ed. James Harry Smith and Edd Winfield Parks, 3rd ed. (New York: Norton, 1951), 514.

10. James H. Hart, Journal, L. Tom Perry Special Collections, Harold B. Lee Library, Brigham Young University, Provo, Utah (hereafter cited as Perry Special Collections). Hart wrote this entry in longhand, but his journal contains a great deal written in shorthand.

11. Hart to *Deseret News*, September 4, 1883.

12. A copy of this printing of the poem and footnote is pasted in Hart's scrapbook, in James H. Hart, Papers, Perry Special Collections.

"The Private Character of the Man Who Bore That Testimony": Oliver Cowdery and His Critics

Larry E. Morris

*D*uring the cold, wet spring of 1829, Oliver Cowdery and Samuel Smith made their way from Palmyra, New York, to Harmony, Pennsylvania, enduring freezing nights, impassable roads, and frost-bite to reach the Prophet Joseph. They arrived on 5 April 1829, and Joseph and Oliver met for the first time. As Lucy Mack Smith sum-marized: "They sat down and conversed together till late. During the evening, Joseph told Oliver his history, as far as was necessary for his present information, in the things that mostly concerned him. And the next morning they commenced the work of translation, in which they were soon deeply engaged."[1]

Over the next few months, Oliver transcribed most of the Book of Mormon and was the first "Mormon" to be baptized. He and Joseph also testified of receiving the priesthood from heav-enly messengers, witnessing the appearance of Moroni, seeing the plates, and hearing the voice of God. Oliver is rightly described as the cofounder of Mormonism. So it is not surprising that treatments of early church history pay special attention to Oliver Cowdery's background and character. In this article I examine how LaMar Petersen (*The Creation of the Book of Mormon*), Robert D. Anderson (*Inside the Mind of Joseph Smith*), and Dan Vogel ("The Validity of the Witnesses' Testimonies") handle primary and secondary sources related to Oliver Cowdery. Although they approach Oliver from quite different angles, none of the three takes advantage of the rich wealth of primary documents so relevant in judging Oliver's character and his reliability as a witness of the Book of Mormon.

Oliver's Excommunication and Methodist Affiliation

A couple of years ago, I was on a book-buying spree at Benchmark Books when I picked up a copy of Petersen's book. I garnered a good bit of bibliographic information by checking the footnotes in this book. Petersen implies (without actually saying as much) that Joseph Smith created the Book of Mormon. He also implies—again, without explicitly stating it—that Oliver's testimony of the Book of Mormon is suspect because of his excommunication, his joining the Methodist Church, his supposed denial of his testimony, and his rejection of the Doctrine and Covenants (84–86).

Petersen correctly notes that in April 1838, the high council in Far West, Missouri, upheld the following charges against Oliver: "urging on vexatious Lawsuits," "seeking to destroy the character of President Joseph Smith jr by falsely insinuating that he was guilty of adultery," "treating the Church with contempt by not attending meetings," "for the sake of filthy lucre . . . turning to the practice of the Law," "being connected in the 'Bogus' business [counterfeiting]," and "dishonestly Retaining notes after they had been paid and . . . betaking himself to the beggerly elements of the world and neglecting his high and Holy Calling."[2]

Petersen's point is to show that church officials attacked Oliver's character. This is true enough, but the validity of the charges is another question. Petersen does not mention that Oliver Cowdery did not attend the council and was thus not present to defend himself. Nor does Petersen note that the council rejected the only two charges that Oliver discussed in his letter to Bishop Edward Partridge.[3] Finally, letters that Oliver Cowdery wrote during his decade out of the church shed light on his attitude toward his excommunication. In 1843, Oliver wrote to Brigham Young and the Twelve: "I believed at the time, and still believe, that ambitious and wicked men, envying the harmony existing between myself and the first elders of the church, and hoping to get into some other men's birth right, by falsehoods the most foul and wicked, caused <u>all this difficulty from beginning to end</u>."[4]

Two years later, Oliver wrote to Brigham's brother Phineas:

> But, from your last [letter], I am fully satisfied, that no un-just imputation will be suffered to remain upon my character. And that I may not be misunderstood, let me here say, that I have only sought, and only asked, that my character might stand ex-onerated from those charges which imputed to me the crimes of theft, forgery, &c. Those which all my former associates knew to be false. I do not, I have never asked, to be excused, or exempted from an acknowledgement of any actual fault or wrong—for of these there are many; which it always was my pleasure to confess. I have cherished a hope, and that one of my fondest, that I might leave such a character, as those who might believe in my testi-mony, after I should be called hence, might do so, not only for the sake of the truth, but might not <u>blush</u> for the private character of the man who bore that testimony.[5]

Oliver's sincerity is clearly evident: he was interested in return-ing to fellowship but not at the expense of his reputation—something he was determined to preserve because he took his role as a witness of the Book of Mormon so seriously. His excommunication and his reaction to it thus make him a more credible witness, not the reverse.

Similarly, Oliver's accusing Joseph of adultery can hardly be taken as evidence that he is not a valid witness of the Book of Mormon. To the contrary, his willingness to make such an accusa-tion while still in the church (Petersen mistakenly says he was not) reveals Oliver's independent spirit. The document in question is a letter from Oliver to his brother Warren written in January 1838, three months before Oliver's excommunication. Speaking of Joseph Smith, Oliver wrote, "A dirty, nasty, filthy affair of his and Fanny Alger's was talked over in which I strictly declared that I had never deviated from the truth in the matter, and as I supposed was admit-ted by himself."[6] Oliver was apparently unaware that Fanny Alger had become the first plural wife of Joseph Smith. Regardless of the difficulties between Joseph and Oliver, however, this whole incident has no direct bearing on Oliver's reliability as a witness. It is not clear why Petersen even brings it up.

Next, after claiming that Oliver's joining another church "is not usually acknowledged by Mormon writers" (85), Petersen curiously quotes one of them, Stanley Gunn, to show that Oliver indeed became a charter member of the Tiffin, Ohio, Methodist Protestant Church. Petersen also fails to mention that Richard Lloyd Anderson, Oliver Cowdery's chief biographer since Gunn, freely discusses Oliver's Methodist affiliation in a 1981 Deseret Book publication, *Investigating the Book of Mormon Witnesses* (57).

Several primary documents not mentioned by Petersen bear directly on Oliver's joining with the Methodists. In 1885, eighty-two-year-old Gabriel J. Keen, longtime Tiffin, Ohio, resident and Methodist Church member, signed an affidavit in which he affirmed:

> Mr. Cowdrey expressed a desire to associate himself with a Methodist Protestant Church of this city. Rev. John Souder and myself were appointed a committee to wait on Mr. Cowdrey and confer with him respecting his connection with Mormonism, and the "Book of Mormon." We accordingly waited on Mr. Cowdrey at his residence in Tiffin, and there learned his connection, from him, with that order, and his full and final renunciation thereof. We then inquired of him if he had any objections to make a public recantation. He replied that he had objections; that in the first place it could do no good; that he had known several to do so, and they always regretted it; and in the second place it would have a tendency to draw public attention, invite criticism and bring *him* into contempt. But said he, nevertheless, if the church require it, I will submit to it, but I authorize and desire you and the church to publish and make known my recantation. We did not demand it, but submitted his name to the church and he was unanimously admitted a member thereof. At that meeting he arose and addressed the audience present, admitted his error and implored forgiveness, and said he was sorry and ashamed of his connection with Mormonism. He continued his membership while he re-

sided at Tiffin and became superintendent of the Sabbath-school, and led an exemplary life while he resided with us.[7]

Keen, a respected citizen of Tiffin, clearly believed that Oliver Cowdery had fully renounced Mormonism. Still, certain difficulties remain with Keen's statement: he recorded the incident (apparently for the first time) more than forty years after it happened; his account was never corroborated by other witnesses; and he gave the statement at the request of Arthur B. Deming, the anti-Mormon editor of *Naked Truths about Mormonism* and a man likely to lead his witness. Furthermore, two equally respected citizens of Tiffin claimed that Oliver never discussed Mormonism. "I think that it is absolutely certain that Mr. C., after his separation from the Mormons, never conversed on the subject with his most intimate friends, and never by word or act, disclosed anything relating to the conception, development or progress of the 'Church of Jesus Christ of Latter-day Saints,'" wrote William Henry Gibson, judge, general, orator, businessman, lawyer, and Tiffin's most famous resident.[8]

William Lang, who apprenticed in Oliver Cowdery's law office and later became mayor of Tiffin and a member of the Ohio senate, used similar language: "Now as to whether C. ever openly denounced Mormonism let me say this to you: no man ever knew better than he how to keep one's own counsel. He would never allow any man to drag him into a conversation on the subject."[9]

There are several points to consider here. First, Gibson and Lang were not present during Oliver Cowdery's interview with Keen and Sounder. It is possible that during the interview Oliver made negative statements about Mormonism or Mormons that he never made in Gibson's or Lang's presence. Indeed, Adeline Fuller Bernard, apparently adopted by Oliver and Elizabeth Cowdery and in her twenties when Oliver joined the Methodist Church, later claimed that Oliver made similar statements.[10] However, it is difficult to believe that Oliver could have publicly begged forgiveness for his association with Mormonism (as reported by Keen) without

Gibson or Lang hearing about such an incident. Both are emphatic that he *never* discussed the church.

Second, any negative statements Oliver made privately in Tiffin must be viewed in light of his family's harsh treatment in Missouri. Two months after Oliver's excommunication, on 17 June 1838, Sidney Rigdon delivered his famous "salt sermon," declaring that the "Salt that had lost its Savour"—meaning dissenters Oliver Cowdery, David and John Whitmer, W. W. Phelps, Lyman E. Johnson, and others—and was "henceforth good for nothing but to be cast out, and troden under foot of men."[11] Two days later, eighty-three church members signed a statement warning the dissenters out of Caldwell County: "There is but one decree for you, which is depart, depart, or a more fatal calamity shall befall you. . . . We will put you from the county of Caldwell: so help us God."[12]

The difficulties that began with the failure of the Kirtland Safety Society—where Oliver and David Whitmer both suffered severe financial losses and became embroiled in financial controversy— had now culminated in a death threat. "These gideonites understood that they should drive the dissenters as they termed those who believed not in their secret bands," wrote John Whitmer. "They had threatened us to kill us if we did not make restitutions to them by upholding them in their wicked purposes."[13]

John Whitmer's mention of a secret band of Gideonites was right on the mark. As Leland H. Gentry writes, "All evidence indicates that the Danite order originated about the same time Sidney Rigdon gave vent to his feelings in his 'Salt Sermon.' The original purpose of the order appears to have been to aid the Saints of Caldwell in their determination to be free from dissenter influence."[14]

Not coincidentally, the Danites were originally known as the "Brothers of Gideon," and a key participant was Jared Carter (who actually had a brother named Gideon), a member of the high council that had excommunicated Oliver and also one of the signatories of the "warning out" document. Sampson Avard, who soon became head of the Danites, had been the first person to sign the document. "Avard arrived some time since," Oliver had written in a 2 June letter.

"He appears very friendly, but I look upon [him] with so much contempt, that he will probably get but little from me."[15]

According to John Whitmer, he, David, Oliver, and Lyman Johnson rushed to neighboring Clay County to "obtain legal counsel to prepare to over throw these attachments which they had caused to [be] used against us. . . . But to our great asstonishment when we were on our way home from Liberty Clay Co[unty] we met the families of O. Cowdery and L. E. Johnson whom they had driven from their homes and rob[b]ed them of all their goods save clothing, bedding, &c."[16]

Considering these shocking circumstances, why should it be surprising that Oliver Cowdery, a man who remained devoutly religious his entire life, joined with a community of Christians when he moved to Ohio? As Anderson and Faulring note, "after his expulsion from the Mormon Church in 1838, Oliver and his family had no choice but to fellowship with a non-Mormon Christian group."[17]

Moreover, although Oliver Cowdery's distinction between the "outward government" of the church and its core doctrine, between his enemies and the church leaders he continued to admire, was likely lost on his Tiffin associates, he continued to make such a distinction. In a letter to Phineas Young, Oliver spoke of the "torents [torrents] of abuse and injury that I have received, fomented, no doubt, by those miserable beings, who have long since ceased [to] disgrace the Chu[rch o]f which you are a m[ember]."[18] But three months later, in a letter to Brigham Young and the Twelve, Oliver wrote, "I entertain no unkindly feelings toward you, or either of you."[19] (Significantly, none of the men addressed in this letter—Brigham Young, Heber C. Kimball, Parley P. Pratt, William Smith, Orson Pratt, Willard Richards, Wilford Woodruff, John Taylor, and George A. Smith—had signed the "warning out" document addressed to Oliver and the other dissenters.)

Seen in this context, Oliver's Methodist affiliation, along with any negative statements he may have made about his experience in Missouri, does no damage to his role as a witness—quite the contrary.

Petersen next quotes what he himself calls a "bit of doggerel" that supposedly proclaimed Cowdery's denial of the Book of Mormon:

> Or prove that Christ was not the Lord
>> Because that Peter cursed and swore?
>
> Or Book of Mormon not his word
>> Because denied by Oliver?[20]

Richard Lloyd Anderson has shown, however, that the author of this poem, Joel H. Johnson, had no firsthand experience with Oliver and that Johnson's sentiments therefore have no bearing on Oliver's reliability as a witness.[21]

Finally, Petersen reports (without giving a reference) that David Whitmer claimed that Oliver rejected the Doctrine and Covenants. But why rely on David Whitmer to tell us what Oliver thought when the latter spoke for himself? As Richard Lloyd Anderson points out, Oliver Cowdery edited (and approved of) the Kirtland edition of the Doctrine and Covenants. In his correspondence, he also showed approval for the Twelve (even while he was out of the church) and rejected William McLellin's attempt to begin a new church movement. Finally, Oliver stated that Joseph Smith had fulfilled his mission faithfully, and, on his deathbed, Oliver expressed support for Brigham Young and the other leaders of the church.[22] Such evidence hardly indicates that Oliver rejected the Doctrine and Covenants. Nor does it reflect negatively on Oliver's role as a witness.

Petersen thus opts for secondary accounts and even Joel Johnson's rumor, rather than drawing on primary sources to show us what kind of a person Oliver was. And even when Petersen refers to original documents, he offers no historical context. Given Petersen's extensive bibliography and obvious research, this is disappointing.

Weak Arguments from Robert Anderson

A few weeks ago, I was on a book-checking-out fit at the BYU Library when I picked up a copy of Robert D. Anderson's book. (There sure are a lot of Andersons writing about Mormon history lately.) Whereas Petersen concentrates on Oliver Cowdery's later experiences, Anderson does the opposite—dealing mainly with Oliver's early life. But Anderson creates suspicion about his research by getting basic facts wrong. He says that Oliver was born in Middletown, Vermont, and that in "1803 the Cowdery family, including seven-year-old Oliver, moved to Poultney" (97). However, the record is clear that Oliver was born in Wells, Vermont, on 3 October 1806 and that the family subsequently made the following moves: to Middletown in 1809, to New York in 1810, back to Middletown around 1813, and to Poultney in 1817 or 1818.[23] I understand that Anderson's main topic is Joseph Smith, so I don't expect him to do original Cowdery research—such as ferreting out the fine details of the family history, which have not been widely known. But it is another thing to get Oliver's birthplace wrong and to miss his birth date by ten years, especially when the correct information is easily available in the secondary sources that Anderson himself cites. For me, red flags start popping up when I see mistakes like this because they reflect a lack of precision. So we are off to a shaky start.[24]

Next, Anderson claims that Oliver's father, William Cowdery, "had been enmeshed in a scandal involving magic about 1800 near their home and had used divining rods in seeking treasure" (97). Anderson relies on secondary sources for this information even though a nineteenth-century source is readily available—*The History of Middletown, Vermont,* published by Barnes Frisbie in 1867.[25] A check of Frisbie's history reveals that the author himself cannot speak authoritatively because he was not an eyewitness of the scandal, which became known as the "Wood Scrape"—in which members of the Wood family united with a treasure seeker named Winchell, employing divining rods and proclaiming frightening prophecies. In addition, Frisbie's star witness, Laban Clark—who was in Middletown at the time—describes the incident in detail without once mentioning William Cowdery. This source thus fails to support either of Anderson's claims about William Cowdery (that he was involved in the scandal and that he used divining rods to search for treasure).[26]

I believe the larger question is this: since the Wood Scrape occurred four years before Oliver's birth, what is the point of bringing it up in the first place? Some might reply (and D. Michael Quinn seems to be in this group) that the point is to illustrate that Oliver brought with him an interest in folk magic,[27] which is certainly relevant to his involvement with Joseph Smith. But early church history already stipulates that Oliver had such an interest. "Now this is not all," asserted Joseph in a revelation to Oliver (within weeks of Oliver's arrival in Harmony), "for you have another gift, which is the gift of working with the rod: behold it has told you things: behold there is no other power save God, that can cause this rod of nature, to work in your hands" (Book of Commandments 7:3).[28] It seems likely that critics also raise the Wood Scrape—a scandal in which a visionary man failed to deliver on his promises—to imply guilt by association, to taint Oliver's reputation, and to raise questions about his reliability, with thinking that goes something like this: "Oliver's father was duped by a prophet who used magical means to search for treasure and divine hidden secrets. Like father, like son." Any serious historical investigation rejects such "reasoning."

Another reason for discussing the Wood Scrape is to imply what Frisbie states explicitly: "It is my honest belief that this Wood movement here in Middletown was one source, if not the main source, from which came this monster—Mormonism."[29] However, although Frisbie and Quinn both attempt to link Joseph Smith Sr. (and by implication, Joseph Jr.) with the Wood Scrape, no such link exists.[30] The Wood Scrape is thus of little, if any, value in understanding Oliver Cowdery's reliability as a witness of the Book of Mormon.

Not surprisingly, Anderson next moves to the second point of controversy in Oliver's early history: his alleged association with Ethan Smith, minister of the church Oliver's stepmother once attended (under the previous minister) and author of *View of the Hebrews*.[31] A number of critics have theorized that Ethan Smith's book "provided the concept and outline for much of the Book of Mormon" (98). According to one subtheory, Oliver knew Ethan Smith or read his book (or both) and used this knowledge to help produce the Book of Mormon. Of course, backing up such a scenario involves proving two things: Oliver's knowledge of Ethan Smith's theories and Oliver's contribution to the Book of Mormon.

On the first point, Anderson acknowledges that "there is no documentation that Ethan Smith and Oliver Cowdery had any kind of relationship" (97). Nevertheless, Oliver certainly could have read *View of the Hebrews* before meeting Joseph. The real crux of the matter is whether there is evidence that Oliver helped create the Book of Mormon, and Anderson fails to discuss recent scholarship on this topic—which I see as a serious flaw and another instance of lack of precision. Royal Skousen's study of the original manuscript of the Book of Mormon offers strong evidence that Oliver acted simply as scribe, not coauthor.[32] In addition, witnesses of the translation process, including such friendly individuals as David Whitmer and such hostile individuals as Isaac Hale, agree that Joseph dictated the text. (Nor do any of them mention Joseph and Oliver doing any sort of planning.) Anderson's view of "Joseph Smith and Oliver Cowdery constructing narratives of Joseph's personal life within Ethan Smith's conceptual framework" (98) thus gets no support from the primary sources. Nor is it difficult to summarize Anderson's use of primary documents in his section on Oliver's background. Anderson simply does not use them.

Vogel's Use of Questionable Sources

Next we move on to Dan Vogel. Several years ago, I was on a book-buying binge at Sam Weller's when I came across a copy of *Early Mormon Documents*, Volume 1. When you are reading history, there is no substitute for the original documents. I was impressed with Vogel's textual editing and annotation, and I picked up a copy. I also purchased volumes 2, 3, and 4 when they came out (that is no small investment). Vogel finds a lot of interesting documents in a lot of different places. He also locates vital records, census records, and so on, about most of the people mentioned in the documents. I consider him an expert on primary sources related to early Mormonism and appreciate his considerable research. I took a careful look at what he had to say about the Wood Scrape, for example, and found him to be careful and fair, correctly noting instances where Quinn had overstepped the sources.

But in his article on the witnesses, Vogel does some things that surprised me. First, he quotes nineteenth-century sources like John A. Clark and Thomas Ford in a rather uncritical manner. I don't understand that. I assume Vogel agrees that when it comes to testimony, there is no substitute for getting (to use another equine metaphor) something straight from the horse's mouth. If I want to know what William Clark said about the Lewis and Clark expedition, my best source is William Clark himself. (If I want to know about William Clark's character, on the other hand, my best source is reliable people who knew him well.) Of course, what he said and the accuracy of what he said are two different things. But before I can judge his testimony against other sources and evaluate it, I first need the testimony itself. And witnesses always have the final word on what their testimony is—that is the very nature of testimony.

If such firsthand testimony is not available, we turn to secondhand sources, what in court is called "hearsay evidence" (and is generally not allowed). But it is a dangerous thing to trust expedition member John Ordway for what Clark said about the journey. We now have to ask a whole slew of questions we did not have to ask about Clark—when Ordway recorded Clark's statements, whether his memory was reliable, whether he was a careful transcriber, whether he was honest, whether he had an ax to grind. We also need to compare Ordway's account to other secondhand accounts. History, of course, employs different standards than the courtroom, and historians naturally handle a good deal of hearsay testimony. I just believe they ought to always distinguish between first- and secondhand testimony and openly acknowledge the limitations of the latter.

Well, then, what about Clark and Ford? Both gave reports of what Book of Mormon witnesses supposedly said. Clark was an editor and minister who knew Martin Harris. According to Vogel, "Harris told John A. Clark in 1828 that he saw the plates 'with the eye of faith . . . just as distinctly as I see any thing around me,—though at the time they were covered over with a cloth'" (104). What? This account from a secondhand witness raises some interesting questions about Martin Harris.[33]

But let us look at the source. Here is the context of the above quotation, taken from a letter from John A. Clark to *The Episcopal Reader*: "To know how much this testimony [of three witnesses] is worth I will state one fact. A gentleman in Palmyra, bred to the law, a professor of religion, and of undoubted veracity told me that on one occasion, he appealed to Harris and asked him directly,—'Did you *see* those plates?'"[34]

This won't do. Vogel's claim that "Harris told John A. Clark" is not accurate. This is not secondhand testimony but thirdhand— "he said that he said that he said." If secondhand evidence is problematic, thirdhand evidence is hugely more so. As if that weren't enough, Clark does not name his source—making it impossible to judge that person's honesty or reliability. What we have is a thirdhand, anonymous account of what Martin Harris supposedly said. (I think that is called a rumor.) Either through neglect or intent, Vogel has represented an anonymous, thirdhand account as being an identified, secondhand account—and there is a vast difference. And since we have Harris's firsthand account—it is printed in the Book of Mormon—and several recorded interviews from both friendly and hostile sources (see *Early Mormon Documents*, vol. 2), there is no reason to rely on a thirdhand account.[35]

This is not to say that anonymous accounts can never be taken seriously. Lewis and Clark scholars, for example, have noted two anonymous accounts that Meriwether Lewis tried to commit suicide as he traveled down the Mississippi River in September 1809. Major Gilbert C. Russell, commander of a fort near present-day Memphis, Tennessee, wrote that members of the keelboat crew told him of the attempts. Similarly, Amos Stoddard, a friend of Lewis's who was in the area, wrote that he heard of Lewis's suicide attempts on the boat. Both reports are treated seriously, not simply as rumor, even though neither man identifies his sources. (Most scholars believe Lewis made good on these threats a month later at an inn southwest of present-day Nashville; others believe Lewis was murdered.)

But some interesting differences distinguish Lewis's case from that of the witnesses: first, Russell was a secondhand witness—that is, he talked to someone who saw Lewis try to kill himself. Clark on the other hand (and I mean John A., not William) is a third-hand witness because his account involves a quotation—he talked to someone who reported what Martin Harris had said. Second, historians necessarily turn to Russell and Stoddard because no other accounts are available, but first- and secondhand testimony abounds with Martin Harris. In my own research, I am inclined not to use thirdhand accounts at all, unless simply to show what rumors were circulating. There is just too much room for error—like the military exercise, or parlor game, where a piece of information changes as it goes from person to person.

Vogel doesn't make any bones about Thomas Ford's account being anonymous and thirdhand. The governor of Illinois at the time Joseph and Hyrum Smith were killed, Ford wrote an account of how Joseph basically tricked unnamed witnesses into seeing the plates—after a prolonged session of fasting and prayer (and ridicule from Joseph). As Vogel says, "Ford claimed that his account came from 'men who were once in the confidence of the prophet' but did not identify his sources" (102–3). This could actually be fourth-hand testimony—Ford (4) may have talked to men (3) who talked to someone else (2) who talked to the witnesses (1). Vogel then points out the weaknesses in this document but mysteriously insists that "the essence of the account contains an element of truth" (103).

I am not comfortable with that kind of reasoning. In the first place, historical methodology ought to eliminate Ford's claim as valid evidence—it is anonymous on two levels because neither the sources nor the witnesses are named; in addition, it involves an unknown number of links. It is pure rumor. Secondly, Ford's account contains an element of truth only if one presupposes certain things about the witnesses. But isn't the point to begin without presuppositions and see what the documents tell us, or, in Vogel's words, to "try to determine more accurately the nature of [the witnesses'] experiences" (79)? Again, Vogel expresses a desire to "examine the historical nature of these events" (79). Again, I agree. But why take a main thread of the discussion from a thirdhand, anonymous account when there are identified first- and secondhand accounts available? What sense does it make to conclude (based partly on Ford's "hearsay hearsay") that the Eight Witnesses "may have seen the plates through the box" (104) in a purely "visionary" experience when such a conclusion is flatly contradicted by the witnesses' firsthand testimony: "As many of the leaves as the said Smith has translated we did handle with our hands; and we also saw the engravings thereon."[36] The fact that the witnesses' statement does not include the time and place of their experience, nor the complete details of that experience, does not disqualify it as historical evidence, as Vogel seems to imply. It is a firsthand document, and its language is unequivocal.

Although strict legal standards do not apply to history, *some* standards do. Thirdhand and anonymous is thirdhand and anonymous, and fair is fair. The Clark and Ford accounts are too far removed from the source to qualify as solid evidence, especially with more direct evidence available. Therefore, I believe they have historical value chiefly as an indicator of what kind of rumors were circulating, not as reliable accounts of witness testimony. I apply this same standard to thirdhand accounts of Oliver Cowdery, in a packed courtroom, bearing his testimony of Moroni's visit, and I agree with Vogel that "the claim rests on less than satisfactory grounds."[37]

Oliver's Religious Experience

In regard to the Second Elder, Vogel takes quite a different tack than Petersen or Anderson. "At least during this early period of his life," Vogel writes, Oliver Cowdery "was known to be unstable and given to obsessive and morbid thoughts. Also, like Harris and Whitmer, he had a history of visions prior to late June 1829. . . . Considering his state of mind and visionary predisposition, his obsessive thoughts may have carried him to the point of delusion;

at least, this possibility should be taken into consideration when assessing his role as one of the three witnesses" (95–96).

Vogel offers four examples of these "obsessive and morbid thoughts": (1) Oliver's intense preoccupation with the story of the gold plates when he was boarding with the Joseph Smith Sr. family; (2) a letter to Joseph Smith in which Oliver expressed his "longing to be freed from sin and to rest in the Kingdom of my Savior"; (3) a second letter to Joseph telling of his "anxiety at some times to be at rest . . . in the Paradice of God"; and (4) a revelation received by Oliver in which he compared the word of God to a "burning fire shut up in my bones," declaring that he was "weary with forebearing" and "could forebear no longer." Let us look at these in context.

(1) Lucy Mack Smith relates that Oliver boarded with the Smiths after accepting a position as a school teacher. Joseph Smith had received the plates a year earlier, and Oliver "had been in the school but a short time, when he began to hear from all quarters concerning the plates, and as soon began to importune Mr. Smith upon the subject, but for a considerable length of time did not succeed in eliciting any information."[38] When Joseph Sr. had gained trust in Oliver, he told him about the plates. Not long after that, Oliver told Joseph Sr. and Lucy that he was delighted at what he had heard and believed that he would have the opportunity of writing for Joseph Jr. The next day, Oliver mentioned his intention of going to Harmony to see Joseph Jr., saying, "I have made it a subject of prayer, and I firmly believe that it is the will of the Lord that I should go. If there is a work for me to do in this thing, I am determined to attend to it."[39]

Joseph Sr. advised him to seek for his own testimony, "which [Oliver] did, and received the witness spoken of in the Book of *Doc. and Cov.*"[40] Joseph Jr. later recalled Oliver's statement that "one night after [Oliver] had retired to bed, he called upon the Lord to know if these things were so, and that the Lord had manifested to him that they were true."[41] In his 1832 autobiographical sketch, Joseph Jr. told more about this manifestation: "[The] Lord appeared unto a young man by the name of Oliver Cowdery and shewed unto him the plates in a vision, also the truth of the work, and what the Lord was about to do through me his unworthy servant."[42]

These accounts make it clear that Oliver was a religious individual who had a powerful experience that convinced him of the truth of Joseph Smith's claims (although Oliver left no detailed description of this epiphany). Given Oliver's conviction that he was about to participate in the divinely appointed restoration of ancient scripture, it seems perfectly fitting that he was "so completely absorbed in the subject of the Record, that it seemed impossible for him to think or converse about anything else."[43] Who wouldn't have been? But note the difference between Lucy's language—"completely absorbed in the subject"—and Vogel's, "obsessive and morbid." Although he is using Lucy Mack Smith as his source, Vogel is wresting her text by introducing negative connotations not present in her history. Furthermore, there is every indication that Oliver competently completed his term of teaching before leaving for Harmony. Oliver's functioning normally in the everyday world is another sign that his preoccupation with the plates was intensely religious but not unhealthy or psychotic.

(2) During November and December of 1829, while he was in Manchester, New York, Oliver wrote two letters to Joseph, who was in Harmony, Pennsylvania. In these letters, Oliver expresses some of his deep religious reflections. "My dear Brother," he writes in the first, dated 6 November,

> when I think of the goodness of christ I feel no desire to live or stay here upon the shores of this world of iniquity only to to ser[v]e my maker and be if posible an instriment in his hands of doing some good in his cause with his <grace> to assist me when I consider and try to realize what he has done for me I am astonished and amaised[.] [W]hy should I not be[?] [F]or while I was rushing on in sin and crouding my way down to that awful gulf he yet strove with me and praised be his holy <and> [=] <Eternal> name he has redeemed my soul from endless torment and wo not for any thing that I have me[r]ited or any worthyness there was in me for there was none but it was in and through his own mercy wraught out by

his own infinite wisdom by prepareing from all Eternity a means
where<by> man could be saved on conditions of repentance and
faith on that infinite attonement which was to be mad[e] by a great
and last sacrif[i]ce which sacr[i]fice was the death of the only begot-
ten of the Father[,] yea the eternal Father of Heaven and of Earth
that by his reserection all the Family of man might be braught back
into the presance of God if therefore we follow christ in all things
whatsoever he comma[n]deth us and are buried with him by baptism into death that like as christ was raised up from the dead by
the glory of the Eternal Father[,] even so we also should walk in
newness of life and if we walk in newness of life to the end of this
probation at the day of accounts we shall be caught up in clouds
to meet the Lord in the air but I need not undertake to write of
the goodness of God for his goodness is unspeakable neither tell
of the misteries of God for what is man that he can comprehend
and search out the wisdom of deity for great is the misteries of
Godliness therefore my only motive in this writing is to inform
you of my prospects and hopes and my desires and my longing to
be freed from sin and to rest in the Kingdom of my Savior and my
redeemer when I begin to write of the mercys of god I know not
where to stop but time and paper fails."[44]

(3) In the second letter, dated 28 December, Oliver expresses
similar feelings:

Be asured my c<h>angeing business has not in any degree I trust
taken my mind from meditating upon my mission which I have
been called to fulfill nor of slacking my diligence in prayr and
fasting but but some times I feel almost as though I could quit
time and fly away and be at rest in the Bosom of my Redeemer for
the many deep feelings of sorrow and the many long struglings
in prayr of sorrow for the sins of my fellow beings and also for
those who pretend to be of my faith almost as it were seperateth
my spirit from my mortal body do no think by this my Brother
that I would give you to understand that I am freed from sin and
temptations no not by any means that is what I would that you
should understand is my anxiety at some times to be at rest in the
Paradice of my God is to be freed from temptation &c.[45]

Each meditation thus laments the sinfulness of this world, proclaims the glory of Christ, and expresses the natural Christian desire for what Paul called "a better country, that is, an heavenly" (Hebrews 11:16). Indeed, Oliver's passages are reminiscent of Paul's epistle to Titus, where he writes:

> For we ourselves also were sometimes foolish, disobedient, deceived, serving divers lusts and pleasures, living in malice and envy, hateful, and hating one another. But after that the kindness and love of God our Saviour toward man appeared, Not by works of righteousness which we have done, but according to his mercy he saved us, by the washing of regeneration, and renewing of the Holy Ghost; Which he shed on us abundantly through Jesus Christ our Saviour; That being justified by his grace, we should be made heirs according to the hope of eternal life. (Titus 3:3–7)

Oliver's letters reflect deeply religious contemplations, but they are not "obsessive," which my dictionary defines as "excessive often to an unreasonable degree," or "deriving from obsession," (which is defined as "a persistent disturbing preoccupation with an often unreasonable idea or feeling"), and they are not "morbid"—defined as "abnormally susceptible to or characterized by gloomy or unwholesome feelings."[46] Again, Oliver's ability to function normally in the world of ordinary life is telling. During the time he wrote these letters, Oliver was helping coordinate the printing of the Book of Mormon. Lucy indicates that Oliver took a lead role in this task, working with the printer and ensuring the security of the manuscript. John H. Gilbert, who set the type for the Book of Mormon (and later declared the Mormon Bible to be a "very big humbug"), said that either Oliver or Hyrum delivered pages of the printer's manuscript each morning, that Oliver often read or checked proofs, and that Oliver even set some type at one point. Others who observed Oliver's work with the printer included Pomeroy Tucker, Stephen S. Harding, and Albert Chandler, all hostile to Mormonism. None of these men ever indicated that Oliver acted strangely or irrationally or that he displayed obsessive or morbid tendencies. The historical record instead gives every indication that Oliver acted in a coherent, businesslike manner.[47]

(4) The document in question is a revelation recorded by Oliver and known as the "Articles of the Church of Christ" (later superseded by D&C 20). In this document, Oliver draws on several scriptural sources to define various aspects of church government. As he closes, Oliver writes, "Behold I am Oliver I am an Apostle of Jesus Christ by the will of God the Father and the Lord Jesus Christ Behold I have written the things which he hath commanded me for behold his word was unto me as a burning fire shut up in my bones and I was weary with forbearing and I could forbear no longer Amen."[48] This does not strike me as obsessive or morbid but rather as a devout paraphrasing of Jeremiah 20:9: "But his word was in mine heart as a burning fire shut up in my bones, and I was weary with forbearing, and I could not stay."

While we are on the subject of the Articles of the Church, it is worth noting Vogel's claim that the Three Witnesses were "suggestible, willing subjects" capable of being deceived or hypnotized (97). Similarly, Robert Anderson calls Oliver "an awestruck, encouraging, and supportive individual who responded fully to [Joseph's] charisma" (97). But Oliver showed himself to be much more than a willing subject or awestruck follower. Within weeks of his arrival at Harmony, he was trying to translate the plates himself. Not long after that, he received his own revelation on the Articles of the Church. Then, in the summer of 1830, when Joseph made changes to Oliver's revelation, Oliver commanded Joseph "in the name of God" to delete certain changes.[49] This does not sound like an individual perfectly willing to be deluded. If anything, Oliver's strong will interfered with his relationship with Joseph and was a prominent factor in his leaving the church.

Oliver's Solid Reputation

What of Vogel's claim that Oliver was "known to be unstable" (95)? Checking Webster's again, "unstable" is "not steady in action or movement," "wavering in purpose or intent," "lacking steadiness," or, more to the point, "characterized by lack of emotional control." So the question is, "Known to be unstable by whom?" I don't know of any such reports coming from Vermont, where Oliver lived until he was around twenty. In an 1869 history of Wells, Vermont, for instance, the authors conspicuously decline taking shots at Oliver even though they enjoy poking fun at Mormonism in general: "Oliver the youngest son, was the scribe for Joe Smith, the founder of the book of Mormon. Smith being illiterate was incapacitated to write his wonderful revelations, employed this Oliver Cowdry to perform the duties of a scribe. We well remember this same Oliver Cowdry when in our boyhood, the person who has figured so largely in giving to the world the wonderful revelations that many dupes seek to follow. He attended school in the District where we reside in 1821 and 1822. He then went to Palmyra, N. Y. There with Joe Smith and others in translating mormonism."[50] Similarly, Barnes Frisbie, so intent on linking the origins of Mormonism with the Wood Scrape, has nothing negative to report on Oliver.

What of the people who knew him in New York before he left for Harmony? The school board (which included Hyrum) trusted him to take his brother's place as a teacher; Joseph and Lucy trusted him with details of Joseph Jr.'s obtaining the plates; David Whitmer trusted him to give a candid report on his (Oliver's) meeting with Joseph Smith. What of the Palmyra neighbors so vocal in their condemnation of Joseph Smith? One, David Stafford, stated that "Oliver Cowdery proved himself to be a worthless person and not to be trusted or believed when he taught school in this neighborhood." But Stafford's statement is contradicted by John Stafford, who called Oliver "a man of good character," and by a host of others: "peaceable," said Lorenzo Saunders; "as good as the general run of people," said Hiram Jackway; "His reputation was good," recalled Benjamin Saunders; "greatly respected by all," concluded William Hyde.[51]

Known to be unstable? It surely doesn't sound like it. What about his later life? Did Oliver reveal signs of instability or obsessive or morbid thoughts? Note these comments from the respected Tiffin residents mentioned earlier: "[Cowdery] led an exemplary life while he resided with us."—G. J. Keen. "Cowdery was an able lawyer, and agreeable, irreproachable gentleman"; "He was an able lawyer, a fine orator, a ready debater and led a blameless life, while residing in this city."—William Henry Gibson. "[Cowdery's] life . . . was as pure and undefiled as that of the best of men. . . . Mr. Cowdery was an able lawyer and a great advocate. His manners were easy and gentlemanly; he was polite, dignified, yet courteous. . . . His addresses to the court and jury were characterized by a high order of oratory, with brilliant and forensic force. He was modest and reserved, never spoke ill of any one, never complained."—William Lang.[52]

Others concurred. "Mr. C . . . earned himself an enviable distinction at the bar of this place and of this judicial circuit, as a sound and able lawyer, and as a citizen none could have been more esteemed," wrote John Breslin, an editor who served in the Ohio House. Breslin added, "His honesty, integrity, and industry were worthy the imitation of all." Horace A. Tenney, editor of the *Wisconsin Argus,* described Oliver as "a man of sterling integrity, sound and vigorous intellect, and every way worthy, honest and capable." When Oliver died in Missouri in 1850, the local circuit court and bar honored him with a resolution: "In the death of our friend and brother, Oliver Cowdery, his profession has lost an accomplished member, and the community a reliable and worthy citizen."[53]

All of this from individuals and institutions who had no particular reason to volunteer positive information on Oliver, at a time when anti-Mormonism was raging throughout the Midwest. By contrast, Vogel offers not a single contemporary account indicating that Oliver Cowdery was unstable or likely to be deluded.

Vogel's Circular Reasoning

"The important question," argues Vogel, "is not whether the witnesses were trustworthy or if they continued to maintain their belief in the Book of Mormon throughout their lives. The central question . . . concerns the nature of their experiences and if their statements are distinguishable from those claiming similar religious testimonies" (79–80).[54] Again, "To emphasize Harris's business ethics or Cowdery's intelligence or Whitmer's good citizenship is irrelevant to their potential to be inclined to see visions" (97).

It seems that Vogel is acknowledging that Oliver was honest and intelligent—he simply allowed his "visionary predisposition" and his "obsessive thoughts" to carry him "to the point of delusion" (96). In other words, Oliver sincerely thought he saw the plates but he was mistaken, misled, deluded. Oliver was deceived or tricked or hypnotized into believing something that was not true. A "delusion" is a "persistent false psychotic belief regarding the self or persons or objects outside the self"; "psychosis" is a "fundamental mental derangement (as schizophrenia) characterized by defective or lost contact with reality." By Vogel's view, this is exactly what happened to Oliver: he had a persistent view (indeed, it lasted the rest of his life) about something that involved a loss of contact with reality (seeing plates and an angel when there were none).

Vogel theorizes that—after a preparatory period of prayer, discussion, anticipation, expectation, and so on—"Smith may have taken three suggestible, willing subjects into the woods and used prayer as a method of induction" (97). In this scenario, the Three Witnesses were deluded by Joseph Smith—they were not co-conspirators with him. So, when Cowdery, Whitmer, and Harris continued to testify of the Book of Mormon throughout their lives, they were in one sense telling the truth: they were reporting the facts as they had perceived them.

If I read Vogel correctly, he is suggesting that Oliver and the others really had some kind of "spiritual" experience—that they really believed that they saw an angel with plates, even though the angel and plates were not actually there. Vogel also expresses a desire to "examine the historical nature of these events" (79). Of course, this is the whole problem, a problem faced by Vogel or any other historian researching the witnesses: history deals with human events that can (at least theoretically) be demonstrated to have occurred or not to have occurred, but visions fall into the realm of the supernatural and are not verifiable in the same manner as ordinary human events.[55]

Take certain experiences of the apostle Paul. When he had a vision of Christ on the road to Damascus, Paul experienced something different from those who accompanied him: "And the men which journeyed with him stood speechless, hearing a voice, but seeing no man" (Acts 9:7). (To make things even more interesting, Paul later reported that "they that were with me saw indeed the light, and were afraid; but they heard not the voice of him that spake to me" (Acts 22:9). Again, Paul claimed, "I knew a man in Christ above fourteen years ago, (whether in the body, I cannot tell; or whether out of the body, I cannot tell: God knoweth;) such an one caught up to the third heaven" (2 Corinthians 12:2).

Joseph Smith expressed the same kind of impressions, even echoing Paul: "The heavens were opened upon us, and I beheld the celestial kingdom of God, and the glory thereof, whether in the body or out I cannot tell" (D&C 137:1). To take an example particularly relevant to the present discussion, note what Joseph said about his experience of seeing the plates with Martin Harris: "We now joined in prayer, and obtained our desires, for before we had yet finished, the same vision was opened to our view—*at least it was, again to me, and I once more beheld and heard the same things.*"[56] I have always taken this as a candid acknowledgment that visions have a different nature than normal human experience. It is also the kind of admission not likely to be made by a person masterminding an imagined vision.

As I see it, these kinds of religious experiences are not empirical, meaning they cannot be verified or disproved through normal observation or testing. (This is clearly evident in the case of Paul: asking observers what they saw or heard does not get to the truth or the heart of Paul's experience.) I also believe such experiences are not empirical because they involve more than the normal senses—they involve the grace of God and what Paul calls "the eyes of your understanding" (Ephesians 1:18). (I would not claim that visions do not involve the physical senses. I believe they could involve both physical and spiritual means of perception, which seems to be the point David Whitmer was making when he said he saw the plates with both his physical and spiritual eyes.) I would subsequently argue that the visionary experiences of Paul, Muhammad, St. Francis, Joseph Smith, and others are not generally proper subjects of history because history is limited to empirical observation, and visions transcend empirical observation.[57]

Does that leave the historian totally adrift in regard to visions? I do not believe so. While history cannot verify or disprove a vision's veracity, it can tell us a good deal about the lives of the people involved and the times they lived in. Historians must simply do their best with the tools they have. In the case of Oliver Cowdery, history cannot tell us whether he really saw the angel and the plates or not. However, history can help us understand whether Oliver was unstable, given to obsessive thoughts, and likely to be deluded, as Vogel claims.

We investigate such issues through normal historical channels—by checking the accounts of reliable people on the scene. Take another example from the Lewis and Clark era, one particularly applicable because it involves stability—in this case, the stability of Meriwether Lewis in the weeks before he died. Those who argue that Lewis committed suicide claim that he acted in an unstable manner during this period. And how do they make the case for instability? By quoting William Clark, who was worried about Lewis's mental state when the two parted in St. Louis late in August 1809; by referring to a contemporary newspaper that said Lewis was "indisposed" when he reached New Madrid, Missouri, several days later; by mentioning Gilbert Russell's firsthand report of Lewis's drinking and secondhand report of Lewis's suicide attempts; by offering a letter from John Neely (Lewis's companion on the trail called the Natchez Trace) that said Lewis acted unwell during the trip; by quoting Mrs. Griner, caretaker of the inn where Lewis spent his last night, when she said that Lewis acted irrationally and talked to himself in a strange manner.

By contrast, what does Vogel offer in the way of evidence that Oliver Cowdery was unstable? He offers no accounts at all from reliable witnesses.[58] Instead, he simply shows that Oliver was a religious person—as seen by his intense preoccupation with the Book of Mormon and by his devout longing to proclaim the gospel and to be free of the sins of this world. That is the extent of Vogel's evidence, the sum total of his claims concerning Oliver's instability, his obsessive and morbid thoughts, and his tendency to be deluded. This is circular reasoning pure and simple. Oliver's "state of mind and visionary predisposition" (96) are taken as evidence that he was deluded when he saw the plates and the angel.[59] But this is only true if one first assumes that Oliver's earlier spiritual experience was bogus, and on what basis can Vogel possibly make that assumption? As a historian, Vogel has no access to Oliver Cowdery's private religious experiences. Therefore, the best Vogel or any other historian can do is investigate whether Oliver had a previous history (based on the accounts of reliable witnesses) of being "unstable." No such evidence concerning Oliver has come to light. Vogel's claim that Oliver was "known to be unstable" thus collapses because Vogel cannot demonstrate that a single person ever made such an accusation. Vogel's sole evidence that Oliver was unstable is Vogel's own interpretation of Oliver's religious experience, and this does not count as historical evidence.[60] (Personally, I would find it quite refreshing if Vogel would tell us what he thinks about these issues. Does he acknowledge the existence [or at least the possibility] of angels but insist that Oliver did not see one, or does he reject the notion altogether?)

Oliver's Honesty and Intelligence

As Vogel points out, Richard Anderson and other "apologists" have frequently cited primary documents concerning Oliver Cowdery's honesty or intelligence. Rather than arguing this point, Vogel claims that Oliver's trustworthiness is not "the important question" (79), that his intelligence is "irrelevant" to his "potential to be inclined to see visions" (97). In doing so, Vogel seems to agree that Oliver was honest and intelligent.

Whoa, Nellie. Vogel gives the appearance of making a historical claim that Oliver was inclined to see visions or was capable of being deluded, but he immediately disqualifies the type of historical evidence normally used to substantiate or refute such a claim—that is, accounts from reliable people who knew the person in question. Therefore, when a third party like John Breslin or Horace Tenney (neither of whom had apparent ulterior motives) says that Oliver's honesty and integrity were worthy the imitation of all, or that Oliver was a man of sound and vigorous intellect, this—according to Vogel—does not really relate to Oliver's inclination to see visions or be taken in by an "induced" vision. But try as he might, Vogel cannot disassociate Oliver's honesty and intelligence from his claim of visionary experience, or what Vogel thinks is a delusion. Instability, obsessive and morbid thoughts, and a susceptibility to delusion are flaws (either related to character or intelligence), and how would a historian ever identify such flaws if not through the accounts of reliable people who knew the individual well?

That is not all. Vogel concentrates on Oliver's experience as one of the Three Witnesses, basically claiming that Joseph primed Oliver, David, and Martin into a highly excitable state and "induced" a vision. We are to understand this as hypnosis or hallucination that somehow did not manifest itself in normal life. (In Vogel's words, "hallucinators are otherwise indistinguishable from other people and can function normally in society" [97]. If a claim ever cried out for an extensive footnote, this one does, but Vogel does not oblige.) But Vogel would have done well to point out that Oliver Cowdery claimed to have received quite a variety of visions over a considerable period of time. In 1836, for example, seven years after Joseph and Oliver reported the vision of John the Baptist, "The vail was taken from their [Joseph and Oliver's] minds and the eyes of their understanding were opened. They saw the Lord standing upon the breast work of the pulpit before them, and under his feet was a paved work of pure gold. . . . After this vision closed, the Heavens were again opened unto them and Moses appeared before them. . . . After this Elias appeared. . . . After this vision had closed, another great and glorious vision burst upon them, for Elijah, the Prophet . . . also stood before them."[61] This seems to be a vision in the biblical tradition, similar to the Transfiguration, one that Vogel might call "purely visionary."

Moroni's visit was different because it involved the voice of God, an angel, and physical objects. The Three Witnesses said, "We also know that they [the plates] have been translated by the gift and power of God, for his voice hath declared it unto us. . . . an angel of God came down from heaven, and he brought and laid before our eyes, that we beheld and saw the plates, and the engravings thereon" (The Testimony of the Three Witnesses). The plates themselves take this out of the realm of the purely visionary, but David Whitmer reported seeing "but a few feet from us, . . . a table upon which were many golden plates, also the sword of Laban and the directors. I saw them as plain as I see you now, and distinctly heard the voice of the Lord declaiming that the records of the plates of the Book of Mormon were translated by the gift and the power of God."[62] (Looking at David Whitmer's account, I wouldn't call this vision internal, subjective, or purely visionary. A table is hardly required for objects that are imagined or seen in the "mind's eye.")

The visits of John the Baptist and of Peter, James, and John fall into yet another category, one where Joseph and Oliver claimed physical contact with resurrected beings. Concerning the visit of John the Baptist, Joseph wrote, "While we were thus employed praying and calling upon the Lord, a Messenger from heaven, descended in a cloud of light, and *having laid his hands upon us,* he ordained us."[63]

What did Oliver say about these experiences? Rather than referring to them in some mystical, hazy way, he habitually used concrete, definite language to describe them, leaving little doubt as to his absolute conviction that these experiences were genuine:

> On a sudden, as from the midst of eternity, the voice of the Redeemer spake peace to us, while the vail was parted and the angel of God came down clothed with glory, and delivered the anxiously looked for message, and the keys of the gospel of repentance!—What joy! what wonder! what amazement! While the world were racked and distracted—while millions were groping

as the blind for the wall, and while all men were resting upon uncertainty, as a general mass, our eyes beheld—our ears heard. As
in the "blaze of day;" yes, more—above the glitter of the May Sun
beam, which then shed its brilliancy over the face of nature! Then
his voice, though mild, pierced to the center, and his words, "I am
thy fellow servant," dispelled every fear. We listened—we gazed—
we admired! 'Twas the voice of the angel from glory—'twas a message from the Most High! and as we heard we rejoiced, while his
love enkindled upon our souls, and we were rapt in the vision of
the Almighty! Where was room for doubt? No where: uncertainty
had fled, doubt had sunk, no more to rise, while fiction and deception had fled forever![64]

I have been sensitive on this subject, I admit; but I ought to be
so—you would be, under the circumstances, had you stood in the
presence of John, <with> our departed brother Joseph, to receive
the Lesser Priesthood—and in the presence <of> Peter, to receive
the Greater.[65]

I was present with Joseph when an holy angle [angel] from
god came down from heaven and confered or restored the Aronic
priesthood, And said at the same time that it should remain upon
the earth while the earth stands. I was also present with Joseph
when the Melchisideck priesthood was confered by the holy angles [angels] of god.[66]

The Lord opened the heavens and sent forth his word for the
salvation of Israel. In fulfillment of the sacred Scripture the everlasting Gospel was proclaimed by the mighty angel, (Moroni)
who, clothed with the authority of his mission, gave glory to God
in the highest. This Gospel is the "stone taken from the mountain without hands." John the Baptist, holding the keys of the
Aaronic Priesthood; Peter, James and John, holding the keys of
the Melchisdek Priesthood, have also administered for those who
shall be heirs of salvation, and with these ministrations ordained
men to the same Priesthoods. . . . Accept assurances, dear Brother,
of the unfeigned prayer of him, who, in connection with Joseph
the Seer, was blessed with the above ministrations.[67]

In suggesting that Oliver Cowdery's "obsessive thoughts may have carried him to the point of delusion" (96), Vogel has seriously understated the case. If Oliver were deluded, this was not a one-time anomaly, momentary lapse of reason, or single instance of overactive imagination—this was delusion on a grand scale: a prolonged, sustained fantasy by one who maintained belief in the false reality even years after being removed from the environment. If deluded, Oliver Cowdery was seriously out of touch with reality—hearing voices, seeing one angel after another, examining objects, and even feeling hands on his head—all this in the absence of external stimuli. Given the scope of these visions, I believe something has to give—either Oliver's honesty or his intelligence. Either he is lying about all these angels or else his intellect is hardly "sound and vigorous." And yet Oliver's business associates go out of their way to praise both Oliver's integrity and his mind.

Vogel thickens the plot by suggesting that "it would have been possible for [Joseph] to make plates out of tin" (108). Of course, Joseph's manufacturing plates and passing them off as an ancient artifact falls fully in the realm of history. If Joseph did produce such plates, he did it at a specific time and place, with specific material obtained from a specific person or location. All of this would be potentially verifiable through normal historical means—through the journals, letters, or reminiscences of honest people on the scene (or possibly through such documents as receipts or promissory notes for the sale of tin or tools). Certainly it is conceivable that Joseph could have constructed fake plates (although Vogel offers no support for this notion) and kept it a secret. But I'm not sure *how* conceivable this is—the Palmyra neighbors were obviously keeping a close eye on Joseph;[68] why didn't they notice anything? Where and when did Joseph make his plates? Did anyone else know about these plates?

As hard as it would have been for Joseph to keep his manufacture of tin plates a secret while he was alive, is it possible that he could keep the secret after death—that no evidence would come forth after more than one hundred and fifty years (in a society where historical enquiry is actively promoted)? Let us look at another parallel from the same time period in American history. General James Wilkinson received appointments from George Washington and Thomas Jefferson and even became governor of Louisiana. Although some accused him of treason, Wilkinson was never charged with illegal activity. Long after his death, however, a search of Mexican archives revealed that Wilkinson had indeed spied for the Spanish, an offense he would have been executed for. This example points out the difficulty of keeping a plot hidden after one's death, for Wilkinson was a master deceiver.

Getting back to Oliver, Vogel apparently believes that Oliver was sincere—that he really believed he saw visions. But what about the tin plates? As Richard Anderson remarks, "Oliver Cowdery played an extraordinary role in the beginning of The Church of Jesus Christ of Latter-day Saints. . . . no one else stood in the unique position of being able to expose Joseph Smith at all critical points, if he could be exposed."[69] This is doubly true for tin plates, a physical object that has to be transported from place to place. Vogel is apparently suggesting that Oliver, an intelligent, thinking man who must have had countless opportunities to recognize the truth, was taken in by this fraud, that he never caught on that the plates were fake. But such a theory is not compatible with what Oliver himself said about the plates: "I beheld with my eyes, and handled with my hands, the gold plates from which [the Book of Mormon] was transcribed."[70] This is clear language, but look what Vogel does with Oliver's text: "Oliver Cowdery also probably intended to refer to separate occasions when he told a group in Council Bluffs, Iowa, according to Reuben Miller, 'I beheld with my eyes. And handled with my hands the gold plates.' . . . Cowdery probably handled the plates, covered by a cloth, sometime during his residence in Pennsylvania and then simply amalgamated the two experiences" (89).

Vogel is jumping to conclusions not justified at all by the text itself. How does Vogel know that Oliver intended to refer to separate occasions? How does Vogel know that Oliver is talking about touching the plates through a cloth? (Vogel mentions this possibility more than once; Oliver never mentions it.) Oliver doesn't make either of those claims. If anything, Oliver's mention of seeing and handling the plates in the same breath would indicate a single experience, not two. (Could Oliver have seen and handled the plates when he was attempting to translate?) This is another example of where Oliver's honesty and intelligence come very much into play. By Oliver's own account, he saw and handled the plates and thus had the perfect chance to see if they looked genuine. If one assumes the plates were fake, one must ask whether Oliver was lying (sacrificing his honesty) or whether he was actually tricked into believing that crude (how could they have been otherwise?) tin plates were really intricate ancient artifacts (sacrificing his intelligence—how gullible can a person be?). Either of these is a character flaw, but what evidence does Vogel offer that reliable people on the scene, Mormon, ex-Mormon, or anti-Mormon, perceived such flaws in the character of the Second Elder? He offers none.[71]

As I see it, neither Petersen, Anderson, nor Vogel seriously mines the rich source material available on Oliver Cowdery (particularly ironic for Vogel, since his other works show a sound knowledge of those sources). When evaluating eyewitness testimony, historians ask three main questions: (1) Was the witness known to be reliable? (2) Did he record his testimony reasonably soon after the event itself? and (3) Is his account corroborated by other reliable witnesses? For Oliver Cowdery, a man shown by the historical record to be honest, intelligent, and of sound character, the answers to all three questions are yes. If he does not qualify as a good witness, who would?

Notes

Editors' note: This article was originally published in the *FARMS Review* 15/1 (2003): 311–52.

1. Lavina Fielding Anderson, ed., *Lucy's Book: A Critical Edition of Lucy Mack Smith's Family Memoir* (Salt Lake City: Signature Books, 2001), 439. All quotations are from this 1853 version of Lucy Mack Smith's history. The detail that one of Oliver's toes was frozen during the journey is included in Lucy Mack Smith's rough draft but not in the version published by Orson Pratt in 1853. In his 7 September 1834 letter to W. W. Phelps, printed in *Messenger and Advocate* 1 (October 1834): 13–16, Oliver Cowdery stated that he and Joseph Smith met on the evening of 5 April 1829, took care of "business of a temporal nature" the next day, and commenced translating on 7 April.

2.   Donald Q. Cannon and Lyndon W. Cook, eds., *Far West Record* (Salt Lake City: Deseret Book, 1983), 163. The high council excommunicated Oliver Cowdery on 12 April 1838.

3.   Ibid., 164–66.

4.   Oliver Cowdery to Brigham Young and the Twelve, 25 December 1843, Brigham Young Collection, Family and Church History Department Archives, The Church of Jesus Christ of Latter-day Saints (hereafter Church Archives); in Richard Lloyd Anderson and Scott Faulring, eds., *The Documentary History of Oliver Cowdery,* preliminary draft (Provo, Utah: FARMS, 1999), 4:330. When quoting primary documents, I have retained the spelling, underlining, and capitalization of the original (but not crossed-out words).

5.   Oliver Cowdery to Phineas H. Young, 23 March 1846, Church Archives, in Anderson and Faulring, *Documentary History of Oliver Cowdery,* 4:394–95.

6.   Oliver Cowdery to Warren A. Cowdery, 21 January 1838, retained copy, Oliver Cowdery Letter Book, Huntington Library, in Anderson and Faulring, *Documentary History of Oliver Cowdery,* 4:218–19. As Todd Compton points out, several nineteenth-century Latter-day Saints, as well as unsympathetic ex-Mormons, considered Joseph Smith's relationship with Fanny Alger to be a marriage. See Compton, *In Sacred Loneliness: The Plural Wives of Joseph Smith* (Salt Lake City: Signature Books, 1997), 28. See Scott H. Faulring, "The Return of Oliver Cowdery," in *The Disciple as Witness: Essays on Latter-day Saint History and Doctrine in Honor of Richard Lloyd Anderson,* ed. Stephen D. Ricks, Donald W. Parry, and Andrew H. Hedges (Provo, Utah: FARMS, 2000), 162 n. 43 for a discussion of what Oliver Cowdery may have known about the early practice of plural marriage and whether he participated in it.

7.   G. J. Keen, statement to Arthur B. Deming, 14 April 1885, *Naked Truths about Mormonism* 1 (April 1888): 4.

8.   William Henry Gibson to Thomas Gregg, 3 August 1882, in Charles A. Shook, *The True Origin of the Book of Mormon* (Cincinnati: Standard, 1914), 57.

9.   William Lang to Thomas Gregg, 5 November 1881, in Shook, *True Origin of the Book of Mormon,* 56.

10.   Adeline Fuller was born between 1810 and 1820 and apparently lived with the Cowdery family for several years, beginning in Kirtland and moving with them to Far West and Tiffin, Ohio, where she married Lewis Bernard in 1845. (Whether she was related to Oliver's mother, Rebecca Fuller, is not known.) In 1881, when she was in her sixties or seventies, she wrote three letters (4 March, 18 March, and 3 October) to newspaper editor and publisher Thomas Gregg (1808–1892), author of the anti-Mormon book *The Prophet of Palmyra.* In her first letter, Adeline Fuller Bernard claimed, "I have often heard Mr. Cowdry say that Mormanism was the work of Devil" (Adeline M. Bernard to Thomas Gregg, 4 March 1881, typescript, L. Tom Perry Special Collections Library, Harold B. Lee Library, Brigham Young University). Bernard may have been recalling harsh statements Oliver made against those he held responsible for his excommunication— "they themselves have gone to perdition," Oliver wrote (Cowdery to Brigham Young and the Twelve, 25 December 1843, in Anderson and Faulring, *Documentary History of Oliver Cowdery,* 4:330). Bernard's letters are problematic for the following reasons: she apparently dictated the letters to others, and the accuracy of the handwritten transcriptions is unknown (indeed, in the second letter, Bernard herself states that her niece made errors in recording the first letter); no originals are extant for the first two letters, so the

accuracy as well as the provenance of the typescripts is also uncertain; and Bernard's mental stability—as well as the accuracy of her memory and her basic reliability—is also unknown. (She gets certain details right, such as Oliver's living in Tiffin from 1840 to 1847, and gets others wrong, such as the vision of the Three Witnesses occurring at midnight.) This is thus a good topic for further research. Thanks to Richard Lloyd Anderson for sharing his files on Bernard.

11. George W. Robinson, The Scriptory Book of Joseph Smith, 47, Church Archives, in Cannon and Cook, *Far West Record,* 190 n. 1.

12. *Document containing the Correspondence, Orders, &c. in relation to the disturbances with the Mormons; and the Evidence given before the Hon. Austin A. King, Judge of the Fifth Judicial Circuit of the State of Missouri* ([Missouri State Department] Boon's Lick Democrat, 1841), 103–6, in Anderson and Faulring, *Documentary History of Oliver Cowdery,* 4:252, 255. Sidney Rigdon was apparently the author of the "warning out" document, although he did not sign it. A year and a half earlier, in Kirtland (on 7 November 1836), Joseph Smith, Brigham Young, and several other prominent Saints, including Oliver Cowdery, had signed a statement "warning out" the local justice of the peace, although this document specifically noted that "we intend no injury to your person propery or carracter in public or in private." Lake County Historical Society, Mentor, Ohio, in Anderson and Faulring, *Documentary History of Oliver Cowdery,* 3:478.

13. Book of John Whitmer, 86–87, Reorganized Church of Jesus Christ of Latter Day Saints, Archives, in Anderson and Faulring, *Documentary History of Oliver Cowdery,* 4:256–57.

14. Leland H. Gentry, "The Danite Band of 1838," *BYU Studies* 14/4 (1974): 426–27. According to the *Encyclopedia of Latter-day Saint History,* ed. Arnold K. Garr, Donald Q. Cannon, and Richard O. Cowan (Salt Lake City: Deseret Book, 2000), 275, the Danites were a "defensive paramilitary organization sanctioned neither by the state nor by the Church," that their leader Sampson Avard "instituted initiation rites and secret oaths of loyalty and encouraged subversive activities," and that the group "attempted to coerce reluctant Saints into consecrating their surplus money and property to the Church." David J. Whittaker points out, however, that "some groups of Danites were to build houses, others were to gather food, or care for the sick, while others were to help gather the scattered Saints into the community." Whittaker, "The Book of Daniel in Early Mormon Thought," in *By Study and Also by Faith: Essays in Honor of Hugh W. Nibley,* ed. John M. Lundquist and Stephen D. Ricks (Salt Lake City: Deseret Book, 1990), 1:170. Since the term *Danite* had different meanings for different people, attempts to compile lists of Danites inevitably arouse controversy. See, for instance, D. Michael Quinn's list in *The Mormon Hierarchy: Origins of Power* (Salt Lake City: Signature Books, 1994), 479–90.

15. Oliver Cowdery to Warren A. and Lyman Cowdery, 2 June 1838, Lyman Cowdery Collection, Church Archives, in Anderson and Faulring, *Documentary History of Oliver Cowdery,* 4:249–50.

16. Book of John Whitmer, 86–87, in Anderson and Faulring, *Documentary History of Oliver Cowdery,* 4:257.

17. Anderson and Faulring, *Documentary History of Oliver Cowdery,* 4:312.

18. Oliver Cowdery to Phineas Young, 26 August 1843, Oliver Cowdery Letters, Archive of the First Presidency, The Church of Jesus Christ of Latter-day Saints, in Anderson and Faulring, *Documentary History of Oliver Cowdery,* 4:326.

19. Cowdery to Brigham Young and the Twelve, 25 December 1843, in Anderson and Faulring, *Documentary History of Oliver Cowdery*, 4:329.

20. *Times and Seasons* 2 (1841): 482, cited in Richard Lloyd Anderson, *Investigating the Book of Mormon Witnesses* (Salt Lake City: Deseret Book, 1981), 153.

21. R. L. Anderson, *Investigating the Book of Mormon Witnesses*, 153–55.

22. See Richard Lloyd Anderson, "The Second Witness on Priesthood Succession," part 3, *Improvement Era*, November 1968, 14–20. There is no doubt that David Whitmer had serious objections to the Doctrine and Covenants. He may have mistakenly assumed that Oliver agreed with him.

23. Wells, Vermont Town Record, Record of Births, 158–59; Hiland Paul and Robert Parks, *History of Wells, Vermont, for the First Century after Its Settlement* (1869; reprint, Wells, Vt.: Wells Historical Society, 1979), 81; Carl A. Curtis, "Cowdery Genealogical Material," 1970, 1, L. Tom Perry Special Collections; Mary Bryant Alverson Mehling, *Cowdrey-Cowdery-Cowdray Genealogy* (n.p.: Allaben Genealogical, 1911), 186–88; "Historical and Genealogical Material, Poultney, Vermont , Part 1, Historical," 1052, type-script, Poultney town clerk's office, Poultney, Vermont.

24. I don't fault R. D. Anderson for stating—as many previous historians have done—that Oliver once worked as a blacksmith (96). Still, this is a rumor worth dispatching. It apparently originated with Eber D. Howe, the anti-Mormon author of *Mormonism Unvailed*, but Cowdery family documents do not corroborate that idea nor is it consistent with Oliver's studious bent or slight build.

25. Key sections of Barnes Frisbie, *The History of Middletown, Vermont* (Rutland, Vt.: Tuttle, 1867), are reprinted in *Early Mormon Documents*, ed. Dan Vogel (Salt Lake City: Signature Books, 1996), 1:599–621.

26. Frisbie, *History of Middletown, Vermont*, in *Early Mormon Documents*, 1:599–621. For more information on the Wood Scrape, see Richard Lloyd Anderson, "The Mature Joseph Smith and Treasure Searching," *BYU Studies* 24/3 (1984): 489–560; D. Michael Quinn, *Early Mormonism and the Magic World View*, rev. and enl. (Salt Lake City: Signature Books, 1998), 35–36, 121–30; and Larry E. Morris, "Oliver Cowdery's Vermont Years and the Origins of Mormonism," *BYU Studies* 39/1 (2000): 106–29.

27. But, of course, even if William Cowdery's involvement in the Wood Scrape were proved—and it hasn't been—this would still prove nothing about Oliver. Documents relating to the family's religious history would be necessary to show a link between the Wood Scrape and Oliver's use of the rod.

28. Oliver's use of a divining rod does not count as a strike against him. As Quinn points out in *Magic World View*, 34, such use was common among respected people at the time. "From north to south, from east to west, the divining rod has its advocates," revealed *The American Journal of Science and Art* in 1826. "Men in various callings, . . . men of the soundest judgment . . . do not disown the art." It seems that anyone trying to put folk magic in context would mention this, but critics sometimes bring up the Wood Scrape without discussing what Richard L. Bushman has called "the line that divided the yearning for the supernatural from the humanism of rational Christianity." Bushman, *Joseph Smith and the Beginnings of Mormonism* (Urbana, Ill.: University of Illinois Press, 1984), 79.

29. Vogel, *Early Mormon Documents*, 1:621.

30. See Morris, "Oliver Cowdery's Vermont Years," 116–18.

31. See ibid., 122 n. 3 for a list of books and articles discussing *View of the Hebrews.*

32. See Royal Skousen, "Translating the Book of Mormon: Evidence from the Original Manuscript," in *Book of Mormon Authorship Revisited: The Evidence for Ancient Origins,* ed. Noel B. Reynolds (Provo, Utah: FARMS, 1997), 61–93.

33. As Vogel himself points out, however, Clark heard this account in 1828, meaning that even if it could be verified it would prove nothing about Martin Harris's 1829 experience as one of the Three Witnesses.

34. Vogel, *Early Mormon Documents,* 2:270.

35. At the same time, Clark's report of his direct conversation with Martin Harris is an important historical document that relates particularly to the Anthon transcript.

36. "The Testimony of the Eight Witnesses."

37. Vogel, *Early Mormon Documents,* 2:468. One difference between the Cowdery account and the Clark and Ford accounts is this: while Clark's and Ford's sources are not identified, one of the Cowdery versions identifies Robert Barrington as its source. It is therefore potentially verifiable in a way that the others are not.

38. L. F. Anderson, *Lucy's Book,* 432.

39. Ibid., 433.

40. Ibid., 434. As Lavina Fielding Anderson points out, this is probably a reference to Doctrine and Covenants 6:22–24: "Verily, verily, I say unto you, if you desire a further witness, cast your mind upon the night that you cried unto me in your heart, that you might know concerning the truth of these things. Did I not speak peace to your mind concerning the matter? What greater witness can you have than from God? And now, behold, you have received a witness; for if I have told you things which no man knoweth have you not received a witness?"

41. Vogel, *Early Mormon Documents,* 1:74.

42. Scott H. Faulring, *An American Prophet's Record: The Diaries and Journals of Joseph Smith,* 2nd ed. (Salt Lake City: Signature Books, 1989), 8.

43. L. F. Anderson, *Lucy's Book,* 433.

44. Oliver Cowdery to Joseph Smith, 6 November 1829, in Anderson and Faulring, *Documentary History of Oliver Cowdery,* 1:78–79.

45. Oliver Cowdery to Joseph Smith, 28 December 1829, in Anderson and Faulring, *Documentary History of Oliver Cowdery,* 1:80–81.

46. *Merriam-Webster's Collegiate Dictionary,* 10th ed. Definitions quoted in this review come from this edition.

47. For Lucy Mack Smith, see L. F. Anderson, *Lucy's Book,* 460–70. For Gilbert, Tucker, Harding, and Chandler, see Vogel, *Early Mormon Documents,* 2:515–52, 3:62–72, 82–86, and 221–23, respectively.

48. Articles of the Church of Christ, in Anderson and Faulring, *Documentary History of Oliver Cowdery,* 1:66.

49. Joseph Smith History, 1839 draft, Dean C. Jessee, *The Papers of Joseph Smith, Volume 1: Autobiographical and Historical Writings* (Salt Lake City: Deseret Book, 1989), 260.

50. Paul and Parks, *History of Wells, Vermont,* 79.

51. For David Stafford, John Stafford, Lorenzo Saunders, Hiram Jackway, Benjamin Saunders, and William Hyde, see Vogel, *Early Mormon Documents,* 2:57, 123, 134, 115, 139, and 3:197, respectively.

52. For Keen, Gibson, and Lang, see Vogel, *Early Mormon Documents,* 2:506; *Seneca Advertiser,* 12 April 1892; Shook, *True Origin of the Book of Mormon,* 57; and William Lang, *History of Seneca County* (Springfield, Ohio: Transcript Printing, 1880), 364–65, respectively.

53. All references in this paragraph are cited in R. L. Anderson, *Investigating the Book of Mormon Witnesses,* 44–46, 48.

54. It is not clear to me why Vogel's "central question" concerns a comparison with similar religious testimonies. As a historian, does he claim to have access to those experiences? Does he have any way of knowing whether they were genuine or not? And how would the experience of the Book of Mormon witnesses being "distinguishable" prove anything? However, if one is looking for a key difference between the experience of the Book of Mormon witnesses and the religious epiphanies of others, how about this: the plates. How many other religious individuals claimed to have received an ancient artifact from a divine messenger—an artifact seen and handled by several other people? (Similarly, when Scott Dunn—in his *American Apocrypha* article "Automaticity and the Book of Mormon"—asks for "evidence of clear differences" (36) between the Book of Mormon and other texts produced through "automatic writing," it seems to me that Moroni's delivering "the original text" to Joseph Smith is one clear difference.)

55. Of course, even the assumption that historians can demonstrate what did or did not happen in the past is open to debate. What does it mean when two (or more) people perceive the same event differently? Is it even appropriate to speak of "the same event"? Is there such a thing as "objective reality"? Such events as the death of Meriwether Lewis, Thomas Jefferson's relationship with Sally Heming, and the assassination of John F. Kennedy have been the source of endless controversy, even though they involved no supernatural element. Nonetheless, while I believe that epistemological distinctions have value up to a point, I also believe that historians can get at the truth of puzzling events through careful, thorough, open-minded research.

56. Jessee, *The Papers of Joseph Smith,* 1:237, emphasis added.

57. Saying that a vision is different from normal experience is not the same as saying it is, in Vogel's words, "internal and subjective" (86). In the case of the Three Witnesses, Joseph Smith, Oliver Cowdery, and David Whitmer reported having the same visionary experience that involved physical objects. This experience involved the supernatural to be sure (and by my definition it is not empirical), but it was clearly not internal and subjective.

58. While Vogel does quote Lucy Mack Smith in regard to Oliver Cowdery, Lucy hardly supports Vogel's conclusions. Quite the contrary, Lucy clearly believed that Oliver was stable, reliable, and capable of being trusted.

59. The phrase "visionary predisposition" itself reveals Vogel's bias. If Oliver had a genuine spiritual experience or vision while he was contemplating what Joseph Sr. and Lucy had told him about the plates, it would hardly be fair to characterize his subsequent attitude as a "predisposition."

60. On one level, historians do have a basis for judging "religious experience." If, for example, one found reliable evidence that Joseph Smith and the Three Witnesses agreed to concoct a story about Moroni appearing and showing them plates, this would certainly give one good historical reason to reject the testimony printed in the Book of Mormon. Again, if a third party claimed to have tricked Joseph and the others (by pretending to be

an angel and producing fake plates, for example), this would also count as potential historical evidence. (Stephen Harding claims to have tricked Calvin Stoddard in a similar manner; see Vogel, *Early Mormon Documents*, 3:82–86.) Of course, such scenarios involve deceit or insincerity, taking them out of the realm of genuine religious experience.

61. Vision, 3 April 1836, Joseph Smith Diary, in Anderson and Faulring, *Documentary History of Oliver Cowdery*, 3:366–67. Interestingly, this early version of Doctrine and Covenants 110 was recorded by Warren Cowdery, Oliver's oldest brother.

62. Lyndon W. Cook, ed., *David Whitmer Interviews* (Orem, Utah: Grandin Book, 1993), 63.

63. Jessee, *The Papers of Joseph Smith*, 290, emphasis added.

64. Oliver Cowdery to W. W. Phelps, 7 September 1834, in Vogel, *Early Mormon Documents*, 2:420.

65. Oliver Cowdery to P. H. Young, 23 March 1846, in Vogel, *Early Mormon Documents*, 2:492.

66. Reuben Miller Journal, 21 October 1848, in Vogel, *Early Mormon Documents*, 2:494. William Frampton was also present when Oliver bore his testimony at Council Bluffs, Iowa, in October 1848. In a letter written more than fifty years later, Frampton quoted Oliver thus: "I received the Priesthood in connection with Joseph Smith from the hands of the Angel, I conversed with the Angel as one man converses with another. He laid his hand on my head, and later with Joseph received the Melchisedeck Priesthood." Vogel, *Early Mormon Documents*, 2:496.

67. Oliver Cowdery, statement to Samuel W. Richards, 13 January 1849, in Vogel, *Early Mormon Documents*, 2:499.

68. See *Early Mormon Documents*, vols. 2 and 3.

69. R. L. Anderson, *Investigating the Book of Mormon Witnesses*, 37.

70. Vogel, *Early Mormon Documents*, 2:495.

71. Vogel seems to believe that even though Joseph constructed fake plates, no one actually saw those plates—they only felt them through a cloth or hefted them in a box. (This would account for the fact that no one pointed out the obvious: "Hey, these aren't gold plates with intricate engravings—these are tin plates produced in the local blacksmith shop.") Vogel further suggests that whenever a witness "saw" the plates, he was not seeing the tin plates but rather the imaginary plates, which had "the appearance of ancient work, and of curious workmanship." To make this logic work, Vogel makes the astonishing assertion that "Smith may have produced a box containing the plates or perhaps something of similar weight. The witnesses were permitted to lift the box, but their view of the plates was visionary. In other words, they may have seen the plates through the box. Thus, each man could claim that he had both seen and handled the artifact" (104). But does Vogel reach this conclusion based on any statement from the Eight Witnesses themselves? Absolutely not. Instead, he relies on speculation and thirdhand accounts from the likes of Stephen Burnett, Warren Parrish, and Thomas Ford. Vogel thus reaches a conclusion that flies in the face of clear, direct testimony offered by the witnesses themselves: "And as many of the leaves as the said Smith has translated we did handle with our hands; and we also saw the engravings thereon" (The Testimony of the Eight Witnesses). "I thank God that I felt a determination to die rather than deny the things which my eyes had seen, which my hands had handled" (Hyrum Smith, p. 51). "I have most assuredly seen the plates from whence the Book of Mormon is translated,

and . . . I have handled these plates" (John Whitmer, p. 54). See Richard Lloyd Anderson, "Personal Writings of the Book of Mormon Witnesses," in *Book of Mormon Authorship Revisited*, 39–60.

THE RETURN OF OLIVER COWDERY

Scott H. Faulring

On Sunday, 12 November 1848, apostle Orson Hyde, president
of the Quorum of the Twelve and the Church's presiding official
at Kanesville-Council Bluffs, Iowa, stepped into the cool waters
of Mosquito Creek[1] near Council Bluffs and took Mormonism's
estranged Second Elder by the hand to rebaptize him. Sometime
shortly after that, Elder Hyde laid hands on Oliver's head, confirm-
ing him back into Church membership and reordaining him an
elder in the Melchizedek Priesthood.[2] Cowdery's rebaptism culminated six years of desire on his part and protracted efforts encouraged by the Mormon leadership to bring about his sought-after,
eagerly anticipated reconciliation. Cowdery, renowned as one of the
Three Witnesses to the Book of Mormon, corecipient of restored
priesthood power, and a founding member of The Church of Jesus
Christ of Latter-day Saints, had spent ten and a half years outside the
Church after his April 1838 excommunication.

Oliver Cowdery wanted reaffiliation with the Church he helped
organize. His penitent yearnings to reassociate with the Saints were
evident from his personal letters and actions as early as 1842. Oliver
understood the necessity of rebaptism. By subjecting himself to
rebaptism by Elder Hyde, Cowdery acknowledged the priesthood
keys and authority held by the First Presidency under Brigham
Young and the Twelve.

Oliver Cowdery's tenure as Second Elder and Associate President ended abruptly when he decided not to appear and defend himself against misconduct charges at the 12 April 1838, Far West, Missouri, high council hearing.[3] Instead, Oliver sent a terse letter in which he elaborated on his differences of opinion "on some Church regulations." In this defensive communiqué, Oliver implored Bishop Edward Partridge and the council to "take no view of the foregoing remarks, other than my belief on the *outward government* of this Church."[4] President Cowdery regretted that differences existed, but he explained that he was not willing to be dictated to in his temporal business affairs or have his civil liberties abused by those who, he believed, were aspiring for position. The Far West High Council, unsympathetic to Oliver Cowdery's views, sustained six of the nine charges against him, and he was promptly excommunicated.[5] That his disparities were mainly bureaucratic versus theocratic is supported by Thomas B. Marsh's chance meeting of Oliver Cowdery and David Whitmer later that summer. Marsh, by then himself a defector from the Mormon fold, asked the two witnesses if they still held to the beliefs as proclaimed in their published Book of Mormon testimony. Marsh recalled that both David and Oliver answered emphatically, "Yes."[6]

The first encouraging news about Oliver Cowdery after his disaffection came to Nauvoo in a letter written to Joseph Smith from an unidentified Church member in Kirtland. Laura Pitkin, a resident of Nauvoo, shared news gleaned from this Kirtland letter in the postscript of her letter to Heber C. Kimball. Pitkin observed: "Brother Joseph received a letter from Kirtland last week. Martin Harris has come [back] into the church. Oliver Cowd[e]ry is very friendly and they have properous times in that place."[7]

No official action was taken to replace Oliver Cowdery as Associate President until 24 January 1841. In Joseph Smith's first public revelation after being liberated from his Missouri imprisonment, reasons for a reorganization were explained, required in part because of the expulsion of Oliver Cowdery. Hyrum Smith, the Prophet's older brother, was called to fill the office of Church patriarch, replacing

Father Smith, who had died four months earlier. In addition, Hyrum was called to fill the vacancy left by Cowdery as Associate President and given the "same blessing, and glory, and honor, and priesthood, and gifts of the priesthood" once held by Cowdery (D&C 124:95). Since Oliver had defected and isolated himself from the Church, it is presumed that he was not notified of the change.

After leaving Missouri in the fall of 1838, Oliver Cowdery returned to Kirtland, settling close to his non-Mormon brother, Lyman. In early 1840, Oliver was admitted to the Ohio bar as an attorney. He practiced law in Kirtland with Lyman for a short time. Cowdery moved in the fall of 1840 to Tiffin, a town in northwestern Ohio, where he continued as a lawyer.[8] For the next seven years, Tiffin was Cowdery's home.

By December 1842, four and a half years after he had been excommunicated, Cowdery was visited at least three times by his devoted friend and brother-in-law Phineas H. Young. Phineas, who had been away from Nauvoo for five months, was accompanied by Franklin D. Richards and had been sent to Cincinnati to preside over the Church in the southern district of Ohio.[9] While laboring in Ohio, Phineas called on Oliver. It is unclear whether Elder Young was specifically directed by Church leaders to contact Oliver Cowdery or whether he did so on his own initiative. Nonetheless, these visits were the first steps taken to redeem Cowdery from estrangement. Phineas, married to Oliver's half-sister Lucy, started the momentum that would, six years later, result in Oliver's reinstatement. Reporting that Oliver was alive and well, Phineas wrote his brother Brigham and the Twelve informing them that Oliver's "heart is still with his old friends."[10]

Phineas expressed his conviction that the disenfranchised Second Elder would willingly gather with the Saints in Nauvoo if only Brother Joseph understood Oliver's side of the controversy that led to his (Cowdery's) dismissal from Far West. Always Oliver's staunchest supporter and ever the sympathetic observer, Phineas believed that his brother-in-law had been unjustly driven out by jealous, conspiring elders. He expressed his opinion that men such as

Sidney Rigdon, Thomas Marsh, George Hinkle, George Robinson, and others, nurturing ulterior motives, testified against President Cowdery and gave Joseph Smith prejudicial information. Oliver, feeling outnumbered, believed that defending himself against these biased witnesses was futile.

Phineas's December 1842 correspondence with the Twelve clarified several issues raised during Oliver Cowdery's high council hearing four years earlier. Cowdery contradicted persistent reports of his supposed claim that if he left the Church, it would collapse. Phineas reported that Oliver never harbored such a pretentious attitude, that such an arrogant disposition never entered the Second Elder's heart. In addition, Oliver had concerns that promissory notes he once held against Brigham Young and others, which were paid off or settled, had been turned over to Oliver Granger for delivery to the parties concerned. Somehow these obligations were sold or given to Granger's son Gilbert for collection. The fraudulent use of these notes caused Cowdery "great anxiety" because he felt personally responsible for their proper and lawful disposition. These and other issues had not been resolved, and Cowdery felt that they tarnished his reputation and wanted them settled.

Near the end of 1842, although involved with his legal practice in Tiffin, Oliver volunteered to leave home to help prepare a legal defense for Elder John Snyder. Leader of a company of British Mormon converts, Snyder was arrested for mutiny in New Orleans.[11] Cowdery was ready, with the authorization of the Nauvoo High Council, to go with Phineas to New Orleans. Phineas assured Brigham and Joseph Smith's secretary, Willard Richards, that "I am satisfied [Oliver] has no sinister motives in the above proposition, as he is crowded with business continually." It is unlikely that the Twelve responded to Cowdery's offer since Elder Snyder was released from jail by the second week of January 1843.[12]

William W. Phelps, one of the Prophet's personal secretaries and himself a recently reclaimed elder, wrote to Cowdery in March 1843.[13] This was the earliest recorded written contact by a Church representative with Oliver since his defection. For unexplained reasons, Oliver viewed Phelps's letter as a "strange . . . epistle." He told Phineas that Phelps did not request a reply but he planned to write him back anyhow.[14] A week later, Cowdery changed his mind, explaining that since Phelps did not specifically ask for an answer, "I have not written him in return."[15]

During the summer of 1843, Oliver received word from his brother Lyman that Phineas had returned to Kirtland. He looked forward to a visit from his esteemed brother-in-law. Cowdery thought about going to Kirtland, but referred to the difficulty in leaving a professional business to be "absent a few weeks when one has numerous competitors." Oliver bragged that his legal practice was increasing steadily and that nothing stood in his way except his previous involvement with Mormonism. He anguished over this intolerance: "Were it not for this, I believe I could rise to the height of my ambition. But, shame on the man, or men, who are so beneath themselves, as to make this a barrier. My God has sustained me, and is able still to sustain me—and through his own mysterious providence to lift me above all my foes. With his dealings I will be content."[16]

Cowdery was unaware that months earlier, on 19 April, during a routine Wednesday afternoon meeting, Joseph Smith instructed the Twelve to invite their former colleague back into Church fellowship and service. According to Willard Richards, keeper of the Prophet's journal, Joseph directed: "Write to Oliver Cowdery and ask him if he has not eat[en] husks long enough, if he is not most ready to return [be clothed with robes of righteousness], and go up to Jerusalem. Orson Hyde hath need of him."[17] Richards noted that the Twelve immediately drafted a letter that was "signed by the members of the Quorum present." In their invitational epistle, addressed specifically to Oliver as one of the Three Witnesses of the Book of Mormon, the Twelve observed:

> We thought perhaps our old, long esteemed friend might by this time have felt his lonely, solitary situation; might feel that he was a stranger in a strange land, and had wandered long enough from his Father's house and that he might have a disposition to

return. If this is the case, all that we have got to say is, your *breth-ren* are ready to receive you; we are not your enemies, but your brethren. Your dwelling place you know ought to be in Zion—your labor might be needed in Jerusalem, and you ought to be the servant of the living God.[18]

The Twelve told Oliver that they would be "happy to have an answer from you to let us know your feeling" and asked him to respond to quorum president Brigham Young at Nauvoo.

This invitation to return, although composed, signed, and dated April 1843, for unexplained reasons, was not mailed until December. In August, Phineas Young, aware of the invitation, told Oliver about the Twelve's dispatch. Oliver replied: "You say 'the Twelve' say they have written me. I have received nothing from them." Cowdery reminded Phineas that the only communication he had received from Church leaders was the "strange unmeaning letter from my old friend Phelps last spring."[19] Finally, on 20 December, Oliver received the Twelve's epistle, which he noted had a 10 December Nauvoo postmark.

Despite the letter's delay, Oliver took time Christmas day to respond. He admitted his confusion over the detained letter but assumed that "feelings of friendship and kindness therein expressed are the same now, as then."[20] Accepting the Twelve's epistle as a "friendly letter," Cowdery reciprocated their cordial sentiments by asserting that he held "no unkindly feelings" toward them. He read-ily admitted the truth of their observation that he lived a "'lonely, solitary situation—a stranger in a strange land'" and confessed that it "is true, strictly true." Oliver wrote: "It has been a long time, nearly six years—the winds and waves, floods and storms, have been arrayed to oppose me; and I need hardly say to you, that the Lord alone has upheld me, till I have fought up, labored up, and struggled up, to a fair reputation and a fair business in my present profession."[21]

Cowdery longed to put the strife associated with his June 1838 departure from Far West behind him. The situation, he explained, was "painful to reflect on." In a genuine spirit of reconciliation,

Oliver offered his personal interpretation of the circumstances leading to his dismissal. He observed candidly:

> I believed at the time, and still believe, that ambitious and wicked
> men, envying the harmony existing between myself and the first
> elders of the church, and hoping to get into some other men's
> birthright, by falsehoods the most foul and wicked, caused *all
> this difficulty from beginning to end.* They succeeded in getting
> myself out of the church; but since they themselves have gone to
> perdition, ought not old friends—long tried in the furnace of af-
> fliction, to be friends still?[22]

Oliver also told Brigham and the other members of the Twelve
that he did not believe any of them had contributed to his removal
and thus could speak freely with them about returning.[23] In his
reply to the Twelve's invitation, Oliver mentioned a "certain publication," signed by some eighty-three Church members then living in
Missouri, charging him and others with conspiring with outlaws.[24]
Cowdery emphatically denied such a vile indictment. He conceded
that he had not seen the offending declaration but had heard of its
existence and the accusations made in it.

Six months later, near noon on that tragic 27 June, the Prophet
Joseph Smith, while incarcerated in Carthage Jail, was visited by
Almon W. Babbitt. During his stay with the Prophet, Babbitt read a
communication received recently from Oliver Cowdery.[25] Although
the letter has been lost and its specific contents remain unknown, it
can be presumed from Oliver's recent optimistic overtures that his
was a congenial letter.[26]

Cowdery's reaction to news of Joseph's murder was captured in
a statement by William Lang, a Tiffin, Ohio, attorney who studied
law under Oliver's supervision. Lang reported:

> [Joseph] Smith was killed while [Oliver] C[owdery] lived here. I
> well remember the effect upon his countenance when he read the
> news in my presence. He immediately took the paper over to his
> house to read to his wife. On his return to the office we had a
> long conversation on the subject, and I was surprised to hear him
> speak with so much kindness of a man that had so wronged him

as Smith had. It elevated him greatly in my already high esteem, and proved to me more than ever the nobility of his nature.[27]

Phineas Young, traveling east on another mission, spent four days in November 1844 with Cowdery at his home in Tiffin. Soon afterwards, Phineas wrote to Brigham. He conveyed that "[Oliver] sends love to you and all old friends," adding parenthetically that Oliver "sees the folly of Sidney [Rigdon]'s course."[28] In a further attempt to reclaim Oliver Cowdery, Phineas told his brother, "There are many things I want to say . . . therefore I will write somewhat to you on a certain subject that I wish you to disclose to no one, but ponder the same in your heart." With this in mind, Phineas asked Brigham to reflect

> back on the days of sorrow witnessed by our beloved Prophet and his old friend O[liver] Cowdery. Watch their prayers and tears, consider their feelings and friendship for each other, see them in Colesville in their weakness, remember them in Jackson [County], Missouri, in Kirtland, Ohio, all was peace, all was love. Did they ever quarrel? No. Did they ever forsake each other? No. What was the difficulty?[29]

Phineas blamed Thomas B. Marsh and others at Far West in 1838 with conspiracy in driving Oliver Cowdery out of the Church by charging him with apostasy, forgery, and theft. George W. Robinson, Rigdon's son-in-law, was singled out as having driven Oliver from his home in June 1838.[30] Phineas insisted that if the charges "were placed on the heads of those apostates" (that is, Marsh, Robinson, and others), then Oliver Cowdery would admit his short-comings, make amends for his weaknesses, and rejoin the Saints. Phineas encouraged Brigham to publish a statement in the Church's Nauvoo periodical, the *Times and Seasons,* explaining "to the Saints and to the world that these charges were false and instigated by false brethren."[31] Cowdery anticipated returning as a useful, productive member of the Church. He believed that he would not be considered a credible witness of the early events of the restoration without a statement clearing him of the Missouri charges. Brigham, preoccupied with the mounting pressure from apostates and antagonistic non-Mormons that would eventually force the Saints to flee Nauvoo, did not respond to his brother's appeal.

Nearly a year later, in October 1845, during another visit from Phineas, Oliver wrote again to Brigham Young. Once more, he offered his legal and personal services to the Church. This time the matter was the Saints' anticipated departure from Nauvoo and surrounding areas and their journey west into Mexican territory. While together in Tiffin, Oliver and Phineas discussed the probability of the Church needing to send out an "exploring company" to find a less-hostile, uninhabited gathering location. Cowdery sensed the strong national desire to push America's borders farther west to the Pacific and recognized how it could be combined with the Latter-day Saints' need to find refuge in either the uninhabited Rocky Mountains or upper California. He proposed traveling to Washington, D.C., to visit President Polk and other national leaders about dispatching a Mormon colonizing party and, as he said, "if favorably received, ask aid." Oliver, fearing he would be perceived as ambitious or scheming for a leadership position, explained: "I only wish to say, that should you determine on a removal to the west, and wish me to see President Polk, and others as I have stated, you will signify such a wish, and any aid I can render you, will be cheerfully done, as I have said to Brother Phineas."[32]

Brigham Young directed his clerk, W. W. Phelps, to respond to Cowdery's generous but unsolicited offer. In early December, Phelps, in a succinct letter, expressed President Young's current attitude toward federal assistance in their westward trek: "We have concluded to let this rotten government alone, and shall not petition at Washington."[33] It appears that after many frustrating years during which the Saints unsuccessfully sought redress from the national government for their privations in Missouri, the governing Quorum of Twelve had all but lost confidence in the integrity of the federal government and did not want to enter into any entangling agreements with it. This antigovernment assistance stance mellowed by January 1846 when Brigham Young sent his representative, Jesse Little, to Washington seeking

President Polk's support for the Saints' offer to construct blockhouses
and bridges and enlist Mormon military recruits in exchange for government support in their exodus west.[34]

Also in Phelps's reply was a renewed invitation for Oliver to
rejoin with the Saints and go west. Phelps, addressing himself as
"your old associate," entreated his former coeditor of the *Evening
and the Morning Star,* "As to our Exodus, if you believe that we are
Israel, come on and go with us and we will do you good, for the Spirit
says come, and your friends say come, and let him that is athirst say
come, with all things ready."[35]

Oliver Cowdery accepted Phelps's epistle as friendly and
thanked him for writing, but commented to Phineas that the letter
from Phelps was "very short" and "very different from what I had
anticipated." Confiding with Phineas, Oliver shared his prolonged
concern that the old Missouri difficulties had not been resolved, and
until they were, he felt unable to return to full fellowship. In a tone
reflecting both frustration and conciliation, he wrote to Phineas:

> I think some times, that my frequent letters to you on the sub-
> ject of, what I have so often expressed anxiety upon, has led you
> to believe me officious and overanxious; and though I have often
> been disappointed, there is notwithstanding, an act of justice due
> to me, not only for my own, but for the sake and character of my
> friends and relatives; and particularly those who are yet in the
> Church. So far as others are concerned, they care nothing about
> it. Indeed, I sometimes think, they wish it never to be given, as
> that may effectually prevent my return. You know my feelings
> fully on this subject—you will present them to Bro. Brigham—
> tell him I am more and more anxious that matters be settled—the
> sooner the better, of course.[36]

In spite of Cowdery's distress, his name was not immediately cleared
nor was his reputation cleansed of the offending charges.

During the spring of 1846, Oliver's frustration peaked over a
letter he received from Orson Hyde. Cowdery wrote that he did not
fully understand the purpose of Hyde's epistle, admitting that he
either misunderstood or was "[in] spirit misconceived by me."[37]

Although Orson Hyde's letter is not extant, we do know from a letter he sent to Brigham Young in early March 1846 that he believed the ongoing efforts to reclaim Cowdery would eventually pay off. Elder Hyde informed President Young that he had put down those who were advocating Strangism and Pagism; he then mentioned the return of the prodigal Luke Johnson and boldly predicted "Oliver will come next."[38]

Again the former Associate President, in a letter to his brother-in-law, emphasized his anxiety for his reputation. Cowdery mentioned: "I have only sought, and only asked, that my character might stand exonerated from those charges which imputed to me the crimes of theft, forgery, &c. Those which all my former associates knew to be false." In making this statement, Oliver was not expecting to be excused from admitting any real shortcomings or wrongs. He readily admitted he had many faults. In what has become Cowdery's most impassioned plea, one focused on his desire to be considered a credible witness of the early restoration to future generations, he wrote:

> I have cherished a hope, and that one of my fondest, that I might leave such a character, as those who might believe in my testimony, after I should be called hence, might do so, not only for the sake of the truth, but might not *blush* for the private character of the man who bore that testimony. I have been sensitive on this subject, I admit; but I ought to be so—you would be, under the circumstances, had you stood in the presence of John, with our departed Brother Joseph, to receive the Lesser Priesthood—and in the presence of Peter, to receive the Greater, and looked down through time, and witnessed the effects these two must produce,—you would feel what you have never felt, were wicked men conspiring to lessen the effects of your testimony on man, after you should have gone to your long sought rest.[39]

Oliver expressed his confidence that "no unjust imputation will be suffered to remain upon my character" and "I am fully, doubly, satisfied, that all will be right—that my character will be fully vindicated."[40] Having eloquently expressed his concerns, Oliver did not mention the "character" issue again in any of his letters.

Phineas, in a letter written between 5 and 9 March, discussed with Oliver the subject of "2nd Eldership, Counsellorship" and noticed the upcoming Church conference on 6 April. This caused Oliver to reminisce about the organization of the Church of Christ on 6 April 1830. He wrote: "Brother Phineas, [if] I could be with you, and tell you about the 6th of April, 1830, when but six members only belonged [to] the Church, and how we looked forward to a future, I should gladly, but I cannot—only in spirit—but in spirit I shall be with you."[41] From this and other comments one senses a yearning on Cowdery's part to once again be personally involved in and associated with the Church. In this March 1846 letter, Oliver expressed his intention to get out of debt so that he could move west with the Saints. He told his friend Phineas that "The situation of my family is such, that it is not possible for me to come with them, this Spring; but I want to be prepared at the earliest moment." Cowdery concluded this touching letter with his blessing: "M[ay] the Lord God of our Father's bless you, and yours—and the Church, as a body. Such is my prayer—such is my heart. I am yours in the new and everlasting covenant." As with previous letters written during this period, Oliver asked that the contents of his letter remain confidential with the Twelve.

Sometime in July, Oliver Cowdery received a letter from Phebe Jackson, his other half-sister. In her communiqué, she confided to her brother the emotional distress she felt concerning the trials and tribulations anticipated in the trek west. She also expressed personal anxiety with the emerging practice of plural marriage among the Saints. Oliver, evidently uninformed by Phineas about the continuance of polygamy at Nauvoo, wrote an emotional reply to Phebe and her husband, Daniel. A brief excerpt reads,

> Now, brother Daniel and Sister Phebe, what will you do? Has Sister Phebe written us the truth? . . . I can hardly think it possible, that you have written us the truth, that though there may be individuals who are guilty of the iniquities spoken of—yet no such practice can be preached or adhered to, as a public doctrine.[42]

Cowdery's response to this news is intriguing. He spoke from personal experience when he pointed out the imprudence of plural marriage as a "public doctrine." Recorded in historical records are credible witnesses to the fact that Oliver himself was involved in and censured for an unauthorized polygamous relationship during the Church's stay in Kirtland, Ohio, during the 1830s.[43] In this period, Joseph Smith married his first plural wife—Fanny Alger.[44] It is unclear why Cowdery, on his own authority, felt the need to take an additional wife. By 1835, the Mormon Church was being publicly "reproached" for the "crime" of polygamy. In Oliver's carefully worded "Article on Marriage," which first appeared in the 1835 edition of the Doctrine and Covenants, a public statement was made defending the Church against immoral conduct. In this article, polygamy was renounced and monogamy declared to be the belief of the Church. Later in Missouri, one charge preferred against Cowdery was that he accused Joseph Smith of adultery.[45] Two years after this emotionally charged social issue was brought to his attention in 1846, during his lengthy private conversations with Elders Orson Hyde and George A. Smith at Kanesville in October-November 1848, Oliver was evidently brought up-to-date on the Nauvoo-era application of the plural-marriage doctrine.

Also, in his response to Phebe and Daniel, Oliver said that his emigration with the Church depended on circumstances. He did not elaborate on what those situations might be, but his struggles with plural marriage, exhausted finances, and ever-fragile health were relevant concerns. Yet in spite of these concerns, Cowdery was convinced that going west offered a most hopeful prospect. To Phebe and her husband, Oliver wrote optimistically, "So far as going west is concerned, I have thought it a wise move—indeed, I could see no other; and though the journey is long, and attended with toil, yet a bright future has been seen in the distance."[46]

Later, in November 1846, Oliver answered a letter received "a long time since" from Phineas. Cowdery was uncertain his brother-in-law would get the letter given the "confusion and difficulty then existing at Nauvoo." He had been anxiously waiting for answers to specific questions asked in his last letters. It is possible that Oliver was referring to inquiries he had made about the Saints living the doctrine of plural marriage. Preoccupied with his frail health and desiring to better himself professionally, Oliver announced to Phineas that he was selling his Tiffin law practice and moving in the spring.[47]

Sometime between late November and mid-December 1846, Oliver Cowdery traveled to Washington, D.C., where he visited his political contacts. Before departing for Washington, he wrote to Phineas and asked him to find out if the Church leaders wanted information that might be of help to them in their westward migration. Noting that the then-raging war with Mexico would afford an opportune diversion for the Church, Oliver offered his unsolicited advice for handling the politically sensitive situation of wintering on federal lands set aside specifically for the Indians. He explained, "[I] have made the foregoing suggestions out of the deep feelings of my soul, and because the welfare of that church, the foundations of which my own hands helped to lay, is constantly near my thoughts."[48] Cowdery's mid-November letter received notice during a council meeting on 22 December 1846. Brigham Young's history reports, "A favorable letter from O. Cowdery to Phinehas H. Young was read."[49]

At this point, efforts by the Church leaders to facilitate Oliver Cowdery's anticipated reconciliation with the Church went into limbo for nearly a year. Several reasons exist for the delay. First, the Church leaders' attention and the Church's resources were focused on supplying and organizing for the forced westward movement of thousands of Saints. Second, Oliver had not received the expected exoneration from the false charges made against him at Far West, Missouri, in 1838 along with the associated restoration of his reputation. Third, Cowdery did not have sufficient means to outfit a wagon and team for a pioneer trek. Fourth, the Saints' immediate future was uncertain and Oliver, already suffering physically and financially, hoped to rejoin and live with the Saints under less life-threatening conditions.[50] During this interlude, Oliver kept busy as a lawyer. For several months, he was temporary editor of the *Seneca Advertiser* while his editor friend, John Breslin, attended to state political responsibilities at Columbus, Ohio.[51] The Mormon leaders, scattered across the Midwestern plains, turned their focus toward the impending exodus of the scattered Saints from the state of Iowa and Nebraska Territory.

By mid-February 1847, Cowdery wrote again to Phineas. He was deeply concerned because he had not heard from his revered brother-in-law or other relatives in some time. Oliver confided, "For no day passes without our thoughts being turned towards our relatives and once loved friends, who are toiling and struggling in the far-off wilderness, during a cold pitiless winter."[52] Reporting on his recent trip to Washington, Oliver informed Phineas that from his personal conversations with his political contacts and the information he gathered, no one in authority at the federal district planned to give the displaced Latter-day Saints any difficulty with their settling temporarily upon Indians' territorial land. As expected, the executive and legislative leaders in Washington were preoccupied by the ongoing war with Mexico. Oliver pointed out that he perceived a feeling of sympathy in the nation's capital toward the uprooted Saints.[53] Although Cowdery asked to be remembered by his former associates, including Brigham Young, Luke Johnson, and William W. Phelps, he did not discuss rejoining the Saints that spring.

Oliver left Tiffin, Ohio, in April 1847 and went to Wisconsin to explore immediate career options there and to be close to his brother Lyman, who had moved there the previous fall. Oliver saw the Wisconsin Territory, on the threshold of statehood, as a land of interim opportunity. He hoped that southern Wisconsin's climate would be better suited to his fragile health and that a developing economy would possibly improve his struggling law practice. He settled in southern Wisconsin, at Elkhorn, less than twenty miles from the Illinois state line. Oliver's later actions suggest that he was purposefully positioning himself closer to the Iowa exodus camps of the Saints. Within two months of his arrival, brothers Oliver and Lyman were again working together as attorneys.

During the last week of July, William E. McLellin arrived in southern Wisconsin to talk with Oliver Cowdery. McLellin, one of the original latter-day apostles called in 1835, became disillusioned and left the Church in 1836. In the summer of 1847, he was traveling west from his home in Kirtland attempting to "prepare the way for the old ship to unhitch her cables and again sail forth" by gathering the Three Witnesses into his faction.[54] McLellin came to Wisconsin specifically to meet with and possibly persuade the unaffiliated former Second Elder to join his movement.[55] Cowdery received him as a "mutual friend and former co-laborer." During a "lengthy conversation,"[56] they discussed their personal views of priesthood authority and the future of the Church restored through the efforts of Joseph Smith and Oliver Cowdery in 1830. Oliver made no commitments to McLellin. He simply discussed his religious opinions with McLellin and then they parted after a two-day visit.

Prompted by McLellin's visit, Oliver penned a confidential dispatch to his brother-in-law David Whitmer. Cowdery candidly expressed to his fellow Book of Mormon witness his opinion that the Church was "lying to" or inactive "either for want of pilots or hands to work her." He tersely dismissed Sidney Rigdon and James Strang as uninspired men who were not called by God to lead the Church after Joseph Smith was "meanly and unlawfully murdered." As for the Twelve's claim to succession, Cowdery was more open-minded. He considered, "[They] have perhaps not as a matter of choice at first, but of necessity taken such as would adhere to them and fled to the western slope of our continent." In this private letter, Oliver expressed his conviction that he still held the priesthood keys and authority conferred on Joseph Smith and him beginning in 1829. He readily admitted that he did not know whether the Lord would again call David and him to "work in his great cause." As before, Oliver's concern for reputation and character resurfaced. He explained that,

> If ever the church rises again in true holiness, it must arise in
> a measure *upon our testimony*, and *upon our characters as good*

men. Such being the case, . . . some ONE should step forward— capable and worthy, who knew us well, and whose heart the Lord should or has touched, whose duty and office should be to vindicate our characters, and disabuse the minds of the honest of those prejudices which they do and would otherwise labor under. All this must be done without solicitation on our part. And it is expedient it should be done by [some]one who has known us from the beginning.[57]

To his trusted relative, Oliver declared his willingness, when circumstances were appropriate, to be involved again in the building up of the Lord's kingdom. In the letter's conclusion, Cowdery summarized his heartfelt feelings about his involvement in the latter-day work, "I will only say that when *the time comes,* I AM READY! But I am not persuaded that it has yet fully come. Let the Lord vindicate our characters, and cause our testimony to shine, and then will men be saved in his kingdom."[58]

Five weeks after parting with Oliver in Wisconsin, McLellin, while visiting John and David Whitmer in Missouri, obtained a copy of Cowdery's personal letter to David Whitmer along with Whitmer's private response.[59] Eight months later, back in Kirtland, McLellin, without permission from either Cowdery or Whitmer, published the letters in the May 1848 issue of his Ensign of Liberty.

In October 1847, Hiram Page, Oliver's wife's brother-in-law and one of the Eight Witnesses to the Book of Mormon, contacted Oliver Cowdery. Page was also estranged from the Church. He advised Oliver not to commit to any Mormon reaffiliation until they (i.e., Page, the Whitmers, and Cowdery) could counsel together. Probably because Oliver could afford neither the time nor the expense in traveling to Missouri for a meeting, he did not respond to Page's invitation. Whatever his reasons for not replying, within six months Oliver wrote to David Whitmer encouraging him to meet at Council Bluffs so they could settle their differences with the Latter-day Saint Church led by Brigham Young.[60]

By late November 1847, just before the reorganization of the First Presidency, Brigham Young, writing collectively for the Twelve, renewed contact with Oliver Cowdery through his brother Phineas. This epistle from the Twelve was actually written in late November but not dispatched until Christmas 1847, shortly after the reorganization of the presidency, and was hand-carried to Oliver by Phineas. In it Oliver was questioned about his declared interest in the "salvation of Israel in these last days," asked about the testimony that he previously bore with "unshaken confidence," and again invited to be rebaptized. The Twelve's invitation was typically straightforward, yet filled with compassion. They wrote:

> [We] say to you in the Spirit of Jesus, . . . come for all things are now ready and the Spirit and the Bride say come, and return to our Father's house, from whence thou hast wandered, and partake of the fatted calf and sup and be filled, and again be adorned with the Jewels of Salvation, and be shod with the preparation of the Gospel of Peace, by putting your hand in Elder [Phineas] Young's and walking straightway into the Waters of Baptism, and receiving the laying on of his hands and the office of an Elder, and go forth with him and proclaim repentance unto this generation and renew thy testimony to the Truth of the Book of Mormon with a loud voice and faithful heart.[61]

Oliver was offered the assurance that the Saints "will with open arms hail thee as their long lost . . . brother found in the new and everlasting covenant."[62]

On 27 February 1848, in a "private and confidential" letter from Elkhorn, Cowdery replied. With increased enthusiasm, he acknowledged:

> By the hand of Brother Phinehas H. Young I received your epistle of Dec[ember] last, and after reading it carefully and conversing freely with Brother Phinehas, have thought that if circumstances would permit, I would visit you in the early part of the Spring, say as soon as the 6th of April, if possible.[63]

To avoid raising false hopes, Oliver warned that his visit in early April could be delayed due to "certain business" he might be obliged to fulfill. At that time, Lyman Cowdery had drafted a legislative bill that, with assistance, would be introduced in the Wisconsin

Territorial council and house of representatives authorizing Oliver to prepare "a complete Index arranged in Alphabetical order of all the session Laws from the year[s] 1839 to 1848 inclusive." Oliver, through this proposed index bill, had the potential to earn up to $650. This was Cowdery's opportunity to raise the money needed to purchase an adequate team and wagon for the trip west. With support, the bill passed the council on the third, but was negated by the House on 7 March 1848.[64]

In his February letter, Oliver told Brigham that he had just written to David Whitmer "advising him, . . . by all means to be at Winter Quarters on the 6th of April." Oliver felt that he and David needed to meet with "many valuable old friends, and time too, of conversing upon interesting subjects." He promised to explain his objective more completely later.

A month later, after the failure of Lyman's proposed index bill, Oliver informed Phineas that he anticipated leaving Elkhorn for Winter Quarters, but was caught, the previous Saturday, in a thundershower that brought on, as he described, "one of the severest attacks of chills and fever—a regular Sandusky attack." He expressed his disappointment in not being physically able to leave as planned but was optimistic that with a few days' rest, he would regain his health and be on his way. Oliver expected, with the cooperation of his "little nag" and good dry roads, to travel fifty miles a day and make the over four-hundred-mile journey in little more than a week.[65] Unfortunately, this was not to be. Oliver Cowdery's sickness continued for two weeks more, and thus he missed the opportunity to be at April conference.

On 7 April 1848, during the afternoon session of the second day of general conference, Elder Phineas Young was invited to report on his recent mission. The conference was held in the log tabernacle at Council Bluffs. Obviously disappointed by Oliver's failure to arrive as expected, Phineas described his journey east, which included a First Presidency-assigned stop in Wisconsin to visit Oliver Cowdery. Elder Young reported that,

This is the first opportunity of seeing so many since last Xmas—I journeyed to the East—and but recently ret[urne]d . . . I went to see the 2nd El[der] in the C[hurch] of J[esus] C[hrist of] L[atter] D[ay] S[aints] O[liver] Cowd[e]ry and once more invite him to return to his Fat[he]rs house—found him in good health and prep[are]d to rece[ive] the word which I [h]ad from the 1st Pres[idenc]y and the 12—it might be impossible for him to get to this conf[erence], but he wo[ul]d be here bef[ore] the 1st Pres[idenc]y go over the mountains—he is willing to do his 1st works over ag[ai]n[.] he wrote to David Whitmer &c[.] I [h]av[e] not learned that they [a]r[e] on the wa[y]—I bel[ieve] they will all be here as soon as cir[cumstanc]es will permit—he [Oliver Cowdery] conversed freely ab[ou]t the coming forth of this work and was conscious that I [h]ad fulfilled my mission.[66]

Wilford Woodruff, present at the afternoon conference session, noted in his journal his observations about what Phineas said regarding his stay with the Book of Mormon witness. Elder Woodruff emphasized that Phineas mentioned Oliver's feelings for the Saints.[67]

Nine days later, on 16 April, Cowdery addressed a long letter to his friend Phineas. He explained his delay, described his prolonged recovery, and observed that making the journey to Council Bluffs—stopping in Richmond, Missouri, to visit the Whitmers and returning to Elkhorn in time for court—would not be possible in so short a time. Oliver wrote optimistically about their future. He said that he had, for quite some time, determined to move to what he called the "new purchase."[68] During Phineas's visit the previous February, they talked about establishing a fruit tree nursery enterprise in the Salt Lake Valley. In mid-April, Cowdery shared with his brother-in-law his feelings about the proposal. He wrote: "The more I have reflected on it, the more anxious have I been to engage in the business." Oliver recommended they gather a large inventory of seeds, even offering to obtain them in Ohio and bring them with him in the fall.

Cowdery, the forty-two-year-old lawyer, in his personal letter to Phineas declared that he was now planning to make the western migration to the Great Basin in the fall with Bishop Reuben Miller. Sometime that previous winter, Bishop Miller, a reclaimed Church leader from Strang's movement and Cowdery's Wisconsin neighbor, generously offered to outfit a team for the Second Elder and his family to use to go west. Oliver noted that Miller stood ready to grant him any assistance needed for the move.[69]

In this letter, Cowdery anxiously asked for information about the recent Church conference. His most pressing question dealt with whether David Whitmer had responded to his request to be at the conference. He asked,

> Was David there? Were any steps taken towards effecting the reconciliation and union of which we talked, and which is so much to be desired? Tell me plainly on all these. Had I been permitted to have been there, these matters would have engaged my earnest labors. . . . From henceforward, I shall double my efforts in effecting an harmonious, righteous reconciliation—I know what is right, and hope I may soon see that right take place.

Over and over again in his correspondence with Church leaders, Oliver asked whether he should first visit the Church's temporary headquarters at Kanesville in preparation for the move west. As Oliver sought counsel on these decisions and other topics related to his reuniting with the Church, he willingly deferred to either Phineas or Brigham for advice.

During the spring of 1848, Oliver Cowdery had another distraction, unrelated to his declining health, to deal with. He was nominated as the Elkhorn district's Democratic candidate for state assembly of the newly admitted state of Wisconsin. Whether Cowdery sought this position or was simply nominated by supporters, or whether he believed he could win the election is not known. However, the Democrats in Walworth County had gotten to know Cowdery pretty well in the year he lived there. They had unshaken confidence in his political abilities. Several articles supporting his candidacy appeared in Wisconsin newspapers.[70] The Whig opposition, fearing Oliver's growing support, took advantage of Cowdery's most obvious political vulnerability by drawing attention to Oliver's earlier Mormon connection. Especially damning in the opposition's mind was the fact that he was one of the Three Witnesses to the Book of Mormon.[71] Oliver quietly withstood the criticism, campaigned confidently, and lost the election by only forty votes—less than one-tenth of the vote. Immediately after Cowdery's narrow loss, his friend and Democratic ally Horace A. Tenney, editor of the state's major political newspaper, observed: "We regret to learn from the Walworth County Democrat that OLIVER COWDERY Esq. was defeated for the Assembly in the Elkhorn district, by a small majority. He is a man of sterling integrity, sound and vigorous intellect, and every way worthy, honest and capable. He was defeated in consequence of his *religion!*"[72] We can only speculate what Cowdery's future might have been had he been elected to the state assembly. The responsibility and influence of public office may have distracted Oliver from the anticipated move west. Once again, this time in a narrow political defeat, Oliver may have sensed that any future professional success or personal happiness was invariably connected to his association with the Mormon Church.

Near the end of May, Reuben Miller wrote from the upper crossing of the Missouri River, twelve miles northwest of Kanesville, believing that Oliver, whom he had not seen since last winter, was visiting friends and family in Richmond, Missouri, and expected to arrive within days. Miller also assumed that Phineas Young had gone to Missouri to accompany Cowdery to Pottawattamie County.[73] Miller's expectation of Cowdery's departure from Wisconsin and anticipated arrival in western Iowa was premature. Sometime that summer, Miller himself traveled back to Wisconsin. Oliver, on the other hand, remained in Elkhorn throughout the summer of 1848, where he renewed his law practice and became associate editor of the *Walworth Democrat.*

In mid-September 1848, Reuben Miller, journeying south toward the gathered Saints at the Bluffs, visited several of his bygone acquaintances in LaSalle County, Illinois. While there he met Phineas Young, who was traveling north to Elkhorn to retrieve Oliver Cowdery. They spent 18 September together, during which

Miller gave Young more than eighty dollars. Fulfilling his promise made the previous winter, Reuben Miller freely gave to help his friend Oliver move with the Saints and migrate west. Miller noted in his journal that thirty-one dollars was appropriated for Oliver Cowdery.[74]

Phineas Young arrived in Elkhorn by late September or early October. On Monday, 2 October, he witnessed the sale by Oliver and his wife, Elizabeth, of eight lots and an additional acre of land to Jonathan Delap for three hundred dollars.[75] In early October, Strang's nearby *Gospel Herald* commented on Cowdery's recent political and religious activities and, in the process, noticed Phineas Young's presence and his mission. The editorial recognized, "On the whole, Oliver seems to be in good demand and first rate standing. Even Phineas Young is here, telling that brother Cowdery is going with him to Council Bluffs."[76] Within days of the real estate sale, Oliver, Elizabeth, and Maria, their only surviving child, accompanied by Phineas, departed Walworth County for the last time.

They made a hurried trip from southern Wisconsin to the Saints' camp in Pottawattamie County, Iowa. Phineas and the Cowderys arrived Saturday afternoon, 21 October, during a special local conference. They entered the open-air meeting, convened in a grove close to Mosquito Creek in the vicinity of Council Bluffs, while Elder Orson Hyde, the presiding official at Kanesville, was speaking. In addition to Hyde, apostles George A. Smith and Ezra Taft Benson were in attendance. Elder Hyde immediately recognized the presence of the former Associate President. Reportedly, Hyde stopped speaking, came down off the stand and embraced Cowdery. Taking him by the arm, Orson brought Oliver up on the platform. After a brief introduction by Elder Hyde, Oliver was invited to speak to the conference. Cowdery stood for a few moments looking out into the numerous faces in the audience. Oliver recognized some, but most were strangers to him. Finally, after more than a decade's lonely separation from the people he loved, the Second Elder was reunited with the Saints of God.

With overwhelming emotion swelling in his heart, yet in a clear and striking voice, Oliver Cowdery addressed this gathering of nearly two thousand people—the largest Mormon audience he ever spoke to. He bore a spontaneous yet lucid testimony of his personal involvement in the early years of the Mormon Church. Cowdery detailed the coming forth of the Book of Mormon and the restoration of the Aaronic and Melchizedek Priesthoods. He reaffirmed his staunch belief in the Prophet Joseph Smith's divine appointment and mission. Oliver recalled that years earlier he had laid hands on Elder Hyde's head and ordained him to the priesthood and extended to him his call as an apostle. Cowdery unequivocally acknowledged the Twelve's authority to lead the Church. He also commented on the nautical imagery used earlier by Elder Hyde in his conference discourse. Oliver said: "Bro. Hyde has just said that it was all important that we keep in the true channel in order to avoid the sandbars. This is true. The channel is here. The priesthood is here."[77] Another report adds that Cowdery expressed his conviction "that the Priesthood was with this people, and the 'Twelve' were the only men that could lead the Church after the death of Joseph."[78] Given his years both in and out of the Church, Oliver knew firsthand about spiritual "sandbars" and priesthood authority.

The audience's reaction to Cowdery's spontaneous discourse was unanimously positive. George A. Smith noted in a letter to Orson Pratt, "His testimony produced quite a sensation among the gentlemen present, who did not belong to the church, and it was gratefully received by all the Saints."[79] Nevertheless, no immediate action was taken nor motion made during the conference to readmit Oliver Cowdery.

Nine days later, on Monday, 30 October, Oliver spent the evening talking with Elders Orson Hyde and George A. Smith. He wanted to know their feelings toward him. It is supposed that Oliver was willing to respond to any questions or concerns they had about him. Cowdery expressed his willingness to receive counsel from them. They advised him to remain in Kanesville that winter, help Elder Hyde set up the *Frontier Guardian* press, and then migrate west the next spring. During the meeting, Cowdery confided with his two old friends that he had not come to Kanesville for a leadership position. His only desire in returning was to have his membership reinstated and to be one among and live with the Saints. Oliver said, "If Mormonism goes up, I want my name to go up with it, and if it goes down, my name goes down with it."[80] Oliver Cowdery recognized the necessity of being rebaptized and affirmed that he "did not expect to return without it."[81] He knew that baptism was the door back into the Church.

Since Oliver had been gone during a decade of spirited doctrinal development, Elders Hyde and Smith evidently took the time during this evening discussion to bring Cowdery up-to-date. We know little about that aspect of their conversation, but it might have included discussion of such temple-related principles as baptism for the dead and the Nauvoo-era endowment. Given Oliver's previously expressed concern with the Saints' active participation in plural marriage, that topic was discussed and resolved in Cowdery's mind.[82] Before concluding, Elders Hyde and Smith requested that Oliver attend a combined meeting of high priests and the high council the first Sunday in November to review his situation formally and accept him back into the Church.

The Pottawattamie High Council met Saturday, 4 November, at Hiram Clark's home in a preliminary session. Oliver was not invited to this meeting. Orson Hyde raised the issue of Cowdery's readmittance. Several council members commented on the proposal. Elder Hyde mentioned a rumor that Phineas Young had "secretly" rebaptized the Second Elder while visiting in Wisconsin. This discussion was inappropriate since President Brigham Young, in the Twelve's December 1847 epistle, invited Cowdery to be rebaptized by Phineas. Regardless, no evidence exists that Phineas "secretly" or otherwise performed the baptism ordinance before Cowdery's formal return in October-November 1848. George A. Smith offered his personal views on Oliver's readmission and gave an account of his and Elder Hyde's private interview with Oliver Cowdery the previous Monday. Elder Smith also reviewed Oliver's deep involvement in the first decade of the Church and his subsequent apostasy. The high council adjourned, agreeing to meet with the high priests quorum the next day in an unusual joint session.

On Sunday, 5 November 1848, Oliver Cowdery joined with the high priests and Pottawattamie High Council[83] in the Kanesville Log Tabernacle.[84] After some unrelated initial discussion, Orson Hyde addressed the group, noting that Cowdery was present and "wished to come back into the church" and "be identified with us." Hyde requested that Oliver speak to the assembled council. Cowdery responded that he "did not come to speak, but to be a looker on, and to hear. . . . He wishe[d] to come into the Church in an humble manner, an humble follower of Jesus Christ, not seeking any presidency."[85] Although reluctant at first to speak, Cowdery did take the opportunity to express his personal feelings about his prolonged absence from the Church, gave his reasons for leaving, and concluded by acknowledging that those who were the cause of his estrangement had died or left the Church. He said:

> I feel that I can honorably return. I have sustained an honorable character before the world during my absence from you, this tho[ugh] a small matter with you, it is of vast importance. I have ever had the honor of the Kingdom in view, and men are to be judged by the testimony given. I feel to sanction what has been said here today. I am out of the church.
>
> I know the door into the church, and I wish to become a member thro[ugh] the door. I wish to be a humble private member. I did not come here to seek honor.[86]

After Cowdery spoke, George W. Harris motioned that Oliver Cowdery be allowed to be rebaptized. Evan M. Greene seconded the proposal. At this point, an intense discussion erupted. William Snow, president of the high priests, questioned Oliver about his (Cowdery's) July 1847 letter to David Whitmer, published the previous May in McLellin's renegade *Ensign of Liberty*. Harris objected, saying that since Cowdery was asking to come back as a "humble member, no action should be now taken upon that letter." George A. Smith agreed, adding, "I am not afraid of [Oliver] overturning the

Church." Phineas Young, along with several others, spoke in support of Cowdery's readmission without further discussion of the offending letter.[87]

President Snow's concerns centered on Cowdery's bold statements to Whitmer regarding priesthood authority, keys, and succession leadership, such as, "True it is that our right gives us the head" and "We have the authority and do hold the keys." Cowdery explained that the letter was a "private" letter, not for public exhibition and published by McLellin without either his or David's knowledge or consent.[88] Cowdery elaborated that he had, since writing the letter, changed his views on the subject. To this, President Snow asked what had changed his opinion. Oliver responded, "When I wrote that letter I did not know of the Revelation [D&C 124:95] which says, that the keys and power conferred upon me, were taken from me and placed upon the head of Hyrum Smith. And it was that revelation which changed my views on this subject."[89] Evidently during their private discussions with Oliver in late October 1848, Orson Hyde and George A. Smith made him aware of the January 1841 revelation.[90] In closing, Cowdery elaborated:

> I have not come to seek place, nor to interfere with the business and calling of those men who have borne the burden since the death of Joseph. I throw myself at your feet, and wish to be one of your number, and be a mere member of the Church, and my mere asking to be baptized is an end to all pretensions to authority.[91]

Oliver then assured the council: "My coming back and humbly asking to become a member through the door covers the whole ground. I *acknowledge this authority*."[92] Elder Orson Hyde expressed his satisfaction with Cowdery's explanation and called for a vote to the effect that "all past transactions be forgotten and that O. Cowdery be received into this Church by Baptism."[93] A full vote was given and the proposal carried unanimously. Finally, six years after first showing a desire to return, Cowdery was only days away from being rebaptized.

Although trustworthy sources verify 12 November 1848 as Oliver Cowdery's rebaptism date, at least one official Church record implies that he was rebaptized on 5 November. The high council minutes, written within days or weeks of the event, read:

> After some more remarks from different ones of the Brethren, the question was called up and Bro. O. Cowdery was received back again into the church, on his being baptized, by a full vote, and many expressed their gratified feelings on the occasion. About 2 o'clock p.m., he was Baptized by the hand of Bro. Orson Hyde.[94]

Other contemporary sources support Sunday, 12 November 1848, as the actual readmittance date. For unknown reasons, Cowdery was rebaptized a week after his meeting with the combined high council and high priests in the Kanesville Log Tabernacle. Orson Hyde wrote to his fellow apostle Wilford Woodruff on 11 November 1848, explaining that "Bro. Oliver Cowdery has . . . made Satisfaction to the church and has been voted to be rec[eive]d by baptism. I expect to baptize him tomorrow."[95] Cowdery's temporal benefactor, Reuben Miller, writing to a friend, confirmed the later date. Four days after the rebaptism, Miller acknowledged, "Brother Oliver Cowdery is here and has been baptized by Elder Hyde on last Sunday."[96]

His personal restoration to full membership marked a beginning for Oliver. He remained in the Kanesville area for the next two and a half months, during which time Cowdery and his family stayed principally with Phineas Young. Oliver immediately went to work helping Orson Hyde set up the printing press that would eventually publish the *Frontier Guardian*.[97]

By early January 1849, Oliver had decided to take his small family and visit his in-laws, the Whitmers, in Missouri before setting out with the western migration in the spring. Heading southeast to Richmond, they encountered a ruthless snowstorm in northwestern Missouri. Desperately seeking a haven from the blizzard, the Cowderys called at the cabin of Samuel W. Richards, a Latter-day Saint. The Cowdery and Richards families spent two weeks riding out the storm. As Samuel Richards later described his time with Cowdery, "This was not lost time to either of us." Being limited by the inclement weather, they had little to do, so they talked about the Church. Elder Richards asked Oliver about his initial experiences with the Prophet Joseph Smith. Cowdery obliged, describing in vivid detail the working method of the Book of Mormon translation. Richards was definitely impressed; he summarized his feelings about meeting the Second Elder: "This interview with Brother and Sister Cowdery was one of entire freedom and familiarity, although we had never met before; and his experience in connection with the prophet Joseph, when the ministrations of Angels were frequent in restoring Priesthood, and the Keys of Knowledge . . . made it all a most divinely and sacred interview to me."[98]

Before leaving in mid-January, Oliver agreed to return to Council Bluffs in the spring prepared for the early migration to the Great Basin.[99] By late April 1849, while comfortably situated with the Whitmers in Richmond, Cowdery's plans were becoming more tentative. He wrote Phineas Young and explained that he felt it a "bad policy" to compete with the California gold rush teams who were thronging the trail. Cowdery confided, "The idea of being crowded in and mixed up with companies—thousands of gold hunters, would impel me to wait another year, as a preference, if I could not safely go this fall."[100] In June, Cowdery contacted Phineas again, updating him on his intentions: "I have obliged to abandon the idea of going to the Mountains this season." Oliver's concerns were not a wavering of his renewed Mormon affiliation; he wholeheartedly wanted to be with the Church. His anxieties were fueled by persisting financial concerns and worry for his and his family's survival out on the western trail and in the Great Basin.[101] Later, in the early fall of 1849, in his last known letter to his beloved friend Phineas Young, Cowdery reflected: "I am poor, very poor, and I did hope to have health and means sufficient last spring to go west and get some gold, that I might so situate my family, that I could be engaged in the cause of God; but I did not succeed. I was then in hope you could go . . . if I could not. Now, as neither of us went, let us not be discouraged, but press on, trusting in the Lord."[102]

In July 1849, the First Presidency wrote directly to Oliver Cowdery, acknowledging his return[103] and exhorting him to magnify his office by "learning [his] duty towards God and man, and practicing according to that knowledge," also requesting his cooperation with Almon W. Babbitt, Orson Hyde, and John Bernhisel to petition for Deseret to be admitted as a state.[104] They called on Cowdery to accompany Babbitt, their congressional delegate, to Washington and help publicize their statehood aspirations and draft a memorial seeking the admission of Deseret as a free state. It is not known for sure if Cowdery received the First Presidency's request.[105] If he did, Oliver would not have had the physical strength to travel since he was seriously weakened by recurring health problems. Around the first of August, Cowdery suffered an attack of bilious fever and the chills. The fever, which Cowdery described as the "most severe of any in my life," stirred his persistent lung problem.[106] From this time, in late summer 1849, until his death a little more than six months later, his health deteriorated steadily.[107] He would not live to go west, get some gold, start a fruit tree business, or serve the Church as he so nobly wanted.

In spite of a diseased body, Cowdery's mind and spirit were vigorous and alert to the end. A few months before his death, Oliver received a visit from Jacob Gates, an old Mormon acquaintance from before his excommunication in 1838. Gates, heading east on a mission to England, heard that his former priesthood leader was in poor health and stopped in Richmond to renew their friendship.[108] After conversing about troubled times in early Church history, Gates asked Cowdery about his testimony printed in the Book of Mormon. He wanted to know if the testimony was based on a dream, the imagination of his mind, an illusion, or a myth. Jacob wanted the truth. As the account goes, Oliver Cowdery got up from his resting place, retrieved a first edition Book of Mormon, and read solemnly the testimony. Turning to face Gates, he said,

Jacob, I want you to remember what I say to you. I am
man, and what would it profit me to tell you a lie? I know .
this Book of Mormon was translated by the gift and power oi
My eyes saw, my ears heard, and my understanding was touc ⌐ᴜ,
and I know that whereof I testified is true. It was no dream, no
vain imagination of the mind—it was real.[109]

On 3 March 1850, the day Oliver Cowdery died at the Peter
Whitmer Sr. home, he was surrounded by his wife; their only
daughter, Maria; his brother-in-law, David Whitmer; Hiram Page,
his nurse; others of the Whitmer family; his half-sister, Lucy; and
her husband, Phineas Young. Oliver asked to be raised so he could
speak. As he had done hundreds of times before, he bore a resolute
testimony of the Book of Mormon. Phineas reported that Oliver, on
his deathbed, confided in him, "The[re] was no Salvation but in the
valley and through the priesthood there."[110] Thus ended the mortal
life of the Second Elder of Mormonism.

To modern generations, Oliver's legacy lives on because of his
strong character and integrity as a latter-day witness of that ancient
American scripture he assisted in bringing forth. Fellow Book of
Mormon witness David Whitmer related that after Cowdery said
his good-byes and bore his closing testimony, he "died the happi-
est man I ever saw. . . . [Oliver] said, 'Now I lay me down for the last
time, I am going to my Savior,' and died immediately with a smile
on his face."[111]

Notes

Editors' note: This article was originally published in *The Disciple as Witness*, by
Ricks, Parry, and Hedges.

1.   I have taken the position that Cowdery was rebaptized in Mosquito Creek (instead of Indian Creek or the Missouri River) based on the following data: (1) Cowdery's
brother-in-law Phineas Young lived in Cartersville, a settlement on the east side of Mosquito Creek; (2) Oliver Cowdery stayed with Phineas Young during all or most of his
two-and-a-half month sojourn in western Iowa; (3) Cowdery's rebaptism took place a
week after the combined Pottawattamie High Council-high priests meeting on 5 November 1848 that was held in the Kanesville Log Tabernacle; and (4) eleven-year-old
Seymour B. Young, Phineas Young's nephew, was also baptized near Cartersville in late
1848. He related, "Just near by the bank of the creek where the baptism occurred lived

my uncle, Phineas H. Young. I returned to his home after baptism, and there I met with
a man somewhat famous in the history of the Church, namely Oliver Cowdery" Conference Reports, April 1921, 114–15.

2.   Although no contemporary documentation exists for Cowdery's reordination,
the action would be logical since Cowdery had been excommunicated. Several early
sources mention Oliver's reordination. See Brigham Young's remarks in the Sunday
morning session of the October 1870 semi-annual general conference where he remarked, "Oliver Cowdery . . . returned, was baptised and *ordained again* went to visit
his friends in Missouri, and died" (*Ogden Junction*, 12 October 1870, emphasis added).
See also statement by W. W. Blair in "'Mormonism' Reviewed," *Saints' Herald* 23, no. 3
(1 February 1876): 74–75. Blair, a member of the RLDS first presidency, wrote, "We have
been informed by credible witnesses that in [1848], he [Oliver Cowdery] attended a conference at Carterville, a hamlet near Council Bluffs, Iowa, and was there re-baptized,
and *re-ordained to the office of an elder.*"

3.   President Cowdery had been at odds with Joseph Smith and other Church leaders for months preceding his high council trial. Cowdery's difficulties, although not
enumerated at the time, centered principally on personal problems between Joseph and
himself and on "administrative" or "procedural" differences. These difficulties received
notice as far back as September 1837 when Joseph Smith wrote a letter to the Church
leaders in Missouri, which he dispatched by the hand of Thomas B. Marsh. Part of the
Prophet's epistle reads, "Oliver Cowdery has been in transgression, but as he is now
chosen as one of the Presidents or Councilors I trust that he will yet humble himself and
magnify his calling, but if he should not, the Church will soon be under the necessity
of raising their hands against him. Therefore pray for him." See Joseph Smith to John
Corrill and the Church in Zion, 4 September 1837, retained copy in "Scriptory Book of
Joseph Smith Jr." (kept by George W. Robinson), 22, Family and Church History Department Archives, The Church of Jesus Christ of Latter-day Saints (hereafter cited as
Church Archives); published in Scott Faulring, ed., *An American Prophet's Record: The
Diaries and Journals of Joseph Smith* (Salt Lake City: Signature Books, 1989), 165, or
Dean C. Jessee, ed., *The Papers of Joseph Smith*, 2 vols. (Salt Lake City: Deseret Book,
1989–92), 2:219–20. Spelling and punctuation have been modernized in all primary
source quotations used.

4.   Oliver Cowdery to Bishop Edward Partridge, 12 April 1838, included in the
Far West Record, 119–22, Church Archives, emphasis added. The official source of
Cowdery's trial minutes is Far West Record, 118–26; published in Donald Q. Cannon
and Lyndon W. Cook, eds., *Far West Record: Minutes of the Church of Jesus Christ of Latter-day Saints, 1830–1844* (Salt Lake City: Deseret Book, 1983), 162–71. A contemporary
abstract is found in "Scriptory Book of Joseph Smith Jr.," 29–31, Church Archives; published in Faulring, *An American Prophet's Record*, 172–74, and Jessee, *Papers of Joseph
Smith*, 2:228–30.

5.   The six charges sustained against Oliver Cowdery (quoted here with minor mod-
ernization) were (1) For stirring up the enemy to persecute the brethren by urging on
vexatious lawsuits and thus distressing the innocent; (2) For seeking to destroy the character of President Joseph Smith Jr. by falsely insinuating that he was guilty of adultery;
(3) For treating the Church with contempt by not attending meetings; (4) For leaving the
calling, in which God had appointed him, by Revelation, for the sake of filthy lucre, and

turning to the practice of the Law; (5) For disgracing the Church by being connected in the 'Bogus' business as common report says; and (6) For dishonestly retaining notes after they had been paid. It should be pointed out that the Far West Record reports that the fifth charge listed here was only sustained on circumstantial grounds. Seymour Brunson preferred the nine charges against Oliver on 7 April 1838. For the entire list of nine charges, see Far West Record, 118–19.

6.   "History of Tho[ma]s Baldwin Marsh," *Deseret News*, 24 March 1858, 18.

7.   Laura Pitkin to Heber C. Kimball, 18 July 1840, postscript, original in uncataloged letters collection, Daughters of Utah Pioneers Society Archives, Salt Lake City. The entire letter was published in Kate B. Carter, comp., *Heart Throbs of the West* (Salt Lake City: Daughters of Utah Pioneers, 1944), 5:380–82. At the time this letter was written, Elder Kimball was serving with his fellow apostles on a mission in Great Britain. Laura Pitkin later became a plural wife to Heber C. Kimball.

8.   According to William Lang, Oliver first visited Tiffin in the spring of 1840 where, on 12 May, he spoke to a large gathering of local Democratic supporters. Cowdery was, during that time, scouting out a location to practice law. Lang mentions that Oliver moved to Tiffin in the (late) fall of 1840. See William Lang, *History of Seneca County* (Springfield, OH: Transcript Printing, 1880), 364–65, 387.

9.   Phineas served in this position until June 1843, when he was recalled to Nauvoo. Shortly after returning to Illinois, he was sent back east on another mission. See untitled Phineas H. Young manuscript autobiography, Church Archives. A typescript entitled "Life of Phineas Howe Young. Written by Phineas Howe Young," Church Archives is cited herein because it is more intelligible than the manuscript.

10.   Phineas Young, with postscript by Oliver, to Willard Richards and Brigham Young, 14 December 1842, Tiffin, Ohio, Church Archives.

11.   Snyder (also spelled Snider) was sent by revelation to England to raise money for the building of the Nauvoo House and Nauvoo Temple (see D&C 124:22, 62, 70, and uncanonized 22 December 1841 revelation, published in *History of the Church*, 4:483). He departed Nauvoo for England on 26 March 1842 (Jessee, *Papers of Joseph Smith*, 2:343–45, 356, 362, 373). On the return voyage from Liverpool, Elder Snyder had charge of a company of 157 emigrating Saints on board the ship *Henry*. The voyage lasted six weeks, and during the last four weeks, the ship was frequently stalled by lack of winds. Elder Snyder and the ship's commanding officer, Captain Benjamin Pierce, had several disagreements during the voyage. The *Henry* arrived in New Orleans by mid-November 1842, where Snyder was arrested. See Conway B. Sonne, *Ships, Saints, and Mariners: A Maritime Encyclopedia of Mormon Migration 1830–1890* (Salt Lake City: University of Utah Press, 1987), 95–96, and Andrew Jenson, *Latter-day Saint Biographical Encyclopedia: A Compilation of Biographical Sketches of Prominent Men and Women in the Church of Jesus Christ of Latter-day Saints* (Salt Lake City: Andrew Jenson History Company and Deseret News, 1901–36), 3:221.

12.   An entry in Joseph Smith's journal for 23 January 1843 noted the arrival of Snyder in Nauvoo: "Bro. John Snider come home from England, where he had been sent by the Twelve according to Revelation to procure help for the Temple." See "President Joseph Smith's Journal [1842–]1843 as kept by Willard Richards," Church Archives; published in Faulring, *American Prophet's Record*, 295, and edited slightly in *History of the Church*, 5:260.

13. Phelps, along with Cowdery, David and John Whitmer, Luke E. Johnson, and others, became disaffected during the internal Mormon difficulties at Far West in 1838. In June 1840, W. W. Phelps humbly asked for and subsequently received forgiveness from Joseph Smith for betraying the Mormon leader by testifying against him at Judge Austin A. King's hearing at Richmond, Missouri, in November 1838. See Phelps's testimony in *Document Containing the Correspondence, Orders, &c. in Relation to the Disturbances with the Mormons* (Fayette, MO: Boon's Lick Democrat, 1841), 120–25. See copy of Phelps's appeal in Joseph Smith Letter Book, 2:155–56, Church Archives; published in *History of the Church*, 4:141–42. Joseph Smith's compassionate reply, dated 22 July 1840, is in *Joseph Smith Letter Book*, 2:157–58; and is published in Dean C. Jessee, ed. and comp., *The Personal Writings of Joseph Smith* (1984; reprint, Salt Lake City: Deseret Book, and Provo, Utah: Brigham Young University Press, 2002), 508–10.

14. Oliver Cowdery to Phineas Young, 19 August 1843, Church Archives. Phelps's letter to Cowdery has not been located. Near the time he wrote to Oliver, Phelps sent a letter to another disenfranchised elder, Warren Parrish. After encouraging Parrish to come and fellowship with the Saints in Nauvoo, Phelps noted the number of non-Mormon lawyers in the city and hinted that Parrish could come to Nauvoo as a "Mormon" attorney. Perhaps Phelps, in his letter to Cowdery, made the same proposal to Oliver but obscured the meaning or was misunderstood. Phelps mentioned to Parrish that "I want this letter to be an epistle general: as well to Zerrubbabel Snow, Esq. as you and Oliver Cowdery, Esq., if you will give him a hint of it by writing." See transcription of Phelps to Parrish in Walter D. Bowen, "The Versatile W. W. Phelps—Mormon Writer, Educator, and Pioneer" (master's thesis, Brigham Young University, 1958), 111.

15. Oliver Cowdery to Phineas Young, 26 August 1843, Church Archives.

16. Cowdery to Young, 19 August 1843, Church Archives.

17. Joseph Smith's 1843 journal, 19 April 1843; published in Faulring, *American Prophet's Record*, 372. An expanded form of this statement, based on Willard Richards's Quorum of Twelve minutes, was published in *History of the Church*, 5:368, and includes the phrase "be clothed with robes of righteousness" inserted between "If he is not almost ready to return" and "and go up to Jerusalem."

18. Brigham Young and Twelve to Oliver Cowdery, 19 April 1843, Nauvoo, Illinois; retained copy, Church Archives, emphasis in original.

19. Oliver Cowdery to Phineas Young, 26 August 1843.

20. Oliver Cowdery to "Dear Brethren" (i.e., Brigham Young and the Twelve), 25 December 1843, Church Archives, emphasis in original.

21. Ibid.

22. Ibid., emphasis in original.

23. "Them" referred to the addressees of his response, namely Elders Brigham Young, Heber C. Kimball, Parley P. Pratt, William Smith, Orson Pratt, Willard Richards, Wilford Woodruff, John Taylor, and George A. Smith. During his troubles in Far West, 1837–38, Oliver Cowdery was not oppressed or persecuted by any of these men.

24. Actually a public or warning-out letter (ca. 18 June 1838) addressed to the leading dissenters (i.e., Oliver Cowdery, John and David Whitmer, W. W. Phelps, and Lyman E. Johnson). This document warned Cowdery and others to depart Far West with their families within seventy-two hours or "a more fatal calamity shall befall you." A copy of the letter was published as evidence in *Document Containing the Correspondence*,

Orders, &c., 103–6. Sidney Rigdon is suspected as the letter's author. For balanced context to this incident, see Alexander L. Baugh, "Chapter 4: Dissenters, Danites, and the Resurgence of Militant Mormonism," in "A Call to Arms: The 1838 Mormon Defense of Northern Missouri" (Ph.D. diss., Brigham Young University, 1996), 68–101.

25. Willard Richards, "Journal and Memorandum," 27 June 1844, Church Archives; source of comment published in *History of the Church*, 6:613.

26. Church historian Joseph Fielding Smith surmised that the Cowdery letter read at Carthage Jail was written in response to the Twelve's earlier invitation to return. This opinion is entirely speculative since, as President Smith admits, "The contents of that letter I have always regretted I did not know; in the perilous times it was lost and no record was made of it." Joseph Fielding Smith, *Doctrines of Salvation* (Salt Lake City: Bookcraft, 1954), 1:227.

27. William Lang to Thomas Gregg, 5 November 1881, published in Charles A. Shook, *The True Origin of the Book of Mormon* (Cincinnati: Standard, 1914), 56.

28. Phineas Young to Brigham Young, 26 November 1844, postscript, Church Archives.

29. Ibid.

30. Ibid. Rigdon's infamous "Salt Sermon," delivered 17 June 1838, contained veiled threats against Cowdery and the other dissenters, and the subsequent ca. 18 June 1838 letter, addressed to Cowdery, David and John Whitmer, W. W. Phelps, and Lyman E. Johnson, was an explicit warning to them as protagonists to leave Far West or face dire consequences. This letter was signed by George W. Robinson and eighty-two other Mormons. George Robinson is credited with delivering the public warning-out in late June 1838. Robinson's entry in the 1838 Scriptory Book (page 47) reveals his true feelings toward the dissenters:

> I would mention or notice something about O. Cowdery, David Whitmer, Lyman E. Johnson, and John Whitmer who being guilty of base iniquities and that too, manifest in the ages of all men, and being often entreated would continue in their course seeking the lives of the First Presidency and to overthrow the Kingdom of God which they once testified of. Pres[iden]t Rigdon preached one Sabbath upon the salt that had lost its savour that it is henceforth good for nothing but to be cast out and trodden under foot of men, and the wicked flee when no man pursueth. These men took warning and soon they were seen bounding over the prairie like the scapegoat to carry off their own sins. We have not seen them since. Their influence is gone and they are in a miserable condition. (Faulring, *American Prophet's Record*, 187, and Jessee, *Papers of Joseph Smith*, 2:249)

31. Phineas H. Young to Brigham Young, 26 November 1844.

32. Oliver Cowdery to Brigham Young, 7 October 1845, Church Archives.

33. W. W. Phelps to Oliver Cowdery, 1 December 1845, quoted in Cowdery to Phineas Young, 18 December 1845.

34. On this dramatic change of position toward government help, see Richard E. Bennett, *Mormons at the Missouri, 1846–1852: "And Should We Die . . ."* (Norman: University of Oklahoma Press, 1987), 21–22.

35. W. W. Phelps to Oliver Cowdery, 1 December 1845, quoted in Cowdery to Phineas Young, 18 December 1845, emphasis in original. Phelps and Cowdery coedited the *Evening and Morning Star* at Independence, Missouri, from 1832–1833.

36. Cowdery to Phineas Young, 18 December 1845.

37. Oliver Cowdery to Phineas Young, 23 March 1846, Church Archives.

38. Orson Hyde to Brigham Young, 10 March 1846, Church Archives.

39. Cowdery to Phineas Young, 23 March 1846, emphasis in original.

40. Ibid.

41. Ibid.; bracketed words represent material missing from holes in the manuscript.

42. Oliver Cowdery to Daniel and Phebe Jackson, 24 July 1846, original letter unlocated; photographs of original letter, RLDS Archives and Richard Lloyd Anderson research files.

43. In spite of some minor differences in details, the essence of these reports is that Oliver Cowdery learned about plural marriage while serving as the Prophet Joseph Smith's assistant and that he (Cowdery) practiced it without the Prophet's consent during the 1830s. A sample of statements by early Church leaders regarding Oliver Cowdery and plural marriage include: Brigham Young, 26 August 1857, Church Archives, quoted in *Wilford Woodruff's Journal, 1833–1898*, ed. Scott G. Kenney (Midvale, UT: Signature Books, 1983–85), 5:84; Brigham Young in Manuscript History of Brigham Young, 1857, 439 (based on Woodruff's journal entry with added detail), Church Archives; Heber C. Kimball (comment made 24 May 1868) in "Record of the Provo Stake of Zion," Church Archives; Brigham Young in Joseph F. Smith diary, 9 October 1869, Church Archives; Brigham Young in Charles Walker diary, 26 July 1872, Church Archives; Joseph F. Smith, 7 July 1878, in *Journal of Discourses*, 20:29; George Q. Cannon in *Juvenile Instructor* 16 (15 September 1881): 206; and Joseph F. Smith (comment made 4 March 1883) in "Provo Utah Central Stake, Historical Records and Minutes, 1877–1888," Church Archives. This episode of Cowdery's life has been examined recently by several scholars. Not all agree whether Oliver practiced an early form of plural marriage. For instance, Richard S. Van Wagoner, in *Mormon Polygamy: A History*, 2nd ed. (Salt Lake City: Signature Books, 1989), 11, reported that Oliver Cowdery "never became reconciled to Mormon polygamy." I disagree with Van Wagoner's interpretation. I believe that evidence suggests Cowdery believed in and practiced this Kirtland-form of plural marriage (1833–34), got in trouble for it (1834), and for many years (1835–48) was opposed to the practice. This opposition mellowed when he returned to the Church in 1848. Nine days after arriving at Kanesville in October 1848, Oliver had a "lengthy and agreeable interview" with the presiding officials at Council Bluffs—Elders Orson Hyde and George A. Smith. During their evening discussion, Cowdery affirmed that he had come to "listen to [their] counsel and would do as [they] told him." He recognized the need to be rebaptized and bore sincere testimony that Joseph Smith had "fulfilled his mission faithfully before God until death." Oliver assured Elders Hyde and Smith that he sought no position or office in the Church; he only wanted to be "one among us, and live with the Saints." At this point in 1848, it is reasonable to assume that Oliver Cowdery was, if he had not already been, made aware that plural marriage was commonly practiced within Mormon society. Unfortunately we do not know Oliver's reaction, but until his death in 1850, Cowdery was making serious plans to move to Utah. If his deteriorating health had not prevented him, he would have come to Utah and served the Church in whatever capacity they wanted him to serve. It is logical that if Cowdery was as morally offended by the Saints' plural marriage relationship as Van Wagoner and others have suggested, he would not have wanted to immigrate to Utah and live as "one"

among them. During his "interview" with Elders Hyde and Smith, Oliver said that he "was determined to rise with the Church, and if it went down he was willing to go down with it." See George A. Smith to Orson Pratt, 31 October postscript to 20 October 1848 letter, in *Millennial Star* 11 (1 January 1849): 14; and Orson Hyde, George A. Smith, and Ezra Taft Benson, "A Report to Presidents Brigham Young, Heber C. Kimball, Willard Richards and the Authorities of the Church of Jesus Christ of Latter Day Saints," 5 April 1849, 4–5, Robert Campbell, clerk, Kanesville, Iowa, Church Archives.

44. See Todd Compton, "Fanny Alger Smith Custer: Mormonism's First Plural Wife?" *Journal of Mormon History* 22, no. 1 (1996): 174–207, republished in Todd Compton, *In Sacred Loneliness: The Plural Wives of Joseph Smith* (Salt Lake City: Signature Books, 1999), chap. 2; and Danel W. Bachman, "A Study of the Mormon Practice of Plural Marriage before the Death of Joseph Smith" (M.A. thesis, Purdue University, 1975), 81–83.

45. During late 1837 to early 1838, Joseph and Oliver were involved in a prolonged emotional discussion about the alleged "adulterous affair" between Joseph and Miss Fanny Alger. Contemporary references to the Smith-Alger relationship are in Oliver Cowdery to Joseph Smith, 21 January 1838 (retained copy in Oliver Cowdery to Warren Cowdery, 21 January 1838), Oliver Cowdery to Warren Cowdery, 21 January 1838, Oliver Cowdery Letter Book, 80–83, Huntington Library, San Marino, California; Thomas B. Marsh to Joseph Smith, 15 February 1838, in *Elders Journal of the Church of Jesus Christ of Latter Day Saints* 1, no. 3 (July 1838): 45; and Far West Record, 118, 123–24; also in Cannon and Cook, eds., *Far West Record*, 167–68.

46. Cowdery to Daniel and Phebe Jackson, 24 July 1846.

47. Oliver Cowdery to Phineas Young, 12 November 1846, Church Archives. Cowdery's law partnership with Joel Wilson was dissolved on 18 December 1846. See notice in *Seneca Advertiser*, 18 December 1846.

48. Cowdery to Phineas Young, 12 November 1846.

49. "Manuscript History of Brigham Young," 16:526; published in *Manuscript History of Brigham Young, 1846–1847*, ed. Elden J. Watson (Salt Lake City: Elden J. Watson, 1971), 482.

50. By 1846, Oliver and Elizabeth Cowdery had had six children born to them—only one, Maria Louise, survived adolescence. Being frequently ill and impoverished, Cowdery was keenly aware of his limited ability to provide for his wife and child. Oliver made frequent mention in his correspondences of his concern for his "small family" and their temporal survival. He sensed from the reports he received about the Saints' destitute condition that if he joined with them he would be subjecting his family to unknown dangers.

51. Cowdery's involvement was noticed in the *Seneca Advertiser* for 11 December 1846: "The editorial management of the Advertiser will be entrusted to the hands of a capable friend, during the absence of the editor." Two months later, when Breslin returned, he announced:

The Editor has returned to his post.

In looking over the columns of the Advertiser, published during our absence, we felt impelled to congratulate our readers upon the interest and ability parted them by our friend, Mr. Cowdery, to whom we entrusted the management of our paper. Mr. C[owdery] has conducted it in a manner wholly satisfactory to ourselves, and we doubt not to our readers, and our thanks are due him for his attention and kindness. (*Seneca Advertiser*, 19 February 1847)

52. Oliver Cowdery to Phineas Young, 14 February 1847.

53. See ibid.

54. Oliver Cowdery to David Whitmer, 28 July 1847; published in William E. McLellin's *Ensign of Liberty* 1, no. 6 (May 1848): 92, emphasis in original.

55. For the broader context of McLellin's efforts to "get back on the old foundation," see Larry C. Porter, "The Odyssey of William Earl McLellin: Man of Diversity, 1806–83," in *The Journals of William E. McLellin, 1831–1836*, ed. Jan Shipps and John W. Welch (Urbana: University of Illinois Press; Provo, UT: BYU Studies, 1994), 341–46.

56. Cowdery to Whitmer, 28 July 1847.

57. Ibid., emphasis added.

58. Ibid., emphasis in original.

59. McLellin left Wisconsin by late July 1847 and traveled to Nauvoo where he met with Emma Smith, widow of the Prophet. From there, he journeyed to Richmond, Missouri, in an attempt to enlist David Whitmer in his cause. On 6 September, McLellin accompanied Hiram Page and David and Jacob Whitmer to Far West, where they counseled together at John Whitmer's. Two days later, on 8 September while at Far West, David Whitmer replied to Oliver's letter, which he had received at Richmond in late August. McLellin published a detailed report of his western trip in "Our Tour West in 1847," *Ensign of Liberty* 1, no. 7 (August 1849): 99–105. See also Porter, "Man of Diversity," 343.

60. See Oliver Cowdery to Phineas Young, 16 April 1848.

61. Brigham Young to Oliver Cowdery, 22 November 1847, retained copy, Church Archives. The only extant source, a retained copy, is dated 22 November, but evidence supports the late December dispatch date. In his reply, Oliver referred to the letter as bearing a December date. The First Presidency's clerk, Thomas Bullock, noted on the copy that the invitation was personally delivered by Phineas Young. On 7 April 1848, while reporting on his eastern mission before the conference gathered at Council Bluffs, Phineas said, "This is the first opportunity of seeing so many since last Christmas." See Conference Minutes, 7 April 1848, Church Archives. In his autobiography, Phineas indicated that "in Dec[ember] [I] took a mission to Wisconsin." See "Life of Phineas Howe Young. Written by Phineas Howe Young," Church Archives.

62. Brigham Young to Cowdery, 22 November 1847.

63. Oliver Cowdery to Brigham Young, 27 February 1848, Church Archives. On the outside of the letter, Cowdery indicated that the letter was being delivered by Phineas. Phineas returned to Council Bluffs on 26 March 1848. See Young, "History of Phineas Howe Young."

64. "A bill to provide for the publication of a general Index," 3 March 1848, Madison, Wisconsin, Council Bill 45, The State Historical Society of Wisconsin. According to the territorial legislative record, Council Bill 45 passed the Wisconsin Territorial Council on 3 March 1848, but the House of Representatives on 7 March 1848 decided to "strike out all after the enacting clause." See *Journal of the Council, Second Annual Session, of the Fifth Legislative Assembly of the Territory of Wisconsin, held at Madison, February 7th, A.D. 1848* (Madison: Tenney, 1848), 116, 138, 139, 146, and *Journal of the House of Representatives, Second Annual Session, of the Fifth Legislative Assembly, of the Territory*

of Wisconsin, held at Madison, on the Seventh day of February [1848] (Madison: Tenney, 1848), 235–36. Days earlier, on 1 March, Oliver wrote Phineas advising him that he had just received a letter from Lyman expressing great confidence in passage of the index bill. He told Phineas that he would not write to David Whitmer again until he knew the outcome of the bill and whether he would be able to see Whitmer in person. Oliver Cowdery to Phineas Young, 1 March 1848.

65. Oliver Cowdery to Phineas H. Young, 27 March 1848, Church Archives.

66. Conference minutes, 7 April 1848, manuscript notes by Thomas Bullock, Church Archives. These minutes were taken down in Bullock's personal form of shorthand, which allowed him to record near-verbatim notes of the speakers' comments.

67. See Wilford Woodruff journal, 7 April 1848; published in *Wilford Woodruff's Journal*, 3:339.

68. Cowdery to Phineas Young, 16 April 1848, Church Archives. Cowdery's use of the term "new purchase" referred to the land purchased from Mexico as part of the Treaty of Guadalupe Hidalgo (signed 2 February 1848; ratified 10 March 1848) ending the Mexican War. With this annexation, the United States acquired what is now Arizona, California, western Colorado, Nevada, New Mexico, Texas, and Utah.

69. See Cowdery to Phineas Young, 16 April 1848. An informative essay detailing Reuben Miller's contact with Cowdery is in Richard L. Anderson, "Reuben Miller, Recorder of Oliver Cowdery's Reaffirmations," *BYU Studies* 8, no. 3 (1968): 277–93.

70. An example of the endorsements Cowdery received from his local supporters follows. This editorial appeared in the Wisconsin Argus shortly before the elections:

Who is Oliver Cowdry?—*Western Star*. For the information of the editor of the Star, we will tell him. Oliver Cowdery is an honest man and sterling democrat, who has battled "Tippecanoe and Tyler too" hard cider whiggery ever since he was old enough to have a voice in political matters. He is a democrat who possessed the entire confidence of the people of that staunch old democratic strong hold—Seneca county, Ohio . . . We have known Mr. C[owdery] long and favorably by reputation in, that state, as a leading democrat, an eminent lawyer, and a worthy citizen, who is entitled to the fullest confidence of his party. (*Wisconsin Argus*, 11 April 1848)

Cowdery's Tiffin, Ohio, associate, John Breslin offered his belated support:

We are gratified to learn . . . that our esteemed friend and former fellow citizen, O[liver] Cowdery, Esq., has been nominated as the democratic candidate for the House of Representatives in that State. This intelligence has been hailed with the highest satisfaction by his numerous friends here, . . .

Mr. C[owdery] was a resident among us for a period of seven years, during which time he earned himself an enviable distinction at the Bar of this place and of this Judicial circuit, as a sound and able lawyer, and as a citizen none could have been more esteemed. His honesty, integrity, and industry were worthy the imitation of all. . . . Politically, Mr. C[owdery] was a prominent, active and radical democrat, never tiring in furthering the good cause. (*Seneca Advertiser*, 5 May 1848)

71. Examples of secular criticism of Cowdery's connection with the Book of Mormon and what they considered his "youthful indiscretions" with Mormonism are found in the *Milwaukee Daily Sentinel and Gazette*, 13 and 29 April 1848.

72. *Wisconsin Argus*, 16 May 1848, emphasis in original.

73. See Reuben Miller to James M. Adams, 30 May 1848, RLDS Archives. Miller returned to Walworth County by early June 1848 where he sold his farm for one thousand dollars. See Anderson, "Reuben Miller," 291.

74. See Reuben Miller journal, 18 September 1848, Church Archives; transcribed in Anderson, "Reuben Miller," 291.

75. See Deeds, 9:295–96, Oliver Cowdery and Elizabeth Cowdery to Jonathan Delap, 2 October 1848, Walworth County Court House, Elkhorn, Wisconsin. The deed was executed in the "presence of Phineas H. Young and Levi Lee." Lee, a justice of the peace, also notarized the deed.

76. *Gospel Herald*, 5 October 1848.

77. Reuben Miller journal, 21 October 1848, Church Archives. Miller, present at the conference session, took what was later described as a "verbatim report" of Cowdery's address. These notes, no longer extant, were copied into the journal soon afterwards and provided the source for Cowdery's testimony.

78. Hyde, Smith, and Benson, "Report to Presidents," 5 April 1849; see also George A. Smith's remarks in *Journal of Discourses*, 13:347–48.

79. George A. Smith to Orson Pratt, 31 October postscript to 20 October 1848 letter, in *Millennial Star* 11 (1 January 1849): 14.

80. "Report to Presidents Brigham Young, Heber C. Kimball, Willard Richards and the Authorities of the Church," 5 April 1849, Kanesville, Iowa, Church Archives.

81. George A. Smith to Orson Pratt, 31 October postscript to 20 October 1848 letter.

82. See previous discussion about Oliver Cowdery and plural marriage, above in n. 43.

83. Fortunately, three sets of minutes—two official, one unofficial—cover this assembly. Official minutes in Pottawattamie High Council Minutes, 5 November 1848, Church Archives, and Pottawattamie High Priests Quorum Minutes, 5 November 1848, Church Archives. The unofficial account appears in two forms in the Reuben Miller journal, the rough draft pencil notes (40–42) taken during the meeting and Miller's slightly expanded copy (16–18).

84. A physical description of the Kanesville Log Tabernacle is in Bennett, *Mormons at the Missouri*, 212–13. This book has been invaluable in understanding the various Church settlements at Council Bluffs and surrounding environs.

85. Pottawattamie High Priests Quorum Minutes, 5 November 1848.

86. Pottawattamie High Council Minutes, 1848–1851, 5 November 1848; Pottawattamie High Priests Quorum Minutes, 1846–1852, 5 November 1848.

87. Pottawattamie High Priests Quorum Minutes, 1846–1852, 5 November 1848.

88. Evidence of Cowdery's displeasure is found in a letter from Hiram Page to Oliver Cowdery, which reads in part:

It appears there is some things that your mind is anxious about. One is whether Brother David [Whitmer] gave Bro. Wm. [McLellin] liberty to publish private letters; I hear say that there were no such liberties given but he was not to publish anything to the world that did not belong to the world. His publications are so conducted that we have sent to have him discontinue his papers to Richmond. (23 July, 1848, Hiram Page Letters, RLDS Archives)

89. "Report to Presidents Brigham Young, Heber C. Kimball, Willard Richards and the Authorities of the Church," 5 April 1849.

90. Excerpts of this revelation, including the material relating to Oliver Cowdery,

were first published in *Times and Seasons* 2, no. 15 (1 June 1841): 424–29. The complete revelation was included in the 1844 Doctrine and Covenants as section 103. In spite of being published in Nauvoo, Oliver was unaware of the revelation until he came to Kanesville in the fall of 1848.

91. "Report to Presidents Brigham Young, Heber C. Kimball, Willard Richards and the Authorities of the Church," 5 April 1849.

92. See Miller journal, 5 November 1848, 17, emphasis added.

93. Pottawattamie High Priests Quorum Minutes, 5 November 1848.

94. Pottawattamie High Council Minutes, 5 November 1848.

95. Orson Hyde to Wilford Woodruff, 11 November 1848, Wilford Woodruff Papers, Church Archives. The date of Hyde's letter has been misinterpreted by several researchers as "10 November 1848" because the second "1" has an end flourish which gives the number the appearance of a "0." Elder Woodruff received the letter on 19 December and wrote in his diary:

> Among the letters which I obtained yesterday was one from O. Hyde who informed me that Oliver Cowdery had come back to the Church, had made satisfaction, And was voted to come in by the door of Baptism. He was the first man baptized into the Church of Jesus Christ of Latter Day Saints in this last dispensation, under the Hands of Joseph Smith the Prophet but after being out of the church eleven years, he had now returned again. And may the Lord bless him and keep him steadfast unto the end. (*Wilford Woodruff's Journal*, 3:392–93 [20 December 1848])

On 26 December, Wilford passed the news about Cowdery's return on to Elder Orson Pratt who was in Great Britain. See Woodruff to Pratt, in *Millennial Star* 11, no. 3 (1 February 1849): 43.

96. Reuben Miller to Henry Sabey [aka Henry Eriksen], 16 November 1848, Church Archives.

97. See Hyde to Woodruff, 11 November 1848, Church Archives. The first issue of the *Frontier Guardian* was published 7 February 1849. The *Guardian* was a Whig-sympathetic newspaper, which may explain why Cowdery, a staunch democrat, did not stay to help edit the paper.

98. Samuel W. Richards, handwritten statement, 21 May 1907, Church Archives.

99. Ibid.

100. Cowdery to Phineas Young, 27 April 1849, Church Archives, emphasis in original.

101. Cowdery to Phineas Young, 24 June 1849, Church Archives.

102. Oliver Cowdery to Phineas Young, date missing (written between 14 and 22 September 1849 based on evidence in the letter and its postmark), Church Archives.

103. Apparently, in the winter of 1848–49, the westward mail to Deseret slowed down considerably or came to a stop. The presiding officials at Kanesville (i.e., Orson Hyde, George A. Smith, and Ezra Taft Benson) waited until early April 1849 to inform the First Presidency of Cowdery's return. This report was probably hand carried west with one of the first emigration companies. See "A Report to Presidents," 4–5, Church Archives.

104. Brigham Young, Heber C. Kimball, and Willard Richards to Oliver Cowdery, 20 July 1849, retained copy, Church Archives. See also Brigham Young to Orson Hyde, 19 July 1849; Brigham Young, Heber C. Kimball, and Willard Richards to Orson Hyde,

21 July 1849; and Brigham Young, Heber C. Kimball, and Willard Richards to N. H. Felt, 24 July 1849, all retained copies in Church Archives.

105. In mid-September 1849, Oliver wrote to Phineas acknowledging a previous letter from Phineas informing him that the "brethren in the Valley wish me to go to Washington" with Almon W. Babbit. Cowdery to Phineas Young, ca. 14–22 September 1849, Church Archives.

106. From the description of his long-term symptoms, Oliver was probably suffering from chronic pulmonary tuberculosis. Symptoms include fatigue, night sweats and fever, and persistent cough. Hemorrhages of blood occur as the lung tissue is destroyed by the disease. Kathryn L. McCance and Sue E. Huether, *Pathophysiology: The Biologic Basis for Disease in Adults and Children*, 2nd ed. (St. Louis: Mosby-Year Book, 1994), 1174–75. During the last years of his life, Cowdery displayed all these symptoms.

107. See Hiram Page to Warren A. Cowdery, 20 March 1850, published in *Saints' Herald* 33, no. 6 (6 February 1886): 83. Also, Cowdery to Phineas Young, ca. 14–22 September 1849, Church Archives.

108. Jacob Gates (1811–1892) was appointed to a three-year mission during the fall conference of 1849. He departed Salt Lake City on 19 October 1849 and arrived in Liverpool by 6 April 1850. See Jacob Gates, "Items of History of the Life and Labors of Jacob Gates," Church Archives. Paraphrased in Andrew Jenson, *Biographical Encyclopedia*, 1:198. Although not specifically mentioned in his biography, it is conjectured that Gates, who was traveling to St. Louis with Erastus Snow, Franklin D. Richards, and other missionaries, stopped in Richmond, Missouri, during January 1850 and visited Oliver Cowdery. See Franklin D. Richards to Orson Pratt, 8 January 1850, published in *Millennial Star* 12 (1 March 1850): 75–76, and Erastus Snow to his wives, 17 February 1850, Church Archives.

109. Jacob Forsberry Gates (son of Jacob Gates), signed and notarized affidavit, 30 January 1912, Church Archives; published in *Improvement Era* (March 1912): 418–19. These are actually two typewritten affidavits by Gates, separated by a month's interval. The first draft, dated 30 December 1911, Gates signed but left unnotarized. The second statement, dated 30 January 1912, was signed and notarized.

110. Phineas Young to Brigham Young, 25 April 1850, Church Archives.

111. Reported in Joseph F. Smith and Orson Pratt interview with David Whitmer, 7–8 September 1878, draft report, dated 17 September 1878, Joseph F. Smith to "President John Taylor and Council of 12," Church Archives.

THE DEDICATION OF THE OLIVER COWDERY MONUMENT IN RICHMOND, MISSOURI, 1911

Richard Neitzel Holzapfel and Robert F. Schwartz

As one of three witnesses, Oliver Cowdery testified that "an angel of God came down from heaven" to display an ancient record—a record known then and now as the Book of Mormon. Cowdery, Martin Harris, and David Whitmer affirmed in written testimony that they saw "the engravings thereon," and more surprisingly that the voice of God declared Joseph Smith's translation of the record to be true.[1] Even though all three men eventually disassociated themselves from Joseph Smith, later members of The Church of Jesus Christ of Latter-day Saints felt to commemorate Cowdery, Whitmer, and Harris for their role in the Church's genesis. In 1911, Church member Junius F. Wells[2] erected a monument in Richmond, Ray County, Missouri, toward this end (figs. 1, 2).

Wells wrote an account of his efforts to erect the monument, which he published in January 1912.[3] His article focuses on interviews that he conducted in Richmond with the nearest of kin of Cowdery and descendents of Whitmer, as well as on his efforts to gain both their trust and the trust of Richmond's citizens. The present article covers some of the same ground as Wells's published article but adds to the story by using primary source data from Wells's personal papers, held in trust by The Church of Jesus Christ of Latter-day Saints. This article likewise includes photographs taken by George Edward Anderson that capture many events involved in creating and dedicating the monument. Happily, the story provides

Fig. 2. Junius F. Wells, ca. 1924.

Fig. 1. Unveiling ceremony at the Oliver Cowdery Monument, November 22, 1911, Richmond, Missouri, photographed by George Edward Anderson.

George Edward Anderson (1860–1928), the first Latter-day Saint to professionally photograph Church historic sites, began his effort to document the Mormon past through his camera in 1907 on his way to serve a mission in the British Isles. After a year of searching out Mormon sites in the settlements in the West, Anderson arrived in England in 1908. After completing his proselytizing mission in Europe, he sailed for America in August 1911, but he did not return home immediately. He stayed in South Royalton, Vermont, continuing his quest to capture Church history through his glass plate negatives. After ending his six-year mission in 1913, he returned home to Utah.

The complete collection of Anderson photographs related to the Oliver Cowdery Monument may be seen at byustudies.byu .edu. All images in this article courtesy of the Church Archives, The Church of Jesus Christ of Latter-day Saints.

remarkable views of a productive, friendly, cooperative effort between Missourians and Mormons in an area where only a few decades earlier the two parties had been at war with one another.

A Promise to Commemorate Oliver Cowdery

President John Henry Smith, second counselor in the First Presidency of The Church of Jesus Christ of Latter-day Saints, traveled to Independence, Jackson County, Missouri, in 1910, where the Church had only recently reestablished a presence after an absence that began with its expulsion in 1833. President Smith, along with Samuel O. Bennion, John L. Herrick, and Joseph A. McRae, visited nearby Mormon historical sites, and on November 30, 1910, the party visited Richmond, located thirty miles northeast of Independence.

Like Independence, Richmond has a past rich in Latter-day Saint history. Joseph Smith and other Latter-day Saint Church leaders were imprisoned in a makeshift Richmond jail following their arrest at Far West on October 31, 1838. Later, after the Mormons were driven from Missouri in 1838–39, the Richmond area became home to several former leaders of the Church who no longer accepted Joseph Smith's leadership. This group included David Whitmer, Jacob C. Whitmer, Hiram Page, and Oliver Cowdery, each of whom played key roles in the Church's founding events. Cowdery and his wife, Elizabeth Whitmer,[4] moved to Richmond in 1849, shortly before he passed away. Cowdery was estranged from Joseph Smith by 1838 and was excommunicated from the Church in Far West, Missouri. Before his death in 1850, however, Cowdery rejoined the Church and planned to gather with its members in Utah.[5] Maria Louise Cowdery (1835–92), the daughter of Oliver and Elizabeth Cowdery and the only Cowdery child to live to maturity, married Dr. Charles Johnson and died without any living descendants in South West City, Missouri, in 1892.

While in Richmond, John Henry Smith and his party visited local cemeteries, trying to locate the graves of Cowdery, Page, and David Whitmer.[6] President Smith wrote, "We went to the old grave yard to visit the grave of Oliver Cowdery and Hyrum Page but we

Fig. 3. Joseph Smith Jr. birthplace, Sharon, Vermont, 1907, photographed by George Edward Anderson. Junius F. Wells managed the creation and installation of the monument to Joseph Smith in 1905.

could not locate them but were told they were in the north end of the Cemetery."[7] (In fact, Hiram Page was not buried in Richmond. David Whitmer was buried in a different Richmond cemetery.) President Smith and his company apparently came into contact with George W. Schweich. Schweich was the nearest living family member to Oliver Cowdery in the Richmond area as his mother, Julia Ann, was the daughter of David Whitmer, Cowdery's brother-in-law. President Smith promised Schweich that the Church would erect a monument in Cowdery's memory.[8] Schweich and A. K. Raeburn—a ninety-three-year-old former sheriff who claimed to be present when Cowdery was buried in March 1850—aided President Smith in identifying the location of Cowdery's final resting place.[9]

When President Smith returned to Salt Lake City, he approached Junius F. Wells about the possibility of erecting a monument in

Richmond. Wells had already successfully purchased, on behalf of the Church, Joseph Smith's birthplace in Sharon, Vermont, and had erected there a large granite monument in Smith's honor in 1905 (fig. 3).[10] In fact, Wells had already given thought to erecting a monument in Cowdery's honor when Smith approached him. He afterwards wrote, "I had a very clear notion of the kind of monument and suitable inscriptions thereon."[11] He also planned to erect additional monuments at the gravesites of David Whitmer and Martin Harris.[12] The decision to build a monument to Joseph Smith in 1905 and to Cowdery in 1911 reflects broader national trends in monument building that took hold after the Civil War. During this period, a multitude of monuments sprung up at Civil War sites, town squares, and cemeteries throughout the country.[13]

After personal reflection and planning, Wells decided on a text that would honor not only Oliver Cowdery but Joseph Smith and all three witnesses, even though he hoped to erect separate monuments to Harris and Whitmer later. He submitted his proposal for the monument—including inscriptions and cost estimations—to the First Presidency, which at the time included President Joseph F. Smith, Anthon H. Lund, and John Henry Smith. Wells reported, "This was approved by the First Presidency and Twelve, and I was commissioned to carry it out."[14] The text appears in the sidebar below.

Preparing a Monument

Wells immediately set about working to build Oliver Cowdery's monument. He contacted R. C. Bowers, president of R. C. Bowers Granite Company in Montpelier, Vermont, sometime before the middle of February. Bowers was the general contractor who organized the logistical efforts involved in constructing the 1905 Vermont monument. In contracting Bowers, Wells was freed from worrying about the details involved in monument construction such as quarrying, polishing, inscribing, and transporting.[15]

On February 13, 1911, Bowers responded to Wells's inquiry: "Referring to your favor of recent date in regard to design of the monuments, the monument[s] alone would be worth $900.00 each

---

The Text of the Oliver Cowdery Monument

Front of monument:

Sacred to the memory of Oliver Cowdery, witness to the Book of Mormon and to the translation thereof by the gift and power of God.

Born 3rd October, 1806, Wells, Rutland Co., Vermont. Died 3rd March, 1850, Richmond, Ray Co., Missouri.

He was the scribe of the translation as it fell from the lips of Joseph Smith, the Prophet. He copied the original manuscript for the printer's use and was proof-reader of the first edition. He was the first person baptized in the Latter-day Dispensation of the Gospel; and was one of the six members of the Church of Jesus Christ at its organization, on the sixth day of April, A.D., 1830, at Fayette, Seneca Co., New York. Though separated from it for a time, he returned to the Church. He died firm in the faith.

This Monument has been raised in his honor by his fellow-believers; and also to commemorate the Testimony of Three Witnesses, the truth of which they maintained to the end of their lives. Over a million converts throughout the world have accepted their testimony and rejoice in their fidelity. Dedicated 1911.

Reverse of monument:

The Book of Mormon. An account written by the hand of Mormon upon plates taken from the plates of Nephi. Translated and published by Joseph Smith Junior, Palmyra, 1830.

On the other two sides appears the text of The Testimony of the Three Witnesses, printed in the Book of Mormon.

F. O. B. cars here, and would weigh about 36000 lbs. each. The V sunk inscription letters would be worth 18 cents each. If the continuous inscription of 1264 letters is smaller letters, they would be worth from 12 to 15 cents each."[16] Wells agreed, sent a check for $30, and asked for a perspective drawing of the design. It was weeks before he received this note from Bowers: "Just got word from the man that makes our designs that he has been sick but he will get right at your design and lose no time in finishing it. Sorry to have delayed you and hope to send it to you shortly."[17] On April 19, Bowers sent by "express this morning" the examples of the design.[18]

On May 19, 1911, Wells, still in Salt Lake City, formalized his obligations regarding the monument's erection when he signed an agreement with President Joseph F. Smith, promising "to procure the requisite consent of the parties lawfully interested and secure the site in the cemetery at or near the burial place of Oliver Cowdery, to erect thereon a monument of dark barre granite accord to the design and inscription submitted."[19] Presidents John Henry Smith and Anthon H. Lund also signed the document as witnesses.[20]

Soon thereafter, Wells traveled to Richmond for the first time.[21] Wells indicated that he hoped to accomplish several important objectives during this visit: first, visit the cemetery; second, identify Cowdery's grave; third, obtain the consent of the local officials to erect a monument; fourth, obtain approval from the nearest of kin living there; fifth, select a site for the monument; and finally, secure the goodwill of the people of Richmond.

Obtaining the goodwill of the people was not necessarily as easy as it might appear to the modern reader. Controversy surrounding polygamy generated ill will toward the Church's members through the late nineteenth century and into the twentieth. Although the Mormon practice of polygamy had officially ended in 1890, controversy and misunderstanding continued. The situation came to a head in the early years of the twentieth century when Apostle Reed Smoot was elected to the US Senate. Public senatorial hearings regarding his suitability for office ensued, and newspapers nationwide criticized Utah.[22] The years 1910 and 1911 witnessed a significant recurrence of anti-Mormon feeling throughout the country, resulting from the negative fallout generated by Smoot's reelection. It might, indeed, be assumed that the monuments of 1905 and 1911 were constructed partly in the hope of engendering goodwill for the Church.

Wells, contrary to what he might have expected in the political climate, was pleasantly surprised by the welcome he received from the hospitable people of Richmond. He received solid support from George W. Schweich, who emphasized his willingness to help and expressed his feelings about erecting another monument in Richmond to honor his grandfather, David Whitmer.[23]

Wells went to the Old City Cemetery, known today as the Pioneer Cemetery (fig. 4[24]). He described his visit:

> Among the earliest graves within this sacred acre are those of Father Peter Whitmer's family and kindred, whose burying lots appear to have occupied about sixteen by sixty feet, along the east side of a central drive, entering at the north end of the cemetery. Within this boundary, and in the southern part, are buried the bodies of Peter Whitmer, and his wife, Mary Musselman Whitmer—father and mother of the Witnesses,—Jacob Whitmer, one of the Eight, and two more of his daughters, and other members of his family. I counted thirteen graves, most of them unmarked, except by crude stones without inscriptions.[25]

Fig. 4. Old City Cemetery, Richmond, Missouri, November 21, 1911, photographed by George Edward Anderson. More than just a photograph of tombstones, this view reveals the history of the Whitmer family and their relatives in Richmond's Old City Cemetery, known today as the Pioneer Cemetery. Note the tombstone of Jacob Whitmer (1800–56) with the opened book, Book of Mormon (second row, right).

Wells looked specifically for Cowdery's grave. With the help of several individuals, including A. K. Raeburn, he found the site.

After making initial contacts in Richmond, Wells made his way to Vermont to select the stone for the monument. In June 1911, President John Henry Smith, traveling in the East, met up with "J. F. Wells, Ben E. Rich and a Mr. Milne and Mayor Boutwell of Montpelier, Vermont who took us in his Auto to the Joseph Smith Monument where Bro. Brown gave lunch. We planted 6 trees. We called at the Barre Marble Quarries."[26] Apparently, they "selected the stone, and the order was given for the manufacture of the [Cowdery] monument" on this occasion.[27]

During the first week of August 1911, Bowers contacted Wells, who was staying in South Royalton, Vermont. He wrote, "We have your monument all ready to letter and have the lettering drawn up for it, and would be pleased to have you come up at once and look the lettering over as we wish to start lettering it Monday."[28] Due to a misunderstanding, Wells failed to contact Bowers to approve the lettering, causing additional delay.

Days later while on another visit to Richmond, Wells met with several of Cowdery's family members, including Philander A. Page, Julia Ann Schweich, and George W. Schweich, in an effort to obtain their legal consent to erect the monument.[29] Each said they would not oppose Wells's efforts. Page said he "preferred not to sign his approval, as he was not in favor of so much display."[30] The Schweich family, on the other hand, were not only supportive but also helped in every way to assist Wells. Regarding Julia Ann Schweich, daughter of David Whitmer, Wells stated, "She was seventy-six years old in September, and is a very smart, clear-minded lady of remarkable memory, firm convictions, honest, outspoken, and independent. I became much attached to her, and enjoyed repeated interviews with her, in which she told me many things concerning her father, his family and the family connections."[31]

On August 8, Wells obtained the legal consent of Cowdery's relatives to proceed with the project. The document states that Cowdery's relatives "approve of this undertaking and freely consent

to it and thereby authorize Junius F. Wells acting for himself, ourselves and fellow believers in the above testimony [testimony of
the Three Witnesses to the Book of Mormon], to take every necessary step to locate the site of said grave and erect said monument
thereon only hold the undersigned free from expense connected
therewith."[32]

Still concerned that Oliver Cowdery's gravesite had not been
correctly identified, Wells visited the graveyard on August 9, 1911,
with A. K. Raeburn. Wells did this again on August 18 and on
November 23 to gain complete assurance that Raeburn provided the
same description.

After repeatedly hearing Raeburn's description, Wells went to
the cemetery to carefully review what he had been told. He wrote:

> I found by measuring the distance between the graves, and be-
> tween the headstones and footstones, that there were two graves,
> shorter than the grave of a full grown man, north of the depres-
> sion which was supposed to be the grave of Oliver Cowdery. By
> some digging, we found the rotting stones that had supported the
> headstone, which was gone, and six and half feet eastward, a large,
> though crumbling, footstone. This supplied whatever assurance
> was lacking as to the identify of the grave we sought—especially
> as the next grave, seven feet southward, was that of a child.[33]

With written permission of Cowdery's surviving family now in
his possession, Wells met with the mayor of Richmond and some of
the city councilmen and "arranged with the city engineer to establish the grade of the street—Crispin avenue—on the north line of
the cemetery—and to stake out and set the levels of the foundation
of the site selected for the monument."[34] The city engineer billed
Wells $3.00 for survey work and setting the corners.[35] The city's final
approval was granted on August 15, 1911.[36]

Once approved by the city council, preparations at the site itself
continued as J. W. Hagans graded the spot for the monument and
prepared a six-foot-square concrete foundation at a cost of $67.50.[37]
On October 26, 1911, Wells and Schweich placed a metal box in the

foundation—a time capsule that contained a number of books, peri-odicals, pictures, and miscellaneous items.[38]

While efforts in Richmond to erect the monument proceeded, work on the monument itself ceased for a few weeks when unusu-ally hot weather in Vermont "shut down work in the stonecutter's sheds."[39] Since Wells had failed to authorize the lettering of the monument, Bowers wrote: "I am in receipt of your favor of the 18th inst. and regret to say we were delayed two weeks on your monu-ment on account of the lettering not being approved, as I did not feel safe in starting it until I heard from you. The lettering is all that will hold us up now and I assure you that we will do the very best we can in rushing the work out."[40]

Originally, Wells and President John Henry Smith desired to dedicate the monument on October 3, 1911, the anniversary of Oliver Cowdery's birth.[41] However, due to these delays, they set back the date for the dedication.

A few weeks later, Utah portrait and landscape photogra-pher George Edward Anderson visited the workshops at Barre, Washington County, Vermont. In his first photograph related to the erection of the Oliver Cowdery monument, Anderson captured in black and white a craftsman engaged in his work on the monument (fig. 5).[42]

A Change of Plans

President John Henry Smith had been busy during the first half of 1911 fulfilling Church, business, and governmental responsibili-ties. Few knew that his health was failing rapidly. President Smith passed away on October 13, 1911. Wells revealed, "The lamentable death of Elder Smith occurring on the thirteenth [October], caused a complete change in the plans respecting the dedication."[43] Wells decided to work for a date later in the year to coincide with the Mormon Tabernacle Choir's six-thousand-mile national tour, which began on October 23, 1911. Wells hoped to arrange for the choir to stop briefly at Richmond on its return trip to Salt Lake City, follow-ing a scheduled concert in Kansas City on November 21 and before

Fig. 5. Construction of the Oliver Cowdery Monument, October 10, 1911, at R. C. Bowers Granite Company, Barre, Vermont, photographed by George Edward Anderson. Often misidentified as the base of the Joseph Smith monument in Sharon, Vermont, this piece belongs to the Oliver Cowdery Monument.

another scheduled concert in Topeka on November 22. While the choir's tour was generally considered a success, especially in light of the anti-Mormon mood that prevailed nationwide, the choir encountered stiff opposition in various places. In some cases, they could not secure places to perform, and, in the end, incurred a deficit of some $20,000. In the face of the budgetary concerns that surfaced during the tour, Wells needed to demonstrate that a side trip to a small Missouri town would not push the choir further into the red and that they would be received warmly by the local people.

Getting Everything in Place

Assuring that work on the monument was moving forward also consumed Wells's efforts. On October 10, Bowers wrote Wells: "Monument will leave here tomorrow."[44] Once Wells received the notification, he contracted with Thomas B. Blount, a house-moving company in Richmond, to transport the monument from the railway station to the old city cemetery. Wells wrote to Blount, "Accept your offer. Please be ready to receive monument shipped from Montpelier eleventh. I shall be there by twentieth. Make sure that every rope, chain, pulley, and anchor are sound and strong. I may bring men to assist in erection but do not depend on that. Be prepared."[45] The men "had quite a time hauling it on the house-moving trucks and setting it, but finally got it up without accident"[46] (fig. 6). The monument was in place in the Old City Cemetery by November 1, 1911 (fig. 7). The total expense for transporting and setting the monument was $100.00.[47]

Wells still had not yet secured the commitment for the two-hundred-member Mormon Tabernacle Choir to participate in the services. They were already in New York when Wells appealed to George D. Pyper, the choir's tour manager, trying to persuade him to make the necessary arrangements for the proposed stop:

Fig. 6. Transporting the Oliver Cowdery Monument to cemetery from the railway, ca. November 1, 1911, Richmond, Missouri, photographed by George Edward Anderson.

Fig. 7. Oliver Cowdery monument, November 21, 1911, Richmond, Missouri, photographed by George Edward Anderson.

Upon arriving here, I found that they have a very nice little opera house practically new and clean and well furnished, there are actually six hundred orchestra chairs, and other seats for at least four hundred with the boxes and standing up twelve hundred people can be admitted. The people here are sufficiently interested in having you come that they have assured me if I find that you can do so, they will tender us the free use of the opera house, warmed and lighted.[48]

After providing several more issues for Pyper's consideration—including further description of available facilities and necessary costs—Wells concluded: "I sincerely hope that nothing will occur to prevent carrying out this program. It will be very delightful for everybody and will do a lot of good."[49]

Eventually, choir leaders agreed that the choir would perform at the dedication, and Wells began the Herculean task of arranging for the visit of so large a party to Richmond. Additionally, some fifty people, most of them family of the choir members, accompanied the choir on their tour. Their presence brought the total number of Latter-day Saints present on this occasion to about two hundred and fifty. Wells wrote the owner of the local hotel in Richmond: "Dedication service Wednesday morning, twenty-second, ten o'clock sharp. Choir must have breakfast and be seated in Topeka House by nine forty-five. Dinner must be all ready twelve thirty, and over by two. Train leaves two thirty for Topeka."[50]

Wells received an official invitation for the use of the Opera House from Richmond's "principal bankers, merchants, one of the ministers, the Mayor of the City, hotel proprietors, and the owner of the Opera House."[51] Wells was "deeply grateful for this courtesy"[52] and reported to President Joseph F. Smith that there was "a feeling of great interest and enthusiasm, already manifest by the people at the prospect of so large a company being present."[53] Wells awaited President Smith's approval and information concerning who would be present on the occasion. Mindful of the weather, he noted: "If we can only have a pleasant day, it promises to be a very fine affair."[54]

President Joseph F. Smith wrote back that the gathering would be more limited than Wells may have anticipated. He assigned Heber J. Grant of the Council of the Twelve to conduct the affairs of the Church at the services.[55] Wells noted in later reflections why other general church officers were not sent to attend the occasion: "Conditions at home were so forbidding that the Presiding Authorities were not able to go to the service."[56] The conditions referred to were the November municipal elections in Utah. Since 1905, the anti-Mormon third party, known as the American Party, controlled several local governments in the northern part of the state, including Salt Lake City. The two national parties made every effort to defeat the American Party. Mormon Church leaders joined in forces with non-Mormons in both parties to help accomplish the defeat. The campaign successfully brought about the demise of the American Party and allowed political affiliation in the state to be based on political preference instead of Church membership.[57]

President Smith indicated in his letter that he did not feel it necessary to invite representatives from the Reorganized Church of Jesus Christ of Latter Day Saints or the Church of Christ (Temple Lot). This decision is significant because of the Reorganized Church's ties to the American Party. Joseph Smith III (cousin of President Joseph F. Smith) and his son, Fredrick M. Smith, had worked with Frank Cannon and ex-Senator Kearns to form the American Party in Salt Lake City.[58] Moreover, in July 1905, when the American Party first began to take root, Frederick Smith wrote a full-page protest of the Joseph Smith monument that the Latter-day Saint Church had recently erected in Vermont under Wells's supervision.[59]

After receiving President Smith's reply, Wells ordered 750 formal invitations, printed at a cost of $15. The invitations were sent not only to local citizens but to all Church mission, temple, stake, and Church college presidents to notify them of the event.

On November 16, Wells wrote Bowers regarding final payment for the monument and added his impressions regarding the final product: "I think the material and workmanship of the monument are very good, and that it will be much admired."[60] Work began on preparing the ground around the monument for the unveiling ceremony. Wells contracted with Charles E. Prispin to grade the area and Powell Brothers to fence the west and north sides of the cemetery.[61]

The citizens of Richmond not only offered the use of the Opera House for the dedication service, but they also graded streets, paved sidewalks, and laid plank crossings at several corners. Several individuals, especially George W. Schweich, offered more assistance than Wells ever expected. So it was with great hope and a sense of satisfaction that Wells greeted the long-awaited day of the dedication service and unveiling ceremony on November 22, 1911.

The Dedication Services and Unveiling Ceremony

A train of Pullman Palace sleeping cars pulled into Richmond from Kansas City during the early morning hours of November 22, 1911 (fig. 8). While the train sat on a side track, members of the Mormon Tabernacle Choir continued to sleep until sunrise. Wells provided a description of the choir's arrival: "The train bringing the choir from Kansas City arrived during the night, or early in the morning of the 22nd. It was not easy to rouse the weary sleepers, and get them out, under lowering skies, at half-past seven for early breakfast, at the hotel. It was, however, loiteringly accomplished, but not until the prince and power of the air, or whoever has charge of the storm clouds, had taken vicious control and started a downpour of chilling rain that continued for the greater part of the day."[62]

Fig. 8. Mormon Tabernacle Choir Train, November 22, 1911, Richmond, Missouri, photographed by George Edward Anderson. A chartered train brought the choir from Kansas City, where they performed the night before, and took them on to Topeka after the dedication of the monument. Here several members, including Evan Stephens (arms outstretched), pose for the photographer.

Following breakfast at the hotel, the choir made its way to the Farris Opera House. Wells paid $12.00 for Manley & Wading to transport the "choir from the Hotel to the Opera House" in the rain.[63]

Wells had prepared 1,500 programs for the dedication service and unveiling ceremony,[64] and the Opera House "was well filled, there being hardly a vacant seat in the building."[65] Elder Heber J. Grant greeted the crowd, followed by the Tabernacle Choir performing the first hymn: "An Angel from On High"[66] (fig. 9). President Samuel O. Bennion offered the invocation and the Tabernacle Choir sang the anthem "Hosannah!" Then Junius F. Wells "spoke in brief as to why we were assembled, reviewing the story of the coming forth of the Book of Mormon, the life of Oliver Cowdery, the history of the monument itself."[67] In the end, he spoke to the local residents suggesting "that the cemetery be improved and that the citizens of Richmond would regard that monument as a credit to the place."[68]

The Tabernacle Choir sang one of its favorite hymns, "Oh! My Father!" followed by comments from Mayor James L. Farris in behalf of the city: "Take possession of the City of Richmond, today we are your servants."[69] The assembled group then heard brief remarks from George W. Schweich, who represented Oliver Cowdery's family, welcoming everyone present to the occasion.

Heber J. Grant then spoke and noted how pleased President Joseph F. Smith was that a monument had been erected to honor Oliver Cowdery. He went on to relate that he had always admired Oliver Cowdery, David Whitmer, and Martin Harris, who played such crucial roles in establishing the Church. As he drew near to the close of his remarks, Grant "bore his testimony of the gospel to the assemblage, gave words of praise to the Choir for their conduct and singing. Also expressed his pleasure in accepting hospitality of Richmond people. Also stated that on account of the storm they would be unable to go to the cemetery to dedicate the grave."[70]

After Grant's remarks, Wells introduced Katherine Schweich, grandniece of Oliver Cowdery, to the assembled group. He noted that she would unveil the monument when weather permitted. She "very modestly acknowledged the honor before the audience."[71]

Elder Heber J. Grant then dedicated Oliver Cowdery's grave from the Farris Opera House, thanking God "for the feeling of good-will and fellowship that has been manifest by the inhabitants of this City during the erection of this monument and we pray Thee that it may continue and that the bond of love and sympathy between the believers of the Book of Mormon and the people of Richmond and those who read the message may grow and increase in strength every year."[72]

Time was allotted for George Edward Anderson to take a photograph of the event (see fig. 9).[73] George Schweich made the program's closing remarks, saying that he was as proud to be a descendant of David Whitmer as of "any monarch that ever lived."[74] He asked the Tabernacle Choir to perform a few concluding numbers before the program ended, including "Lucia Sextet." The choir performed and Bishop David A. Smith then offered the benediction to close

Fig. 9. Dedication service in the Farris Opera House, November 22, 1911, Richmond, Missouri, photographed by George Edward Anderson. Front row, from left: John J. McClellan (organist), Willard A. Weihe (violinist), George W. Schweich (grandson of David Whitmer), Samuel O. Bennion (Central States Mission President), Bishop David A. Smith (Presiding Bishop's Office), Evans Stephens (Tabernacle Choir director, behind the wooden platform), Elder Heber J. Grant (Council of the Twelve), Katherine Schweich (great-granddaughter of David Whitmer), and Junius F. Wells.

the service. Wells reported that "the visitors [Tabernacle Choir and Church representatives] hurried through the rain to the hotel for dinner, and about half-past one, their train pulled out for Topeka, Kansas. . . . Elders Grant and Bennion accompanied them."[75]

Later in the afternoon, when the weather permitted, Wells and a small party proceeded to the cemetery. George Edward Anderson accompanied them and provided some beautiful black-and-white images of the occasion (figs. 10 and 11).

Wells preserved the details regarding the monument's unveiling: "The following named Elders, Geo. W. Schweich & his daughter Kathryn met with Geo. Ed Anderson & me at about 3 p.m. at the monument and I spoke to them & offered prayer & Kathryn held

Fig. 10. Unveiling ceremony at the Oliver Cowdery Monument, November 22, 1911, Richmond, Missouri, photographed by George Edward Anderson. Katherine Schweich holds the bouquet of flowers following the unveiling of the monument, and Junius F. Wells stands at her right, in the front row.

Fig. 11. Junius F. Wells (standing by the fence) offers a prayer following the unveiling of the monument, November 22, 1911, Richmond, Missouri, photographed by George Edward Anderson.

the flag that veiled the monument while we all had our pictures taken."[76]

Assessment

The local paper in Richmond provided its assessment of the service: "The musical numbers rendered by the choir were excellent and showed their fine training and splendid voices. . . . The remarks by the speakers were to the point and interesting. Apostle Heber Grant of Salt Lake City, made the longest talk and was very interesting. . . . The arrangements and plans were carried out and everything worked smoothly. Mr. Wells had been here for several days and with Geo. W. Schweich, a grand son of David Whitmer, had everything in readiness for the event."[77]

Everyone seems to have been pleased with the events of the day and happy to have participated in celebrating the life of Oliver Cowdery. Wells may have captured, at least on one level, the significance of the day when he talked about the members of the community, including clergymen, bankers, merchants, county and city officials, and the leading citizens who gathered in the Opera House and "wept for joy, as they participated in this song service. They were also admonished in words of stirring testimony and convincing reason of the truth, the life, the immortality and saving grace of the doctrines and government of the Church, as they fell from the lips of descendants of the very men who had been well nigh hounded to death in the public square near by."[78] This day, however, provided a different setting for the interaction between the Latter-day Saints and the people of Missouri as they celebrated together to honor one of their own.

Notes

Editors' note: This article was originally published in *BYU Studies* 44/2 (2005): 99–121.

1. Oliver Cowdery, Martin Harris, and David Whitmer, "The Testimony of the Three Witnesses," in Joseph Smith Jr., *History of The Church of Jesus Christ of Latter-day Saints,* ed. B. H. Roberts, 2nd ed., rev., 7 vols. (Salt Lake City: Deseret Book, 1971), 1:57.

2. Junius F. Wells (1854–1930), son of Daniel H. and Hannah C. Free Wells, was asked to organize the Church's Young Men's Mutual Improvement Association (YM-MIA) in 1875 and became its first president.

3. Junius F. Wells, "The Oliver Cowdery Monument at Richmond, Missouri," *Improvement Era* 15 (January 1912): 251.

4. Elizabeth Ann Whitmer Cowdery (1815–92) was the daughter of Peter and Mary Musselman Whitmer.

5. Richard L. Anderson, *Investigating the Book of Mormon Witnesses* (Salt Lake City: Deseret Book, 1981).

6. David Whitmer is buried in the Richmond City Cemetery, located on Highway 10 just west of Richmond City Center. Oliver Cowdery, along with many other Whitmer relatives, including Peter Whitmer Sr. and Mary Musselman Whitmer, are buried in the Pioneer Cemetery located on Highway 13, just north of the center of town. See Richard Neitzel Holzapfel and T. Jeffery Cottle, *Old Mormon Kirtland and Missouri: Historic Photographs and Guide* (Santa Ana, CA: Fieldbrook, 1991), 215–16.

7. John Henry Smith, Diary, November 30, 1910, John Henry Smith Papers, Family and Church History Department Archives, The Church of Jesus Christ of Latter-day Saints (hereafter Church Archives). All quotations from Smith's diary are from Jean Bickmore White, ed., *Church, State, and Politics: The Diaries of John Henry Smith* (Salt Lake City: Signature Books, 1990).

8. Wells, "Oliver Cowdery Monument," 251.

9. Wells, "Oliver Cowdery Monument," 251.

10. See Keith A. Erekson, "American Prophet, New England Town: The Memory of Joseph Smith in Vermont" (master's thesis, Brigham Young University, 2002).

11. Wells, "Oliver Cowdery Monument," 251.

12. Junius F. Wells to Heber J. Grant, August 26, 1924, Church Archives. All primary source material is found in the Junius F. Wells Papers, 1867–1930, Church Archives, unless otherwise noted. In the letter, Wells maintains that John Henry Smith promised him that additional monuments would be erected. He writes:

In 1918 the matter came up again for completing the plan and after a long consideration and favorable report being made by a committee of the Apostles a contract with me was authorized for the immediate erection at the grave of Martin Harris for the sum of $5800, with the further recommendation that I should also have the contract to erect the one promised at David Whitmer's grave later on—(The promise to do this was originally made by President John Henry Smith & virtually repeated at the dedication of Oliver Cowdery's in 1911.) As I was called to go upon a mission to Europe before the contract for the Harris monument was actually executed, it was decided to postpone the matter until my return. (Wells to Grant, August 26, 1924)

Neither a monument to Harris nor to Whitmer came to fruition under Wells's direction.

13. See Michael Kammen, *Mystic Chords of Memory: The Transformation of Tradition in American Culture* (New York: Knopf, 1991); G. Kurt Piehler, *Remembering War the American Way* (Washington, DC: Smithsonian, 1995); David W. Blight, *Race and Reunion: The Civil War in American Memory* (Cambridge, MA: Harvard University Press, 2001).

14. Wells, "Oliver Cowdery Monument," 251.

15. Erekson, "Memory of Joseph Smith in Vermont," 59–101.

16. R. C. Bowers to Junius F. Wells, February 13, 1911. Bowers's reference to multiple

monuments presumably has to do with Wells's ostensible desire to erect a monument for each witness.

17. R. C. Bowers to Junius F. Wells, April 7, 1911.

18. R. C. Bowers to Junius F. Wells, April 19, 1911.

19. "Agreement," May 19, 1911.

20. Anthon H. Lund (1844–1921) had served as first counselor since April 7, 1910.

21. Wells's published timeline, written nearly six months after the event, does not match the primary source record. Because he made several visits to Richmond within the space of three months, he probably could not recall the exact details of what happened during each visit. See Wells, "Oliver Cowdery Monument," 251.

22. Milton R. Merrill, *Reed Smoot: Apostle in Politics* (Logan: Utah State University Press, 1990), 33.

23. George Schweich to Junius F. Wells, May 27, 1911.

24. George Edward Anderson's notation on the glass plate edge of this photograph proves that this image was taken in 1911 and not, as previously thought, in 1907.

25. Wells, "Oliver Cowdery Monument," 253.

26. Smith, Diary, June 12, 1911, in White, *Church, State, and Politics*, 673.

27. Wells, "Oliver Cowdery Monument," 251.

28. R. C. Bowers to Junius F. Wells, August 4, 1911.

29. Philander Alma Page (1832–1919) was the son of Hiram Page, Cowdery's wife's brother-in-law. Julia Ann Whitmer Schweich (1835–1914) was David Whitmer's daughter and Cowdery's niece. George W. Schweich (1853–1926) was son of Julia Ann Whitmer Schweich, grandnephew of Cowdery.

30. Wells, "Oliver Cowdery Monument," 255–56.

31. Wells, "Oliver Cowdery Monument," 257.

32. "Certificate of Authority," August 8, 1911.

33. Wells, "Oliver Cowdery Monument," 254–55.

34. Wells, "Oliver Cowdery Monument," 259–60.

35. Junius F. Wells to W. A. Mullins, August 18, 1911.

36. "Petition," August 15, 1911; I. R. E. Brown to Honorable Mayor and City Council of Richmond, Mo., August 16, 1911.

37. Junius F. Wells to J. W. Hagans, August 18, 1911.

38. "Certificate," October 26, 1911. The books included the Book of Mormon, Doctrine and Covenants, Pearl of Great Price, and volume one of *History of the Church*. The periodicals included issues of publications then printed by various church organizations as well as a few that were no longer in publication. Wells chose a volume from the discontinued *Contributor* because it contained the history of the coming forth of the Book of Mormon by George Reynolds and a beautiful steel engraving of the Three Witnesses: Oliver Cowdery, David Whitmer, and Martin Harris. The photographs deposited included views of Salt Lake City and portraits of U.S. President William H. Taft, Oliver Cowdery, Joseph Smith, Hyrum Smith, Lucy Smith, Brigham Young, Wilford Woodruff, John Taylor, Lorenzo Snow, Joseph F. Smith, Anthon H. Lund, John Henry Smith, David Whitmer, George W. Schweich, and Julia Whitmer Schweich. The miscellaneous items included statistical information about Utah and the Church (sixty-two stakes, twenty missions, and 690 wards), a current Church directory of officers, programs from an "Old Folks Reception to William H. Taft, President of the U.S." and

the "Proceedings of the Dedication of the Joseph Smith Monument, at his birth place Sharon, Vermont, 1905."

39. See Susan Easton Black, "Pioneer Cemetery: Richmond, Ray County, Missouri," *Mormon Historical Studies* 2 (fall 2001): 183.

40. R. C. Bowers to Junius F. Wells, August 21, 1911.

41. Wells, "Oliver Cowdery Monument," 263.

42. This photograph has been mistaken to be "the base of the obelisk erected in 1905 at Joseph Smith's birthplace in the township of Sharon, Vermont." Richard H. Jackson, "Historical Sites," in *Encyclopedia of Mormonism*, ed. Daniel H. Ludlow, 4 vols. (New York: Macmillan, 1992), 2:592; see also Douglas F. Tobler and Nelson B. Wadsworth, *The History of the Mormons in Photographs and Text: 1830 to the Present* (New York: St. Martin's, 1989), 63.

43. Wells, "Oliver Cowdery Monument," 263.

44. R. C. Bowers to Junius F. Wells, October 10, 1911.

45. Junius F. Wells to Thomas Blount, October 14, 1911.

46. Junius F. Wells to R. C. Bowers, November 16, 1911.

47. Junius F. Wells to Thomas B. Blount, November 4, 1911.

48. Junius F. Wells to George D. Pyper, October 29, 1911.

49. Wells to Pyper, October 29, 1911.

50. Junius F. Wells to H. B. McIntyre, November 9, 1911.

51. Junius F. Wells to Joseph F. Smith, November 11, 1911.

52. Junius F. Wells to J. M. Ferguson and others, November 11, 1911.

53. Wells to Smith, November 11, 1911.

54. Wells to Smith, November 11, 1911.

55. Heber J. Grant (1856–1945) was ordained a member of the Council of the Twelve Apostles in 1882. Later he served as president of the Church from November 1918 to May 1945.

56. Wells, "Oliver Cowdery Monument," 265.

57. See Thomas G. Alexander, *Mormonism in Transition: A History of the Latter-day Saints, 1890–1930* (Urbana: University of Illinois Press, 1986), 16, 29–30, 32–33, 38–39, 201.

58. Alexander, *Mormonism in Transition*, 16, 29–30, 32–33, 38–39, 201.

59. Frederick M. Smith, "Open Letter to All People," *Salt Lake Tribune,* July 1, 1901, 3. Smith's article was actually less of a protest against the monument and more of a polemic against the Latter-day Saint Church's practice of polygamy, including the controversy surrounding Apostle Reed Smoot's senatorial candidacy. His mention of the monument was a foil used to initiate arguments against the church that, given the contemporary political climate and his involvement in the American Party's organization, might have been posed as political concerns that would become the tenets of the American Party.

60. Wells to Bowers, November 16, 1911.

61. Junius F. Wells to Charles E. Prispin, November 23, 1911; "Powell Brothers Receipt," November 23, 1911.

62. Wells, "Oliver Cowdery Monument," 267.

63. "Manley & Wading Receipt," November 23, 1911.

64. Junius F. Wells to L. H. Biglow, November 15, 1911.

65. "Tabernacle Choir Here," *Richmond Conservator*, November 23, 1911.

66. "Minutes of the Dedicatory Service and Unveiling of the Oliver Cowdery Monument," November 22, 1911. Apparently, the report was prepared by Louise Dansie of the Central States Mission Office; see Louise Dansie to Junius F. Wells, November 27, 1911.

67. "Minutes of Dedicatory Service," November 22, 1911.

68. "Minutes of Dedicatory Service."

69. "Minutes of Dedicatory Service."

70. "Minutes of Dedicatory Service."

71. "Minutes of Dedicatory Service."

72. "Minutes of Dedicatory Service." President Grant made a comment regarding David Whitmer being buried in the same cemetery as Oliver Cowdery, but this is inaccurate. Whitmer was in fact buried in the New City Cemetery west of Richmond.

73. George Edward Anderson was apparently not the only photographer present for the occasion. On November 23, Wells paid John Encoe $8.40 "for pictures." John Encoe, Receipt, November 23, 1911. Anderson and Encoe were well acquainted, having met in 1907 when Anderson was taking his first photographs of Church historical sites in Missouri. Richard Neitzel Holzapfel, T. Jeffery Cottle, and Ted D. Stoddard, *Church History in Black and White: George Edward Anderson's Photographic Mission to Latter-day Saint Historical Sites* (Provo, UT: Religious Studies Center, 1995), 75–76.

74. "Minutes of Dedicatory Service."

75. Wells, "Oliver Cowdery Monument," 272.

76. Junius F. Wells, Notes, November 22, 1911.

77. "Tabernacle Choir Here."

78. "Six Thousand Miles with the 'Mormon' Tabernacle Choir," 448.

Fig. 1. Patrick A. Bishop discovered this daguerreotype while perusing the Library of Congress Prints and Photographs Division. Preliminary comparisons to other known images of Oliver Cowdery suggests that this is an original daguerreotype of Cowdery. Courtesy Prints and Photographs Division, Library of Congress.

An Original Daguerreotype
of Oliver Cowdery Identified

Patrick A. Bishop

During my graduate studies I took on the project of obtaining photographic images of each apostle of this dispensation. The task proved difficult, but I found photographic likenesses for all but seven members of the First Presidency and Quorum of the Twelve Apostles of The Church of Jesus Christ of Latter-day Saints. My interest in collecting daguerreotypes has continued since that day, and it has led me to the discovery of what I believe is an original daguerreotype of Oliver Cowdery.

One criterion for authenticating an image is to see if the clothing fashions worn in the photo correspond to the person's age in that time period. Many Web sites have viewable copies of daguerreotypes. One of the best sites to find photographs of early clothing styles is the Library of Congress Prints and Photographs Division. On the evening of February 6, 2006, I was studying images thought to contain 1840s clothing styles, when daguerreotype 1363 (fig. 1) came up. This original daguerreotype, located at the Library of Congress Archives in Washington, DC, was entitled "Unidentified man, half-length portrait, with arm resting on table with tablecloth." There were also more facts about the daguerreotype on the information page.[1] I surmised that the portrait may contain the image of Oliver Cowdery. As I gave more consideration to this newly discovered image over the next few days, I decided to do a preliminary comparison between the image and other likenesses of Oliver Cowdery.

Fig. 2. Junius F. Wells. All images courtesy   Fig. 3. James H. Hart.
LDS Church Archives, Salt Lake City,
© Intellectual Reserve, Inc., unless noted.

Fig. 4 (left). Engraving of the Three
Witnesses printed for the October
1883 issue of the *Contributor*. This
engraving of Cowdery was taken
from an original daguerreotype
that was destroyed in a fire.

Fig. 5 (above). Painting of Cowdery
by John Willard Clawson. Courtesy
Joseph Smith Birth Home, Sharon,
Vermont.

Known Likenesses of Oliver Cowdery

In 1883, Junius F. Wells (fig. 2) decided to make an engraving of the Three Witnesses for publication in the October issue of the *Contributor*.[2] Images of Martin Harris and David Whitmer were obtained quite easily. Obtaining Oliver Cowdery's image, however, proved to be much more difficult. After much research, Wells discovered that Cowdery's daughter, Mrs. Charles Johnson, had both a portrait painting and a daguerreotype of her father. Elder James H. Hart (fig. 3) was sent by Junius F. Wells to obtain the daguerreotype.

After obtaining the image, Elder Hart gave the daguerreotype to H. B. Hall and Sons Engravers in New York to make a copy and the subsequent engraving that was published in the October 1883 *Contributor* (fig. 4). Elder Hart then returned the daguerreotype to the Johnsons' home. Not long after, the Johnsons' home was destroyed by fire, and both the original portrait and the daguerreotype of Cowdery were destroyed. Hence, the only portraits available are based on the engraving in the *Contributor*.[3]

Probably the best of these portraits is the one painted by John Willard Clawson that hangs in Joseph Smith's birth home in Sharon, Vermont (fig. 5). This portrait image was used for the program cover for the 1911 dedication of the Oliver Cowdery memorial monument in Richmond, Missouri.

One of the most popular images of Oliver Cowdery is the Charles W. Carter image (fig. 6). Some have assumed that this image is an actual photograph of Cowdery. The image appears to stem from the original that was destroyed by fire. The features

O. Cowdery

Fig.6. It is believed that Charles W. Carter took this photograph of an original daguerreotype of Oliver Cowdery, which was owned by Mrs. Charles Johnson. The original daguerreotype was subsequently destroyed in a house fire.

are not as sharp and defined as the portrait
by John Willard Clawson or the engraving by Hall and Sons. Ronald E. Romig,
head archivist of the Community of Christ
Library-Archives, indicated that the Carter
image given me was a copy of the glass-plate
negative of Cowdery (also by Carter) that is
held in the LDS Family and Church History
Department Archives. I then contacted
William W. Slaughter, photo archivist of the
LDS Church, and he confirmed that there is
not a record of what image Carter used for
his photograph. It is obviously not an original picture of Oliver while living, as Oliver
had died a decade before Carter started taking photographs. There is no known record
of Carter ever coming into contact with the
Johnsons to copy the daguerreotype.

Carter's photograph is most likely
taken from a copy of the original daguerreotype. It was a common practice in those
days to photograph paintings or other photos and make copies to be distributed. For
example, Carter took a photograph of an
oil painting of Joseph Smith that is now
owned by the Community of Christ (fig. 7).
That photograph is sometimes mistaken for
an original daguerreotype of Joseph taken
while he was living (figs. 7a, 7b).[4]

Regardless of the origin of the Carter
photo of Oliver, it is another witness to the
reliability of the other renderings of the
original Oliver Cowdery daguerreotype.
Because each image is so similar, examin-
ers have a very good knowledge of what he

Fig. 7 (top). Oil paint-
ing of Joseph Smith.
Courtesy Community of
Christ Library-Archives,
Independence, Missouri

Figs. 7a (middle), 7b (bottom). These two images are
often mistaken for original
daguerreotypes of Joseph
Smith while living.

looked like. All these likenesses provided the means necessary to identify the newly discovered daguerreotype.

Provenance

The most disappointing part of the discovery is the lack of provenance for the image. As seen on the notes from the Library of Congress, the image was sold to them in 1999 by Anthony Barboza, a photograph collector who currently resides in New York City. Because the image did not become available to public view until 1999, it is likely that no attempt was made to identify it until now. I contacted Anthony Barboza to ask him where he had obtained the image. He indicated that he bought most of the images in the 1970s and sold them to the Library of Congress. He kept no records from where or from whom he had purchased them. Since he bought the images thirty years ago, Barboza could not remember where he had obtained this particular daguerreotype.

I decided to contact the Library of Congress again and ask if I might schedule a trip to Washington, DC, to view and study the image. I had high hopes that the image contained some other clue to positively match the image to Cowdery. My desires were met with much resistance; I was told that because the original was so fragile, the only image they allowed anyone to view was a surrogate copy.

I called again later, hoping to finally prevail, but the request was again denied. This time, however, I persuaded the head curator to study the original image. The only additional information was given via e-mail on February 27, 2006. It included the measurements and type of case the image is contained in.[5] All other information about the image is given on the information page of the Web site.[6] Thus the quest to positively trace the image from the Library of Congress back to Oliver Cowdery ended rather quickly.

Proximity of Oliver Cowdery and J. P. Ball

Engraved on the brass plate just below the image of Cowdery is both the name of the daguerreotypist, James Presley Ball (fig. 8),

Fig. 8. James Presley Ball, a daguerreian who may have had contact with Oliver Cowdery. Courtesy Ester Hall Mumford, *Seattle's Black Victorians*

and the city of Cincinnati where he was employed. "A black daguerreian," J. P. Ball reportedly first learned the process in 1845. . . .

In the same year Ball opened a studio in Cincinnati, Ohio. In the spring of the following year, penniless, he closed his gallery and moved to Pittsburgh, Pa., and then to Richmond, Virginia, taking a job as a hotel waiter. When he accumulated a little money, he opened daguerreian rooms there.

In 1846–1847, he traveled as a daguerreian in Virginia and Ohio, and in 1847 opened Ball's Daguerreian Gallery of the West in Cincinnati, Ohio.[7]

From 1847 to 1850 Ball operated his studio alone. In 1851 his brother-in-law Alexander Thomas became his partner, and in 1858 the studio was renamed "Ball and Brothers" or "Ball and Thomas."[8] During the 1850s, it is likely that all the daguerreotypes the studio produced etched the names of Ball and Thomas into the case, as seen in many of the daguerreotypes housed in the Library of Congress. As the identified photo has only Ball's name engraved on the case, it is strong evidence that Ball took the daguerreotype sometime between 1845 and 1850 in Cincinnati or while he traveled in Ohio in 1846.

After Oliver Cowdery was excommunicated from The Church of Jesus Christ of Latter-day Saints in 1838, he moved back to Kirtland, Ohio, to study and practice law. In 1840 Cowdery moved to Tiffin, Ohio, where he practiced law and became a prominent civic leader and ardent Democrat.[9] Richard Lloyd Anderson writes of these years:

> Several remarkable estimates of Cowdery as a person stem from his political activities in two states while out of the Church. In Tiffin, Ohio, he was regularly before the public as an active party worker, public speaker, and occasional candidate for civil office. In 1842, 1844, and 1845, he was elected by the party township

meeting as delegate to the Democratic county convention. In all these years he was named on the resolutions committee at the county convention because of his characteristic role as an articulate party spokesman. He was regularly sent to political rallies as a persuasive stump speaker. In 1845 he was elected as one of three township trustees, defeating his nearest opponent by a twenty-six percent vote margin. In his last year of political activity in Tiffin, 1846, Cowdery was promoted for the office of state senator at a tri-county convention by a dozen delegates who were loyal to him through two ballots.[10]

If the daguerreotype is of Oliver Cowdery, it was undoubtedly taken during the years from 1845 to 1847. No hard evidence has been found yet placing J. P. Ball and Oliver Cowdery in the same place on the same day; this research is ongoing. However, the following information is worthy of note: First, J. P. Ball's studio was in operation in 1845 while Cowdery was being "regularly sent to political rallies" around the state. It is not unlikely that Cowdery would have gone to Cincinnati for one of these rallies. Second, J. P. Ball was traveling the state of Ohio taking photographs in 1846. Oliver Cowdery would have been a prime photographic candidate as a prominent civic leader and a respected lawyer in Ohio. Finally, while Junius F. Wells was trying to ascertain whether a photo existed or not, some friends of Oliver Cowdery indicated that a daguerreotype had been taken four years before his death.[11] This information would date the daguerreotype to 1846. After Hart received the now-lost daguerreotype from Mr. Johnson to make the engraving for the *Contributor,* the Johnsons and the Whitmers stated that that image of Cowdery was taken when he was about age forty-two, dating it to 1848.[12] Could it be that the newly identified daguerreotype is the one Cowdery's friends reported being taken in 1846? Some may argue that in this new image Cowdery appears older than in the 1848 image obtained from the Johnsons. It should be noted that the extant image from the Johnsons is a copy; engravers and portrait artists often leave out the aging features of the face, such as wrinkles and scars.

Cowdery had traveled to Cincinnati, Ohio, in response to a revelation stating, "And again, verily I say unto you, my servants, Sidney Rigdon, Joseph Smith, Jun., and Oliver Cowdery, shall not open their mouths in the congregations of the wicked until they arrive at Cincinnati" (D&C 61:30).

Two revelations are all that directly connect Cowdery to Cincinnati. They are both given in August 1831, fifteen years before the daguerreotype would have been taken. It is common, however, for one to go back to places of importance to visit or reflect on significant events in the past. Perhaps Cowdery was drawn to visit Cincinnati because of past events or associations made in that city.

Dating the Clothing and Photograph

As stated above, one criterion for authenticating an image of a person is to match the clothing fashions worn in the time period to the age of the person in the photo. It follows that the man in the image should be wearing mid-1840s clothing:

> 1840's men's fashion was marked by tightly tailored coats and trousers. . . . The coats were noticeable for their fitted sleeves and often featured oversized buttons. Frocks and cutaway coats were the most common style.
>
> Vests were still de rigueur and are seen in both notch and shawl collar variants as well as single and double breasted styles. Shirts featured a high straight collar, though some did appear with a slight turn-down over the cravat.
>
> At the outset of the decade cravats were relatively thin and often worn in the familiar bow tie style. But by the end of the decade, gentlemen wore very wide cravats, some of which featured frames to hold the fabric in place throughout the day. . . .

Fig. 9.

In contrast to the 1840's, the 1850's reflected a marked preference for bolder styling particulary seen in frock coats with wider lapels and looser cuts. Waistcoats became fancier with bold patterns and metal buttons. In the early part of the decade, gentlemen wore extravagant, heavily starched, assymetrically tied cravats, which subsided later in the decade to reflect softer styling. At the beginning of the decade many gentlemen wore their hair parted on the side styled with an extreme frontal wave on top, but once again this subsided toward the end of the decade.[13]

The daguerreotype concurs with these criteria for the clothing Cowdery would have worn in the mid-1840s. The man in the image (fig. 9) has a tightly fitted coat especially in the arms, a high collar, and a thinner cravat tied in a simple bow tie style. In 1846, Cowdery would have been forty years of age, matching the approximate age of the man in the image.

Facial Identification

In the mid-1990s Ephraim Hatch published a book entitled *Joseph Smith Portraits: A Search for the Prophet's Likeness.* In his book, Ephraim used a gridline system to verify whether or not facial features from portraits of Joseph Smith were a match to his death mask. This system is a good starting place. In doing a gridline comparison,

Fig. 10. This gridline comparison of facial features matches with exactness.

Fig. 11. Without the gridlines, each individual feature can be examined.

the engraving from the original daguerreotype of Cowdery was used, as it provides the most accurate comparison. As seen in fig. 10, the newly found image and the engraving match with exactness.

As the above method only takes into account the spatial orientation of the facial features, each individual feature should be examined closely. Again using the above two images with the gridlines removed (fig. 11), each feature will be examined.

Starting with the hair and moving down it can be seen very clearly that the hairline in both images match with a slight widow's peak. The hairstyle is also an exact match in both images, with the part on the same side, the slight wave on the comb-over in the front, and the sides combed forward with a distinctive "winged" look. The shape and size of the eyes and eyebrows are also excellent matches. Both noses are long and wide at the base, having the same shape from top to bottom. The lips on each are wide but thin, having a "clenched mouth" with slight creases in each corner of the mouth. Finally, the chin in both images is broad and gently pointed.

William Lang, an associate partner of law with Cowdery, wrote of his impressions of Cowdery while writing a history of Seneca County, Ohio. In that work, Lang produced the following description:

> Mr. Cowdery . . . had an open countenance, high forehead, dark brown eye, Roman nose, clenched lips and prominent lower jaw. He shaved smooth and was neat and cleanly in his person. He was of light stature, about five feet, five inches high, and had a loose, easy walk. With all his kind and friendly disposition, there was a certain degree of sadness that seemed to pervade his whole being.[14]

As one reads this description by William Lang it seems to be describing this newly found daguerreotype in every way.

Research Is Ongoing

While the observations in this article are not absolute, they do provide convincing evidence that this is indeed a heretofore-unknown image of Oliver Cowdery. Hopefully this preliminary study will be used as a platform to bolster further research and prove conclusively that the image is that of Oliver Cowdery. To establish a better provenance, further evidence might be collected by searching newspaper clippings, advertisements of the day, or other public records to see if Oliver Cowdery and J. P. Ball can be connected more substantially. Searching the journal entries of friends and family from both parties may also prove helpful. A facial recognition expert could further authenticate the image. These are beyond the realms of my capabilities at present.

This year, 2006, will mark the two-hundredth anniversary of Oliver Cowdery's birth. I hope that this newly identified image will be accepted and used as widely as possible to celebrate the accomplishments of this great man and his witness to all the key events of the restoration of The Church of Jesus Christ of Latter-day Saints.

Notes

Editors' note: This article was originally published in *BYU Studies* 45/2 (2006): 100–111.

1. Library of Congress, Prints and Photographs Online Catalogue, lcweb2.loc.gov/pp/dagquery.html (accessed February 6, 2006).

TITLE: [Unidentified man, half-length portrait, with arm resting on table with tablecloth]

CALL NUMBER: DAG no. 1363

MEDIUM: 1 photograph : quarter-plate daguerreotype.

CREATED/PUBLISHED: [between 1847 and 1860]
CREATOR: Ball, James Presely, 1825–1905
NOTES: Case: back only - Rinhart 108.
Barboza number: 6019.028.
Stamped on brass mat: J. P. Ball, Cincinnati.
Purchase; Anthony Barboza; 1999; (DLC/PP-1999:022).
Forms part of: Daguerreotype collection (Library of Congress).
REPOSITORY: Library of Congress Prints and Photographs Division,
Washington, DC 20540 USA
CARD #: 2004664581.

2.   For a full account of this story see Junius F. Wells, "The Three Witnesses," *Contributor* 5 (October 1883): 34–36.

3.   Junius F. Wells, "The Engraving of the Three Witnesses," *Improvement Era* 30 (January 1927): 1024.

4.   Ronald E. Romig and Lachlan Mackay, "What Did Joseph Smith Look Like?" *Saints Herald* 141/12 (December 1994): 9.

5.   Personal e-mail from Library of Congress Prints and Photographs Division to Patrick A. Bishop, February 26, 2006, copy in author's possession, as follows: "The daguerreotype #1363 has the following measurements: Length (top to bottom) 12 cm or 4 3/4 inches. Width (side to side) 9.5 cm or 3 3/4 inches. Height (thickness) 1 cm or 3/8 inches. The front cover of the case is missing. The back cover has an embossed design of flowers. All other marks and other unique information have been included in the online bibliographic record. There are no other marks etched, embossed, engraved or otherwise written on the back case. Since the front cover is missing, I am unable to tell you of anything that may have been included in the interior of the case."

6.   lcweb2.loc.gov/cgi-bin/query/D?ils:40:./temp/~pp_BLYW:: (accessed October 2, 2006).

7.   Craig's Daguerreian Registry: The Acknowledged Resource on American Photographers 1839–1860, www.daguerreotype.com (accessed February 18, 2006). See Deborah Willis, *Reflections in Black* (New York: W. W. Norton, 2000), 4–5; and Willis, *J. P. Ball, Daguerrean and Studio Photographer* (New York: Garland, 1993), xiv–xv.

8.   Willis, *J. P. Ball, Daguerrean and Studio Photographer*, 303.

9.   Richard Lloyd Anderson, "Cowdery, Oliver," in *Encyclopedia of Mormonism*, ed. Daniel H. Ludlow, 4 vols. (New York: Macmillan, 1992), 1:338.

10.   Richard Lloyd Anderson, *Investigating the Book of Mormon Witnesses* (Salt Lake City: Deseret Book, 1981), 42–43.

11.   Wells, "Three Witnesses," 34.

12.   Wells, "Three Witnesses," 35.

13.   Gentleman's Emporium, "Gentleman's Portrait Gallery 1840's," www.gentlemansemporium.com/1840-victorian-photo-gallery.php (accessed February 5, 2006).

14.   William Lang, *History of Seneca County* (Springfield, OH: Transcript Printing, 1880), 365.

Reuben Miller, Recorder of
Oliver Cowdery's Reaffirmations

Richard Lloyd Anderson

One of the spectacular events of Latter-day Saint history unfolded as Oliver Cowdery walked into a conference session in progress at Council Bluffs in 1848 and was personally escorted to the stand by his friend Orson Hyde. That his remarks on that occasion were a striking vindication of Mormon claims is shown in all recollections of the event. George A. Smith wrote within ten days: "His testimony produced quite a sensation among the gentlemen present who did not belong to the church, and it was gratefully received by the Saints."[1] No one in the latter group seems to have been more impressed than Reuben Miller, who at the same meeting had made his own public reconciliation with the Church. At least, no one else is known to have recorded the Cowdery remarks in such detail. The reality of the return of the former "Second Elder" does not rest alone on the Reuben Miller account, since a score of solid historical references disprove an anonymous "confession" describing the astounding feat of impersonating Cowdery before hundreds of his former intimates. But while the return itself is abundantly attested, no historical source but the Miller account adequately reveals Oliver Cowdery's public testimony upon his return to the Church.

The Miller-reported speech recounts the irony of Cowdery's humble return contrasted with the presiding and initiating power that he once held; he reiterated Orson Hyde's observations that any successful career in the Church must be based on loyalty to the true priesthood leaders. There is a considerable amount of historical information about Cowdery while he was out of the Church that portrays the cofounder of Mormonism in just this light, as one who took a good deal of personal pride in his spiritual experiences in founding the Restored Church and as one who was considerably pained by his separation from its people. The main interest of his returning speech, however, is doctrinal. He discounted the Spaulding story as totally inconsistent with his own experience as secretary to Joseph Smith during the production of the Book of Mormon. He publicly reaffirmed the chief facts within his knowledge of the founding of the Church:

> I wrote with my own pen the entire Book of Mormon (save a few pages) as it fell from the lips of the Prophet. . . I beheld with my eyes, and handled with my hands, the gold plates from which it was translated. I also beheld the Interpreters. . . .
>
> I was present with Joseph when an holy angel from God came down from heaven and conferred, or restored, the Aaronic Priesthood and said at the same time that it should remain upon the earth while the earth stands.
>
> I was also present with Joseph when the Melchisedek Priesthood was conferred by the holy angels[2] of God, which we then confirmed on each other, by the will and commandment of God.[3]

An occasional anti-Mormon writer has denied the accuracy of this discourse on the grounds that it was not printed until a decade after the event, but it appears in Miller's journal, a contemporaneous document. In printing this journal account later, Miller insisted that he made notes at the time and consequently had a "verbatim report."[4] Whether that is believed obviously depends upon whether or not one trusts Miller. And in investigating that question, what emerges is not only his individualistic integrity, but also his experience as a reporter and his unusual interest in both the visions of the Restoration and in Cowdery as a person.

Prominence in Utah

Coincidence brought Cowdery and Miller together in the Kanesville conference session of October 21, 1848. In the following year, Cowdery was stricken with his last illness in Richmond, Missouri, while Miller had migrated to Salt Lake Valley and was beginning his one-third century's prominence there as a farmer, businessman, civic leader, and pioneer bishop. In his second year of residence in the valley he was appointed bishop of the Mill Creek Ward and held this position until his death in 1882.[5] The year after he became bishop he entered county government as a select-man, the equivalent of today's commissioner. This post he also held until his death. John Taylor, then President of the Church, spoke at his funeral, paying tribute to him as a "highminded, honorable man." Another speaker at Miller's funeral was the perceptive and candid Elias Smith who, as probate judge, had been chairman of county government for the entire time of Miller's tenure. Something of Miller's personal character merges in Smith's estimate: what impressed him was Miller's "wide practical experience coupled with the best of judgment, to say nothing of his uprightness and honesty, which he possessed to an eminent degree."[6] Biographical sketches of Miller verify his prominence and effectiveness as a pioneer and community leader in Utah and describe other facets of his life, such as his successful farming and business operations[7] and his large and able family.[8] The Church newspaper editorialized on these quali-ties at his death: "He was an active and capable man, with a strong individuality, and both as Bishop and Selectman, was an able public servant, whose services and experience were of great value to the community."[9]

No doubt his contributions to Utah merit further study, but it is the story of Reuben Miller's religious convictions and conflicts in the pre-Utah period that shows why he would be an accurate reporter of Cowdery's recollections of the supernatural events of the founding of Mormonism.

Miller's Conversion

As a young man Miller migrated from his Pennsylvania birth-place to Illinois, where he became first a millwright, then a substan-tial farmer in Ottawa, La Salle County. There, as an undoubtedly

respected member of the community,[10] he became a Mormon convert (1843) while in his early forties. That he was early given important Church positions demonstrated his ability and reliability. The
year following his baptism, he was selected as bishop in the formal
organization of the Latter-day Saints in his area.[11] A machine dupli-
cation exists of a Miller letter dated July 29, 1845, which describes
what must be typical activities of the period of this early bishop-
ric. He reports to William Clayton that he is about to leave La Salle
County for Chicago to facilitate transportation of several wagon
loads of goods (particularly glass) to Nauvoo, and that he will use
three yoke of oxen taken in tithing. Miller's own summary of his
early performance in the Church was made in 1846 and lists a call
to settle at Nauvoo, an assignment as collection agent for tithing and
building funds, and appointment as "the leader of a company to go
West in the coming Spring."[12] The pursuance of this calling was the
beginning of an episode in Reuben Miller's life that is but faintly disclosed in published sketches and yet is the key to his intense interest
in Oliver Cowdery's words at the time of his return.

Belief in Strang's Revelations

James J. Strang maintained that Joseph Smith wrote a letter
appointing him as successor, that this appointment was effected
through the visit of an angel, and that the location of ancient plates
was also revealed. By the Urim and Thummim he translated their
message: the "forerunner" (Joseph Smith) would be slain, but the
translator of the records (James J. Strang) would be a "mighty
Prophet." The documents embodying these revelations were printed,
along with the testimony of witnesses to Strang's plates, in the initial number of the *Voree Herald* in January, 1846, immediately
before Reuben Miller's first contact with Strang. Both men were in
northern Illinois, Miller attempting to effect the gathering west and
Strang attempting to prevent it. The most detailed account of their
confrontation is found in the Strangite *Chronicles of Voree*, the manuscript history of this movement. Miller is introduced in that record
as "a man of distinguished worth and sterling integrity."[13] The nar-

rative relates that William Marks was instrumental in introducing Miller to Strang's disciples, who arranged that he should hear Strang present his claims, with the privilege of refutation allowed. On January 12, 1846, this meeting took place before an audience of about sixty. Strang spoke four hours "in his rapid manner," and Reuben Miller was impressed:

> High Priest Reuben Miller said that the main points and principles which had been set out were well sustained by the authorities referred to in the Book of Doctrines and Covenants, that he was not able to contend against the force of them. Strang had all the authorities on his side. And as nothing but truth would do them any good he consented then to learn the truth by all their testimonies which God had given and should give them and to receive the truth, whatsoever it might be.[14]

Miller queried Strang closely on the details of his appointment by divine manifestations. Sincere if somewhat naive, he determined to "go to Nauvoo and see What discoveries I could make in regard to Joseph's writing such an appointment and the claims of the Twelve to the Presidency of the Church."[15] Admittedly "mired in Strangism,"[16] *he approached Brigham Young on January 30, 1846. The leader of the Twelve grasped* the central issue, Miller's search for direct revelation to establish divine authority:

> Yesterday I had some conversation with Reuben Miller of Ottowa, he being considerably bewildered by Strang's new fangled revelation—rendered him almost devoid of reason although apparently honest in what he was doing, and said the word of the Lord would be decidedly satisfactory to him—whereupon I said, Thus saith the Lord unto Reuben Miller through Brigham Young—that Strang is a wicked and corrupt man and that his revelations are as false as he is—there-fore turn away from his folly—and never let it be said of Reuben Miller that he was ever led away and entangled by such nonsense. Thus saying, I left him, my time being too precious to be spent in hearing and even talking about such trash.[17]

Still believing in the reality of Strang's vision of appointment, Miller publicly lectured some six weeks longer in Nauvoo for the new cause; thereafter, he left for Strangite organizational conferences in Wisconsin.[18]

Miller's thinking at the point of Strangite conversion is revealed not only in the Strang records and the Journal History of Brigham Young, but also in his own accounts of the experience. His recollections minutely agree with these two contemporary records in stressing "a divine appointment through Joseph"[19] as the foundation upon which acceptance of Strang was built. Miller alludes more than once to the initial number of the *Voree Herald,* which he examined "carefully."[20] Since this issue contained the basic documents alleging Strang's divine commission, Miller's emphasis upon it shows that he regarded the visitation of heavenly messengers as conclusively establishing authority to represent God: "The Voree Herald was placed in my hands; I read it with care, and at that time not having a very great knowledge of the Law of the Church or the Book of Doctrine and Covenants—I considered his appointment and his arguments reasonable."[21]

It is evident that Reuben Miller thought that these documents would impress other Latter-day Saints, for he shortly brought out 3,000 copies of a tract entitled *A Defence of the Claims of James J. Strang to the Authority Now Usurped by the Twelve; and Shewing Him to be the True Successor of Joseph Smith, as First President of the High Priesthood.*[22] The pamphlet is characteristic of Miller's frame of reference. He regards divine manifestations as the source of authority and uses the approach of merely reprinting the "historical" basis of Strang's authority, with a minimum of comment.[23]

Disbelief in Strang's Revelations

Miller was soon disenchanted with Strang and came to doubt the integrity of his divine commission. The pamphlet defending Strang was in the press in February 1846, about a month after his conversion. His commitment then was serious enough not only to publish this pamphlet, but also to be agent in notifying the Twelve of their impending excommunication by Strang, and to participate in the event as high councilman in the Strangite April Conference, when he was sustained as "President of the Stake at Voree."[24] In repeated organizational meetings, Miller frequently served as a clerk in recording minutes of speeches and transactions.[25] But this close and official contact with Strang only hastened disillusionment. In a later pamphlet Miller explained that in the beginning Strang took the clear position that the appointing angel merely appeared and announced his authority, and did not perform any ordaining ceremony through the laying on of hands. Miller thus expected the proper ordination to follow in Strang's organizational conferences, since he knew that Strang was merely an elder and held no keys of priesthood leadership. When no such ordination materialized, Miller temporarily held his peace until he heard that Strang now claimed that an elaborate ordination ceremony had accompanied the initial angelic visitation. Miller bluntly accused Strang of manufacturing a new story "that was entirely contradictory to his former remarks (on this subject) to myself and others." In the same pamphlet Miller reveals his own thinking upon being confronted with the second, contradictory version of Strang's visitation:

> I came to the conclusion, irresistibly, that I had embraced an error, a delusion, and one that would be handed down on the pages of history, as a monument of his folly and of the corruption and wickedness of the human heart; and that it was a duty which I owed to God and to his people, to resign my station as President over the Stake, and my place on the High Council, and give my reasons for the same to the brethren. This I done on the 27th of June last, at the meeting ground in Voree.[26]

The Strang collection at Yale contains detailed notes of a Miller speech dated July 25, 1846, the essence of which is his insistence that Strang's authority and revelations do not measure up to the patterns of Joseph Smith's priesthood and the testimony of the witnesses of the Book of Mormon.[27]

Miller now resolutely retraced his steps. The trustees at Nauvoo communicated with Brigham Young on October 20 that Reuben

Miller had been baptized the previous day.[28] In response to a later summons by Strang to defend his membership, Miller issued a terse ultimatum of his own. Insisting that he had told nothing but the truth about Strang, he requested "the favor to cut me off immediately." In his blunt critique of Strang, Miller saw a single issue: "You hold no authority to remove me from the Church of Christ or to give or take the priesthood of the Son of God. So go ahead."[29]

Missionary to the Strangites

Not content with verbal and local disassociation with Strang, Miller took unhesitating steps to set the printed record straight. Because of "a duty which I conscientiously believed I owed to God and to his church" he published in September 1846 the pamphlet, *James J. Strang, Weighed in the Balance of Truth, and Found Warning. His Claims as First President of the Melchisedek Priesthood Refuted.* He challenged Strang's "appointment" as fraudulent and his witnesses of plates inadequate in comparison to those of the Book of Mormon.[30] He perceived Strang as the inventor of false experiences: his ordination by "an unknown messenger" is a defective "picture to hand down upon a church record to future generations."[31] Later, Miller was outraged by John C. Bennett's version of Strang's appointment, and before February, 1847, he published his second attack upon Strang's legitimacy: *Truth Shall Prevail: a Short Reply to an Article Published in the Voree Herald (Reveille), by J. C. Bennett; and the Willful Falsehoods of J.J. Strang, Published in the First Number of Zion's Reveille.*[32] Again, Miller was preoccupied with documentation. Affidavits of prominent Strangites were given to show that Miller was correct in maintaining that Strang had switched stories on his ordination. The printed revelations of Joseph Smith were cited to prove that the laying on of hands characterized the restoration of both the Aaronic and Melchizedek Priesthoods. As for Strangite impeachments of Miller, he retorted: "They cannot injure me with their lies and hellish spirit of revenge. *I hold the documents in my hands.*"[33]

With their taste and talent for polemics, Strang and his associates lost no time in excoriating Miller. They answered his first pamphlet with the sneer, "Reuben 'is a great man of the kind,' but the *kind* is very peculiar, Brighamite, and terrestrial."[34] Bennett's answer to the second pamphlet was a general denial, prefaced by the significant admission, "I have heretofore regarded Mr. Miller as a man of unquestioned probity."[35] Even though Miller stirred up bitter charges of misrepresentation, it must be admitted that his character fared surprisingly well in Strangite circles. After most of the issues ceased to be current, Strang still referred to him as one of the "several men of talent and influence [that have] separated from me . . ."[36] This is an important point in assessing Miller's trustworthiness as a recorder of Cowdery's returning discourse. Miller proved his independence by dissenting openly both in Nauvoo and Voree; he also proved his reputability by earning the grudging respect of the leaders of both camps who differed from his position. An enlightening confirmation of the sincerity of such respect comes from the letters to Strang of "Louisa," in Dale Morgan's phrase "a superb woman." She first doubted Strang because her high opinion of Miller postulated "some very good and substantial reason" for his dissent, although her revulsion of polygamy kept her from following Miller in his loyalty to the Twelve. She said of Miller: "I have known him for a long time, and his conduct has always been such as to give me a high opinion of his integrity and uprightness. I cannot believe that he would intentionally do wrong or suffer himself to be influenced by any improper motives."[37]

Reuben Miller's lot was now cast with the people whom he regarded as holding true authority: "I have truly and sincerely repented of my course and conduct, and have traveled 270 miles and was baptized for the remission of sins, and had my priesthood confirmed."[38] His source of authority and direction was the Twelve, with whom there seems to have been considerable mutual respect. Even during his days as the emissary of Strang in Nauvoo, he reports a cordial relationship:

[I]n justice to the Twelve I must say, while investigating their claims to the Presidency of the Church, and that of Mr. Strang; they treated me kindly, and affectionately, and as brothers; reasoned with me, and remembered me in their prayer meetings, and done all that was required at their hands as servants of God in my case, to save me from what they said they knew to be a delusion of the blackest die. But I could not see the force and power of their argument, for I was completely mired in the spirit of apostacy, and when they shook hands with me the last time I saw them, they blessed me in the name of the Lord, and said I would return to the bosom of the Church again.[39]

His correspondence in the Church Historian's Office reveals a deep though not abject desire to be reinstated to his former status of trust with the leaders of the Church. On November 17, 1846, he wrote from Nauvoo to Elders Young and Kimball, "I have examined myself and believe I acted in honest sincerity." He further stated, "I come before you in all confidence, believing as I do that God has forgiven me," and called the attention of "Bro. Brigham" to their last conversation, when "you told me I would see my error before six months and would again return to the bosom of the Church." He sought approval for his missionary activities among the Strangites, whom he now sought to reclaim.

Miller's private correspondence from Wisconsin shortly before rejoining the migrating Saints consistently emphasizes the double theme of honoring his priesthood authority, all the more important now after the risk of losing it, and of reaching anyone in his former status of a deceived believer. His letter to Brigham Young on April 21, 1847, insists:

Brother Young, my object is to do good and be useful in the day and generation in which I live, magnify my priesthood, and assist to build up the kingdom of God, and truly as far as in me lies be a servant of the Lord. Therefore I consider it right to use all honorable means to redeem the Saints from the spiritual darkness in which the devil has thrown them and bring them back to the true fold and the principles of immortal glory.

A similar letter to Brigham Young on February 5, 1847, reiterates Miller's strongest theme, underlined by himself: "And by the grace of God that priesthood *shall be magnified.*" This means to Miller an intensified campaign of disseminating his writings among the Strangites. This letter asks for some official reaction to his first pamphlet and states that in the absence of direction, "I consider it for the welfare of the cause of God to publish my second epistle," which was enclosed with this letter. He admits that his publications might be seen as too contentious, but insists that the best way to reach those deceived is by printing the truth.

On Reuben Miller's side, his writings seem to have been a substantial influence in disillusioning Strang's followers. The letter just quoted states that the initial pamphlet against Strang produced "a great revolution. . . among the honest Saints." "Whole branches" were affected, and requests were received "almost daily" for the publication. That Miller's publications had such an effect is revealed in Strangite correspondence. For instance, Lester Brooks wrote from Ohio to the Wisconsin headquarters on January 12, 1847, that on his recent stopover in New York he found the branch in a "most stupid condition. They have a pamphlet written by Reuben Miller against Brother Strang. They are inclined to think there is something quite wrong."[40] Another Strang adherent wrote him by way of deploring dissent from him, reviewing as a major crisis the fact that "that paper Miller put out was circulated with triumph."[41]

Miller's Contact with Cowdery

Miller's own motivation was the sole reason for his publications, since he received no encouragement from the leaders of the Church. At the time of his reconversion they had written him,[42] but in the next six months no other letter was received.[43] On April 21, 1847, as just discussed, Miller appealed for direction once more, describing his past publishing activities. In addition, he reported rumors of a planned Strangite mission to England and indicated that he was countering it by preparing a documentary communication for the British Mission "in which is embodied some of the visions and

revelations of Mr. Strang," together with "the full history" of their
newly established secret ceremonies. While former information from
Miller seems to have been received without complete enthusiasm,[44]
this last letter provoked the bluntest direction from the Church leaders. It was not delivered until some five months later on the Platte
River, and was answered by Willard Richards "as an individual" after
the Council had declined to answer Miller formally. Richards' answer
of September 17, 1847, assumes that Strang's claims are patently ridic-
ulous and thus takes a dim view of Miller's writings as useless controversy. Richards further alludes to "the many calls of the council
for you to come home" and chides Miller for "wasting so much time
with your pen" instead of acting on their advice. One who reads this
letter will realize that Miller was given a stinging rebuke, despite, in
Richards' words, the "spirit of kindness that has dictated it."[45]

Some ten miles from Reuben Miller's residence near Burlington,
Wisconsin, was Elkhorn, Wisconsin, to which Oliver Cowdery had
moved shortly before Miller was told in no uncertain terms of his
duty to migrate west.[46] The two men were now in remarkably similar circumstances, for the reconciliation of Oliver Cowdery had been
effected through the means of Phineas Young (Brigham's brother
and Cowdery's brother-in-law), and the invitation to be baptized
and gather with the Saints was extended in a letter to Cowdery of
November 22, 1847, sent from Winter Quarters by Elders Young and
Richards for the Twelve.[47] Thus both Miller and Cowdery were in
close proximity in the winter of 1847, and both were making plans
to dispose of their properties and join the Saints migrating west.
Cowdery's response (February 27, 1848) to Brigham Young expresses
his hope to be present at April Conference at Winter Quarters.[48]
Because of a combination of poverty, ill health, and personal proj-
ects, Cowdery did not fulfill this plan, and he explained to Phineas
Young in a letter of April 16, 1848, that he still planned to migrate
but was counting heavily on help from Reuben Miller:

> Brother Miller has manifested the right spirit on the subject of
> my going West, nor does he know but I am now on my way, or

there, ere this, and he said that he will furnish me with a team, if I
went in the fall, and go up when he does, as he intends to go if he
succeeds in making a sale. He will do that at any rate, if I wish it,
and as much more as you shall say is the wish or advice of Brother
Brigham.[49]

The financial condition of the two men on the eve of their
return to the Church as portrayed in the foregoing letter of Cowdery
is confirmed by the existing deeds on file in Walworth County,
where both resided. Miller had sold farmland on June 10, 1848, for
a recited consideration of $1,000, which probably did not constitute
his total assets.[50] On the other hand, Cowdery held title only to his
Elkhorn residential property, then subject to mortgage, and did not
locate a buyer until long after the above letter. The sale was made,
for a recited consideration of $300 on October 3, 1848, and there is
reason to assume that debts encroached upon this small sum.[51]

Cowdery's deed of sale marks an approximate time of departure
for his return to the Church at Council Bluffs, inasmuch as one of the
witnesses on the deed is "Phineas H. Young," his brother-in-law, in
Elkhorn to assist in his return to the Church. Reuben Miller had left
with his family for Council Bluffs some three weeks earlier, noting
in his journal the departure from the Burlington, Wisconsin, area
on September 12, 1848. Miller traveled through La Salle County,
Illinois, where he stopped with former acquaintances in this area
of his initial career in the Church. At this point the most important entry of the journey appears under the date of September 18,
1848: "Here we met Bro. Phineas H. Young and stopped with him
the remainder of the day. I paid to him 30 dollars in money, and 31
dollars on Bro. Oliver Cowdery, making in all 81 dollars."[52]

From the Cowdery deed of sale in Elkhorn two weeks after this,
it is clear that Phineas Young was on his way then to get Cowdery and
his small family.[53] The Miller journal entry fits precisely the earlier
Cowdery letter representing Miller's willingness to contribute money
to Cowdery's return. Because of his earlier departure Reuben Miller
arrived in Kanesville, according to his journal, in the late afternoon
of Sunday, October 15, 1848. Cowdery arrived just six days later,

proceeding immediately to the session of conference that he addressed. Just before Cowdery's arrival, Miller had himself addressed the conference, making public acknowledgment of his mistake in believing Strang's revelation.[54] It is obvious that he was necessarily interested in the parallel situation of Cowdery's return, especially in the reiteration of Cowdery's solemn witness to the reality of the revelation that stood as the foundation of Mormonism. The proof of this is a private letter from Reuben Miller to his friends in La Salle County, Illinois, after his own return to the Church in Kanesville. No letter of the Apostle Paul to his converts is more ecstatic. Miller insists that his faith has found nothing but confirmation:

> Yes, true it is the church has been nourished and fed according to the word of God. And the kingdom of our God has moved steadily on amidst all the opposition of the apostates and wicked and corrupt men. I can say to you and to all my friends and brethren that I have come *home*. And never felt more at *home* in all my life. It really appears as though the trees, Bluffs, and every thing around us are praising King Immanuel. While the *holy priesthood* is swaying a scepter in *righteousness* that will sooner or later arouse the nations of the earth from their *midnight slumber of ages*. Yes, there is a *spirit* and *power* with this people that no mortal arm can withstand, or any nation or kingdom overthrow.[55]

Reuben Miller had once detected inconsistent testimony from James J. Strang and fallen into deepest disillusionment. The profound conviction of the Kanesville letter of November 16, 1848, rests in no small part upon the consistent reaffirmations of the "Second Elder" on his return, for the postscript of this letter of elation reads: "Brother Oliver Cowdery is here and has been baptized by Elder Hyde on last Sunday, is again restored, and bears a strong and positive testimony. This people are *united*, and are a *good, great,* and *mighty* people."

Conclusions

In summary, an informed reader of the Reuben Miller account of Cowdery's speech on his return to the Church will recognize the following insights into Miller's personality, interests, and abilities: (1) No religious vagabond bent on exploiting Mormon factions, Miller changed his affiliation once and was recognized by associates in both groups then and throughout later life as a man of independence and honesty. (2) Because of his conversion to and deconversion from Strang's claims of visions, he was intensely interested in the validating evidence of the revelations of Joseph Smith. (3) His specific religious interest, revealed in his pamphlets, is in the question of priesthood authority through the physical presence and ordination of resurrected beings. His general interest is in the integrity of supernatural experience, including the reality of the plates of the Book of Mormon. (4) In his own words, he was concerned with "a church record" for "future generations" and was highly sensitive to what "would be handed down on the pages of history." His experience of being deceived by contradictory documents led him to this position. (5) His experience in writing (including the publication of three pamphlets) and minute-taking demonstrates some skill in recording the essentials of public speeches. (6) He contributed financially to Oliver Cowdery's return and was vitally interested in him because of proximity and similar circumstances in returning to the Church. (7). Because of a Miller letter written four weeks after Cowdery's return and while Cowdery was still at Kanesville, there is clear evidence independent of the journal that Miller was at the time deeply impressed with the "strong and positive testimony" of the returning Second Elder.

No one in 1848 had more access to the facts of the modern dispensation than Oliver Cowdery. And no one in his audience that October had better motivation and capacity to record Cowdery's reaffirmations than Reuben Miller.

Notes

Editors' note: This article was originally published in *BYU Studies* 8/3 (1968): 277–93.

1.   Letter of George A. Smith to Orson Pratt from Council Bluffs, October 31, 1848, cited in *Millennial Star* 11 (January 1, 1849): 14.

2.   This term, plural in the original Reuben Miller Journal, was made singular in the

initial *Deseret News* printing of the incident. Later changes adding the plural form have been wrongly interpreted as tampering with the text.

3.   Reuben Miller Journal, Family and Church History Department Archives, The Church of Jesus Christ of Latter-day Saints, Salt Lake City, Utah (hereafter cited as Church Archives). As noted, the text differs in some minor wording from the initial publication during the life of Reuben Miller, *Deseret News*, April 13, 1859, 48. All quotations made from original documents in this article are exact, with the exception of punctuation and spelling corrections.

4.   *Deseret Evening News*, April 13, 1859, 48.

5.   Andrew Jenson, *Encyclopedic History of the Church of Jesus Christ of Latter-day Saints* (Salt Lake City: Deseret News, 1941), 504.

6.   *Deseret Evening News*, July 26, 1882.

7.   See Frank Esshom, *Pioneers and Prominent Men of Utah*, vol. 2 (Salt Lake City: Utah Pioneers, 1913), 1040: "He was known to be a hard worker and a keen business man, and succeeded in accumulating considerable worldly goods."

8.   Andrew Jenson, *Latter-day Saint Biographical Encyclopedia*, vol. 3 (Salt Lake City: Western Epics, 1971), 166–67, gives details of his wives and children. In 1918 total descendants were 360. The National Historical Record Company's *Biographical Record of Salt Lake City and Vicinity* (Chicago: National Historical Record Co., 1902), published biographies of Miller and five sons who were active in business and community affairs.

9.   *Deseret Evening News*, July 26, 1882. One instance is Miller's service as a delegate to the convention for forming a state constitution, January 20, 1862. Orson F. Whitney, *History of Utah*, 4 vols. (Salt Lake City: G. Q. Cannon & Sons, 1893), 2:39.

10.   In his pamphlet exposing Strang, *James J. Strang, Weighed in the Balance of Truth, and Found Wanting* (Burlington, W. T. [i.e. Wisconsin Territory]: s.n., 1846), 5, Miller challenged anyone doubting his integrity to "write to Ottawa, LaSalle Co., Illinois." Later called on a mission to this area, he wrote (Ottawa, LaSalle Co., Ill., January 24, 1870) that he was personally well treated; in spite of basic prejudice against his message, many came to hear him preach "for respect to an old neighbor" (*Deseret Evening News*, February 8, 1870).

11.   The date, October 23, 1844, and basic facts agree in Joseph Smith, *History of The Church of Jesus Christ of Latter-day Saints*, ed. B. H. Roberts, 2nd ed. rev., 7 vols. (Salt Lake City: Deseret Book, 1971), 7:311–12, and in Miller's résumé, 1 (cited in the previous footnote).

12.   Ibid. See Journal History of the Church, September 24, 1845, Church Archives (hereafter cited as Journal History), microfilm copy in Harold B. Lee Library, Brigham Young University, Provo, Utah, where Reuben Miller is listed with several dozen local leaders to effect the exodus to Nauvoo.

13.   *Chronicles of Voree*, 52, microfilm negative at the State Historical Society of Wisconsin.

14.   Ibid., 52–53.

15.   Miller, *James J. Strang*, 1.

16.   Ibid.

17.   History of Brigham Young, January 30, 1846, Church Archives, cited by S. Dilworth Young, "An Experiment in Feeling," Brigham Young University, *Speeches of the Year*, January 17, 1967, 11.

18. Miller's activity in Nauvoo and complete commitment to Strang at this period are recorded both in his *James J. Strang*, 2, and also a letter written to Strang from Nauvoo, February 15, 1845, Strang Collection, Yale University Library, New Haven, Connecticut (hereafter cited as Strang Collection).

19. Reuben Miller, *Truth Shall Prevail* (Burlington, W. T. [Wisconsin Territory]: s.n., 1847), 6.

20. Ibid., 4.

21. Miller, *James J. Strang*, 1.

22. Proof of Miller's authorship and the fact that the pamphlet basically reproduces the initial number of the *Voree Herald* are discussed by Dale Morgan, "A Bibliography of the Church of Jesus Christ of Latter-day Saints [Strangite]," *Western Humanities Review* 5 (winter 1950–51): 51–52.

23. Only four pages out of sixteen are original, and even these are highly documentary. Two pages treat "The Doctrine of Primitive Mormonism" and another two pages contain "Irresistible Conclusions," all of which is really an argument for Strang based on the laws of succession from the Doctrine and Covenants.

24. References to these and other less important events in Miller's Strangite period in the *Chronicles of Voree* (n.p.: n.d.) attest to his prominence: 24, 63–64, 67–68, 76, 85. By p. 99 Miller is conspicuous by his absence at the September 1, 1846, conference.

25. Ibid., 67, 76, 85.

26. Miller, *James J. Strang*, 3–4.

27. Miller speech, July 25, 1846, Strang Collection. It is likely that either the Miller or Strang manuscript date is wrong and that the two speeches are the same, since the content Miller describes corresponds exactly to the main outline of the speech of the Strang manuscript. For further evidence of Miller's outspoken opposition see also two letters from John C. Bennett from Burlington, Wisconsin, on August 18 and August 20, 1846, Strang Collection, recognizing the impact of "the whole Miller conspiracy."

28. Journal History, November 4, 1846; see also ibid., November 11, 1846, 3, which quotes a letter of John M. Bernhisel of November 4, 1846: "Reuben Miller has recently been here, was baptized and ordained again, and then returned to Voree to enlighten his benighted and deluded brethren."

29. Letter from Reuben Miller to James Strang, Burlington, Wisconsin, Dec. 23, 1846, Strang Collection.

30. Miller, *James J. Strang*, 10, 16.

31. Ibid., 14.

32. The date of the pamphlet is known from Bennett's rebuttal, written February 1, 1847. Miller's letter of February 5, 1847, Church Archives, alludes to the recent publication of "my second epistle." See Morgan, 113n22. Although no copy was found by Morgan, two were published in Chad J. Flake and Larry W. Draper, eds. *A Mormon Bibliography, 1830–1930: Books, Pamphlets, Periodicals, and Broadsides Relating to the First Century of Mormonism*, 2nd ed., rev. and enl. (Provo, UT: Religious Studies Center, Brigham Young University; American Fork, UT: Covenant Communications, 2004). Since the complete copy is signed by Brigham Young, it probably is the pamphlet sent him by Miller.

33. Miller, *Truth Shall Prevail*, 11; emphasis in original.

34. *Voree Herald*, October 1846.

35. *Zion's Reveille*, February 4, 1847.

36. Ibid., August 12, 1847.

37. Letter of "Louisa" to James Strang, from Ottawa, July 15, Strange Collection. The fact of Miller's disillusionment with Strang makes an 1846 date virtually certain. Morgan's opinion of the quality of this woman is given in his typewritten notes to the letter. See also his commentary to Ms. 159, where he justly calls the author "wise and witty" and identifies her signature on that letter as "Louisa S." This is a correction of Milo M. Quaife's incorrect reading in his biography of Strang. The Morgan reading is confirmed by several similar "S" capitalizations in the letter. Morgan suspected that "Louisa S." of Ottawa was Louisa Sanger. This is now clear from the fact that two letters of James Strang to Louisa Sanger are preserved in the Church Archives (December 5, 1844, and March 10, 1845) that fit minutely into the dialogue between Strang and this correspondent. From the Patriarchal Blessing file her birthdate can be determined, March 20, 1812. She was thirty-four years of age when she gave the quoted opinion of Miller. The 1850 census indicates that she was then unmarried. LaSalle County histories speak of the family as respected and indicate that Louisa had died by 1877. Elmer Baldwin, *History of La Salle County* (Chicago: Randy McNally, 1877).

38. Miller, *Truth Shall Prevail*, 6.

39. Miller, *James J. Strang*, 2.

40. This letter from the Strang Collection is quoted in full by Milo M. Quaife, *The Kingdom of Saint James* (New Haven: Yale University Press, 1930), 243–45 (punctuation added).

41. Letter of John Macauley to James Strang, from Galena, Illinois, June 29, 1849, Strang Collection.

42. Journal History, November 14, 1846, notes that Brigham Young heard a letter that "he had written in behalf of the Council to Reuben Miller, giving him advice in relation of his future movements."

43. Two of the letters quoted above from the Church Archives, written from Burlington, Wisconsin, to Brigham Young, establish Miller's lack of contact with the Twelve. The letter of February 5, 1847, reads: "Bro. Haywood has been here a few days since and informs me that you have written to me, but I have never received anything from any of the brethren in the camp. And I feel bad enough. Nevertheless I must do the best I can and act according to the best light and knowledge that God may, bless me with." The letter of April 21, 1847, begins: "I have written to you from time to time, but as yet have received nothing from you. But I am not discouraged. Believing that you have not given me over as one unworthy of your notice, I expect something soon."

44. See the Journal History entries of November 16, 1846, and December 22, 1846, which seem to have connotations of skepticism concerning the value of Miller's work in Wisconsin.

45. The letter is quoted in full in the Journal History, September 17, 1847, 2–5, writer's copy at Church Archives.

46. Cowdery's name first appears as attorney of record in Elkhorn, Wisconsin, in a case filed May 20, 1847; however, the firm of Cowdery and Wilson tried numerous cases throughout July of the same year in Tiffin, Ohio. This data published by Stanley R. Gunn, *Oliver Cowdery* (Salt Lake City: Bookcraft, 1962), 186–90, can be supplemented by further facts. Cowdery wrote one letter from Madison, Wisconsin, on May 18, 1847,

printed in *Seneca Advertiser*, June 18, 1847; his next published letter was written from Elkhorn, Wisconsin, on August 15, 1847, printed in *Seneca Advertiser*, September 3, 1847, and indicates receipt of "some four numbers" of the weekly *Advertiser* in Wisconsin prior to that time. This implies that his residence was in Elkhorn, Wisconsin, by mid-July of 1847.

47. Cited by Gunn, *Oliver Cowdery*, 191–92.

48. Cited in full, ibid., 268–69. Journal History, February 27, 1848, copies the letter in full, original at Church Archives.

49. This letter, not in the Journal History, was copied from the original by Stanley R. Gunn and is printed in full by him, *Oliver Cowdery*, 255–57. In addition to the paragraph quoted, the urgency of Cowdery's financial reliance on Miller is underscored by the request that Phineas Young "say a word to Brother Miller, in your next letter to me, as I know he stands ready to render me any aid I want, on your suggestion." The postscript reiterates the point: "As I determine to come even if I do not dispose of my place, it is important that you enclose to me a word to Bro. Miller. This will enable me to go about it in good time, and not suffer a disappointment."

50. Deed of Reuben Miller to Edward E. Prindle and Others, June 9, 1848, recorded at Walworth County, Courthouse, Elkhorn, Wisconsin, June 16, 1848.

51. Deed of Oliver Cowdery to Jonathan Delap, October 2, 1848, recorded at Walworth County Courthouse, Elkhorn, Wisconsin, January 8, 1848.

52. Reuben Miller Diary, Church Archives.

53. In Strang's community of Voree, but a few miles from Cowdery's residence at Elkhorn, the presence of Phineas Young in the area was noted: "Even Phineas Young is here, telling that brother Cowdery is going with him to Council Bluffs" (*Gospel Herald*, October 5, 1848). Young must have arrived some days before such a published notice.

54. Letter of George A. Smith to Orson Pratt from Council Bluffs, October 20, 1848, *Millennial Star*, January 1, 1849.

55. Letter of Reuben Miller to Brother Sabey [Henry Sabba Erekson] from Council Bluffs, November 16, 1848, a photocopy of which was furnished by Vaughn Erekson of Salt Lake City, Utah. The original is now in the Church Archives. All underlining is Miller's in the original letter.

Further Reading and Selected Bibliography

Richard Lloyd Anderson has long been considered the dean of Cowdery scholars. As the bibliography makes clear, he has published widely on many aspects of Oliver Cowdery's life. We recommend all of his work and three items in particular: *Investigating the Book of Mormon Witnesses*, an excellent starting point for anyone interested in Cowdery (or any other of the witnesses); "The Mature Joseph Smith and Treasure Searching," for information on Oliver and treasure seeking; and "Attempts to Redefine the Experience of the Eight Witnesses," for a response to recent attacks on those witnesses.

As noted in the bibliography, Richard Anderson and Scott Faulring's documentary history of Oliver Cowdery is forthcoming. This multivolume series will contain an unparalleled treasure trove of Cowdery documents (with meticulous annotation) and will be an excellent companion to the Joseph Smith Papers. In the meantime, however, researchers can find several important Cowdery documents in volume 2 of Vogel's *Early Mormon Documents*.

As the editor of the Book of Mormon Critical Text Project for almost twenty years, Royal Skousen has conducted exhaustive research on the original and printer's manuscripts of the Book of Mormon, as well as on textual variants in the Book of Mormon, all of which bear directly on Oliver's role as scribe. Skousen's transcriptions and analyses are invaluable for any student of the translation and publication of the Book of Mormon. Oliver also played a vital role in early Church publishing, and Peter Crawley's *Descriptive Bibliography* offers crucial information on that aspect of Oliver's career.

Lucy Mack Smith and David Whitmer both provide detailed first-person accounts of Oliver's involvement in the Restoration. See

Lavina Fielding Anderson's *Lucy's Book* and Lyndon Cook's *David Whitmer Interviews* for their stories. Milton Backman's *Eyewitness Accounts* includes first-person narrations of early Church history from many different participants, while Larry Porter's *Study of Origins* and Richard Bushman's *Beginnings* give valuable overviews of the 1805–31 time period. See Dean Jessee's *Papers* and *Personal Writings* for the writings of Joseph Smith himself.

Like Richard Anderson, Daniel Peterson and Matthew Roper, both of the Neal A. Maxwell Institute for Religious Scholarship, have vigorously defended Oliver Cowdery and the other Book of Mormon witnesses from a variety of attacks from critics. See Peterson's "Not So Easily Dismissed" and Roper's "Comments" for excellent examples.

Anderson, Lavina Fielding, ed. *Lucy's Book: A Critical Edition of Lucy Mack Smith's Family Memoir*. Salt Lake City: Signature Books, 2001.

Anderson, Richard Lloyd. "Attempts to Redefine the Experience of the Eight Witnesses." *Journal of Book of Mormon Studies* 14/1 (2005): 18–31.

———. "Book of Mormon Witnesses." In Ludlow, *Encyclopedia of Mormonism*, 1:214–16.

———."The Credibility of the Book of Mormon Translators." In Reynolds, *Book of Mormon Authorship*, 213–37.

———. "Did Oliver Cowdery, one of the three special Book of Mormon witnesses, express doubt about his testimony?" I Have a Question. *Ensign*, April 1987, 23–25.

———."The Impact of the First Preaching in Ohio." *BYU Studies* 11/4 (1971): 474–96.

———. *Investigating the Book of Mormon Witnesses*. Salt Lake City: Deseret Book, 1981.

———. "The Mature Joseph Smith and Treasure Searching." *BYU Studies* 24/4 (1984): 489–560.

———. "Oliver Cowdery." In Ludlow, *Encyclopedia of Mormonism,* 1:334–40.

———."Oliver Cowdery, Esq.: His Non-Church Decade." In *To the Glory of God: Mormon Essays on Great Issues,* edited by Truman G. Madsen and Charles D. Tate Jr., 199–216. Salt Lake City: Deseret Book, 1972.

———. "Oliver Cowdery's Non-Mormon Reputation." *Improvement Era,* August 1968, 18–26.

———. "Oliver Cowdery's Voice in Modern Scripture: Priesthood Restoration, Book of Mormon, and the Articles of Faith." Provo, UT: FARMS, 1997.

———. "Personal Writings of the Book of Mormon Witnesses." In Reynolds, *Book of Mormon Authorship Revisited,* 39–60.

———. "Reuben Miller, Recorder of Oliver Cowdery's Reaffirmations." *BYU Studies* 8/3 (1968): 277–93.

———. "The Second Witness of Priesthood Restoration." *Improvement Era,* September 1968, 15–24; and November 1968, 14–20.

———. "The Second Witness on Priesthood Succession." *Improvement Era,* November 1968, 14–20.

———. "The Smiths Who Handled the Plates." *Improvement Era,* August 1969, 28–34.

———. "Who were the six who organized the Church on 6 April 1830?" I Have a Question. *Ensign,* June 1980, 44–45.

———. *Witness of the Second Elder: The Documentary History of Oliver Cowdery,* 4 vols. Forthcoming. With Scott H. Faulring.

Arrington, Leonard J. "Oliver Cowdery's Kirtland, Ohio, 'Sketch Book.'" *BYU Studies* 12/4 (1972): 410–26.

Backman, Milton Vaughn. *Eyewitness Accounts of the Restoration.* Salt Lake City: Deseret Book, 1983.

Bishop, Patrick A. "An Original Daguerreotype of Oliver Cowdery Identified." *BYU Studies* 45/2 (2006): 101–11.

Bradford, M. Gerald, and Alison V. P. Coutts, eds. *Uncovering the Original Text of the Book of Mormon: History and Findings of the Critical Text Project.* Provo, UT: FARMS, 2002.

Bushman, Richard L. *Joseph Smith and the Beginnings of Mormonism.* Urbana: University of Illinois Press, 1984.

———. *Joseph Smith: Rough Stone Rolling.* New York: Knopf, 2005.

Cannon, Brian Q., and BYU Studies Staff. "Seventy Contemporaneous Priesthood Restoration Documents." In Welch, *Opening the Heavens*, 215–63.

Cannon, Donald Q., and Lyndon W. Cook, eds. *Far West Record: Minutes of The Church of Jesus Christ of Latter-day Saints, 1830–1844.* Salt Lake City: Deseret Book, 1983.

Cook, Lyndon. *David Whitmer Interviews: A Restoration Witness.* Orem, UT: Grandin Book, 1991.

Crawley, Peter. "A Bibliography of The Church of Jesus Christ of Latter-day Saints in New York, Ohio, and Missouri." *BYU Studies* 12/4 (1972): 465–537.

———. *A Descriptive Bibliography of the Mormon Church.* Vol 1. Provo, UT: Religious Studies Center, Brigham Young University, 1997.

Faulring, Scott H. "An Examination of the 1829 'Articles of the Church of Christ' in Relation to Section 20 of the Doctrine and Covenants." *BYU Studies* 43/4 (2004): 57–91.

———. "The Return of Oliver Cowdery." In Ricks, Parry, and Hedges, *The Disciple as Witness*, 117–73.

Gunn, Stanley R. *Oliver Cowdery, Second Elder and Scribe.* Salt Lake City: Bookcraft, 1962.

Harper, Steven C. "'A Pentecost and Endowment Indeed': Six Eyewitness Accounts of the Kirtland Temple Experience." In Welch, *Opening the Heavens*, 327–71.

Hart, Edward L. "James H. Hart's Contribution to Our Knowledge of Oliver Cowdery and David Whitmer." *BYU Studies* 36/4 (1996–97): 119–24.

Holzapfel, Richard Neitzel, and Robert F. Schwartz. "The Dedication of the Oliver Cowdery Monument in Richmond, Missouri, 1911." *BYU Studies* 44/3 (2005): 99–121.

Jessee, Dean C. "Joseph Knight's Recollection of Early Mormon History." *BYU Studies* 17/1 (1976): 29–39.

———, ed. *Papers of Joseph Smith.* 2 vols. Salt Lake City: Deseret Book, 1989.

———, ed. *Personal Writings of Joseph Smith.* Salt Lake City: Deseret Book, 2002.

Ludlow, Daniel H., ed. *Encyclopedia of Mormonism.* 4 vols. New York: Macmillan, 1992.

Morris, Larry E. "Oliver Cowdery's Vermont Years and the Origins of Mormonism." *BYU Studies* 39/1 (2000): 107–29.

———. "'The Private Character of the Man Who Bore that Testimony': Oliver Cowdery and His Critics." *FARMS Review* 15/1 (2003): 311–51.

Packer, Cameron J. "Cumorah's Cave." *Journal of Book of Mormon Studies* 13/1–2 (2004): 50–57.

Peterson, Daniel C. "A Response: 'What the Manuscripts and the Eyewitnesses Tell Us about the Translation of the Book of Mormon.'" In Bradford and Coutts, *Uncovering the Original Text of the Book of Mormon,* 67–70.

———. "Editor's Introduction—Not So Easily Dismissed: Some Facts for Which Counterexplanations of the Book of Mormon Will Need to Account." *FARMS Review* 17/2 (2005): xi–xlix.

Porter, Larry C. "A Study of the Origins of The Church of Jesus Christ of Latter-day Saints in the States of New York and Pennsylvania." PhD diss., Brigham Young University, 1971. Provo, UT: Joseph Fielding Smith Institute for Church History, 2000.

Reynolds, Noel B., ed. *Book of Mormon Authorship: New Light on Ancient Origins*. Provo, UT: BYU Religious Studies Center, 1982.

———, ed. *Book of Mormon Authorship Revisited: The Evidence for Ancient Origins*. Provo, UT: FARMS, 1997.

Ricks, Stephen D., and Donald W. Parry and Andrew H. Hedges. *The Disciple as Witness: Essays on Latter-day Saint History and Doctrine in Honor of Richard Lloyd Anderson*. Provo, UT: FARMS, 2000.

Roberts, B. H., ed. *History of the Church*. 7 vols. Salt Lake City, 1st ed., 1902; 2nd ed., 1950.

Roper, Matthew. "Comments on the Book of Mormon Witnesses: A Response to Jerald and Sandra Tanner." *Journal of Book of Mormon Studies* 2/2 (1993): 164–193.

———. "The Mythical 'Manuscript Found.'" *FARMS Review* 17/2 (2005): 7–140.

Skousen, Royal. *Analysis of Textual Variants of the Book of Mormon, Part 1: 1 Nephi – 2 Nephi 10*. Provo, UT: FARMS, 2004.

———. *Analysis of Textual Variants of the Book of Mormon, Part 2: 2 Nephi 11 – Mosiah 16*. Provo, UT: FARMS, 2005.

———. *Analysis of Textual Variants of the Book of Mormon, Part 3: Mosiah 17 – Alma 20*. Provo, UT: FARMS, 2006.

———. "History of the Critical Text Project of the Book of Mormon." In Bradford and Coutts, *Uncovering the Original Text of the Book of Mormon*, 5–21.

———. "John Gilbert's 1892 Account of the 1830 Printing of the Book of Mormon." In Ricks, Parry, and Hedges, *The Disciple as Witness*, 383–405.

———. *The Original Manuscript of the Book of Mormon: Typographical Facsimile of the Extant Text*. Provo, UT: FARMS, 2001.

————. *The Printer's Manuscript of the Book of Mormon, Part 1: 1 Nephi 1 – Alma 17.* Provo, UT: FARMS, 2001.

————. *The Printer's Manuscript of the Book of Mormon, Part 2: Alma 17 – Moroni 10.* Provo, UT: FARMS, 2001.

————. "The Systematic Text of the Book of Mormon." In Bradford and Coutts, *Uncovering the Original Text of the Book of Mormon,* 45–66.

————. "Translating the Book of Mormon: Evidence from the Original Manuscript." In Reynolds, *Book of Mormon Authorship Revisited,* 61–93.

Vogel, Dan. *Early Mormon Documents.* 5 vols. Salt Lake: Signature Books, 1996–2003.

Welch, John W. "The Miraculous Translation of the Book of Mormon." In Welch, *Opening the Heavens,* 77–213.

————, "Oliver Cowdery's Response to Alexander Campbell." In *The Disciple as Witness,* 435–58.

————, ed. *Opening the Heavens: Accounts of Divine Manifestations, 1820–1844.* Provo, UT: Brigham University Press and Deseret Book, 2005.

Name Index

About the Authors

Richard Lloyd Anderson, Professor Emeritus at Brigham Young University, received doctorates of law and ancient history from Harvard and the University of California, respectively. He has published widely on both the history of the ancient church and the history of the Restoration. Among his works are *Understanding Paul* and *Investigating the Book of Mormon Witnesses*.

Leonard J. Arrington, who received his bachelor's degree from the University of Idaho and his PhD in economics from the University of North Carolina, served as Church Historian for The Church of Jesus Christ of Latter-day Saints and Director of the Joseph Fielding Smith Institute of Church History at Brigham Young University. He is also the author of several books, including *Brigham Young: American Moses*; *Great Basin Kingdom: An Economic History of the Latter-day Saints*; and, with David Bitton, *The Mormon Experience: A History of the Latter-day Saints*. Brother Arrington passed away in 1999.

Patrick A. Bishop is Church Educational System Coordinator for the Casper, Wyoming, Seminary and Institute. He received his master's degree in human development from Utah State University in 2004.

Brian Q. Cannon, who received a BA from BYU, MA from Utah State University, and PhD in history from the University of Wisconsin, is Associate Professor of History and Director of the Charles Redd Center for Western Studies at Brigham Young University.

Scott H. Faulring, formerly a research historian with the Joseph Fielding Smith Institute for Latter-day Saint History at Brigham Young University, is coeditor of *Joseph Smith's New Translation* *of the Bible: Original Manuscripts* and also coeditor (with Richard Lloyd Anderson) of a forthcoming documentary history of Oliver Cowdery. He received a BS in history from BYU and an MPA from Troy State University.

Steven C. Harper is Associate Professor of Church History and Doctrine at Brigham Young University and an editor of the Joseph Smith Papers. He did his undergraduate work at BYU and received a PhD in history from Lehigh University.

Edward L. Hart, Professor Emeritus of English, Brigham Young University, is well known for his poetry and essays. He is also the author of a hymn in the current LDS hymnbook, *Our Savior's Love*. He received a BS in economics from the University of Utah, an MA in English from the University of Michigan, and a DPhil from Oxford.

Richard Neitzel Holzapfel is Professor of Church History and Doctrine at Brigham Young University and Photographic Editor at *BYU Studies*. He received his MA and PhD degrees from the University of California at Irvine and received his BA at Brigham Young University. He has published several books on the New Testament and is coauthor of *Jesus Christ and the World of the New Testament: An LDS Perspective.*

Larry E. Morris, a writer and editor with the Neal A. Maxwell Institute for Religious Scholarship at Brigham Young University, is the author of *The Fate of the Corps: What Became of the Lewis and Clark Explorers After the Expedition* (Yale University Press) and is now writing a book on John Colter for the University of Nebraska Press. He received an MA in American literature from BYU.

Matthew Roper, who has an MS from Brigham Young University, is a resident scholar at the Neal A. Maxwell Institute for Religious Scholarship at Brigham Young University. He is editor and compiler of *Book of Mormon Publications, 1829–44*, a forthcoming Maxwell Institute publication covering all newspaper articles printed about the Book of Mormon during Joseph Smith's lifetime.

Robert F. Schwartz is an associate with Allen & Overy in London. He received a BA from Brigham Young University and a JD from the University of Virginia. He was a 2002–2003 Fulbright scholar at Warsaw University.

Royal Skousen received his PhD in linguistics from the University of Illinois, Champaign-Urbana, and is a professor of linguistics and English language at Brigham Young University. Since 1988, Skousen has served as the editor of the Book of Mormon Critical Text Project.

John W. Welch is Professor of Law at the J. Reuben Clark Law School, Brigham Young University. He earned an MA in Greek and Latin at BYU and a JD at Duke University. He is Editor in Chief of *BYU Studies* and serves on the development council of the Neal A. Maxwell Institute for Religious Scholarship at BYU.